EDUCATIONAL KNOWLEDGE

SUNY series

FRONTIERS IN EDUCATION

Philip G. Altbach, Editor

EDUCATIONAL KNOWLEDGE

CHANGING RELATIONSHIPS BETWEEN
THE STATE, CIVIL SOCIETY, AND
THE EDUCATIONAL COMMUNITY

Edited by
THOMAS S. POPKEWITZ

State University of New York Press

Grateful acknowledgment for excerpts from chapter 8, "Rethinking Decentralization and the State/Civil Society Distinctions: The State as a Problematic of Governing," *The Journal of Educational Policy* 11, 1 (1996): 27–51.

Published by
State University of New York Press, Albany

© 2000 State University of New York

LC 71
.L 335
2000

* o 40869780*

For information, address State University of New York Press,
State University Plaza, Albany, N.Y., 12246

Production by Marilyn P. Semerad
Marketing by Nancy Farrell

Library of Congress Cataloging-in-Publication Data

Educational knowledge : changing relationships between the state,
  civil society, and the educational community / edited by Thomas S.
  Popkewitz.
      p.   cm. — (SUNY series, frontiers in education)
    Includes bibliographical references and index.
    ISBN 0-7914-4403-1 (hbk : alk. paper). — ISBN 0-7914-4404-X
  (pbk. : alk. paper)
      1. Education and state Cross-cultural studies.   2. School
  management and organization Cross-cultural studies.   3. Education–
  –Social aspects Cross-cultural studies.   4. Educational change Cross-
  cultural studies.   I. Popkewitz, Thomas S.   II. Series.
  LC71.L335   2000
  379—dc21   99-20650
                                                                   CIP

10 9 8 7 6 5 4 3 2 1

Contents

Preface

The book began as a small symposium at the University of Wisconsin–Madison concerning international reforms in education. The symposium was organized to bring historical and social sciences perspectives into strategies for comparative educational research. The book's authorship has broadened since that original meeting but the theoretical purpose has been maintained. The concern is to place educational discourses into a dialogue with a number of important intellectual currents in the fields of sociology, anthropology, political science, and history.

The contributors to this volume consider changes in the operation and objectives of national states, social groups within nations, and educational communities, as they exist within and among nations. The focus on the international setting underscores the interrelatedness of state practices with larger sets of cultural and economic relations that exist among nations.

The focus on the international setting in which national policies are formulated is intended to underscore the interrelatedness of state practices with larger sets of political, cultural, and economic relations that exist among nations. We seek an understanding of changes that are occurring within the international arenas that are pertinent to national educational reform. Our attention to the State as an organization and the state as an analytical concept is intended to provide historically specific case studies that can be used to refine our understanding of national educational practices. This distinction between theoretical deployments will be signaled in this book with the distinction between capitalized *State* as an organization, and *state* as a problematic of governing. By focusing on educational reforms as an arena of political conflict, we are interested in a development of social theory that is historically grounded.

Tied to the study of policy and practice is the treatment of educational knowledge as a social practice related to issues of power. The concern with knowledge is to consider how policy and pedagogy are governing practices through the rules and standards applied in educational problem solving. Knowledge is viewed as an integral part of the social phenomena that bear upon the framing of educational policy and the restructuring of education. In an almost Durkheimian sense, we can think of current national and international efforts to reform education as constituting a reformation of the patterns of governing by which the State, civil society, and economy are related.

vii

Two approaches to comparative studies are maintained. One is to explore multiple countries as the case. The comparison among different countries is guided through an interaction between the historical phenomena under scrutiny and theories that enable an exploration of differences and similarities among the different phenomena. The second approach is case study of national educational phenomena. Local, national practices are examined in relation to international, global patterns of change. This approach also weaves together the theoretical interests in comparative studies with local practices. The use of case studies makes it possible to understand the particular nuances and tensions that are implicated through the struggle for educational change.

Four tentative observations organized the themes that are taken up by the book:

1. We believe that conventional notions of the State that emphasize institutional structures and stability are inadequate for the task of assessing change in education. The blurring of boundaries through economic changes in world capitalism, the global circulation of discourses about social and educational change, and suprastate organizations such as the European Union call for a nuanced analysis that rethinks the idea of the state as a governing mechanism.

2. An understanding of interrelation of local, national systems and international systems is central to the development of our understanding of change in education. Historically, demands that are placed upon national educational systems are best understood within a complex set of relations with international systems. This relation is best expressed linguistically as globalization/regionalization in which the two terms are viewed as mutually tied to each other and thus conceptually as one.

3. The exploration of the governing patterns of education is important to interpreting the changes that are taking place. By governing, this book is concerned with two layers of educational practices. One refers to the state administrative and policy practices such as changes resulting through neoliberal policies related to school choice, teacher certification, and the training of teachers. A second use of governing relates to the discursive practices of education. The second notion of governing is tied to the discursive practices whose distinctions and categories order the world, define the place of individuals, and establish rules and standards by which expression and practices are made possible. Whereas the first theme of governing focuses on the constraints and restraints imposed through institutional relations, the second theme enables an exploration of how power is deployed through the rules and principles that order knowledge.

Many of the chapters in the book deploy Foucault's concept of "governmentality" to consider the nonbinary relations in the study of change. It is argued that the processes of modernization involve new responsibilities, expectations, beliefs, and attitudes about the individual who is to participate in education. These aspects of "the educated subject" are embodied in educational discourses of policy and pedagogy. Then new conception of the "self" is one who has a national identity as well as an international identity as a member of a larger political/economic body that transcends the geography of the nation-state. A discourse about "professionalism," for example, can be viewed as related to these processes of modernization. Professionalism has been introduced to many countries that previously had no comparable word or concept. The discourses of professionalization are to establish a teaching corps seemingly with a particular expertise that transcends local boundaries and whose allegiance is to competence rather than ideology.

If we treat discourses about reform as governing practices, then it is possible to consider how the rules, standards, and styles of reasoning of education are also injunctions as to how individuals should speak, think, and act in their everyday world. These injunctions are part of the social processes in which they occur: responsive and productive of power relations.

4. The changing patterns of state steering of education and governing draw attention to the social location of intellectuals. Social theorists and social historians have enabled us to understand that *the social sciences are the sacred knowledge of modernity*. What were formerly questions of the rabbi and the priest are now questions of the economist, the criminologist, the psychologist, and the educational researcher. The effects of social science can be found in the ways that individuals construct boundaries for themselves, define categories of good/bad, and envision possibilities. The ordering procedures of social science are elements in the production of power, as they have the potential effect of normalizing institutional patterns and social distinctions about "others"—that is, those who do not have the power to define, categorize, or order.

A characteristic of current educational reform is the mobilization of research communities in a manner that seems to transcend national boundaries. Proposals for reform and strategies for evaluating national school systems are presented as though they incorporate universal characteristics. There is a certain international commonality in the strategies for rationalizing school systems, as well as in the development of international groupings of intellectuals who are concerned with alternative and antisystem projects. The development of international scholarly groups in education, the international movement of researchers at all levels of academia, and the increased market for translated books in the social sciences, all produce a circulation of ideas that have different potentials when brought into national contexts.

While the chapters in the book continually take up these themes that relate education and power within a global and local context, the chapters do not have a single notion of power or knowledge, an issue that I discuss in the introductory chapter.

Thomas S. Popkewitz

Acknowledgments

The writing of this book began with a small international symposium held at the University of Wisconsin–Madison in June 1993. The meeting was an intellectual joy as the conversations raised important issues and elaborated central problems for the study of comparative education. That conference was made possible through the encouragement and financial support of the School of Education. I wish to thank the former Dean of the School of Education, Henry Trueba, for making the symposium possible. Andrea Kazamias co-organized the meeting and his friendship and understanding of the comparative educational field has continually been a source of inspiration to me over the past years. I appreciate his agreement to write a foreword to this book.

I also need to thank Lynn Fendler who has worked in the preparation of the book, but even more so, as someone whose intellectual sensibility and critical eye has continually challenged my thoughts. The Wednesday Group, an informal but ongoing graduate student seminar at the university, has also helped to clarify theoretical issues that form the underlying themes to organize this book. No literature passes by this group without a careful and deep reading that leaves no ideas unscathed. Some of the members of this group have written chapters for this book. Finally, I have to thank Joann Foss, whose recent retirement from the department has forced me to remember how valuable she has been over the years in keeping me on track as well as maintaining an organization between my multiple intellectual and departmental interests. This book would not be possible without her organizing the communication among authors on multiple continents, providing important guidance in the preparation of the manuscript, as well as administratively maintaining the files for the book in a way that I would have surely messed up.

List of Contributors

Thomas S. Popkewitz
Professor, Department of Curriculum and Instruction
University of Wisconsin-Madison

António Nóvoa
Professor, Faculdade de Psicologia e de Ciências da Educação
Universidade de Lisboa, Portugal

Marianne N. Bloch
Professor, Department of Curriculum and Instruction
University of Wisconsin-Madison

Benita Blessing
Visiting Researcher, HEC
Instituto Universitario Europeo, Italy

Carlos Alberto Torres
Professor, Latin American Center
University of California-Los Angeles

Geoff Whitty
Professor, Department of Policy Studies
University of London, UK

Sharon Gewirtz
Lecturer, Social Policy
The Open University, UK

Tony Edwards
Emeritus Professor, Education
University of Newcastle-upon-Tyne, UK

Stephen T. Kerr
Professor, Education Communication and Technology
University of Washington

Inés Dussel
Doctoral Candidate and Researcher, Department of
Curriculum and Instruction University of Wisconsin-Madison;
FLASCO (Facultad Latinoamericana de Ciencias Sociales
Sede Académica), Argentina

Guillermina Tiramonti
Researcher, Educación
FLASCO (Facultad Latinoamericana de Ciencias
Sociales Sede Académica), Argentina

Alejandra Birgin
Researcher, Educación
FLASCO (Facultad Latinoamericana de Ciencias
Sociales Sede Académica), Argentina

Gunilla Dahlberg
Professor, Department of Educational Research
Stockholm Institute of Education, Sweden

Frances Vavrus
Lecturer, International Studies Program
University of Wisconsin-Madison

Lisa Hennon
Doctoral Candidate, Department of Curriculum and Instruction
University of Wisconsin-Madison

Johan Müller
Professor, University of Cape Town Middle Campus
South Africa

Peter Drewek
Professor, Institut für Allgemeine und Vergleichende Pädagogik
Freie Universität Berlin

Jürgen Schriewer
Professor, Institut fur Allgemeine Pädagogik
Humboldt-Universität zu Berlin

Part I
Introduction

CHAPTER 1

Globalization/Regionalization, Knowledge, and the Educational Practices

Some Notes on Comparative Strategies for Educational Research

THOMAS S. POPKEWITZ

The globalization of economies and cultures and the emergence of new nationalisms that are associated with schooling have sharpened the problem of the governing of education. Educational reform has become a central item on the agendas of national governments and international agencies (such as the OECD, UNICEF, and European Union's Task Force on Human Resources, Education, Training, and Youth) that are concerned with modernization as well as research projects such as the International Evaluation of Educational Achievement (IEA). In most nations, educational "reform" is considered to be a strategic site for intervention that can promote the modernization of nations, enhance the viability of economic systems within world markets, and link macro issues of regulation with micro patterns of socialization and child rearing.

This chapter is concerned with comparative strategies that consider the relation of knowledge, power, and educational practices. This focus on knowledge underscores an important facet of contemporary life. Power is exercised less through brute force and more through the ways in which knowledge (the rules of reason) constructs the "objects" that comprise the issues, problems, and practices of daily life. The discussion is organized around three themes:

1. The relation of global and local, national practices in the construction of power in education, with attention to how the global and local forms overlap

3

2. The transformation of educational systems as problems of governing and governmentality
3. The relation of intellectuals and knowledge in the problem of educational change

Through these three themes, certain conceptual distinctions that have ordered comparative studies are critically analyzed. Among the concepts explored are those of power, the State versus civil society, globalization versus regionalization, and social inclusion versus exclusion.

Globalization/Regionalization and the Reconstituting of Education Practices

My discussion joins with a broader sociological and historical literature about the relation of local changes to global culture and world systems (e.g., Featherstone 1990, 1995; Robertson 1992; Wallerstein, 1991; Wagner, 1994). My discussion highlights the importance of knowledge in considering the social practices through which schooling is being revisioned in both global and national contexts. To underscore the issue of knowledge, I focus on the relation and overlay of global and local or national practices using the concept of globalization/regionalization as a single concept with multiple overlapping dimensions. I pursue this overlapping of relations through considering the *hybridization* or amalgamation of educational practice and the concept of the *indigenous foreigner*. The latter considers the relation of new international heroes and heroic discourses that function to produce national imaginaries about the citizen and participation.

Knowledge, Power, and Schooling: Some Shortcomings and Directions to Comparative Approaches in the Study of Globalization

The globalization literature has tended to point to the relation of cultural changes but has tended to gloss over the theoretical implications of relations among knowledge, power, and changing social patterns. At one level are correspondence theories that relate changes in world economies to the analysis of the relative autonomy of cultural and social movements in the processes of globalization. Balibar and Wallerstein (1991), as one example, consider current interests in multiculturalism and ethnicity as the product of changes in the world system of nationalism and capitalism in the late nineteenth century. But when such analyses are brought into current transformations, there is little differentiation of the distinctive differences in the world capitalist economies among, for example, East Asia, Eastern Europe, Scandinavia, and the United States (see, e.g., Boyer & Drache, 1996).

Nor is there an elaboration of how knowledge produced in education and cultural spheres is a constructive element in the "innovative, health, growth and productivity at a society-wide level" (Boyer, 1996, p. 104). Featherstone (1995), for example, asserts that the narratives produced by intellectuals are important elements in defining the boundaries and distinctions of the conditions of globalization, which he calls "post-modernity." But once this rudimentary yet provocative observation is made, there is no sustained analysis of the function of knowledge as an effect of power. (For a counterexample, see Shapiro, 1997.)

What is more central to this volume is that schooling as an institution has produced systems of governing that tie the local and national with the global through pedagogical practices and knowledge (see, Donald, 1992; Hunter, 1994; Meyer et al., 1992, 1997). Schooling not only constructs the national imaginaries that give cohesion to the idea of the national citizenry. It also constructs the images of cosmopolitan subjectivities that travel across multiple boundaries that form the worlds of business, politics, and culture (see, e.g., Bourdieu, 1996). In multiple countries, curriculum reforms are concerned less with the specific content of school subjects and more with *making* the child feel "at home" with a cosmopolitan identity that embodies a pragmatic flexibility and "problem-solving" ability. The omission of schooling from most cultural studies of globalization and regionalization is odd.

Hybridity and Globalization/Regionalization

While the nation-state is the most common subject of research, national reform practices are simultaneously an overlay of a complex web of global and local relations. The histories of colonialization have depicted this relation as one that is unidirectional or univocal, leading from the colonizer to the colonialized. But recent scholarship has rethought this relation as one of hybridity; that is, as an overlay or scaffolding of different discourses that join the global and the local through complex patterns that are multiple and multidirectional (see, e.g., Gilroy, 1993; Young, 1995; Anderson, 1991; Spivak, 1992; Dhillon, 1999). The idea of hybridity is underscored in the formation of political agendas for the new South Africa. Its politics embody fluid and pragmatic relations within a field of multiple power relations. The results are practices that are "a residue of Marxism, a spoonful of Chicago economics, a dash of West European social democracy, and much local spice. Like post-communists everywhere else" (Ash, 1997, p. 33).

The concept of *hybridization* makes it is possible to think of educational reforms as plural assumptions, orientations, and procedures in which the practices of reform are effected. The hybridity of discourses is evident within the political imaginary of European Union "unity." Current reforms give reference to Europe as a continent of diversity, with those "inside" the Union built by the Maastricht Treaty having different national traditions of 'reasoning' about social policy, and separated from those outside "the walls" (Silver, 1994). Educational reforms in Argentina can also be understood as embodying a complex scaffolding of techniques and knowledge that are not exerted though fixed strategies and hierarchical applications of power that move uncontested from the center nations of the world system to the peripheral and less powerful countries (Dussel et al., in this volume). Rather, Argentinian reforms embody processes of mediation and transformations of "the space of political rationalities to the modality of techniques and proposals that are used in particular locales." Further, the governing patterns embodied in the new constructions of EU's Europe entail new reconfigurations in the nexus of nationality-sovereignty-citizenship that cannot be taken for granted in studies of "European identity" but need to be explored through the new principles of governing produced.

The concept of hybridity, then, enables us to consider the relation of knowledge and power as not hierarchical, moving uncontested from the center nations of the world system to the peripheral and less powerful countries. Rather, the global and the local are intricately joined through complex patterns that are multiple and multidirectional. My chapter, for example, points to the differences in how seemingly universal discourses of centralized/decentralized systems of educational reforms are deployed variously as multiple global and local discourses intersect in South Africa, Russia, Sweden, and the United States (also see Kerr's chapter). Bloch and Blessing's chapter, as well, points to the complexity in which Eastern European centralized patterns of the state and foreign interventions through international grants interweave with local "cultures." While not using the word *hybrid*, Bloch and Blessing point to discourses that join what is analytically distinct: liberalism, neoliberalism, and collective, social ideologies of the welfare state. In these contexts, the overlapping discursive practices make it difficult to apply traditional ideological categories of conservative, liberal, or left. The chapter by Whitty et al., as well, gives a historical specificity to the British discourses of neoliberalism as entailing a cross-Atlantic movement that has no center but different sets of relations as policy is realized. The reform policy discourse continually moves between the United States and Britain with no apparent originary authorship.

Hybridization, then, provides a way to consider the interrelation of processes of globalization and regionalization as constituted through fluid, multiple, and historically contingent patterns. At the same time, we need to recognize that the playing field in which these processes of change occur is not level. In one context, Latin America and African national reforms may be positioned in relation to international funding agencies and other centers such as Europe/North America.

The ideas of hybridization pertain in different contexts. While the rhetorical constructions of today's reforms speak of giving marginal groups "voice" in schools, there is no natural voice. There are only mediated distinctions and divisions which are the historical effects of multiple discourses through which subjectivities are constructed. The construction of voice is an effect of power and never outside of the power relations in which it is positioned.

Hybridity also provides a way to consider globalization as not merely an issue of hegemony and the dominance of the powerful over the less powerful—a power that moves from the "core" nations to the periphery. There is not some non-European "voice" that exists in some pristine state to be deployed to counteract the colonialism of the European. As recent historical discussions of colonialization illustrate, there are slippages and processes of translations of ideas of the colonial metropolis as discourses are rearticulated in different contexts from which they were originally produced (see, e.g., Moore-Gilbert, 1997). At the same time, the metropole is itself reconstructed in a manner that is still relevant today. Europe, for example, was made by its imperial projects as much as the colonial encounters were shaped by conflicts within Europe itself (Cooper & Stoler, 1997). Nóvoa's chapter discusses the inclusions and exclusions through which the nineteenth-century European nations refashioned notions of citizenship, sovereignty, and participation cannot be adequately understood without exploring the relation of European practices to Asian and African political movements as well as self-doubts about the moral claims of liberalism in the face of the colonial enterprises.

Current Tanzanian reforms can illustrate the hybridity. Current Tanzanian educational reform about national unity and community overlap national purpose with the subjectivity of the individual (Vavrus, in this volume). The reform discourse appears indigenous as it refigures and reformulates the national imaginary through notions of "self-reliance" and African unity. But the Tanzanian reforms embody hybrid relations as colonial and "postcolonial" discourses collide. The discourses of African unity and nationalism inscribe the historical construction of European State (see, e.g., Badie & Birnbaum, 1983). Its notions of history and "public sphere" assume historicism, agency, and gendered quality that are themselves of European construction (Prakash, 1994; also see Pateman, 1988).[1] The double relations become important to the reading of contemporary literatures that focus on curriculum change.

The Production of Memory/Forgetting in National Imaginaries

In the previous section, I referred to the concept of hybridity in relation to national imaginaries. This section will explore this idea, with the following section pursuing the idea of the *indigenous foreigner* to explore how global discourses circulate without a history of time and place.

The idea of a nation and of a citizen is not one that is naturally produced through a common language, race, or geographical boundary. Nation-ness, as a community, is formed through discourses that project individuals into a collective narrative that enables people to know, understand, and experience themselves as members of a "community" (Balibar, 1991, p. 49). Discourses of public policy and theories of the social sciences, for example, generate images of the attitudes, dispositions, and capabilities of the "citizen" who contributes and participates in a nation. Anderson (1991) has called this institution of an imaginary unity an "imagined community," one in which cultural representations are historically fabricated to produce a "nation-ness."

The fabrication of the citizen and nation-ness is not only important for its construction of national imaginaries through which identities are constructed. The images and narratives of nation-ness produce new memories. These memories of the past, however, are not of the past that is more adequately represented in the present. The narratives of nation-ness recuperate national memories through the forms of representation constructed. "The past is not simply there in memory but it must be articulated to become memory. Memory is *recherché rather than recuperation*" (Huyssen, 1995, p. 11).

The new images of the citizen, however, do not provide the missing conception of identity for groups that demand recognition. Rather, the new conceptions of identity are forged out of the relations constituted in the new cultural practices. Cultural anxieties are formed as old identities are estranged and one's "home" (identity) is no longer located where one thought it was (Wald, 1995). As older conceptions of one's "home" are juxtaposed with new images that are being imagined into existence, there are ambiguities and contentions assembled in the new cultural territories (see, e.g., Chatterjee, 1993; Wald, 1995). Adjustments to national imaginaries "conjur away" various aspects of disorder and disjuncture through the consolidating languages of solidarity and coherence (see, e.g., Shapiro, 1997). In Argentina, for example, public discourses have inserted a notion of *reconciliation* as a way to develop a consensus about the past in the present conjuncture (see Dussel et al., in this volume). The discourse of *reconciliation* is embedded in debates about where and how to build monuments and museums that are to produce new memories and new reading of the past through the articulation of new heroes to think about national identities.

The production of memory, then, "is not some natural generality of forgetting that could be contrasted with through some form of a more reliable representation itself. Memory is given in the structure of representation itself" (Huyssen, 1995, p. 11).

The "making/remaking" of national imaginaries is also the producing of cultural anxieties. The constructions of memory entail a deconstitution of old images as people must be dissociated from the old collective identities and reimagined with another collective narrative (Balibar & Wallerstein, 1991).

The struggles over identity that exist over minority rights and gender, for example, have produced new exclusions and taboo zones, as monolithic notions of identity clash with the convictions of identities that are heterogenous. Current discussions in the United States about revising the school curriculum to include concepts of multiculturalism, for example, can be understood as transforming the geopolitical imaginaries and notions of community. Such discussions can also be examined as altering the forms of representation and images through which the culture constructs and lives in its temporality (Popkewitz, 1998).

In the construction of national distinctions and divisions is a forgetting practice as the new reorganizations of the notions of unity, community, and individuality "make" other histories disappear or appear as not relevant for action and participation. And as discussions about "the cultural wars" indicate, the forms of representations contest the home in which one is to locate identity. In part, the imagined unity is instituted against other possible unities, as well as interpretive contentions and analytic capacities of people (see, e.g., Shapiro, 1996).

The construction of "national imaginaries" is deeply embodied in the reflexivity inscribed in the social and educational sciences. The discourses of science have historically embodied the imagining (reimagining) of the conception of personhood and identity in the production of narratives of nationness (see, e.g., for general discussion Anderson, 1991; Hacking, 1995; in teacher education, see, Popkewitz, 1993a; Wagner, Wittrock, Weiss & Wollman, 1991; also see Herbst, 1965). The European and North American discourses of the social sciences linked the individual to political rationalities of a citizenry and collective social purpose in the nineteenth century.[2] Further, the disciplinary constructions of history, social and educational science, and anthropology centered a particular European historicism as their point of reference in the administrative reforms, although the discourses of "reason" are continually mediated and transformed in cultural contexts (see, e.g., Chakrabarty, 1992).[3]

The construction of national imaginaries provides a way to think about the discourses of educational reform and research. They should not be thought of as descriptive of change but as embodying a deep reshaping of the images of social action and consciousness through which individuals are to relate to the multiple global and local contexts in which they participate.

The Indigenous Foreigner

At this point, I would like to pursue the idea of national imaginaries further through the idea of the indigenous foreigner. I use this concept to direct attention to a particular type of hero and heroic discourses that bring global discourses of change into a relation with particular national discourses through which national imaginaries are constructed. I view the indigenous foreigner as particularly important in contemporary understandings of the relation of knowledge and power.

It is common in national policy and research for the heroes of progress to be "foreigners" who are immortalized in the reform efforts. The names of the "foreign" authors, for example, appear as a sign of social, political and educational progress of the national debates. The turn-of-the-century American philosopher John Dewey and the Russian psychologist Lev Vygotsky, for example, have become icons in the educational reforms that circulate among many countries. Dewey and Vygotsky appear as universal heroes to explain the "new" principles of pedagogy in South Africa, Spain, the Scandinavian countries, and the United States, among others. In critical social theory traditions, the names of the German Frankfurt School social theorist, Jürgen Habermas, the Brazilian Paulo Freire, and the French philosopher Michel Foucault, among others, are inserted into national debates to provide principles for social change, and, in some cases, educational planning. In most cases, these "foreign" traditions appear in discourse as if they were indigenous or universal.

While the heroes and heroines circulate as part of global discourses of reform, such heroes and heroines are promoted in national debates as indigenous or what appears as a seamless movement between the global and the local. The foreign names or concepts no longer exist as outsiders but with an indigenous quality that erases any alien qualities. The invocation of the indigenous foreigner functions to bless the social reform and nation with the images of the harbinger of progress. The discourses in which the foreigner appears are seen as opening up new intentions as new concepts are available for opportunities and interactions.

But when the narrative of the indigenous foreigner is examined closely, it is found to be a narrative without specific historical references and practices. It is a discourse that is *empty of history*. There appears an abstract, serial continuity rather than a series of specific historical contingencies in which the discourses of education are produced. The empty history of the educational reforms has no social mooring to the interpretations and possibilities of action. Dewey, Vygotsky, and Foucault are read not as writers whose ideas are produced in other, foreign fields of power relations but as local "saints" who forge an apparent continuity and evolution in the governing systems.

In the new systems of reasoning, the "saints" appear to produce emancipatory projects. The constructive pedagogy of the "problem-solving" teacher and child employs the names of Dewey and Vygotsky, for example, in what appears to be a serial continuity of the past, present, and future (Popkewitz, 1997). From critical traditions, the German Frankfurt critical theories overlay with the Italian Gramscian's language of "hegemony" and the Brazilian Catholic worker heritage of Freire's "critical consciousness" and "dialogics" to become a discourse that promises universal liberation and empowerment.

The indigenous foreigner can be examined in Latin American discourses about "action research" in teacher education, and about decentralization and marketization of educational practices. The distinctions, which emerge in relation to different ideological positions, coexist in the reform literature as part of the local efforts to modernize schools (see, Dussel et al. and Torres, in this volume). Action research, decentralization, and marketization, sometimes separately and sometimes within the same policy discussions of educational change, construct the new manifest destiny of the country through claims of economic prosperity, personal liberation, and/or social reconstruction.

But these categories of reform and policy are not solely those of Latin America. The policy and research reports often deploy literature from Spain to justify the approaches taken. Here, though, the complexity of the discursive deployments of the foreigner as an indigenous practice does not end. The Spanish educational literature is itself one that is transmogrified, built on translations of British and American texts but this "origin" is not longer evident in the discussions of the reforms. Importation and translation no longer appear as either. The discourses become inscribed as the internal "logic" through which the ongoing national dialogue of educational change is discussed. The national narratives circulate as if they were local and with no history except in the logic of the principles that the categories are to represent: the *problem-solving* child, the *progressive* curriculum, the *professional* teacher, and the *decentralized* school.

The transmogrification of the indigenous foreigner is the effect of power. The indigenous foreigner appears in the form of universal categories that order the interpretations and possibilities of national practices—the paths that one must take toward salvation and emancipation. The universal principles, however, are not universal but embody specific social and cultural forms. The national imaginaries that speak of emancipation and empowerment tend to inscribe principles of a "liberal democracy." These universal, inalienable principles embody particular sets of European, bourgeois norms about human rights and political freedom. But the specific cultural and psychological conditions that are woven into the principles of "liberalism" are concealed, as they seem to exist as preconditions for the actualization of individual capacities (Metha, 1997). Thus, while it is important to recognize that the principles of liberalism have been important in producing major social and political changes around the world, it is also important to recognize that the narratives of rights and democracy are also woven into the production of violence both within European nations and in colonies.

My concern with the indigenous foreigner is to recognize how the local and the global become overlayed in the production of power. If the discourses of reform and science are thought of as a form of storytelling, then the indigenous foreigner inscribed in national debates is part of the power relations embodied in the stories of global/regional relations. The importance of the indigenous foreigner, then, is not the individuality of the person who is made the heroine, per se, but in the deployments of the hybridity of discursive principles that order the memory about progress and that divide "reason" from nonreason. National discourses of policy and research embody multiple historical trajectories as principles for governing action and participation are produced. The indigenous foreigner is the effect of power.

Professionalization: An Example of Indigenous Foreigner in Global/ Local Relations

The indigenous foreigner and the construction of memory/forgetting can be explored through the discourses of professions and professionalization that circulate internationally. The professional teacher seems to cross ideological positions. That image is found in liberal and neoliberal reforms to decentralized school decision making through teachers who have more autonomy and relation to local community "cultures." From the left, the professionalization of teachers is to promote the emancipatory, empowering potential of education for a democracy. The professional teacher participates with the community and the child in order to reconstruct the society (see, e.g., Popkewitz 1993b).

When examined comparatively, the discourses of professionalization are seen to produce an empty history that embodies the power relations of globalization and regionalization. The discourses of professions and professionalization are neither singular nor universal. The idea of professional occupations that is embodied in current reform literatures is particular to European and North American constructions. While there are distinctions between the European continental and Anglo-American traditions of professions, it is the Anglo-American one that is dominant in the reform literature (see, e.g., Popkewitz, 1992). Anglo-American traditions of professions emphasize an ideal type of the expert knowledge of the teacher and occupational control of members. This Anglo-American ideal of the professional is a historical construction of the relation of the state and civil society in these countries. The noncentralized legal/administrative traditions of the United States and Britain produced particular occupational groups with strong cultural and social authority that existed alongside the state legal-administrative apparatus. The social sciences and "helping" professions, including teaching, linked the governing patterns of cultural and social life with the governing patterns of the state.

In continental Europe, in contrast, the concept of "professional" is historically different from that of Britain and the United States (see, e.g., Jaraush, 1990). One can compare, for example, the German or Russian traditions where the word *profession* had multiple meanings, ranging from particular occupations to any kind of employment. Discussions in France, as well as in Britain, have attempted to avoid the "expert knowledge" conceptions of professions through the introduction of the word *professionality*. The "ity" of the word gives emphasis to a quality or a state unlike the "ism" that relates to a system or doctrine. This is a semantic move however, and does not differentiate historically about the nature of expert knowledge and experts.

Latin America involves different state traditions through which discussions of the teacher-as-professional occur as a particular, historical hybrid of the global/local (see Dussel et al. and Torres, in this volume). The Latin American state was built on a Borbonic tradition. This involved strong state-centered policies that defined the progress of society as a movement from top to bottom. In this state tradition, citizenship was an achievement that was to be reached through state mass education. With this background, the welfare state that emerged by the second half of the twentieth century did not construct citizenship in the liberal terms of the European welfare state, but in a Catholic antienlightenment tradition that left little room for the formation of the modern individual; rather, it was distrusting/disregarding of civic participation, contemporary culture, and the construction of the teacher as found in Britain and the United States. Thus, the idea of professionalization in Latin America has a different trajectory from that found in Europe and English-speaking North America.

Discourses of professionalization, then, provide an exemplar of the global/regional relations that seem to go unnoticed in research. The discourses of the professions travel across national boundaries in the form of universal principles that govern particular aspects of social and cultural life. The discourses appear to have no apparent "origin," but are not global or universal. They emerge from particular national or local interests but become part of the authorized discourses of world systems of reason about social and educational reform. But the movement is one that embodies the local in the global and back to local or national arenas. What seems global in policy and research discourses is brought back into different local contexts and deployed within fields of power.

It is here that there is a need to return to the circulation of ideas and power as embodying a *hybridity* rather than the hierarchical application of power. Hybridity draws attention to how the different sets of distinctions and conditions of the professional, for example, are those of power with a specific historicity in relating state traditions and expert systems of knowledge in the governing of populations. In one sense, the circulation of ideas requires attention to issues of power, as certain discourses do become authorized as the "reason" of reform, such as those related to professionalism discussed above. But to complicate matters further, the inscription of discourses of professions in current educational reform, then, is regionalized within different social fields, cultural traditions, and social relations. The discourses of reform, then, are not one of an ideal to pursue but of changing power relations concerned with governing patterns that link political rationalities with identities. These changes in power relations cannot be assumed but must be interrogated for their implications, assumptions, and consequences.

The complex field that relates knowledge and social relations compels us to rethink the legacies of the nineteenth century that embodied binaries such as that of global and regional. This rethinking of binaries in social theory, however, is not only of geographical distinctions but of the dichotomies of political philosophy and social science such as the state/civil society and inclusion/exclusion, ideas taken up later in this chapter.

Methodologically, the relation of knowledge, institutions, and power in the comparative understanding of educational systems is elegantly drawn in Schriewer's chapter. He explores the challenges of a comparative social research program that is premised upon a theoretical understanding of historical changes in knowledge and structures that cannot be reduced to ideas of the state and the boundaries of the nation, but which require historical specificity. Schriewer helps us recognize that movements of ideas and practices that cross national boundaries cannot be explained through examinations that are limited within national contexts.

Transformation of Educational Systems as Problems of Governing and Governmentality

The previous discussions focused on the relation of knowledge and power through issues of memory/forgetting and hybridity. Two different notions of power were used that I want to explore more explicitly here. One focus is on the knowledge of policy and pedagogy as benefitting or excluding different social actors. I will call that a *sovereignty concept of power*. The second concept of power relates knowledge to the rules generated for action and participation. This notion of power can be viewed as the effects of power in that it examines the outcome of the relations of knowledge in governing the problematic or rules through which choices and possibilities are generated—what Foucault (1979) called *governmentality*. Where the sovereignty notion of knowledge identifies how knowledge represents and represses social interests, power as governmentality focuses on ways in which the individual is disciplined to act through discursive practices. The two different concepts of power and knowledge involve different strategies for understanding the governing practices of the state as well as for thinking about the politics of social change.

Knowledge, Policy, and the State: Sovereign Power

In contemporary social and educational analysis is found a view of power as something owned or possessed to dominate, repress, and oppress. Implicitly or explicitly, the idea is that power is something possessed by "the rulers," which enables their rule and, in principle has to be undone so as to provide a more equitable context in which people can equally "negotiate" how resources are allocated. When notions of "resistance" are inserted into discussions of power, it usually focuses on those groups who are dominated and oppressed and how they resist the demands and expectations of those who rule.

This concept of power can be viewed as one of sovereignty in that there is assumed a source or origin to the control mechanism of society. One side of the sovereignty concept of power is pluralist and elitist traditions that emphasize "power over" groups and individuals. The idea of "power over" tends to focus on structural forces and groups that have the power to exert their values as those of the society as a whole, such as capitalism, the State, and racism. Studies of schooling, within this tradition of power, look for how the daily practices and policies correspond to perserving or resisting the structural agents who have power over the decision making and value allocations in society. A different side of sovereignty power is "power to," which stresses the collective capacity of groups to negotiate power relations and thus privilege dimensions of consensus. Much of the progressive pedagogies of group processes embody the "power to" concept. In both "power over" and "power to" conceptions, the idea of sovereignty assumes that there is an actor where power originates that needs to be addressed to change in the distribution of production and consumption among groups.

If the State is taken as a key concept in contemporary social and educational analysis, it is assumed that the State acts as a sovereign power in the restructuring of education (Green, 1990; Torres, in this volume). Analyses examine, for example, how the State's monopoly (sovereignty) weakened hold over the economy has produced new cultural forms as pragmatic responses to the reduction of public funding and local specific pressures created by economic, demographic, and social needs (Bakker & Miller, 1996). In current educational and social theory, the new State is described as "neoliberal" to focus on the mixture of centralized and decentralized practices that benefit or repress structural agents (actors).

The sovereignty notion of power produces particular strategies toward policies about social *inclusion*. Equity is a practice to share ownership of the power that has an identifiable essence. Since power is considered to have a source or origin, the problem of inclusion is one of equity; that is, how schools provide for greater social access and representation of those groups and individuals who previously lay outside the ruling practices.

The idea of inclusion is analytically separated from exclusion in the sovereignty concept of power. Studies of inclusion are to identify access to social practices and values, to include others within the power arrangements. Exclusion is something separate from inclusion, something that is corrected through, for example, better policies that give representation (or "voice") to the varied social interests. Research on policies related to school choice in Britain and the United States, for example, points to uneven effects of efforts to increase parent options and involvement in the schools, as well as in State policies to decentralize school decision making (Whitty, 1997).

Power as sovereignty provides a form of problem solving that searches for the origin of control and seeks to eliminate repressive forces and mechanisms that limit equal representation in social practices. Equity assumes the redistribution of ownership among groups. When questions of knowledge are introduced into research, they are investigated as an epi-phenomenon to understand how the groups who have power (its origins) affect their will or are resisted by others.

Knowledge and Power: Governmentality

A different concept of power is one that considers the knowledge or rules of "reason" as generating the principles by which individuals act and participate in the world as a "knowing" being. The notion of power looks to the effects of knowledge in governing social practices, subjectivities, and possibilities. The relation of knowledge to power is in its disciplining and producing of the "self," who operates in the world as a "reasoned" person. This disciplining element of knowledge is what Foucault (1979) called *governmentality*. Governmentality calls attention to the tactics of regulating society through the disciplining of the dispositions, sensitivities, and "problem solving" through which individuals judge their competence and achievements. Knowledge, in this sense, is productive and an active, material practice in constructing the world, rather than negative, repressive, or as an epi-phenomenon of the world.

Power-as-effects, or as governmentality, can be thought of as it relates to the categories and distinctions of the order and divides social and personal life. The categories of "the terrible twos," or the health choices made through the tables of ingredients on the back of a package embody systems of reason, and these categories are important in that they give order to "our" perceptions of "reasonable" actions in dealing with children or buying foods. The systems of classification embodied in these practices are not of our making but historically constructed and expressed through our actions. To put this somewhat differently, the knowledge that orders and gives meaning to experiences is formed through power relations and is the effect of those relations. Joan Scott (1991), in her essay on the politics of experiences, persuasively argues that what are taken as "natural" experiences are socially constructed identities tied to power.

How "reason" and "the reasonable person" are constructed are the effects of power. Power in modern political regimes is exercised less and less by brute force, and more and more through the circulation of knowledge that ties political rationalities to the governing principles of our individuality. The "educated subject" in the contemporary world is also one that relates political rationalities to the governing of the "self." One just needs to look at the debates about the national curriculum standards in social studies to understand this relation of knowledge, power, and the idea of the educated subject. Rarely, however, are the rules through which we "know" about the world questioned or thought of as the effects of power.

The idea that knowledge is an effect of power can be explored if I return to the discussion of the State that I began in the previous section. The state in nineteenth-century intellectual and social thought extends its role of protecting territories and ensuring physical borders. The care of the state's territory shifted to include care for its population. The nineteenth-century state linked the development of social institutions to the development of the person. Power in this new constellation is reversed from its traditional moorings of sovereignty. Power no longer operates from the top or apex of society through the sovereign rulers. Rather, knowledge is linked to power by the microprocesses through which individuals construct their sense of self and their relations to others. Power functions through an individualization that disciplines and produces action rather than merely repressing action.

The problematic of governmentality provides a way to focus on the relation of the global and the local in social and educational studies. Like the new institutions of health and employment, the school tied the new social welfare goals of the state to a particular form of scientific expertise that organized the "knowing" capacities of the productive citizen (Wagner, 1994; Rueschemeyer and Skocpol 1996; also, see, e.g., Popkewitz, 1992, 1993a). Pedagogy would transform children into modern citizens who were self-motivated and self-responsible.

The idea of governmentality enables a rethinking of the binary of State/ civil society that was embodied in the previous discussion of the State as distinct from that of economy or culture. Rather than focus on the State as a sovereign entity separate from other social actors (such as economy and culture of the civil society), the state can be thought of as the historical relations through which principles of governing are produced. This notion of the state provides a way to consider how multiple institutions overlap as the discourses of, for example, state-governmental agencies, philanthropic organizations, and international lending agencies, as well as professions, provide the technologies and discourses to fashion subjectivities. This multiple set of relations can be understood in recent transformation of Eastern European policy related to women, child care, children, and education. The hybrid discourses relate national and global discourses in the construction of the subjectivities of teachers, children, and parents, as Bloch and Blessing analyze. The state, in this context, is treated as an epistemological category to study the relations in which discursive practices construct governing principles (see, e.g., Popkewitz, 1996).

At this point, I can return to the distinction between the sovereignty concept of power discussed earlier and the current discussion of governmentality.

Whereas the sovereignty concept focuses on the negative, repressive side of power, the idea of governmentality considers knowledge as disciplining and productive through the rules that are generated for actions (see, Popkewitz & Brennan, 1998). While I make the analytical distinction between two different orientations to the concept of power, the two concepts sometimes collide in the concrete case studies. The work of Spivak (1992) in postcolonial studies, Fraser (1989) in feminist philosophy, Hall (1986), and the critical pedagogy tradition in the United States that draws on the Frankfurt School (Lather, 1991), are examples of discussions that maintain a certain Marxist structuralism while adopting a view of power as governmentality in exploring the concrete social relations.

Rethinking the Concept of Inclusion/Exclusion

In the previous discussions of equity, one side of the binary of inclusion/exclusion is taken as a moral principle to judge the effectiveness of policy. If I return to the production of memory and forgetting in pedagogical practices, I find that the "memories" deployed to reason about the child embody normalizations about "being." That is, the discourses of pedagogy sanction the norms of health, attitudes, dispositions, and problem-solving abilities of the inner self of the individual. The categories and distinctions of pedagogy stand to "tell" what is to be valued and sought as successful, inner characteristics of the child.

But this memorialization of the child simultaneously forms a system that excludes as it includes. This can be illustrated in the U.S. idea of "urban education" that circulates within reforms (Popkewitz, 1998b). Contemporary U.S. reforms in teaching and teacher education "draw" distinctions and divisions to differentiate the *urban* children from those children who are *not* urban. The "urbanism" in educational discourses constructs a particular normalized space or "map." Urbanness outside of education is tied to ideas of cosmopolitan and modern, while urban education is historically mobilized to give attention to those who are to be socially administered because of their subjectivities. Practices were designed to help and save the *urban* child. However, *urban* signified something that was absent in the *urban* child, and, at the same time, these absent qualities were presumed necessary for success. The distinctions and divisions about what is present yet absent in the being of the *urban* child made it not possible for that child to ever be normal and "of the average."

The normalization of the urban child is at the level of the inner qualities, dispositions, and sensitivities that enable and disenable action. The ability of the child and parents to act properly (of the home to provide books and reading time), to have positive self-esteem, and to participate in appropriate and successful ways in school activities appear as the product of a natural and universal reason about learning (Popkewitz, 1993a). The distinctions of children's problem-solving capabilities are not universal but particular distinctions, tastes, and problem-solving strategies that are historically bounded. The particular distinctions of pedagogy are produced by particular social actors within a social field whose dispositions and sensitivities authorized as the reason of schooling (see, e.g., Bourdieu, 1984, 1996). What is taken as the universal capabilities of problem solving in pedagogy inscribe the divisions in a manner that makes the normalcies seem natural and unproblematic. It is at this level of inscription of dispositions and sensitivities that the inclusions/exclusions occur; that is at the level of "being."

It is in light of contemporary discourses of urban education in the United States that we can locate the significance of Hennon's chapter. While she focuses on the changing relation of power and knowledge in the construction of "urban" in the United States, she signals a way to comparatively understand how systems of inclusion/exclusion are produced. While there are different discursive forms through which normality and abnormality are established among the countries represented in this book (see Dussel et al. discussion of the "needy" in Argentina), Hennon's innovative approach enables us to begin to understand how certain historical rules and standards of reason about pedagogy are mobilized and overlay with those of social, psychological, and political discourses. The effect is to place the inner characteristics of certain children as inhabiting spaces that are outside of normality and in which the children can never be "of the average," no matter how much rhetorical energy is spent in talking about "saving" children.

This function of knowledge as producing systems of inclusion/exclusion is also important when examining the circulation of global discourses of reform. The policies of The World Bank, USAID, The European Union's Tacis, Swedish SIDA, and semiprivate international foundations, for example, can be thought of as constructing not only social and economic programs but as governing discourses that relate to the capabilities and being of the modern citizen, the teacher, and the worker in the "assisted" countries. The discourses of reform function in a manner similar to urban education in the United States. The World Bank and International Monetary Fund policies use a similar rhetoric as found in European and North American reform about modernization and saving the nation through saving the child. But the reforms do not take into account the particular social fields in which the dispositions and sensitivities of the teacher and child are constructed. The practical work of the apprenticeship models in teacher education found in the recipient countries of international funding agencies has different distinctions for the teacher than those found in the university educational systems of the donor countries. One can conjecture that the effects of these different sets of distinctions in the current World Bank restructuring policies may disqualify certain segments of the "assisted" country's population through the divisions produced in the "being" of the teacher and child. (The qualifying/ disqualifying functions of such policies can be intuited in Torres' chapter.)

To summarize, my concern with issues of inclusion and exclusion is to place them within a single continuum through which knowledge differentiates and divides. It is this continuum that structural analyses of inclusion and the sovereignty concept of power overlook in their focus on the origins of power. Power, in the sense of the production of principles that exclude as they include, is located in the classifying and dividing practices at the level of the being of the child and teacher. My concern, then, with the problem of inclusion/exclusion is to provide a comparative strategy by which to understand global and national relations as hybrid systems of reasoning constituted in an unequal playing field, in the sense of the principles generated about the being of the child and teacher.

Intellectuals, Governing, and Transformations in the Registers of Social Administration and the Freedom of the Citizen

This discussion of globalization and regionalization of knowledge has been infused with questions of power and the practices of educational research. Yet studies by academics tend to restrict their focus to the production of ideas within national boundaries. The history of the social sciences, for example, attends to how ideas are produced in response to national policy and a particular cultural milieu. The discussion of the European intellectual migrations prior to World War II focuses on the immigrants' contributions to the local economy of ideas (see, e.g., Coser, 1984). The myopia is also exhibited in current social and cultural studies discussions of the relation of postmodern theories to French intellectuals. Anglo-American critics identify this phenomenon as "the faddism" of French thought without questioning how the *indigenous foreigner* has settled into national discourses as processes of both globalization and regionalization.

Historically, the social sciences and social scientists have linked political rationalities about progress with a particular redemptive culture about social reform and individual salvation and liberation (Popkewitz, 1998a). The linking of social sciences with a redemptive culture entails a complex set of relations between the global and the local. This was expressed earlier in the European Union efforts to fund research related to "European Identity."

The idea of governmentality introduced earlier provides a different set of strategies for considering the politics of knowledge and social change. In one sense, knowledge produces distinctions, differentiations, and divisions that function to normalize and discipline action. With this in mind, to paraphrase Foucault, all discourses are dangerous, including intellectual production, but all discourses are not necessarily bad. I have argued elsewhere that one reflexive strategy to this recognition that the political is knowledge is to focus on the concrete historical forms of reason through which the acting, sovereign subject is constituted as an effect of power (see, e.g., Popkewitz, 1996; also Fendler, 1998). Bauman (1987) called the stance as moving from the intellectual as a legislator who establishes the rules of social and the personal action to one of thinking of the role of knowledge and the researcher as a problem of an interpreter.

This position is different from seeing research as eliminating bias, stereotypes, or ideologies, at least the bad ones. Each of these strategies assumes that there is some final essence or universal principle of truth that can be obtained through either the proper methodology or theory. Science, it is assumed, is to improve the school or to emancipate! An irony in these ways of reasoning about social and educational research is their constructions of memory and forgetting. These constructions of purpose and fulfillment forget the relation of nineteenth-century social scientific knowledge to the formation of the modern welfare state in the social administration of freedom (Wagner, 1994). Also forgotten is the historical relation between policy and policing that emerged in the nineteenth century. It also forgets that statistics (state arithmetic) and the deployment of populational reasoning in thinking about children was produced to provide administration of the state in its disciplining of individuals. (Early statistics involved both qualitative and quantitative approaches to data collection.)

This selective forgetting has enabled researchers to view themselves as producing both the critique and planning of a progressive society through the policy sciences. In the global/regional contexts where knowledge circulates as part of the governing process itself, this joining of the interpretive, critical discourses with strategic tasks has to be questioned as itself as an effect of power (see Müller, in this volume). But as Callewaert (1999) suggests, the view of research as "action" for policy and planning is a political strategy of intellectuals that needs to be questioned epistemologically and ideologically. This questioning of the function of intellectuals in defining the political, however, is not to forego the use of reason or action for social change but to make the doxa that inscribes the academic's vision of progress onto "others" as the problematic of research (see, e.g., Buenfil-Burgos, 1997; Popkewitz, 1998a).

The issue of globalization/regionalization of intellectual work is taken up in multiple chapters, from Schriewer's discussion of comparative social research to the final section of this book. Drewek's historical analysis of the German academic debates about pedagogy in the 1930s and again in the 1960s, for example, enables us to consider pedagogical theory in relation to historical cultural changes as well as a reaction to the new position of Germany within an emerging world system. Rather than deploying a notion of the teacher as a professional, the German debates were structured around the concept of *Bildung*, a particular German concept related to "self-cultivation" of the person. Drewek explores how Bildung is reinterpreted as the institutional demands of the German educational system change. In the post–world war changes that include educational expansion as well as the internationalization of pedagogical discourses, the older discourses of pedagogy are no longer appropriate, although residues of the older forms of representation remain.

Drewek's chapter compels us to rethink the epistemological principles of academics as related to social, political, and economic arenas. We can think of the paradigmatic debates that are expressed in the chapters of this book as not only descriptive and interpretive of the changes occurring. The discussions of power-as-sovereignty and power-as-effects are also linked to changes in social movements and political projects that have emerged after World War II (Popkewitz, 1996).

Further, one can read current discussions in this book as exemplars of not only the comparative questioning of policy but also as questions about the ideas of the rational administration of progress and the redemptive role of research (Popkewitz & Brennan, 1998). The previous discussions of the changes in the welfare state, economy, and culture are homologous to the epistemological challenges that are circulating in the humanities, social sciences, and educational research. The important article by Stuart Hall (1986), about Marxism without guarantees, epitomizes a rethinking about the role of knowledge and the researcher as a problem of an interpreter or a legislator. The postmodern social and political theories in which the discussion of governmentality is situated also refocuses the knowledge of intellectual as an interpreter rather than as a legislator.

It is with this last thought that I conclude this chapter. My focus has been on a strategy for thinking about comparative studies. In that process, I have focused on knowledge as a central problematic to understanding issues of power as the global and the local relate. My discussion explored how certain binaries of social thought (State/civil society; inclusion/exclusion, memory/forgetting) are, in fact, mutually related and thus require different conceptual strategies for understanding the function of knowledge as a material practice. The idea of the indigenous foreigner, for example, was deployed to direct attention to how power circulates through the methods of problem solving. I have not emphasized terms such as *postmodern* or *modern* to classify the debates and paradigmatic distinctions about power, although one might find much of my analysis on "governmentality" as drawing upon the former to develop the argument about historicizing "reason" in educational studies. Yet, in making this analytical move, I do recognize that the debates are not only about labels and slogans but about the conditions in which power and change are located.

Notes

As I wrote this chapter, I appreciated comments from a number of friends who are also colleagues. I have come to continually value their ideas and wish to acknowledge this debt to Mimi Bloch, Inés Dussel, Lynn Fendler, Kent Löfgren, António Nóvoa, and Miguel Pereyra, Geoff Whitty, Fran Vavrus, and The Wednesday Group, an ongoing seminar at the University of Wisconsin–Madison. The last, The Wednesday Group, provides an intellectual environment and continual questioning that is important to my intellectual life.

1. The issue of globalization/regionalization raised in this postcolonial literature is not to eliminate European Enlightenment ideas of bourgeois equality, citizen rights, and self-determination within the sovereign nation-state, but to challenge the historicism that projects the West as History. This argument is not relativistic, but rather documents how reason/science/universals of the Enlightenment are mobilized in historically and culturally specific practices in which the claims to empower are produced in circumstances that have also engendered violence.

2. It is also worth recalling that the pioneers of the social sciences were explicitly engaged in the understanding and governing of colonial people as in the British case; or, in the United States, the social scientists were often sons of missionaries who related research to social policy that would rescue immigrants and marginalized people for "civilization."

3. One can look at the Latin American discourses, for example, about "action research" in teacher education, and decentralization and marketization of educational practices. The distinctions in the reform literature appear as part of the local efforts to modernize the schools. But these categories of reform and policy are not solely of Latin America. The policy and research reports deploy literatures from Spain to justify the approaches taken. Here, though, the complexity of the discursive practices do not end. The Spanish literature is itself one that is transmogrified, built on translations of British and American texts that are no longer evident in the discussions of reform. Importation and translation no longer appear as either. They become inscribed as the internal "reason" through which the ongoing national dialogue of educational change is discussed.

References

Anderson, B. *Imagined Communities: Reflections on the Origin and Spread of Nationalism.* Rev. ed. London: Verso, 1991.

Ash, T. "True Confessions." *New York Review of Books* 44 (1997): 33–38.

Badie, B. & P. Birnbaum. *The Sociology of the State.* Chicago: University of Chicago Press, 1983.

Baker, B. "Childhood-as-Rescue in the Emergence and Spread of the U.S. Public School." In *Foucault's Challenge, Discourse, Knowledge and Power in Education,* ed. T. Popkewitz and M. Brennan. New York: Teachers College Press, 1998.

Bakker, I. & R. Miller. "Escape from Fordism: The Mergence of Alternative Forms of State Administration and Output." In *States against Markets: The Limits of Globalization*, ed. R. Boyer and E. Drache. New York: Routledge, 1996, pp. 334–56.

Balibar, E. & I. Wallerstein. *Race, Nation, Class: Ambiguous Identities*. Trans. Chris Turner. New York: Verso, 1991.

Ball, S. *Education Reform: A Critical and Post-Structural Approach*. London: Open University, 1994.

Barry, A., T. Osborne & N. Rose. *Foucault and Political Reason: Liberalism, Neo-Liberalism and Rationalities of Government*. Chicago: University of Chicago Press, 1996, p. 20.

Bauman, Z. *Legislators and Interpreters: On Modernity, Post-Modernity and Intellectuals*. Ithaca, N.Y.: Cornell University Press, 1987.

Bourdieu, P. *Distinction: A Social Critique of the Judgment of Taste*. Cambridge: Harvard University Press, 1984.

Boyer, R. "State and Market: A New Engagement for the Twenty-First Century?" In *States against Markets: The Limits of Globalization*, ed. R. Boyer and D. Drache. New York: Routledge, 1996, pp. 84–116.

Boyer, R. & D. Drache (eds.) *States against Markets: The Limits of Globalization*. New York: Routledge, 1996.

Callewaert, S. "Philosophy of Education, Frankfurter Critical Theory and the Sociology of Pierre Bourdieu." In *Critical Theories in Educational Discourse*, ed. T. Popkewitz and L. Fendler. New York: Routledge, 1999, pp. 133–60.

Chakrabarty, D. "Provincializing Europe: Postcoloniality and the Critique of History." *Cultural Studies* 6 (1992): 337–57.

Coleman, J. *Foundations of Social Theory*. Cambridge, Mass.: Belknap Press of Harvard University, 1990.

Cooper, F. & A. Stoler. *Tensions of Empire: Colonial Cultures in a Bourgeois World*. Berkeley: University of California Press, 1997.

Coser, L. *Refugee Scholars in America: The Impact and Their Experiences*. New Haven, Conn.: Yale University Press, 1984.

Dhillon, P. "(Dis)locating Thoughts: Where Do the Birds Go after the Last Sky?" In *Critical Theories in Educational Discourse*, ed. T. Popkewitz and L. Fendler. New York: Routledge, 1999, pp. 191–207.

Donald, J. *Sentimental Education; Schooling, Popular Culture and the Regulation of Liberty*. London: Verso, 1992.

Elzinga, A. "Research, Bureaucracy and the Draft of Epistemic Criteria." In *The University Research System: The Public Policies of the Home of Scientists*, ed. B. Wittrock and A. Elzinga. Stockholm: Almquist and Wiskell International, 1985, 191–220.

Featherstone, M. (ed.). *Global Culture: Nationalism, Globalization and Modernity*. London: Sage, 1990.

———. *Undoing Culture: Culture, Postmodernism, and Identity*. Newbury Park, Calif.: Sage, 1995.

Fendler, L. "Making Trouble: Prediction, Agency and Critical Intellectuals." In *Critical Theories in Educational Discourse*, ed. T. Popkewitz and L. Fendler. New York: Routledge, 1999, 169–188.

————. "What It Is Impossible to Think: A Genealogy of the Educated Subject." In *Foucault's Challenge, Discourse, Knowledge and Power in Education*, ed. T. Popkewitz and M. Brennan. New York: Teachers College Press, 1998.

Foucault, M. "Governmentality." *Ideology and Consciousness* 6. (1979): 5–22.

Fraser, N. *Unruly Practices: Power, Discourse and Gender in Contemporary Social Theory*. Minneapolis: University of Minnesota Press, 1989.

Gee, J., G. Hull & C. Lanskear. *The New Work Order: Behind the Language of the New Capitalism*. Boulder, Colo.: Westview Press, 1996.

Gilroy, P. *The Black Atlantic: Modernity and Double Consciousness*. Cambridge, Mass.: Harvard University Press, 1993.

Hacking, I. *Rewriting the Soul: Multiple Personality and the Science of Memory*. Princeton, N.J.: Princeton University Press, 1995.

Hall, S. "The Problem of Ideology: Marxism without Guarantees." *Journal of Communication Inquiry* 10 (1986): 28–43.

Hamilton, D. *Towards a Theory of Schooling*. London: Falmer Press, 1989.

Haskell, T. *The Emergence of Professional Social Science: The American Social Science Association and the Nineteenth-Century Crisis of Authority*. Urbana: University of Illinois Press, 1977.

Heilbut, A. *Exiled in Paradise: German Refugees, Artists and Intellectuals in America*. Boston: Beacon Press, 1983.

Hunter, I. *Rethinking the School; Subjectivity, Bureaucracy, Criticism*. New York: St. Martin's Press, 1994.

Jarausch, K. *The Unfree Professions: German Lawyers, Teachers and Engineers, 1900–1950*. New York: Oxford University Press, 1990.

Kliebard, H. *Struggle for the American Curriculum*. New York: Routledge and Kegan Paul, 1987.

Krohn, C. D. *Intellectuals in Exile: Refugee Scholars and the New School for Social Work*. Amherst: University of Massachusetts Press, 1987/1993. Trans. R. & R. Kimber.

Kuttner, R. *The End of Laissez-faire: National Purpose and the Global Economy after the Cold War*. New York: Alfred A. Knopf, 1991.

Lather, P. *Getting Smart: Feminist Research and Pedagogy within the Postmodern*. New York: Routlege, 1991.

Lekachman, R. *Greed Is Not Enough: Reaganomics*. New York: Pantheon, 1982.

Metha, U. "Liberal Strategies of Exclusion." In *Tensions of Empires, Colonial Cultures in a Bourgeois World*, ed. F. Cooper and A. Stoler. Berkeley: University of California Press, 1997, pp. 59–86.

Meyer, J., A. Benavot, Yun-Kyung Cha & D. Kamens. *School Knowledge for the Masses: World Models and National Primary Curricular Categories in the Twentieth Century*. Washington, D.C.: Falmer Press, 1992.

Moore-Gilbert, B. *Postcolonial Theory: Contexts, Practices, Politics*. London: Verso, 1997.

Myrdal, S. "Teacher Professionalism and National Culture: Reconstruction of the Icelandic Teacher." In *Professionalization and Education*. Research Report 169 ed., edited by H. Simola and T. Popkewitz. Helsinki, Finland: Department of Teacher Education, University of Helsinki, 1996, pp. 183–99.

Pateman, C. *The Sexual Contract*. Stanford, Calif.: Stanford University Press, 1988.

Popkewitz, T. *Paradigm and Ideology in Educational Research: Social Functions of the Intellectual.* London & New York: Falmer Press, 1984.

———. "Social Science and Social Movements in the U.S.A.: State Policy, the University and Schooling." In *Education in the Late Twentieth Century: Essays Presented to Ulf P. Lundgren on the Occasion of his Fiftieth Birthday,* ed. D. Broady. Stockholm: Stockholm Institute of Education Press, 1992, pp. 45–79.

———. (ed.). *Changing Patterns of Power: Social Regulation and Teacher Education Reform.* Albany: State University of New York Press, 1993a.

———. "Professionalization in Teaching and Teacher Education: Some Notes on Its History, Ideology and Potential." *Teaching and Teacher Education* 10 (1993b): 1–14.

———. Systems of Ideas in Historical Spaces: 'Constructivism,' Educational Reform and Changing Patterns of Governing the 'Self.' Paper prepared for the conference, "Democracy, Citizenship and Education," University of Turku, Finland— May 24–25, 1996.

———. "A Changing Terrain of Knowledge and Power: A Social Epistemology of Educational Research." *Educational Researcher* 26, 9 (December 1997).

———. *Struggling for the Soul: The Politics of Schooling and the Construction of the Teacher.* New York: Teachers College Press, 1998.

Popkewitz, T. & M. Brennan (eds.). *Foucault's Challenge: Discourse, Knowledge and Power in Education.* New York: Teachers College Press, 1998.

Prakash, G. "Subaltern Studies as Postcolonial Criticism." *The American Historical Review* 99 (1994): 1475–90.

Robertson, R. *Globalization, Social Theory and Global Culture.* Newbury Park, Calif.: Sage, 1992.

Rose, N. & P. Miller. "Political Power beyond the State: Problematics of Government." *British Journal of Sociology* 43 (1992): 173–205.

Rueschemeyer, D. & T. Skocpol (eds.). *States, Social Knowledge and the Origins of Modern Social Policies.* Princeton, N.J.: Princeton University Press, 1996.

Shapiro, M. *Violent Cartographies: Mapping the Culture of War.* Minneapolis: University of Minnesota Press, 1997.

Silva, E. & S. Slaughter. *Serving Power: The Making of the Academic Social Science Expert.* Westport, Conn.: Greenwood Press, 1984.

Simola, H. & T. Popkewitz (eds.). *Professionalization and Education.* Vol. Research Report 169. Helsinki: University of Helsinki, 1996.

Spivak, G. "The Politics of Translation." In *Destabilizing Theory: Contemporary Feminist Debates,* ed. M. Barrett and A. Phillips. Stanford, Calif.: Stanford University Press, 1992, pp. 177–200.

Streeck, W. "Public Power beyond the Nation-State: The Case of the European Community." In *States against Markets: The Limits of Globalization,* ed. R. Boyer and D. Drache. New York: Routledge, 1996, pp. 299–316.

Torres, C. "Critical Theory and Political Sociology of Education: Arguments." In *Critical Theories in Educational Discourse,* ed. T. Popkewitz and L. Fendler. New York: Routledge, 1999, pp. 87–115.

Wagner, P. *The Sociology of Modernity.* New York: Routledge, 1994.

Wagner, P., C. Weiss, B. Wittrock & H. Wollman (eds.). *Social Sciences and Modern States: National Experiences and Theoretical Crossroads.* New York: Cambridge University Press, 1991.

Wallerstein, I. *Geopolitics and Geoculture.* New York: Cambridge University Press, 1991.

Whitty, G. "Creating Quasi-Markets in Education." In *Review of Research in Education*, ed. M. Apple. Vol. 22. Washington, D.C.: American Educational Research Association, 1997, pp. 3–48.

Wittrock, B., P. Wagner & H. Wollman. "Social Science and the Modern State: Policy Knowledge and Political Institutions in Western Europe and the United States." In *Social Sciences and Modern States: National Experiences and Theoretical Crossroads*, ed. P. Wagner, C. Weiss, B. Wittrock, and H. Wollmann. Cambridge, UK: Cambridge University Press, 1991, pp. 28–85.

Young, R. *Colonial Desire: Hybridity in Theory, Culture and Race.* London: Routledge, 1995.

Part II

Globalization and The Restructuring of Education

The State and the Restructuring of Teaching

CHAPTER 2

The Restructuring of the European Educational Space

Changing Relationships among States, Citizens, and Educational Communities

ANTÓNIO NÓVOA

This chapter deals with education in "Little Europe," that which has been named by the European Union, and which has its headquarters in Brussels. This is a "royal" Europe that cannot be talked about by itself without reference to other Europes not only outside of, but also inside the wall built by the Maastricht Treaty: the Europe with new forms of discrimination and with groups that have no voice in our communication-based society. As Jacques Attali comments, Europe doesn't exist: it is not a continent, a culture, a people, or a history. That is why the language system that supports the notion of European "unity" must be seen as essentially problematic. Europe cannot be defined by a single border or by a common dream or destiny. And, it is possible (and ironic) to analyze this "unity" as an effect of power exercised by colonies on the colonizers. In fact, there are only Europes, which need to take into account their differences:

> It is necessary that Europe(s) thinks of itself as the *continent of diversity*, and not as a peninsula in the process of becoming homogenized; that Europe(s) would be able to organize a peaceful coexistence between their peoples without imposing an unifying model: plural is the greater trump of this singular continent. (Attali, 1994, p. 11)

David Coulby (1996) is right when he states that the theme of *Europeanization of Education*, espoused by the various bureaucracies of the Union, is based on the assumption of stable and readily recognized boundaries to the continent, but in fact these boundaries are far from clear, whether considered in political, economic, or cultural terms. European frontiers are not specified because they are perennially shifting subjects of dispute, lacking any confines in the Eurasian East, such as the Atlantic Ocean has provided in the West. Nowadays, we tend to refer only to the Member States of the European Union when we say "Europe," which is a way of speaking that needs to be questioned (Hayward & Page, 1995).

Europe, Citizenship, and Educational Policies: Sociological Approaches

The analysis of educational policies within the European Union is not easy. There is, on the one hand, an official discourse issuing from Brussels and the different Member States which implies that education will continue in the future as it has in the past, to fall into the domain of each Member State, which is an idea that precludes from the outset any harmonization of laws and regulations or construction of common policies. Nevertheless, the Community has been adopting, on a regular basis, a number of communitywide acts which, although without constraining legal value, have either a direct or indirect impact on educational affairs. Finally, it is important to take note of a pro-European rhetoric, produced both within political circles and in scientific milieux, which constitutes an obligatory reference point for communitywide educational action.

In order to accomplish this, I will initially try to explain the sociohistorical context of the educational policies of the European Union, in order to identify the contradictions and the paradoxes that characterize them. Following this, I will attempt a synthesis of the principal measures taken in the area of education, notably between the first resolutions of the 1970s and the initiatives that have been taken since the signing of the Maastricht Treaty. I finish this section with a reference to the rationalities that organize the educational discourse of Brussels, which tend to define a regulatory ideal for both national and communitywide actions in the field of education.

The Sociohistorical Context of Educational Policies within the European Union

In November, 1994, the European Commission published a declaration entitled *Cooperation in Education in the European Union (1976–1994)*. After an initial phase marked by hesitation, the Community adopted a series of coordinated actions that culminated in articles of the Maastricht Treaty dealing with education and vocational training. The list presented by the Commission mentions hundreds of documents which sketch out a *European educational policy*, although each passage recalls the exclusive competence of the Member States in this field. This is a precaution justified by the conviction, largely shared by the different countries, that education is, by definition, the space within which national identity is constructed; public opinion places education first on the list of those sectors in which decision-making power should remain primarily on a national level (cf. *Eurobarometer*). Nevertheless, the Community does, in fact, intervene fairly frequently in educational matters, although this takes place through an "indirect" educational strategy. This intervention consists, on one hand, of the construction of categories of thought, of organizing language and proposing solutions, which become the dominant schemes for approaching educational problems, and, on the other hand, of acting in a variety of other areas (work, vocational training, professional qualifications, etc.) which involve reconfigurations of the educational system.

Political scientists, especially academics in comparative politics, have studied the possible perversions resulting from this type of policy (Brown, 1994; Hix, 1994). It has been frequently noted that the European Court of Justice has played a crucial role in shaping the European Community (Shapiro, 1992). Furthermore, the articulation between the different levels of decision making within the European Union has always attracted the attention of the social and political sciences; Anthony Smith (1991), for example, is interested by the sui generis characteristics of this new type of transnational political association, which he defines as a condominium of powers—that is, a voluntary agreement to hand over certain powers to a series of central institutions, with overlapping jurisdictions, empowered to make binding decisions for all within carefully circumscribed parameters. Concerning these two aspects—the legal nature of the Community decisions and the architecture of the powers in the European Union—I identify two types of perversions provoked by the way political intervention into education was adopted by Brussels.

The definition of education through the bias of an expanded concept of vocational training. The first type of perversion comes from a definition of education through the bias of an expanded concept of vocational training. For a long time it was assumed that the absence of explicit mention of education in the Treaty of Rome meant that the powers of the Community were limited in this regard. Nevertheless, legal scholars and, especially, the judges of the Court of Justice in Luxembourg, have interpreted the silence of the treaty in this respect to mean the opposite: that the powers of the Community in this connection were not limited by the law (Shaw, 1992).

Using a subtle legal argument, Koen Lenaerts, judge in the Court of Justice, justifies this position, which is evident in the majority of the decrees issuing from the Court in Luxembourg. He supports, first of all, the legitimacy of a Community intervention in order to assure the legitimation of certain aspects of the treaties, especially the common market: "Any reasonable exercise of that power must be tolerated by the Member States, even if this affects aspects of the national educational policy" (Lenaerts, 1994, p. 12). Later he considers Community jurisdiction inasmuch as it concerns the recognition of professional diplomas, which, in many respects, depends on a coordination of policies concerning educational and training policy. Finally, and this is perhaps the most important step in his reasoning, Koen Lenaerts explains that the Court of Justice has been obliged to adopt a very expansive understanding of the concept of vocational training, in a way that includes virtually all forms of education that go beyond basic compulsory instruction. Referring to the Maastricht Treaty, he affirms that the "detour" via the expression "vocational training" is no longer necessary in order to allow the Community to pursue an educational policy, because all forms of education, irrespective of their relevance from the point of view of access to the labor market or to an occupation, warrant the same attention from the Community.

At the end of the 1980s, Bruno De Witte did not hesitate to affirm: "If there is a Community law of education, there is also a Community educational policy" (1989, p. 9). However, it is also important to recognize that this policy was legitimated, in the majority of cases, by a sort of extension of actions taken in the area of vocational training, which enclosed education within an excessively restricted definition. A whole range of discursive formations, and not only the logic of the market, supports the vocational bias, but at this point I would like to stress the overdetermination of education by the economic context, by the job market, and by qualifications for the workforce.

Today, nothing justifies a failure to take into account all forms and modalities of education, regardless of their importance for gaining access to the job market. Even if the Maastricht Treaty restricts the powers of the European Union in matters pertaining to education, we are facing a new situation, which permits a more open (and participatory) view of educational policies and initiatives. Questions of education cannot be discussed only on the basis of training and qualifications, and they need to address issues of personal, cultural, and social development. In this sense, it is advisable to examine the *vocational bias* and to adopt more nuanced perspectives to approach educational matters at the European level.

The development of a semiclandestine educational policy. The second perversion results from the European Union's institution of an uncontrolled educational policy, which tries to remain invisible and does not submit itself to democratic regulation and control. This is a covert educational policy, which cannot be spoken of in public and, as a consequence, does not permit participation, discussion, or judgment by any of the concerned parties. In fact, this situation of "legal semiclandestinity" (Frediani, 1992) experienced by the Community in the domain of education has prevented the initiation of any real debate in this area. Strongly based on a logic of expertise and resting on a technical rationality, the actions undertaken by Brussels have valued normative and adaptive strategies to the detriment of a more *political* attitude.

The question deals with the architecture of powers within the European Union, which leads directly to the principle of *subsidiarity* and to the structuring of decisions at the national, supranational, and subnational levels. Frequently this debate has been framed in a simplistic manner, as if power was a *thing*, a thing which one could divide, add, subtract, give away, or keep. However, simple arithmetic does not work in the field of power, as we can see from the example of the process of European integration. The work of Michel Foucault is very useful to understand this question; namely, when he comments that "power is not a substance" or some "mysterious attribute which origins need to be searched," but a series of strategic and complex relationships (Foucault, 1994). He understood power not as "a fixed quantity of physical force, but rather as a stream of energy flowing through every living organism and every human society, its formless flux harnessed in various patterns of behavior, habits of introspection, and systems of knowledge, in addition to different types of political, social, and military organization" (Miller, 1993, p. 15).

Reference is made to the importance of understanding how the alchemy of power is produced within the European political arena. This way, even as they lose some privileges traditionally linked to the exercise of sovereignty, certain States are using the European project to develop their own identity— see for instance, the case of Greece, or the "new" Germany (Marquand, 1994; Taylor, 1991). In addition, the fact of transferring a part of their prerogatives to the European Union does not prevent certain national executives from acquiring an accrued legitimacy, which comes to them from the fact of being seated at the decision-making table at Brussels—see, for example, the case of Portugal or Spain (Milward, 1992; Sbragia, 1992). Finally, let us take into account the fact that if it is true that there is a supranational consolidation of decision-making routines, there is also a reinforcement of power on a subnational level, that is to say local and regional—see, for instance, the cases of Belgium, France, or Italy (Cornu, 1993; Schnapper, 1994).

These tensions and contradictions appear in the field of education (Coulby, 1993). In the peripheral countries, references to Europe play a central role in the legitimation of national educational policy initiatives and in the imposition of certain laws that would otherwise have been unacceptable; for these States, the fact of participating in the European Union stimulates them to an *imagination-of-the-center*—that is, the idea that they belong to the political center of one of the great regions of the world (Santos, 1994). However, in forming themselves as models for those outside, the central countries have also been able to acquire an additional source of internal legitimacy. This double role is illustrated in the first case by the Spanish and Portuguese political reforms of the 1980s, and in the second case by attempts to export German or Danish systems of vocational training.

Talking about power is not possible without asking questions about participation. In this respect, Jürgen Habermas (1992) effectively demonstrates the way in which decisions made in Brussels are taken by a new European bureaucracy that is aloof from democratic process. He questions the "provisional" character of the imbalance between the increasing number of decisions made at the supranational level and the relatively feeble level of participation by populations. What interests him is whether or not it is possible to reverse this situation, or whether we are facing a permanent orientation in which a suprastate bureaucracy will predominate and put into place a strategy based on criteria of economic rationality that tends to transform politics into a problem of administration and management (Dinan, 1994; Imbert, 1993).

This question takes on an accrued pertinence in the field of education, given the absence of an "assumed" policy on the European level, which involves a deficit in participation. The creation of conditions for an open discussion about the future of Europe is very important so as to question the potential and limits of this project, clearly assuming its political, ideological, and cultural dimensions. Otherwise, the European integration will continue to be seen as a "technical" (and bureaucratic) problem that follows in the course of the options taken about the economy's domain, emphasizing the participation and democracy's deficit—that is, the barrier between decision spaces (at European level) and the various conditions of civic intervention. In fact, it is necessary that the European integration not be seen as an inexorable process organized independently of the debates, contests, and popular opinion, as well as of the communities. Reference is made to the fact that there is not one but many European opinions, and that all of them must be a cause for contest and face-to-face ideas, in order that the forms of power exercised by the new discursive constructions be analyzed rather than obscured, as they would be by analytical tools appropriate for older patterns of political power.

The Formulation of Educational Policies within the European Union

Brussels has taken measures in matters concerning education, since the beginning of the 1970s, through a diversified panoply of instruments: Community acts (decisions, recommendations, resolutions, etc.), Community programs (Erasmus, Petra, Lingua, Socrates, Leonardo, etc.), subsidies and economic aid, and so forth. There is a long list of documents that define *orientations* at the same time that they construct a *language* to talk about and to think about education in Europe. It is impossible at this point to give this inventory in detail, although this has, by the way, already been collected in two indispensable documents: *Cooperation in Education in the European Union, 1976–1994* (European Commission 1994) and *European Educational Policy Statements* (Council of the European Communities, 3 volumes, 1987–1993).

This literature is traversed with certain continuities but also with certain changes, most notably concerning policies dealing with vocational training and the placement of young people in the job market, the European dimension in education, the initiation of certain cooperation programs, higher education, or the mobility of teachers and students. Now, in the 1990s it is important to point out the importance of documents such as *Guidelines for Community Action in the Field of Education and Training* (May, 1993); *Green Paper on the European Dimension of Education* (September, 1993), *White Paper on Growth, Competitiveness, Employment* (December, 1993), and definitions concerning the new "generation" of European programs (*Socrates, Leonardo, Targeted Socio-Economic Research*, etc.). The Maastricht Treaty then, represented a turning point in the formulation of an educational policy, even if its consequences were less significant than one might have thought at first, resulting, undoubtedly from the difficulties in the process of European construction.

Using a necessarily simplified model, it is possible to group into five major domains the decisions made on the European level:

- *Vocational training:* Measures taken regarding career or vocational training, as well as the preparation of young people for careers, the transition from education to the workplace, the correspondence between professional qualifications and the schooling of young people, migrant workers, and migrant populations.
- *Higher education:* Decisions concerning higher education, most notably in order to assure the mobility of students, connections between the university and industry and the recognition of diplomas; in the articulation between "professional training" and "higher education" it is also important to take into account preservice and inservice training of teachers.
- *Cooperation and exchange:* A group of initiatives designed to stimulate cooperation and exchanges such as the introduction of new technologies into education, the development of distance education, the inception of European schools and multilateral educational partnerships, or the organization of exchange programs for young people, so that a number of diverse measures address, for example, the fight against illiteracy, or equal educational opportunity for boys and girls.
- *Information and control:* The construction of information and control technologies, such as the organization of standards, the dissemination

of statistics and information about different educational systems, the evaluation of Community programs, or control over the quality of teaching (notably, higher education).

• *European curriculum:* The organization of aspects which affect the development of a European curriculum, the most important of which relate to the European dimension of education, especially the teaching of foreign languages, although these include initiatives in the areas of consumer education, health and environmental education, and propositions concerning decreasing rates of school failure, promoting equal opportunities, and favoring the integration of handicapped students into regular school programs.

This systematization into five major domains only scratches the surface of Community action in the area of education. In a general sense, the Commission has justified its intervention by the need to catalyze action within the different Member States. At the same time, the objectives of economic and social cohesion have been omnipresent in the definition and the contents of European educational policy. The rhetoric pertaining to the "exclusive powers" of the Member States and excluding "any harmonization of laws" coexists with practices which harmonize language, categories, and systems of reasoning. Several documents explain that even if the European Commission cannot intervene explicitly for *harmonization* in the field of education, it does not eliminate the possibility that actions undertaken in other areas have consequences for education and training. A very interesting footnote, placed in a document issued by the Presidency of the European Commission is very clear under this matter: "The new Articles 126 to 129 of the European Union Treaty in the area of education, vocational training and youth, culture and public health will explicitly rule out harmonization of laws and regulations of Member States. . . . This does not mean that the pursuit of other Community objectives through Treaty articles other than 126 to 129 might not produce effect in these areas."[1]

But even in the field of education, several documents issued in Brussels do not hesitate to make a broader interpretation of the Maastricht Treaty, even if they always feel obliged to restrain their proposals in order to avoid further criticisms: "The stakes are high. Without investment in the skills and versatility of the present and future workforce, the Community will not be competitive on the world stage. Equally, without a high quality education service throughout the Community, the cohesiveness of the European Community will be impaired and the capacity to act together in harmonious (but *not* harmonized) concert will be endangered."[2]

These interpretations are very important because they underscore the consequences of the European construction, namely of issues related with economic integration for the educational policies of the different Member

States. Attempts to seize the initiative in educational policy for the European Union are, above all, attempts to make sense of the sometimes contradictory and often unexplained equilibrium between the "full respect for the responsibility of the Member States" and the need for a stronger cooperation and agreements; namely, in what concerns professional qualifications and workers' mobility. For this reason it is necessary not only to describe *contexts* and identify *contents*, but also to interpret the organizing rationalities embedded in the discursive practices which support these policies.

Rationalities behind the Educational Discourse of Brussels

There are several ways of alluding to the rationalities that organize the discursive practices relative to education which are coming out of Brussels. On the one hand, they reiterate themes already present in various national educational arenas, which have been summed up by authors such as Geoff Whitty (1993) or Sigurjón Myrdal (1993): the former presents five themes coming out of the reform movement of the 1980s (quality, diversity, parental choice, school autonomy, and responsibility); the latter deals with reference ideas in the European context (equality, privatization, quality control, return to the market, centralization-decentralization, and professionalization). On the other hand, these rationalities can be understood through the concept of *social regulation*, to the extent that educational reforms are the result of a change in the technology of regulation between the State, civil society, and the economy. On the *macro* level, it is important to deal with new modalities of organizing the State and articulating policies within the framework of the European Union; at the *micro* level, it is necessary to underline the utilization of new forms of "governing" education (Popkewitz, 1996). In both cases it is necessary to understand the production of discourses and practices that encourage a reappraisal of education and training patterns, not only in each Member State but also on a European basis.

Martin McLean (1995) asserts that the content of education, for some, is the vehicle for the creation of a European cultural identity, while for others, the curriculum is the ultimate defense of national and, indeed subnational, identities, which the European Union must respect. These issues are as much practical as ideological. It is necessary to understand the significance of an administrative system—followed up either in the national States or in Brussels—which will go on establishing and legitimizing a series of interventions in the field of education. It refers to a "false evidence" imposing solutions and languages that define perspectives and solutions for the problems of education. Therefore, it is necessary to deconstruct the rhetoric of education as the last barrier in defense of a national identity and understand the whole complexity of the current process of delocalization/relocalization of identities. And that is why we need to analyze a conflict between: "On the one hand, the centripetal force of Europeanization pulling culture and knowledge towards the metropolitan center and, on the other hand, the centrifugal forces of local, regional and even national identities pulling towards the preservation and reformulation of heterogeneity" (Coulby & Jones, 1995, p. 133).

Economic logic. Policies concerning education and vocational training are founded, first of all, on an *economic logic.* Community documents unceasingly repeat the necessity of preparing "qualified human resources" to respond to "economic challenges" and "technological mutations." The educational reflections that take place in these European forums are dominated by an economic viewpoint, its tasks being seen as providing vocational training, preparing people for working life, and helping them to adapt themselves to new social structure. The language of *human capital theory* is central for these debates, because the education and training programs have as one of their common aims increasing European competitiveness: "There is a growing consensus throughout the European Community, as in other parts of the world, that so-called "intangible capital" is the most vital resource of advanced economies, without which the natural endowments of nations, their financial power and fixed capital will become dwindling resources."[3] In this sense, the European Commission advocates the need for improving the quality and quantity of professional/vocational qualification, for linking education and training with economic life and competitive realities, and for the development of European training products and Europe-oriented qualifications. Surely enough this *language* is not only a way of talking about "preexisting" problems, but represents the imposition of certain theoretical frameworks and discursive practices that define the dominant perspective for approaching educational issues.

This logic has restrained the scope of educational measures, while at the same time trying to present the Member States with a fait accompli: European economic necessities and the internal market would lead inevitably to agreements and accords on the level of the organization of national systems of education (length of studies, level of qualifications, curriculum, etc.). In this concern, the conclusions of the Council and the Ministers for Education meeting within the Council of 6 October 1989 are quite clear: reaffirming that it is necessary to "respect the fundamental powers of the Member States in matters of general education policy," the document states that "the establishment of the internal market will affect the educational policies of the Member States." This kind of reasoning is current in most of the documents published under the auspices of the European Community (now European Union). Martin McLean (1990) even feels that "a pan-European curriculum may emerge from the pressure of localized consumer demand, driven by the logic of European economic union, which all the governments are legally committed to achieve.

This economic rationality is accompanied by a neoliberal orientation, which serves to frame discourses pertaining to privatization, free choice, and even participation. The *White Paper on Growth, Competitiveness, Employment* (1993) stresses the convergence among the Member States on the necessity of a *greater implication of the private sector* in educational systems and vocational training, and in the formulation of policies for education and training, to take into account the needs of the market and local circumstances. Neoliberal perspectives cannot be reduced to an economic register, in the sense that corporate (and vocational) discourse includes religious work ethics, shifts in disposition, redefinitions of "pleasure in work," new constellations of social affinities, and changes in the meaning of "family life." Educational policies are being reconstructed around ideas of "choice," "standards," "competencies," "European values," and "real knowledge" as a way to legitimize the growing pressure to make the perceived needs of business and industry into the primary goals of the school (Apple, 1996).

As Thomas Popkewitz argues in the introduction to this volume, metaphors of privatization and marketization are employed for the restructuring of schools as markets (the idea of choice). Nevertheless, it is important to recognize that neoliberalism is not a universal and constant policy but an interweaving of multiple practices that do not fit neatly into any ideology. Popkewitz's ideas remind us that our analyses of economic logics must be complex, that the relations between schools and work are not universal, and that we need to go beyond a simplistic vision of this connection.

In fact, this is rhetoric that attempts to reconstruct education as a private space, but which is frequently incompatible with the European Union in dealing with the structure of the articulation of powers of the different Member States. Using a number of different approaches, several authors have shown the contradictions which presently exist between the neoliberal perspectives and the authoritarian orientations of a great number of state policies in the educational sector—that is, the contradictions between the free-market, consumerist approach to education and the authoritarian drive for social order. The words of Michael Apple are well adapted to the European situation: "One of the major effects of the combination of marketization and strong state is to remove educational policies from public debate" (1996, p. 29). And this is a very important issue to understand questions related to European citizenship, and the way this concept is entailing new patterns of inclusion/exclusion.

In a time when so many people have found from their daily experience that the "grand narratives" of progress are deeply flawed, is it appropriate to return to yet another grand narrative, the market? (Cf. Apple, 1996.) In fact, the metaphor of the "market" is a part of a political rhetoric that carries with it a binary language (State/civil society, freedoms/constraints, public/private) that is not adequate to furnish the intellectual instruments necessary to understand the problematic of governmentality in the arena of education (Popkewitz, 1995).

Discourse about quality. Discourse about quality constitutes another rationality structuring the Community's actions concerning education. The first objective of Article 126 of the Maastricht Treaty states that "the Community shall contribute to the development of quality education by encouraging cooperation between Member States and, if necessary, by supporting and supplementing their action." The introduction of the concept of *quality* in the treaty must be seen as the achievement of a logic implemented for several years within the European Community. Going through the *European Educational Policy Statements* issued in the beginning of the 1990s one can find a constant reference to this point: quality in teacher training (1990), quality assessment in higher education (1991), quality in the field of education and training (1992), quality of professional/vocational qualification (1993), and so on.

Since Maastricht this discourse has increased, as we can see in the attempts of the *White Paper on Education and Training* to identify the guidelines for action in the pursuit of objectives to build up high-quality education and training: "Giving priority to quality in education and training has become vital to the EU's competitiveness and to the preservation of its social model; indeed Europe's very identity over the next millennium depends on this" (1996, p. 28). In a reconciliation with the ideology of efficiency and effectiveness, one can find the most important aspect of the discourse concerning quality. No doubt, the use of this discourse is integrated into a greater redefinition of educational policies, in the sense that it renews the value placed on the economic payoff of education connected to the need to implement higher educational standards to the detriment of cultural and social factors. Michael Apple, in his work *Official Knowledge,* characterizes this discourse in a particularly expressive way:

> Economic modernizers, educational efficiency experts, neo-conservatives, segments of the New Right, many working and lower-middle-class parents who believe that their children's futures are threatened by a school system that does not guarantee jobs, and members of parts of the new middle class whose own mobility is dependent on technical and administratively oriented knowledge have formed a tense and contradictory alliance to return us to "the basics" to "appropriate" values and dispositions, to "efficiency and accountability" and to a close connection between schools and an economy in crisis. (1993, p. 119)

Discourse about quality must be decoded in the context of this diffuse project, which attempts to replace the objectives of social equity with a reinforcement of academic technologies for educational selection. Therefore, it is important to maintain a tension between the objectives of social equity and those of quality, especially in a period in which the economic situation tends to value "overall quality" over "quality for all" (Lowe, 1992). In fact, current meanings of "quality" now signify some instrumental effectiveness toward tacitly accepted (and somehow inarticulated) goals. It is an approach that is unable to understand the historical undertones of this concept: the "search for quality" has been a problem for all generations of educators, which have defined their own aims and goals, and that is why this concept cannot be taken for granted. In this regard, João Barroso (1995) shows very well that a political action based on the definition of "quality patterns" is a strategy of rationalization and a process of social homogenization; the educational use of the concept of quality tends to create new forms of social exclusion in the school; the adoption of a discourse about quality is a way to introduce a logic of marketization and to client-led strategies that are innacurate in education. The discourse about quality helps to constitute a goal-steering pattern of power in relation to educational policies, which reinforces neoliberal orientations and produces a "new" rhetoric of citizenship. This rhetoric, each time more active in the European circles, tends to form a strategy designed to somehow overcome the barrier between the political decision and the social participation. It deals with a strategy allowing that educational matters continue to be articulated in economic terms, even though multiple arenas contribute to the construction of the "new" European educational policies.

Another aspect of this strategy, particularly salient in the European context, concerns the establishment of educational policies, more on the level of *criteria* than objectives and propositions. By *criteria*, I mean a whole series of instruments for evaluation and control (norms, standards, models, etc.), which tend to envision education as a problem of management and organization, and not in terms of social and political issues. Hans Vonk is entirely right when he points out that this is an essentially bureaucratic perspective: "These proposals are mainly bureaucratic, i.e. management-oriented in nature. In current society bureaucrats define many social, educational and other problems in terms of management instead of content. Management seems to have the appearance of 'the panacea' for all problems in education, in the same way as curriculum development in the sixties" (1991, p. 134). This tendency, which is strongly evident in the European Community, is not limited to a posteriori control, but also contributes to the construction of solutions and to the imposition of a certain way of approaching educational problems.

Rhetoric of citizenship. Since the ratification of the Maastricht Treaty, European citizenship has functioned as a useful reference point in educational discourse. Raymond Aron's response to this concept is well known: "Though the European Community tends to grant all the citizens of its member states the same economic and social rights, there are no such animals as 'European citizens.' They are only French, German, or Italian citizens" (1974, p. 653) Jacques Delors's concept of citizenship with a *variable geometry* is also important. This concept is thought provoking, especially as it does not limit itself to the idea of doubling a sense of national reference with a European affiliation, but instead suggests a diversification of loyalty and belonging (Badie, 1995). As W. H. Taylor puts it: "Individuals can and usually have many cultural identities, a Gaelic speaker being simultaneously a Highlander, a Scot, a Briton and a European: this list can expand in both directions. Having a European identity does not mean abandoning other identities" (1993, p. 437).

As long as the discussion takes place on a philosophical level, the impact on education is relatively limited, but if we invest the debate with a political dimension, this fact changes. In this respect, the approach of Jürgen Habermas (1992) is particularly interesting, especially when he denounces populations' *deficit of participation* in the European construction, while at the same time demonstrating that, at the moment, there is an obvious connection between legal, civil, political, and social rights. Participation thus becomes, the sine qua non condition of European citizenship (Imbert, 1993; Marquand, 1994). This is what permits us to break away from the determinism of an education that is enclosed within the interior of a nation-state, and to open our imagination to educational practices that are more European even as they are rooted in local space and communities. The point is made by Rob Gilbert, in a broader analysis of citizenship, education, and postmodernity, when he suggests the expansion of the idea of citizenship from civil, political, and welfare entitlements to greater participation in the cultural and economic dimensions of everyday life:

> A citizenship education would not be distracted by national symbols or flag or parliament, but would focus on concrete principles of rights and the practices of political action. It would not succumb to self-interested political calls for loyalty to the symbols of hierarchical economic or political power, nor to the abstract ideals of a past golden age, however well intentioned. . . . It could further show the value of conventional forms of citizenship in civil, political and social rights, and the need to extend these more fully to the economic sphere. In doing so it would illustrate the significance of citizenship in an increasingly important mode of experience of postmodernity. (1992, p. 66)

This same question is addressed by Paul Close is his attempt to list the conceptual features of citizenship. He underlines that, besides a status and a set of rights, citizenship is a relationship with the State and with other people, which is a multistranded relationship, being not just legal but also political, economic, and otherwise social. Defining citizens' relations as power relations characterized by process and change, he presents a view that "implies and anticipates the unstoppable progress of the European Union towards a supra-national organization; towards a federal union or United States of Europe; towards the establishment of State apparatus at the level of the European Union, and so, above the state, at Member State level; towards the Union's consolidation as a *supra-state*" (1995, p. 279).

That is why the initiatives intended to promote a European dimension in education must be seen in the light of a political restructuring, and not only as a new rhetoric on citizenship. It is not enough to state that "Education systems are not limited to ensuring the continuation of their own cultures; they must also educate young people for democracy, for the fight against inequality, to be tolerant and to respect diversity. They should also educate for citizenship; and here, Europe is not a dimension which replaces others, but one which enhances them" (*Green Paper on the European Dimension of Education*, 1993, p. 6). Therefore, the need for definition of measures and policies with a concrete meaning, to achieve this intention. This matter goes through an idea of citizenship participation, which means a more effective presence of the various actors in defining educational policies, as well as organization and administration of schools. Otherwise, rhetoric of citizenship is formed by a kind of "veneer" serving to hide the deficit of participation (and of democracy) existing in the European Union, in the Community field and within each Member State. The result is a certain "folklore" which is simultaneously political and intellectual, frequently legitimated by an *expert* label, which tends to create the illusion that struggling against a "nationalist ideology," by contrasting it with the "European dimension," is the best way of assuring peace and development (Bell, 1991; Edwards, Munn & Fogelman, 1994; Heater, 1992; Husén, Tuijnman & Halls, 1992; Ryba, 1995).

It is not sufficient to identify the "added value" of Community action in the sphere of education. But it is necessary to clarify decision and action strategies in order to achieve the ideals referred in the *Green Paper on the European Dimension of Education*: "This 'added value' would contribute to a European citizenship based on the shared values of interdependence, democracy, equality of opportunity and mutual respect; it would also help to extend the opportunities for improving the quality of education; and finally, it would help pupils towards social integration and a better transition to working life" (1993, p. 5). For the time being, it is important to recognize that the rhetoric of citizenship has mainly become part of a certain political folklore in the Community spheres and a certain intellectual folklore within the academic ones, so not an element of consolidation of new identities and belongings, in local regional, national and European fields (cf. Bell, 1991; Heater, 1992; Ryba, 1995). This way, discursive eurocentric practices are sometimes strengthened, which leads to new forms of discrimination: "Consequently, the European dimension in education must not be organized as a eurocentral and isolationist speech, but shaped from the tolerance, the interdependence, and promotion of the European multicultural or intercultural pedagogy" (Pereyra, 1994, p. 15).

In the field of education these discursive rationalities are seizing the key themes of educational reforms in several European countries and relocating them within the framework of the European community: curriculum reform, school autonomy, and the professionalization of teachers. As far as the curriculum is concerned, there is a discourse dealing with values and the socialization of young people as European citizens, which is frequently accompanied by a reference to multiculturalism and respect for diversity. Democracy, tolerance, or solidarity are all part of a language that legitimates political efforts through the construction of a history of Europe as the enlightened center of civilization. This "colonial" perspective conceives the future of Europe as the continuation of a past that is imagined to be glorious: "I think that if today [there] exists a group, or a cultural enclave capable of guiding this new planetary civilization, this group is, precisely, the European continent" (García Garrido, 1994, p. 12).

For this reason, I think it is important to point out that "neither Europe nor its culture are unitary," resulting that great precautions should be taken as to any "attempt to impose unity on heterogeneity" (Coulby & Jones, 1995, pp. 130–31). As such, it is useful that teachers, as cultural intellectuals, refuse to accept the politics of identity as given, and critically examine how representations of Europe and Europeans are constructed, for what purpose, by whom, and with what components: in fact, "many Euro-enthusiastic educationists are hitching their theorizing and research (not to mention careers) to the EU band-wagon, proclaiming—too uncritically—the virtues of the Union" (Sultana, 1995, p. 133).

The issue raised by Zygmunt Bauman is useful to understand how "Europe" works as the privileged center and "enlightened" guardian of the world: "From at least the seventeenth century and well in to the twentieth, the writing elite of Western Europe and its footholds on other continents considered its own way of life as a radical break in universal history. Virtually unchallenged faith in the superiority of its own mode over all alternative forms of life contemporaneous or past allowed it to take itself as the reference point for the interpretation of the telos of history (1987, p. 110). Often, the assumptions of European intellectuals are embedded in a mythological "unitary past" that neither history nor geography can confirm. In fact, the so-called European unity is partially formed by the colonies (African, Asian, and American) whose perspective might not differentiate among European nations. Postcolonial discussions show the importance of the European "identity": inside Europe, people define themselves as French, German, or Italian, but outside Europe, the sense of belonging as European is stronger. Moreover, the discursive practices of non-Europeans tend to define the idea of what it means to be European. The irony of the colonizers constructing their "unity" through the mirror image of the colonized is quite appealing.

The increasing rhetoric of *participation* must be seen as a strategy followed by different States to adopt new regulations, and to regain control over the reformation process. In this sense, it is very important to understand the discourses on decentralization and professionalization as part of a broader process of reorganization of the educational arena, in order to deal with multiple identities, from local to national and European levels. The discussions of state decentralization, the devolution of state practices, and multiculturalism are examples of deeper changes in the modernization of schools that are understood through considering dimensions associated with the *identity* of teachers. Furthermore, teachers are being asked to help redefine new identities in the context of a *post–nation-state* Europe.

Europe functions as a *regulatory ideal* influencing the educational policies of its Member States, even if the different countries interpret it in different ways. For central countries (like France or Germany), this is viewed as a strategy for imposing solutions and principles that are capable of ensuring their hegemony under the European "construction." For peripheral countries (like Greece or Ireland), it is often a question of replicating patterns and solutions adopted by the most developed countries, and thus imagining themselves as participating in decisions at the European "core." Interpreting this feeling, a former Portuguese prime minister was proud to say that his country was "a good pupil of Europe." Raising this same kind of issue, it is interesting to note that the document discussed during the meeting between the ministers of education from the European Union and from Eastern European countries (European Commission, April 1997) was entitled, "Towards a Common House of the European Education." The recuperation of this metaphor stressed that the idea of a European "unity" was in great measure assured by an educational endeavor. The recuperation of this metaphor gives the concept of "regulatory ideal" new explanatory possibilities for interpreting the restructuring of European educational space.

However, to enable education to prepare for a citizenship that does not coincide exclusively with national borders, and in order that educational policies may be able to integrate local and global references (that is, to express themselves inside as well as outside of the nation-state), it is essential to effect major changes that reconceptualize the very structure of national educational systems. In order to accomplish this, it is crucial to rediscover a way of thinking that encourages rupture and does not enclose educational debates within an inert consciousness; such a way must be critical, theoretical, engaged, and capable of addressing complex issues.

Recent Developments in the European Union: The Emergence of "New" Educational Policies?

Continuities and Changes in European Educational Policies

During the last years, the three rationalities discussed earlier were structured in post-Maastricht Europe. A series of documents and political initiatives amply confirm the analysis previously made. Looking, for instance, at the resolutions concerning the new generation of Community programs (Socrates, Leonardo, etc.), the documents published during the European Year of Lifelong Learning (1996), the *Green Paper "Living and Working in the Information Society"* (1996), the Report from UNESCO International Commission on Education for the Twenty-First Century (*Learning: The Treasure Within,* 1996), and above all the *White Paper on Education and Training* (1995) and the *Report "Accomplishing Europe through Education and Training"* (1996). In all this documentation one understands a continuity regarding previous logics, even if some rupture and political changes are also announced.

From the continuities' point of view, the foci are the extension of an *economic logic,* a *discourse about quality,* and a *rhetoric of citizenship.*

Economic logic. Problems related to unemployment, mainly youth's unemployment and competitive matters, caused greater worries concerning an economic logic. From documentation issued in recent years, it is clearly necessary to examine education and training in the context of employment: "Education and training have now emerged as the latest means for tackling the employment problem" (*White Paper on Education and Training* 1995, p. 1).

Discourse about quality. Extending the previous outlook, these documents insist that the watchword should be quality, this concept being assumed as a structuring component of educational policies: "Quality assurance basically means placing the client or user of a service at the center of concern, rather than the perspectives and practices of service providers" (*Report "Accomplishing Europe through Education and Training,"* 1996, p. 22). It is very interesting to note that in stressing the idea that education and training systems need to be more user oriented, these documents identify the companies, and not the students, as the *users.* According to this report, "the problem is how to get our systems to take greater account of business sector requirements and thus offer learners the skills and qualifications companies need." In this sense, students still remain apart from the main trends of policy formulation, which reconstitutes their lives and careers without taking into account their own positions and dispositions.

Rhetoric of citizenship. Finally, most discourses are followed up by a principle of citizenship, which tends to be redefined in the logic of political action. So, the intention to emphasize the idea that logics of economy, quality, and citizenship are not incompatible:

> To examine education and training in the context of employment does not mean reducing them simply to a means of obtaining qualifications. The essential aim of education and training has always been personal development and the suc-

cessful integration of Europeans into society through the sharing of common values, the passing on of cultural heritage and the teaching of self-reliance." (*White Paper on Education and Training* 1995, p. 3)

Nevertheless, "personal development" is now seen as vocational training, and "self-reliance." means dependence on corporate social and political structures. The *Cresson's Report* envisages four orientations for action that intend to articulate these different (and somehow contradictory) trends: "constructing European citizenship; reinforcing economic activity and preserving employment; maintaining social cohesion in Europe; fully utilizing the opportunities offered by the Information Society." (1996, p. 11)

However, besides these continuities, there are also some changes worth identifying, concerning new action political logics in the European Union. The first one refers to an endeavor of rethinking *education* and *training* concepts, as well as relations between education and work. In this field, it is useful to distinguish between the articulation of the concepts, trying to understand them completely: "Education and training, will increasingly become the main vehicles for self-awareness, belonging, advancement and self-fulfilment. Education and training whether acquired in the formal education system, on the job or in a more informal way, is the key for everyone to control their future and their personal development" (*White Paper on Education and Training,* 1995, p. 2). The *Cresson's Report* goes far beyond, as far as it defines two major requirements for an education strategy aside from the need to strengthen European competitiveness: the need to appreciate the difficulties of the current situation, insofar as we are witnessing a crisis in the traditional institutions of society, particularly the family and the State; and the need to respect the basic principles of education, whose aims go far beyond a purely utilitarian perspective. In this sense, it is acknowledged that among the potential changes identified, the following should be noted: the transition from objective to constructed knowledge; the transition from an industrial to a learning society; the change in educational mission from instruction to the provision of methods for personal learning; the increasing (and perhaps, in the future, dominant) role of technology in the communication process and in knowledge acquisition; and the shift away from formal educational institutions such as schools and universities toward organizational structures for learning that have yet to be determined. Evident in these ideas is the intention to redefine some educational perspectives, which is reinforced by two statements: the position of everyone in relation to their fellow citizens in the context of knowledge and skills will be decisive; and lifelong learning has to be a priority.

The second change refers to the architecture of powers in the European Union. A need to recognize more openly the beginning of a European action in the field of education was engendered post-Maastricht. Little by little—in addition to the implicit intervention schemes that always existed—suggestions were brought forward for better coordination between the different Member States. The *White Paper on Education and Training* talks about "an overall approach capable of assembling the efforts of Member States and those of the European Union, each acting within its area of competence" (1995, p. 1). And the *Cresson's Report* is still more assertive when it asks for guidelines for Union action on education and training and states the need to "proclaim a general European aim that serves as a *guide* for the different systems" (1996, p. 78). This kind of statement, which would have been impossible before 1993, has become increasingly common, figuring a more precise political definition of European action in the field of education. Obviously, this concerns a change with great consequences, regarding the way education and training systems operate and the way different educational actors are involved. No doubt, these changes will entail new regulations between state, citizens, and educational communities. That is why it is so important to understand these changes in relation to a broader process of globalization that is reorganizing state practices in education, and also in connection with changing patterns of state steering of education inside each country.

All these changes are taking place in an educational space invaded by discourses that state the importance of education from the collective and individual point of view. Due to the failure of traditional economic forms and conceptions of education, having as a main purpose the preparation for the world of work, ways and alternatives are being sought. It is in this light that the following declaration should be understood: "*The society of the future will therefore be a learning society.* In the light of this it is evident that education systems—which means primarily the teachers—and all of those involved in training have a central role to play" (*White Paper on Education and Training*, 1995, p. 2). And the the *Cresson's Report* did not hesitate to write that "establishing a genuine learning society will require major changes in our education and training establishments" (1996, p. 11).

Challenges for the Future

The idea of a *learning society* marks the most recent European discourse in the field of education. *Toward the learning society*: this is the subtitle of the *White Paper on Education and Training,*[4] which introduces a very important debate when mentioning the problem of education and citizenship from the perspective of participation—"There is therefore a risk of a rift in society, between those that can interpret; those who can only use; and those who are pushed out of mainstream society and rely upon social support: in other words, between those who know and those who do not know" (1995, p. 9)— and ends with a strong statement about the role of the school: "Naturally, everything starts at school, which is where the learning society has its roots. . . . School has to adapt, but nevertheless remains the irreplaceable instrument of everyone's personal development and social integration. Much is asked of it because it has such so much to offer" (1995, p. 27).

It is very curious to note the return to typical assertions from the beginning of the twentieth century, with school and teachers being called to an essential role in reorganizing the European society. The need for profound transformations in education and training has been imposed, as part of a reorganization of the dynamics of the European states (Vaniscotte, 1996). Some authors even add the perspective of a Europe of knowledge (and not only of information and communication) as the biggest future project.

A second challenge of great meaning within the European context consists of the linking of the concepts of lifelong learning and training. It does not mean the traditional concept of lifelong learning, but just globally redefining the sense of educational and training trajectories. Is does not mean to suggest a kind of continuous training (after an initial period of schooling), but integrating the educational process as a whole, which is developed throughout life. It doesn't mean to separate formal learning (in schooling context) from informal learning (in professional context), but to join these contexts and others for constructing a new idea of education.

This reflection leads me to the last change, which I would like to mention briefly: the necessity for a new understanding of the relations between education and work. Closely following the analysis of Jose A. Correia (1997), one notes the existence of a *logic of exteriority* characterized, first, by a relative *autonomy* between these two universes, and, after the 1960s, by a *subordination* of the educational system to the world of work. Nowadays, we face contradictory logics, characterized by instability and uncertainty phenomena, through the perturbation of relations between people and social and professional spaces, between training, work, and employment, and between local and global dimensions in the management of the training-working systems. We are placed before a reinterpretation, not only of relations between education *and* work, but also in what concerns the concepts of *education* and *work*.

The debate about European educational policies must be seen from this perspective, emphasizing the set of contradictions going through them. If some discursive practices are pointing to new understandings of the concepts of education and work, it is not less true that in many European documents the school continues to be seen in its nineteenth-century form and the world of work is being defined either in a Taylorist logic or in a Fordist version. The time we are living through in the European Union is profoundly contradictory, in all regards. But it is also for this reason that the restructuring of the European educational space is very stimulating as a field of inquiry and intellectual thinking.

Notes

The first draft of this text was written in the United States, in 1994 and so some references to the Maastrict Treaty are out-of-date. It owes a lot to the collaboration and criticism of colleagues at the University of Wisconsin–Madison, especially Thomas Popkewitz and Andreas Kazamias. The final version was written in Paris, during an important stay at the History of Education Service (National Institute for Pedagogical Research), whose director is Pierre Caspard. I would also like to thank Jürgen Schriewer, Marc Depaepe, Boaventura de Sousa Santos, and the colleagues and students of the *Thursday Group* (University of Lisbon) for their support and suggestions. A final word of thanks is due to Dory Lightfoot for her translation and editing of this text. Major support for the research on which this article is based came from a JNICT grant (project PCSH/C/CED/908/95).

1. I am referring to the document *Overall Approach to the Application by the Council of the Subsidiarity Principle and Article 3b of the Treaty on European Union*, issued by the Presidency of the European Commission (Edinburgh, December 12, 1992).

2. Commission of the European Communities, *Report from the Commission to the Council, the European Parliament and the Economic and Social Committee—EC Education & Training Programmes, 1986–1992—Results and Achievements: An Overview*, Brussels, May, 1993.

3. Commission of the European Communities, *Report from the Commission to the Council, the European Parliament and the Economic and Social Committee—EC Education & Training Programmes, 1986–1992—Results and Achievements: An Overview*, Brussels, May, 1993.

4. Curiously, the *White Paper* is organized around the concept of *learning society* in the English version, a concept that appears in the French version as *société cognitive* (cognitive society). This terminological difference is very interesting and gives origin, in fact, to two very distinct readings of the document.

References

Adick, C. "Education in the Modern World System: An Attempt to End the Mythology of the Concept of Education as a Colonial Heritage." *Education* 40 (1989): 30–48.

Allum, P. *State and Society in Western Europe.* Cambridge: Polity Press, 1995.

Anderson, B. *Imagined Communities: Reflections on the Origin and Spread of Nationalism.* London and New York: Verso, 1983.

Apple, M. W. *Official Knowledge: Democratic Education in a Conservative Age.* New York: Routledge, 1993.

———. *Cultural Politics and Education.* New York: Teachers College Press, 1996.

Aron, R. "Is Multinational Citizenship Possible?" *Social Research* 41 (1974): 638–56.

Aronowitz, S. *The Politics of Identity: Class, Culture, Social Movements.* New York and London: Routledge, 1992.

Attali, J. *Europe(s).* Paris: Fayard, 1994.

Badie, B. *La fin des territoires*. Paris: Fayard, 1995.

Barroso, J. Perspectiva crítica sobre a utilização do conceito de qualidade. Paper presented at the Third Conference of the Portuguese Association of Educational Sciences (Lisbon, December, 1995).

Bauman, Zygmunt. *Legislators and Interpreters*. Cambridge: Polity Press, 1987.

Bell, G. "European Citizenship: 1992 and beyond." *Westminster Studies in Education* 14 (1991): 15–26.

Bourdieu, P. (ed). *La misère du monde*. Paris: Éditions du Seuil, 1993.

———. *Raisons pratiques: Sur la théorie de l'action*. Paris: Éditions du Seuil, 1994.

Brown, C. (ed.). *Political Restructuring in Europe*. London and New York: Routledge, 1994.

Carnoy, M. et al. *The New Global Economy in the Information Age: Reflections on Our Changing World*. Philadephia: Pennsylvania State University Press, 1993.

Chartier, R. & D. Julia. "L'école: Traditions et modernisation." In *Transactions of the Seventh International Congress on the Enlightenment*. Oxford: The Voltaire Foundation.

Close, P. *Citizenship, Europe and Change*. London: Macmillan, 1995.

Cornu, M. *Compétences culturelles en Europe et principe de subsidiarité*. Bruxelles: Bruylant, 1993.

Correia, J. *Formação e Trabalho: Contributos para a construção de uma epistemologia da mediação*. Porto: University of Oporto, 1997.

Coulby, D. "Cultural and Epistemological Relativism and European Curricula." *European Journal of Intercultural Studies* 3 (1993): 7–18.

———. "European Culture: Unity and Fractures." In *Challenges to European Education: Cultural Values, National Identities, and Global Responsibilities*, ed. T. Winther-Jensen. Frankfurt am Main: Peter Lang, 1996, 241–52.

Coulby, D., and C. Jones. *Postmodernity and European Education Systems: Cultural Diversity and Centralist Knowledge*. London: Trentham Books, 1995.

———. "Postmodernity, Education and European Identities." *Comparative Education* 32 (1996): 171–84.

Déloye, Y. *Ecole et Citoyenneté*. Paris: Presses de la Fondation Nationale des Sciences Politiques, 1994.

Der Derian, J. & M. Shapiro (eds.). *International/Intertextual Relations: Postmodern Readings of World Politics*. Lexington, Mass.: Lexington Books, 1989.

De Witte, B. (ed.). *European Community Law of Education*. Baden-Baden: Nomos Verlagsgesellschaft, 1989.

Dinan, D. "The European Community, 1978–1993." *The Annals of the American Academy of Political and Social Science* 531 (1994): 10–24.

Edwards, L., P. Munn & K. Fogelman (eds.). *Education for Democratic Citizenship in Europe: New Challenges for Secondary Education*. Lisse: Swets & Zeitlinger, 1994.

European Commission. *Proceedings from the Conference of the European Ministers of Education in Varsovie, April 22–24, 1997*.

Foucault, M. *Dits et Écrits*. Vol. 3. Paris: Éditions Gallimard, 1994.

Frediani, C. "La politique de la Communauté européenne en matière d'éducation et de culture." *L'Europe en Formation* 284 (1992): 51–64.

Garcia Garrido, J. L'avenir de l'éducation dans une Europe unifiée. Communication présentée au 16 ᵉᵐᵉ Congrès de al CESE (Copenhague, 1994).

Gellner, E. *Nations and Nationalism.* Ithaca, N.Y.: Cornell University Press, 1983.

———. *Encounters with Nationalism.* Oxford: Blackwell, 1994.

Giddens, A. *The Consequences of Modernity.* Stanford, Calif.: Stanford University Press, 1990.

Gilbert, R. "Citizenship, Education and Postmodernity." *British Journal of Sociology of Education* 13 (1992): 51–68.

Green, A. "Education and State Formation Revisited." *Historical Studies in Education* 6 (1994): 1–17.

Habermas, J. "Citizenship and National Identity: Some Reflections on the Future of Europe." *Praxis International* 12 (1992): 1–19.

Hayward, J. & E. Page (eds.). *Governing the New Europe.* Durham, N.C.: Duke University Press, 1995.

Heater, D. "Education for European Citizenship." *Westminster Studies in Education* 15 (1992): 53–67.

Hix, Simon. "The Study of the European Community: The Challenge to Comparative Politics." *West European Politics* 17 (1994): 1–30.

Husén, T., A. Tuijnman & W. Halls (eds.). *Schooling in Modern European Society.* Oxford: Pergamon Press, 1992.

Hutmacher, W. *L'école dans tous ses états.* Genève: Service de la Recherche Sociologique, 1990.

Imbert, C. "Identité européenne: Le complexe de Prométhée." In *Les nouvelles frontières de l'Europe.* Paris: Economica, pp. 33–41.

Jung, H. "Editor's Introduction to a Special Issue about 'Postmodernity and the Question of the Other.' " *Human Studies* 16 (1993): 1–17.

Lenaerts, K. "Education in European Community Law after 'Maastricht.' " *Common Market Law Review* 31 (1994): 7–41.

Lowe, J. "Education and European Integration." *International Review of Education* 38 (1992): 579–90.

Marquand, D. "Reinventing Federalism: Europe and the Left." *New Left Review* 203 (1994): 17– 26.

McLean, M. *Britain and a Single Market Europe: Prospects for a Common School Curriculum.* London: Kogan Page, 1990.

———. "The European Union and the Curriculum." *Oxford Studies in Comparative Education* 5 (1995): 29–46.

Meehan, E. "Citizenship and the European Community." *The Political Quarterly* 64 (1993): 172– 86.

Meyer, J., D. Kamens & A. Benavot (eds.). *School Knowledge for the Masses.* London: Falmer Press, 1992.

Meyer, J., F. Ramirez & Y. Soysal. "World Expansion of Mass Education, 1870–1980." *Sociology of Education* 65 (1992): 128–49.

Miller, J. *The Passion of Michel Foucault.* New York: Simon and Schuster, 1993.

Milward, A. *The European Rescue of the Nation-State.* Berkeley: University of California Press, 1992.

Morin, E. *Penser l'Europe.* Paris: Gallimard, 1987.

Myrdal, S. "Centralization, Decentralization and the Reprofessionalization of the European Teacher." Paper presented at the Symposium "Educational Systems and the Restructuring of the State" (Granada, 1993).

Pereyra, M. "La Comparación, una empresa razonada de análisis: Por otros usos de la comparación." *Revista de Educatión* (Los usos de la comparacion en Ciencias Sociales y en Educacion) (1990): 24–76.

————. "La construcción de la educación comparada como disciplina académica." In *Manual de Educación Comparada*—ed. by J. Schriewer and F. Pedro. Barcelona: PPU, +1993, 255–323.

————. "The Social Participation in the Construction of the European Dimension in Education." *CESE Newsletter* 36 (1994): 12–21.

Phillips, D., (ed.). *Aspects of Education and the European Union*. Oxfordshire: Triangle Books, 1995.

Pisani, E. "Où va l'Europe?" *L'événement européen* 14–15 (1991): 181–83.

Popkewitz, T. *A Political Sociology of Educational Reform: Power/Knowledge in Teaching, Teacher Education, and Research*. New York: Teachers College Press, 1991.

————. "Policy, Knowledge and Power: Some Issues for the Study of Educational Reform." In *Transforming Schools: Trends, Dilemmas and Prospects*, ed. P. Cookson and B. Schneider. New York: Garland Press, 1995, pp. 413–57.

————. "El Estado y la administración de la libertad a finales del siglo XX: Descentralización Estado/sociedad civil." In *Globalización y descentralización de los sistemas educativos*, ed. by M. et al. Pereyra. Barcelona: Ediciones Pomares-Corredor, 1996, 119–68.

Rohrs, H. "A United Europe as a Challenge to Education." *European Journal of Intercultural Studies* 3 (1992): 59–70.

Rust, V. "Postmodernism and Its Comparative Education Implications." *Comparative Education Review* 35 (1991): 610–26.

Ryba, R. "Unity in Diversity: The Enigma of the European Dimension in Education." *Oxford Review of Education* 21 (1995): 25–36.

Santos, B. *Pela Mão de Alice: O social e o político na pós-modernidade*. Porto: Edições Afrontamento, 1994.

————. *Toward a New Common Sense*. New York: Routledge, 1995.

Sbragia, A. (ed.). *Euro-Politics: Institutions and Policymaking in the "New" European Community*. Washington, D.C.: Brookings Institution, 1992.

Schnapper, D. *La communauté des citoyens: Sur l'idée moderne de nation*. Paris: Gallimard, 1994.

Schriewer, J. *World System and Interrelationship Networks: The Internationalization of Education and the Role of Comparative Inquiry* [in this volume], 1995.

Shapiro, M. "The European Court of Justice." In *Euro-Politics: Institutions and Policymaking in the "New" European Community*, ed. A. Sbragia. Washington D.C.: Brookings Institution, 1992, pp. 123–56.

Shaw, J. "Education and the Law in the European Community." *Journal of Law and Education* 21 (1992): 415–42.

Smith, A. *The Ethnic Origins of Nations*. Oxford: Basil Blackwell, 1986.

————. *National Identity*. Reno: University of Nevada Press, 1991.

Soysal, Y. *Limites of Citizenship: Migrants and Postnational Membership in Europe.* Chicago and London: University of Chicago Press, 1994.

Soysal, Y. & D. Strang. "Construction of the First Mass Education Systems in Nineteenth-Century Europe." *Sociology of Education* 62 (1989): 277–88.

Sultana, R. "A Uniting Europe, a Dividing Education? Eurocentrism and the Curriculum." *International Studies in the Sociology of Education* 5 (1995): 115–44.

Taylor, P. "The European Community and the State: Assumptions Theories and Propositions." *Review of International Studies* 17 (1991): 109–25.

Taylor, W. "Educating British Children for European Citizenship." *European Journal of Education* 28 (1993): 437–44.

Tilly, C. *Coercion, Capital, and European States, A.D. 990–1992.* Cambridge, Mass.: Blackwell, 1992.

———. "States and nationalism in Europe 1492–1992." *Theory and Society* 23 (1994): 131–46.

Tyack, D. & W. Tobin. "The "Grammar" of Schooling: Why Has It Been So Hard to Change?" *American Educational Research Journal* 31 (1994): 453–79.

Vaniscotte, F. *Les Écoles de l'Europe: Systèmes éducatifs et dimension européenne.* Paris: INRP, 1996.

Vibert, F. *Europe: A Constitution for the Millennium.* Brookfield: Dartmouth, 1995.

Vonk, H. "Some Trends in the Development of Curriculum for the Professional Preparation of Teachers in Europe." *British Journal of Educational Studies* 39 (1991): 117–37.

Wasser, H. "The European Mind and EC 1992." *History of European Ideas* 17 (1993): 11–17.

Whitty, G. "New Schools for New Times? Education Reform in a Global Context." Paper presented at the Symposium "Educational Reform: Changing Relationships between the State, Civil Society, and the Educational Community" (Madison, Wisconsin, 1993).

Winther-Jensen, T., ed. *Challenges to European Education: Cultural Values, National Identities, and Global Responsibilities.* Frankfurt am Main: Peter Lang, 1996.

Wistrich, E. *The United States of Europe.* London and New York: Routledge, 1994.

Some European Documents

Commission of the European Communities. Green Paper on the European Dimension of Education. Brussels, COM (93) 457 final, 29 September 1993.

———. Report from the Commission to the Council, the European Parliament and the Economic and Social Committee—ED Education & Training Programmes 1986–1992—Results and Achievements: An Overview. Brussels, COM (93) 151 final, 5 May 1993.

———. *White Paper,* "Growth, Competitiveness, Employment: The Challenges and Ways Forward into the Twenty-First Century." Brussels, COM (93) 700 final, 5 December 1993.

———. *White Paper,* "Education and Training—Teaching and Learning: Towards the Learning Society." Brussels, COM (95) 590 final, 29 November 1995.

————. *Green Paper,* "Living and Working in the Information Society: People First." Brussels, COM (96) 389 final, 24 July 1996.

Council of the European Communities. European Educational Policy Statements. Luxembourg: Office for Official Publications of the European Communities.

European Commission. Cooperation in Education in the European Union, 1976–1994. Luxembourg: Office for Official Publications of the European Communities.

————. Targeted Socio-Economic Research. Brussels.

Study Group on Education and Training (dir. Edith Cresson). Report "Accomplishing Europe Through Education and Training." Brussels, December, 1996.

UNESCO-International Comission on Education for the Twenty-First Century (dir. Jacques Delors). Learning: The Treasure Within. Paris: Unesco.

CHAPTER 3

Restructuring the State in Eastern Europe

Women, Child Care, and Early Education

MARIANNE N. BLOCH AND BENITA BLESSING

Welfare Policies toward Families and Children in East-Central Europe during the Post–Soviet Transition

The collapse of the Soviet Union in the late 1980s and early 1990s resulted in enormous and varied changes in the former Soviet and Soviet-bloc countries, including those of Eastern and Central Europe. During the early transition years, the Communist governments or those that replaced them in Eastern and Central European countries began to move toward market economies with aid from international organizations, businesses, and banks. The global, regional, national, and local discursive environment appeared to support a transition toward a "market-oriented" and "democratic" system of governance. Eastern and Central Europeans individually, in small groups as members of civil society, and in the form of national and regional debate have nevertheless questioned the wisdom of different discursive models for rebuilding social, political, and economic institutions and laws—searching for their own way to define democracy or "market economy." The urgency associated with dialogue and reform in all spheres, new opportunities (e.g., entry into NATO or the European Union) as well as the difficulties associated with rapid change led to quick policy changes and reversals in governments, policies, laws, practices, and the lives and opportunities for different economic, political, and social groups.

In this chapter, we explore the ways in which diverse discourses have provided different ways of reasoning as a foundation for dialogue within and across the countries of East/Central Europe during this transition period. We especially attend to the ways in which different actors and texts have generated temporary truths about which social, economic reforms or scenarios for a region or country might be best for different interest groups, for majority as well as minority groups, for the short term and for the long term. We argue that the rapid disintegration and changes in policies, institutions, and practices that had been taken for granted for approximately forty years under Communism (approximately 1950 to 1990), represented here as new systems of governing and governance, have resulted variously in uncertainty, impoverishment for many, and, in some instances, to new visions and opportunities.

Our focus here is on changing discourses represented in proposed and recently enacted reforms in welfare policies related to the care and education of young children, with particular attention to the experiences and debates that have occurred in the East/Central European countries of Hungary, Poland, and Bulgaria, where research was conducted in 1993 and 1995. We argue that reforms related to families, and the care and educational systems organized for young children, represent a complex intermixing of global, regional, and local discourses related to new conceptions of family and individual "needs," conceptions of dependency, and independence[1] for the newly imagined communities and citizens of East/Central Europe. This chapter also reveals how reforms currently taking place embody selective images of liberalism, welfare, the market, democracy, and the role of the state and civil society in governance, especially in relation to the family, women, and the care and education of the young child as citizen.

In examining recent reforms in East/Central Europe, it is important to look at how global as well as more localized discourses come to govern through new reasoning created in reform laws and policies, immersed in changing local practices and the language used to promote interests and beliefs by different groups and individuals within the state and civil society "complex." We argue that new governing discourses affect the way State and nonstate, public and private groups and individuals have come to act and reason about themselves and others. The new ways to reason include implications about what men and women are to be and do, where and how children are to be cared for and educated, the formation of schools for different age children, and the role of governments in caring for the well-being of citizens, particularly, women and children.

Governance and governmentality. Foucault's theoretical concept of governance and governmentality[2] frames the presentation of our research on East/Central European social and educational reforms. Foucault used the concept of governance, simultaneously in relation to *governance of others* and *governance of the self.* Governance refers to macro- and micro-social forms that aim to shape, guide, manage, or regulate the conduct and ways of reasoning embedded in institutions, laws, reports, groups and individual language, conduct, and even reflections or the "soul."[3]

Foucault proposed the notion of *governmentality* as a blurring of boundaries between the state and all quarters of civil society and blurring the boundaries between the self and the society. The governmentalized subject views himself or herself not merely as a self-governed individual but also as "citizen." Governance is also political—not through particular actions of the *State*, institutions, or particular actors (e.g., a sovereign power) but by the varieties of political reasoning that come to order the affairs of a territory and its population to ensure its well-being or welfare. The creation of ways to reason can result in what appears as "natural" divisions between the proper spheres of action of different types of authority, roles, or responsibilities; for example, the way we reason about the divisions in authority between State and civil society, or the responsibilities of State, schools, and family.[4] The creation of artificial distinctions in reasoning hides governance that is subtle, diffuse, and complex.

Here we argue that patterns of global, national, and local discourses, embodied in everyday language, reforms, media, statistics, scientific "knowledge," educational pedagogy and texts, and our reflections create understandings of words, divisions, and actions. These reasonings represent power/ knowledge relationships that have differential effects, that include and exclude, allowing different opportunities for participation in different social groups.

Governance and changing political rationalities about the "welfare" of citizens. Philosophies of welfare from the above perspective then embody ways of reasoning based upon complex interactions in and across societies at particular historical/cultural moments. Conceptions of welfare embody ways of reasoning that bring together a legal as well as a common sense understanding of the rights of individuals in balance with those of the rights of the collective (Hindess, 1996). In the examination of changing governing strategies and rationalities in East and Central Europe, as these relate to the welfare of families and young children, we illustrate how the circulation of global, regional, and local discourses has begun to shift reasoning about welfare for children and their families since the post–Soviet transition.

Constructing Conceptions of Welfare in Eastern and Central Europe

Reasonings and governance prior to 1990. Although many individuals, groups, and institutions were expected to be influenced by changes, families—especially women and children—were expected to be vulnerable to the post–Soviet transition toward a market economy. Under Communist governments, collective welfare was to take precedence over individual opportunity.

Thus, families were guaranteed minimum family incomes, universal health benefits, access to universal family allowances and child care, and a variety of other entitlements and social benefits that ensured them at least minimum acceptable economic welfare.

The Communist command economy virtually assured and, indeed, forced employment by all adult male and female citizens. Under Communist governments, child care and other family financial supports facilitating, especially, women's ability to reproduce and produce were important. Families were supported through a variety of intricate family allowances that were based on the number of children in a family, age of the child, and the premise that society needed to support care and education for children while supporting (men's and) women's work outside the home. From birth to three years of age, care for children was guaranteed through maternal leave policies, family allowances that allowed mothers to stay at home with young children from one to three years, and creches (day care) for infants to three year olds whose mothers "needed" to work. Mothers went back to their employment with virtually free State child care ("kindergartens") for three to six year olds.

The political discourse that surrounded this conception of collective "cradle to grave" safety and welfare, and gender equity in the workplace for women was never fulfilled, and it varied significantly both within and across countries of the former Communist bloc. There was less equity in the workplace than ideologically promised; while there was a minimum income provided to all, along with health care and so forth, there were still wide resource variations as well as discursive limitations on liberties that became well known. In addition, by the mid-1980s, the Soviet planned economy that organized markets and prices across the entire set of Soviet bloc countries had suffered economic setbacks, stagnation of industries and agriculture, and gradual increases in black-market activity. It was in this context that new discussions of competition, "freer markets," and "democracy" began to emerge. Since 1990, there have been rapid changes in national economic and political pictures and in the everyday economic, social, and cultural lives of families, women, men, and children. Income disparities have grown along with uncertainty for many who have lost jobs and other guarantees of minimum welfare for their families.

Discursive shifts in governance since 1990. The sense of collective welfare gave way to a discursive environment that encouraged "individualism," opened up discussions of poverty, and allowed some to be impoverished while others were applauded and encouraged to compete for wealth. Long-term economic growth became discursively the most important collective goal, with short-term poverty suddenly acceptable. The new context also produced a sense that "democratization" would allow for economic and political independence, new freedoms of speech and participation, recognition of individual rights and choices, and an ability to participate actively in civil society as voters and decision makers. The expectation for "democracy" was that the new possibilities would be all-inclusive in a way that socialist/communist governance failed to accomplish, especially once the long-term goals for economic development and modernization were accomplished. With new expectations came governance including new ways of self-reflection and self-action.

National Culture and History. Global and European discourse supported a transition to a more market-oriented and "democratic" system of governance, including saving money through a nonuniversal, "need"-based, liberal welfare model targeted particularly at the poorest families and dependent children. Nevertheless, a strong undercurrent of national and local debate in East/Central Europe (and the former Soviet Union) also directed the language of governance—its policies, reforms, and practices. Sometimes these appeared to include liberal market discourse, and at other times the discourses supported socialist politics and social welfare-state discourse, often with elected Communist/Socialist government leadership.

No countries, perhaps, are better examples of these issues than Bulgaria, Hungary, and Poland, each of which has had multiple governments since 1990. The latter two have been approved for NATO inclusion and will be two of the early candidates for entry into the European Union. Bulgaria, on the other hand, according to statistical/media reports from the early 1990s, was represented as a "less advanced" country in terms of its transition toward a growth-oriented market economy and was slated for "later" inclusion in NATO and the European Union.

While all three provide a glimpse of regional economic changes, the three also provide examples of countries where international, regional, national, and local history and culture combine, resulting in significant historical and current distinctions between countries. In the next section, we use world economic reports on the three countries to represent some of the ways new global discourses have begun to emerge and merge with national-local history, old welfare discourses, and new conceptions of welfare and well-being for families and children.

Bulgaria, Hungary, and Poland: Shifting Governing Strategies

Of the three countries, Polish citizens, especially through the Solidarity Union movement, seemed to be the most eager and "ready" to make a break toward the West in the late 1980s. They were also the first to make a break with Communist Party leadership and with the former Soviet Union's leadership. In contrast, the Bulgarian government and citizens seemed to be politically and economically most tied to the Communist regime and command economy of the former Soviet Union. Poland, Hungary, and Bulgaria each had different economic possibilities with respect to competing for Western resources, funds to privatize companies, and different industrial strengths and weaknesses, when the transition began in the late 1980s. Each had different histories of state control and different groups representing new visions of democracy, the economy, and welfare.

Poland, for example, had resisted state ownership of agricultural land to a much greater extent than the other countries under the Communist government. It was also more heavily influenced by the Roman Catholic Church than the other two countries. The women's movements, while repressed in all three countries, were significantly different in the more conservative religious environment of Roman Catholic Poland than in the less religiously conservative Hungary.[5] Poland's strategic geographic location and history pushed it politically and economically toward the West and Western markets. Given its history of war with Russia, it also had eyed the security of NATO as well as the relative wealth of Western European neighbors from a close range. Poland had used black-market activity with the West to begin accumulating funds, which became instrumental in its radical approach to price liberalization in 1990. Bulgaria, on the other hand, was more reluctant at first to break with the Soviet Union and its continued reliance during the early 1990s on the Soviet command economy. Its debt and relative poverty and distance from the West also made it less attractive than Poland or Hungary to outside Western investors.

Politically, all three countries had elements of civil society available to begin work toward "democracy" and, with different histories, geographic, political, and economic possibilities, work toward developing open markets, and more competitive and "efficient" economic systems. Poland began its transition, however, with what became known as "shock therapy"; under the guidance of international advisors, they decided to open markets quickly, to restrict or eliminate government subsidies, and to allow rapid price inflation to occur. Government policy makers, with international guidance from Harvard University economists, decided to thrust the country into "shock," assuming there would be quick pain, with rapid economic growth thereafter and recovery. Hungary and Bulgaria, on the other hand, with traditions that tied them more closely to socialist beliefs and policies, assumed that a slower transition toward the West would minimize the pain of the transition, particularly for the least well-educated or able citizens; both countries initially assumed that a welfare model that maintained social/family benefits and a minimum of standards for families would be crucial for a successful transition and for a "softer landing" into the West.

New discourses within countries as well as from the outside to "privatize," develop "open markets," and become "efficient" and "competitive," provided important governing contexts that allowed East/Central European countries to become "receptive" to multinational companies from the West that began to examine possibilities for privatization or joint ventures. During the early transition years, each of the former Soviet bloc countries competed for international donor funds and for multinational funds to buy state companies or to develop joint-venture schemes. Within this economic and discursive framework, each of the countries was interested in developing an economic and political context that would make it favorable to future funds and investments, as well as to joining NATO and the European Union.

Other economic discourses—"competition," "choice," "privatization," "efficient and free markets"—circulated within and around the East/Central European region throughout the period 1990 to 1995 when this research was conducted. The discourses of "freedom," "autonomy," "individualism," and "democracy" were linked with the concept that competition was good, open markets were needed, efficient markets were important even at the cost of social provisions for citizens. To become "democratic" and "economically competitive" became important and these discourses became important at the broad as well as at the local levels. They could be heard in the ways individuals spoke, the reasoning they used, and the actions they performed.

International economic reports: Statistical reasoning. Statistics in international reports, as descriptive and neutral as they seem, are part of the changing governing strategies that have been occurring during the transition toward a market economy in East and Central Europe. In fact, in the West and East, statistics have been a form of social administration since the late nineteenth and early twentieth century. Statistics were used to define and describe groups that could be "treated" or intervened with, groups to whom social policies could be directed. We can see this reasoning at work in statistical assessments of the "health" of a nation, or a "people," or when classifications such as "poor," "under the poverty line," or "single parent"[6] come to be used to describe a group of individuals. Group names, or statistical categories, also focus attention toward classification of difference—who is normal and abnormal, which countries are developed/undeveloped, modern/nonmodern.

In the case of international discourse that describes the transitional period in East/Central Europe (and the former Soviet Union), the international banks and donor agencies selected labels and statistical indicators that represented progress toward goals characteristic of a healthy free-market economy and a liberal perspective on welfare. In the following pages, we present statistics representing the economic and social contexts in Bulgaria, Hungary, and Poland over the past few years to provide examples of the international discursive environment that constituted regional, national, and local reasoning.

Domestic product, investment, and debt. Reports emphasize per capita "domestic product," or "Gross Domestic Product" (GDP), internal and external

TABLE 3.1
Annual Percentage Change in GDP, 1990–1995

	1990	1991	1992	1993	1994	1995[7]
Bulgaria	–9.1	–6.9	–5.7	–3.7	2.2	2.5
Hungary	–3.3	–11.9	–3.0	–0.8	2.9	2.0
Poland	–11.6	–7.0	2.6	3.8	5.0	7.0

investment, and debt. Looking at table 3.1 above, GDP statistics indicate that Poland was the first of the three to have a positive GDP, but that, by 1994, all three countries had positive economic growth, with Poland appearing to be "first" in production. The growth in efficiency and competitiveness represented by GDP were positively construed in reports as the right directions toward a market economy.

A successful transition was also construed as one in which foreign investment would occur. Foreign companies saw the transitional countries as opportunities; Eastern and Central European countries needed help to "modernize" companies, to become competitive in a free-market economy. One construction on foreign investment was "aid" to modernize inefficient, noncompetitive companies (and countries). Another construction, rarely included in international bank/donor reports, was that foreign investment constituted the growth of dependencies between the West and Eastern and Central European countries.

In the early years of the East/Central European transition, foreign investors were being enticed into countries with a variety of low-cost incentives including the ability to disregard traditional welfare guarantees. The complex ways in which economic progress was entangled with the "need" for outside investment, privatization, and need for budgetary "efficiency" pushed each country in the region to market itself as a modern (i.e., open, free-market) economy, and to look aside when traditional social guarantees such as child care, traditionally offered by factories in the Soviet period, were ignored or shut down by foreign companies.

The differences in the three countries followed the same pattern observed in GDP with Bulgaria receiving less foreign monies than Hungary and Poland (Bulgaria went from $20 million to $220 million in foreign investment from 1990 to 1995; Hungary went from $311 million to $1511 million in foreign investment between 1990 and 1995; Poland went from $88 million to $1300 million in foreign investment from 1990 to 1995).[8]

While international donors, banks, and multinational companies were pushing investment, privatization councils within the three countries were eager to compete for investments. It was understood that it was good to attract investment, (almost) no matter what the cost. The relation between investment and social benefit maintenance or provision is represented by the comment of a young male American international consultant in Hungary who stated that firms were being urged to get rid of all of their "social assets" as quickly as possible (including nurseries, kindergartens, etc.), as these only detracted from the firm's or factory's value, were cumbersome and costly, and not typical of Western business benefits to employees. It was this type of mentality that constituted the discourse of development in social policy reforms related to welfare and well-being.

International banks and donor agencies not only provided resources for emerging and emergency needs, but "guided" policy development with strict rules, regulations, incentives, and threats, in return for loans. While adding to external debt, international donor requirements/pressures to reduce internal debt stimulated many countries in East/Central Europe to be concerned with the amount of social benefits and services they were providing, as these services and benefits were interpreted as being too costly in a declining economy, and when factories were closing or unable to pay wages. While some of these concerns were reasonable, there are choices as evidenced by recent debates between labor unions and governments in France, Italy, and Scandinavia where many social benefits for families have been maintained. In many other countries of the European Union, and countries of East/Central Europe that aspired to be in the European Union, there were attempts to reduce social benefits in order to bring debt down to a uniform targeted 3 percent level. Thus, the discourse of membership in the European Union provided reasonable justification for policies that decreased welfare benefits.

Unemployment, professional mothers, and the discourse of choice. Unemployment rates and changes in unemployment again become the criteria of economic illness or health, and the history of debates about social policy was forgotten or obscured. Liberal philosophies of welfare supported a "safety net" only for those most in need, while socialist welfare philosophies supported a discourse of universal entitlements to jobs, child care, and the like.

The emergence of statistics documenting employment and unemployment was an important discursive shift. Changes in unemployment are represented in tables 3.2 and 3.3 and suggest that the rise in unemployment had subsided in all three countries by 1995, but that the *registered* unemployment rate was high.[9] The new method by which employment was measured is another embodiment of a shift in the system of reasoning.

TABLE 3.2
Annual Percentage Change in Employment, 1990–1994

	1990	1991	1992	1993	1994,Q2[10]
Bulgaria	–6.1	–13	–8.1	–6.0	–3.5
Hungary	–3.1	–9.6	–9.3	–5.9	–2.6
Poland	–4.0	–5.9	–4.2	–0.6	–1.2

TABLE 3.3
Unemployment Rates, 1990–1994

	1990	1991	1992	1993	1994,Q2[11]
Bulgaria	1.7	11.1	15.3	16.4	13.3 (June)
Hungary	1.7	8.5	12.3	12.1	11.0 (June)
Poland	3.5	9.7	13.3	15.7	16.9 (June)

Women's employment. Between 1989 and 1992, female employment participation fell from 93 percent to 66 percent in Bulgaria, from 78 percent to 66 percent in Hungary and from 70 percent to 60 percent in Poland.[12] Female/male unemployment rates, in contrast, did not indicate differences between male and female unemployment rates in the three countries, though industry rates varied. With factories closing, being sold or privatized, many lost employment, took "involuntary vacation," or took child-care leave.

The discursive effect was the increase in maternity leave. Registration for unemployment, the statistical indicator most heavily used in international reports for unemployment, does not include unemployment if one is on child-care leave, nor does it include those on "involuntary vacation." Thus, while many had been fearful that women would be forced out of jobs first in the transition toward a free market liberal philosophy economy, the unemployment statistics never showed large inequalities. However, women were discursively encouraged to become "professional mothers" and to take child-care leave while remaining officially and discursively "employed." They were also not eligible for unemployment benefits while on small parental leave allowances, nor, as they were still "employed," were they eligible for retraining possibilities. The maintenance and, at times, augmentation of maternity leave allowances or leave time, at low cost to governments and factories, supported a statistical picture of low female unemployment, while at the same time saving money and eliminating a portion of the workforce during this period.[13]

In all three countries, from 1990 to 1995, social policies, media, and other institutional, legal, and civil society groups, including local academic feminists,[14] developed laws in support of more years for maternity and child-care leaves and supported this with the discourse of "professional motherhood," giving women the "choice" to be at home, according to some women's groups, for the first time in fifty years.

Initially, in 1993, "professional mothers" were being offered the choice to go home with their children for extended periods; in Hungary, one proposed law (never passed) suggested child-care leave could extend until the youngest child in a family was eight years old (the law stated three years). By 1995, new laws were proposed, and eventually passed, limiting child-care leave to only one year in order to reduce factory stipends to mothers and to minimize the "social costs" of factories employing women. Laws in Hungary, as well as the other countries, were also instituted stipulating that no benefits had to be paid to short-term employees. It was possible to hire temporary or short-term employees with no guarantees or social benefits. Many women who had lost jobs or who were looking for new or additional jobs were hired under the classification of temporary or short term.[15] With rising costs, women generally continued to need to work, but had to pay their own increasing fees for child care, or use relative or unregulated family day care, a system of care that grew after 1990.

Poverty and economic differentiation. The growth in official and unofficial unemployment, by industrial sector, geographical region, and by gender (as well as age and ethnicity), was matched by growth in poverty, diminishing average real wages, price inflation, and increasing economic and social differentiation. This is indicated statistically by the percentage of people considered to be under the poverty line or "in poverty," as calculated by international agencies. These statistics suggest that between 1989 and 1994, 40 percent of the Polish population and 30 percent of the Hungarian population were considered to be officially under minimum income levels, or "in poverty" (the international reports examined gave no comparable figures for Bulgaria);[16] the growth in this statistic was also discursively important as prior to 1990 in the Communist regimes there had been no published reports of "poverty."

There have been many arguments about the number of people considered to be "in poverty" in each country, related to proposed changes in social reforms. Such arguments were most visible in Hungary during the research conducted in 1995. Here the new minister of finance (Bokros), under pressure to reduce debt from the International Monetary Fund (IMF) and the World Bank, had proposed to eliminate universal family supports and allowances and to replace universal entitlements with a new need-based system of social benefits based on estimates of family income. Earlier reforms in Hungary supported "professional motherhood" and the choice to be at home through a proposal to extend maternity leave and allowances . In 1995 discourse about "professional motherhood" and the choice to be at home was no longer so evident (see earlier discussion); discourses surrounding "need" and supporting those under the poverty line emerged in the Bokros Plan.

There was considerable debate about the proposal; an interview with one woman in the Institute for Nurseries in Hungary in 1995 suggested that there was no uniform "voice" responding to the international discourse to reform social policy, nor one model:

As of July 1, the new social policy orchestrated by the Minister of Finance, with no consultation with anyone else, will begin. [It was] passed into law. As a result of this the Minister of Welfare and another resigned as they had been trying to implement policies that would safeguard many social benefits while saving money, while the Minister of Finance policy removes many benefits, and will be need based. For example, it used to be that 0–3's were covered by a family policy and benefits, and these benefits will be reduced to families with 0–1 year olds only. Other benefits will disappear entirely unless a family can qualify (need based). While instituted by the Minister of Finance alone, it was probably stimulated by pressures from the IMF and/or the World Bank, . . . *But many more families will need day care and family day care will be needed; many more families have applied for day care.*[17] (emphasis added)

There was also debate about how many people would be cut out of receiving benefits by the proposed plan. As the finance minister's goal was to save money, the new benefits' reform had to leave some people out. However, the debates surrounded how high to estimate the "poverty line." While most in the Social Democratic Party, representing a socialist vision of welfare, were adamantly opposed to the sharp reductions in support, some nonetheless stated that the policy would have little effect. Maria Zam, a former deputy minister of welfare, for example, and adamantly opposed to the Bokros Plan suggested that the "poverty line" selected would still include nearly 80 percent of the Hungarian population because so many people earned so little.[18] In July 1995, the law was stopped from implementation by the courts, and the minister of finance was forced to resign.

The statistics and discourses reviewed above present the new mentalities that have been created in the reasoning in and about countries, groups, and individuals in Eastern and Central Europe. Now progress is represented by Gross Domestic Product, and by rates of international investment. It is now acceptable to have "unemployed," "people in poverty." Universal welfare is no longer a reasonable justification for an economic policy. It is good to have "professional mothers" who choose to stay at home. It is good to reduce social benefits to become efficient and competitive. In the next section, we look at the impact of these discursive shifts on the provision of child care.

Child Care, Kindergartens, and Education

As suggested earlier, full provision of either maternity leave or nurseries for infants to three year olds and mandatory provision of kindergarten places for all three to six or three to seven year olds had been a part of the discourse of universal provision in all of the former Soviet block countries, including Bulgaria, Hungary, and Poland. In the postcommunist transition period, proposals for reductions in maternity leave, other social subsidies and services nurseries for infants to three year olds and kindergartens for three to six year olds were part of the global and regional discourse, and indeed services for infants to six year olds were early targets in social and economic policy reforms.

Nonetheless, there were important differences among the three countries even before 1990 and important changes in provisions across the region and within each country since 1990. These are represented in table 3.4; no entries were made where data for particular years, typically prior to 1990, could not be located.

The statistics on nursery and kindergarten "coverage" (percent of age group enrolled in nurseries or kindergartens) suggest what other interviews and data confirm (see Fernandez & Bloch, 1993): while nurseries and kindergartens began to decrease prior to 1990, they were closed in greater numbers after 1990; also the number of children enrolled in the institutions declined over the same period, though, in some cases, more children were combined into fewer nursery and kindergarten programs. The exception was in Hungary, where kindergarten provision remained fairly constant between 1990 and 1995.

A close examination shows that kindergartens and nurseries began closing before 1990 in all three countries, with, in Bulgaria and Hungary, a significantly greater percentage covering children in 1980 and even in 1985 than in 1990; in Poland, while the percentage differences look similar (55 percent coverage in 1980 and a decline to 47 percent in 1990), the sheer numbers of children no longer enrolled in kindergarten declined sharply, both before 1990, and again after 1990 (again, see Fernandez & Bloch, 1993, for greater discussion here). Nurseries, always much smaller in number because of the history of maternity leave and child allowances in each country, closed in greater proportion than kindergartens in Bulgaria and Poland, and were proposed to close or be restructured significantly as an effect of the 1995 Bokros Plan in Hungary.

National-local debates concerning child care. There are many factors that can account for the described changes in provision for and attendance in

TABLE 3.4
Percent Nursery and Kindergarten Coverage, 1980, 1985, 1990, 1993, 1994

	1980	1985	1990	1993	1994
Bulgaria					
Nurseries—0–3				11.7	9.2[19]
Kindergartens—3–6		100	93	67–80	60–82
Hungary					
Nurseries—0–3		14.8	11.1	11.1	11.2[20]
Kindergartens—3–6	96	91	84.9	86.6	86.3[21]
Final Yr. Kind.—5 yrs.					95
Poland					
Nurseries—0–3		5.2	5.1	4.2	4
Kindergartens—3–6	55	51	47.1	42.6	42.7
Zero class—6 yrs.					96

nursery and kindergarten programs in the three countries. These include declining economic production in the 1980s resulting in the beginnings of the transfer and closing down of nurseries and kindergartens associated with factories, as well as falling birth rates and increasing fees for child care at the same time that unemployment (especially female) and poverty were increasing. In addition, from the 1990s, as we've discussed earlier, international and regional market discourses along with national and local women's groups' pressures for more flexibility to stay at home with young children promoted the conception that women might stay at home, that it was no longer necessary to provide extensive and expensive social benefits; the "causes" were complex, with no single factor or discourse appearing to dominate.

In the next section, we look at different arguments at international, regional, national, and local levels, policies and responses to new regulations—showing the possibilities for complex debate, local actions, meanings, and resistances. Examples from our research on Hungarian regulations about kindergarten, women's groups in Russe, Bulgaria, or policy implementors in local communities that kept "social assets" represent the importance of looking at local meaning and action.

Local meanings: The language of reform policies. Some of the explanation for trends in child care can be examined through the wording of reform policies and the variations in actions and words during the 1990 to 1995 transitional period. Some of the explanation can be seen by looking at a longer history of discourse surrounding the provision of care/education for infants to six-year-old children.

Historically, there have been rules since the early twentieth century in all three countries that distinguished policy for child care for infants to three-year-old children from policy for kindergartens. In most countries, nurseries or creches for infants to three-year-old children were administered in health and welfare ministries, while kindergartens for three-to-six- or three-to-seven-year-old children were administered in ministries of education. Thus, there was a discourse of health and custodial care, rather than education, surrounding institutions for the youngest children. Also, maternity leave and mothers' allowances were the most frequently used alternative by parents during this period, with nurseries typically accounting for at most 15 percent of the infant to three-year age group in Hungary, for example, in 1980, while kindergartens in Hungary during the same period provided care for 80 percent to 90 percent of the three-to-six-year-old children. Thus, women were seen as the principle caretakers for young children, and their ability to move in and out of the (out-of-the home) labor market had been established over the twentieth century in social science policy formation, despite a counterrhetoric of "full employment" for men and women under the Communist governments that were in control from approximately 1950 to 1990.[22]

In contrast, in kindergartens for three to six year olds, which were administered and supervised in special preschool units in ministries of education from the beginning of the twentieth century in all three countries, there was a historical discourse associating, and at the same time *dis*associating, young three-to-six-year-old children's care and education with the formation of schools and schooling. For example, while primary schooling was mandatory, kindergarten attendance was not mandatory for children in any of the countries. Unlike nursery schools for infants to three-year-old children, government regulations mandated provision of kindergarten centers and places for parents who requested/needed it. Coupling this with full employment policies and a discourse supporting universal provision, the majority of parents wanted kindergartens, and governments had to respond. In fact, in Bulgaria and Hungary, with long historical traditions of educational experimentation with kindergartens that predated the Communist period, the policies requiring kindergartens for all children resulted in 80 percent to 90 percent of the three- to-six-year-old children having places in kindergartens in both countries by the 1980s. In Poland, a much larger, more rural, and more politically conservative country than the other two, finances were never made available to fully enact the policy of providing kindergartens for all three to six year olds; therefore, kindergarten provision reached only 55 percent to 60 percent of the three to six year olds, even at the peak of provision in the 1970s.[23]

While the historical differences are very important, they also manifested themselves in different transitional policies during the 1990 to 1995 period. In all three countries, new regulations and policies were passed during this period that supported the continuation of maternity leave and other allowances for infants to three-year-old children (and in Hungary by 1995 the proposed law to provide leave only for mothers with infants to three-year-old children) and legislation that supported the desirability but not the necessity of providing "places" in creches or nurseries for infant to three-year-old children; the choice of providing nursery places would be left to local governments. In contrast, in all three countries, new regulations were passed that reinforced the state mandate to provide kindergartens for those who wanted them. However, again, local governments were to put these regulations into place. In Poland and Bulgaria, the mandates were written into regulations in the strongest form for the year prior to primary school, "that communities must provide kindergarten for the year preceding entry into the public school . . ." with slightly weaker language for kindergarten provision for three- and four-year-old children.

In Hungary, in contrast, ministry of education officials in the preschool section charged with policy related to kindergarten education lobbied for and helped to pass legislation mandating that communities had to provide kindergartens for all three-to-six-year-old children as kindergartens were the first step of publicly provided "school." By changing the conception of kindergarten from an educational institution for young children *outside* the school (or preschool) and by associating kindergartens with the public school, the Hungarian officials merged kindergarten into general and accepted discourse on "schooling" rather than the more flexible, disposable, and separate/separatable early education, preschool, or kindergarten schooling. The result of the shift in language used in the legislation was to force communities to maintain kindergartens for three-to-six-year-old children in Hungary, while in Bulgaria and Poland, the protection was only for the final pre-public school year. In the case of nurseries, the legislative wording was even weaker in all three countries, providing *choice* to economically strapped communities as to whether to continue to keep nurseries open for families who requested space.

The Language of Regulation: Decentralization and Choice

The subtlety of the shifts and differences in ways laws and regulations referred to the need to provide nursery/creche or kindergarten care (openings) for families signals the ways in which subtle shifts in reform discourse enact broader discourses (e.g., that of choice) or form resistance. In this case, the new regulations were being formed as a response to a certain discourse of "democracy" that included notions of strategies of decentralization, local control, and increasing autonomy. While the state continued to provide broad "steering" and maintained some control of finances, prioritization of needs and specific financial allocations were shifted to local municipalities, in part because neither the central nor the local governments had enough money to continue to finance all prior services. They were also a response to discourse supporting the desirability or need to privatize, and as a response to the broad international and regional discourses concerned with local autonomy, choice, and democracy.[24]

In the 1980s, state factories were among the earliest to see the advantage of shifting child care (nurseries and/or kindergartens) from their own budgets to those of local municipalities, which were also responsible for providing state nurseries and kindergartens; the first major changes in kindergarten/nursery provision, then, was in who was in nominal control at local levels, while the government maintained central control of curriculum and finance. The second major change occurred in the early 1990s, when partial financing and decision making was handed over by the central governments to local municipalities in new laws related to local municipality control. This change, combined with the changes in the wording of regulations about providing nursery and kindergarten places for children, allowed some municipalities to keep existing nurseries or kindergartens open, while others did not—they closed or sold buildings, or reduced the number of children who had access to public programs.

One vice mayor of a district in Budapest described some of the ways in which the financing and decentralization policies, as well as the new regulations on nurseries (creches) and kindergartens, resulted in a discourse that appeared to give greater "choice" and local control to families, women and men, and communities, while at the same time regulating and reducing "choice," autonomy, and control.

> Before the transition, they (the government) thought there was no need for creches, but [it is] just the opposite. There's unemployment of men and women who want to keep jobs and so they want children in creches. But the creches aren't growing. We thought we could give an allowance for mothers to stay at home, but it's not enough. Social insurance, 5,000 Forints for each mother to stay at home, but (it is) not enough, so mothers are still trying to go to work.
>
> The state gives subsidies for Kindergartens, roads, or whatever a municipality needs; but they just give money. It's not obligatory how municipalities should do the task—Greatest stress is the subsidy, (but it is) not enough to cover tasks . . . especially in poorer communities. Start with creches— no specific subsidies are set aside for creches—so we have to find sources for this: All costs—energy, operating costs are theirs [the municipalities] now. . . . If we wanted to hold a vote, we can't because we do not have enough money, so [we] cannot hold a vote.[25]

Discourse and Acts of Privatization

New privatization laws restored State-owned property to their pre-Communist-era owners, allowed State-owned companies to be sold along with their "social assets" (including kindergartens/nurseries), and allowed municipalities to sell their buildings, including all those connected with social services, if they chose to do so. These moves constructed the particular market discourses of the region—that privatized companies were more efficient and productive than state companies; many sales were instituted by economic need or difficult choices by poorer municipalities with too many services and needs to pay for (see the vice mayor's points above). The restitution of private property returned many state kindergarten or nursery buildings to earlier owners who often converted the buildings from kindergartens to houses or other businesses. While one of the bigger previous owners, the church, often kept kindergartens open for educational purposes, when restored to the church, they were now nonstate, private, and included a sectarian education; in other words, they were no longer universal, public, or accessible to everyone, and the justification for this move had shifted from universal welfare to market efficiency.

In Bulgaria, in 1995, an interview with a government consultant concerning the number of kindergarten buildings that had been sold or closed down suggested again, however, that the broader discourses were met with local sites of resistance to sale, closing, or privatizing of kindergartens. One has to understand the local context to understand what lies beneath the statistics and forced cutbacks of social services:

> [Recently there was a] strike by mothers in one city when a kindergarten was sold and was to be used as a business. The population was so shocked that the structure was closed, although their children were probably changed to another kindergarten. Also there were other initiatives of other private entrepreneurs to open other kindergartens. [The strike was] shown on TV and in the news . . . probably no other mayors will sell kindergartens. The kindergartens are under municipal ownership and they should keep them. Probably the mayor was corrupt and this was the problem.[26]

Conclusion

In this chapter, we have tried to examine how governing patterns are changing in Eastern and Central Europe with a particular focus on changes in social policies and practices related to young children's care and education. Central to the analysis has been an examination of the language used that, we argue, defines, governs, and regulates the actions of families, what men and women are to be and do (e.g., the conception of the "professional mother," men and women as productive laborers outside the home), where and how children are to be cared for and educated, and the role of society in caring for the well-being of private citizens, particularly children. The comparative strategy used to make this examination included looking at discursive practices in three countries in the same region during the first five years after the breakup of the Soviet Union—the beginning of a transition away from Communist social policies that had been in place for nearly forty years.

In the final sections of this chapter, we look to our new understandings and emergent questions with regard to family, mothers' and fathers' roles and responsibilities, the changing patterns of early education and child care, and the shifting discourses related to society's role in taking care of children.

"Family, women," "professional motherhood," and "choice." In this chapter, we have concentrated on a narrow examination of "family" that focuses on parents, mothers and fathers roles and responsibilities, and young children. Even within this narrow definition or construction, we see arguments about the relationship between the state and "family," what "mothers/fathers" should look like and act, how they are governed, and in what ways and with what understandings parents govern themselves.

Eastern European women writers, for example, have suggested that "the family" became the primary center for individual definition in socialist/communist Eastern Europe, and a site of resistance to what was thought of as central state governance in the period prior to 1990. As one writer suggested, "Family and friends filled the space where civil society could not exist; the private sphere was the only space for the development of individual initiative and autonomy."[27] In this space, Eastern European women writers have also suggested that women took refuge in the assigned double burden, in motherhood and in care for young children, along with mandated employment outside the home, in order to remain more autonomous from state intrusion, to have space to resist state intrusions, to be in some ways freer of state intrusion than men were allowed to be.

In the post-Soviet period, this perspective is still influential. While there are many differences in perspectives and material conditions, one common written perspective in the Eastern women writers' work cited above expressed support for "choice" and the concept of "professional motherhood," where having the choice to remain at home might have advantages for some women by providing a desired space to be with and rear children, a space to develop autonomy, and different forms of participation in civil society, including, for example, more time to participate in children's schooling. Others interviewed during the course of the 1993 and 1995 research, some cited in this chapter, stated that "choice" to be at home with young children, might be desirable and possible for some, but impossible for others; thus, there were a variety of perspectives with most women interviewed centering on the need to continue employment outside the home, particularly in the unstable economic, political, and social circumstances of the "transition" period.

While there is no single feminism (East or West, apparently), nor an essential "women's voice, perspective, or experience," Western feminist writers from the period of 1993 to 1995, in contrast to some of the Eastern women writers from the early 1990s, wrote that their Eastern "sisters" could be disadvantaged in the short and long term in the transition to a market economy. They have worried that the transition policies would erase many of the social benefits that women in the West are still trying to get or are worrying about maintaining. Funk and Mueller (1989), for example, reject 1989 as a "turning point" for women in East/Central Europe, noting a growing "neoconservatism" throughout Europe and a larger pattern of unemployment as the roots of antifeminist and, by extension, antiwomen discourse.[28] Others suggested that the ever increasing unemployment level coupled with decreasing public funds would result in changes in the workplace that relate to the exclusion of women, pushing them back to the family and the home. Indeed this is a pattern that we did observe occurring in research in Bulgaria, Poland, and Hungary. Similarly, Sen, writing about Bengal policy, described patterns we observed in East/Central Europe: "Today compulsory creche and maternity benefit legislation has, in pushing up the transactional costs of employing women, provided a significant argument for pushing them out of the organized work force. The 'nationalist' empowerment of women as mothers serves to justify the denial of social, economic and political entitlements to women."[29] In Bulgaria, Poland, and Hungary, as firms tightened which workers could get benefits, as industries reduced "social assets," including child-care centers, the "transactional costs" of employing women, especially, were decreased, in what Sen called the "denial of social, economic, and political entitlements to women."[30]

Family, men and women, professional parenthood, and choice. While the arguments above are crucial to our understanding of these issues and their consequences in the lived reality of families, women's, men's, and children's lives, the discussions, observations, and debates are even more complex than pictured above. Choice is still depicted, for example, as individual choice; in contrast, our conception of governance and self-governance looks to the ways in which choices are a reflection of a broad governing system that includes the way we come to regulate ourselves, make our own decisions, think about our own opportunities and choices. With this example in mind, we question the simple dichotomies suggested in the arguments above—the sharp distinction between state and family, between public and private, the notion of "autonomy" or "choice," the way we begin to conceive of "professional" mothers, to construct "needs." What, for example, does it mean to be a "nonprofessional" mother who chooses to stay employed/remaining apart from young children, especially when wages are low and employment is necessary? Does it always mean the same thing, at all times, or for all people?

While the debates and observations of the previous section are valid and important observations, related to policy and governance patterns in East/ Central Europe, as elsewhere, here we return to our examination of how we come to reason, and to accept what is natural. To illustrate this point further, we again look at "family," parental, and societal roles and responsibilities.

In many of the debates of Eastern and Western women writers mentioned earlier, the policy debates were viewed as women's individual issues—whether to allow women the "choice" to be at home with young children, or whether to allow them the opportunity to earn a family living, develop as a professional, or participate more actively in civil and political society outside the home. Yet we didn't question the individual nature of the decision, nor the discourse surrounding *women* and children that defined women primarily as the caretakers of children—in relation to men's or other societal members' roles.

By writing so frequently about women, family, and child care, we have often seemed to essentialize as well as normalize the roles/actions and opportunities available to both women and men. The construction of social/family policies primarily aimed at women, in fact, negates the construct that the family typically consists of more than one adult, most often a father and mother, and that the need to rear future citizens must be constructed as public/private responsibility. By focusing on women as employed/unemployed, or as "surplus labor," while encouraging the mentality of a social policy that includes gendered and class-related discourses ("families in poverty, or "in need"), one accepts a gendered and classed discourse that regulates freedom, various identities, and important long-term possibilities. By focusing on a liberal welfare policy that accepts that the gains of a few will eventually "trickle down" to the rest, that allows unemployment or poverty to become "natural," there is also a naturalized sense of acceptability, perhaps inevitability to such a "model" as a model of development, modernity, and progress. In this chapter, we are questioning such a model.

Local actions and debates. Modern governing in the late twentieth century is complex as are the relationships between governing, power, and knowledge. Here we have begun to describe a network of discourses (for example, the market discourses of privatization and choice, the political discourses of liberal and social "democracy," independence and choice, religious discourses on motherhood, gendered discourses of "Eastern" and "Western" writers, and classed discourses on different "needs") that contextualize how the definition and conduct of "family" has begun to change in Eastern/Central Europe, how members of families are beginning to rethink their public and "private" family conduct and responsibilities–including the divisions between "private" and "public." In addition to the reshaping of the roles and definitions of "good" mother (and relationally the good father) in new discourses, the new and best places for good child care and education, we have also examined the ways in which the role of government in children's care is being reconstructed to care particularly for those families "in need."

But it would be too simple to end on this note. We need to remember that governing is complex, and that discursive practices are multiple and multilayered, resulting in a variety of new ways of reasoning, of constructing power and knowledge relations. Power/knowledge relations are productive, not simply repressive or oppressive. By examining words and texts, we construct new ways of reasoning, new ways of questioning, new possibilities for action. We also remember the importance of history, cultural debates, and the importance of local actions and local contingent meanings and actions—the argument to keep kindergartens from closing in Bulgaria, the debates in Hungary over reductions in social benefits, and the actions in education ministries to protect children and child care through changes in the words used in new laws and regulations. These are the complexities of global and local governance and action that we need to understand as we move to the next century.

Notes

This chapter is a result of two research projects conducted by the first author in Bulgaria, Hungary, and Poland in 1993 and 1995. The first was done with Margarethe

Fernandez of Price Waterhouse International, through funding to Price Waterhouse by the U.S. AID's Women and Development Bureau. The second visit in 1995 was funded through a sabbatical leave and a research fellowship from the Land Tenure Center, University of Wisconsin–Madison. Benita Blessing provided research assistance in the United States related to European social and educational policy; she is currently completing a dissertation on educational history in East Germany. dissertation research on education in East Germany.

1. The social construction of "need" and "dependency" has been examined by Nancy Fraser and Linda Gordon in several pieces (see Fraser, 1989; Fraser & Gordon, 1994). See a similar argument in Hungary in Haney, 1997.

2. See Foucault (1979/1991), for a recent discussion.

3. See Gordon (1991) and Rose (1990).

4. See Foucault (1991) and Hindess (1996).

5. The outlawing of abortion in Poland but not in the other countries is a symbolic and extremely important example of this point.

6. See Hacking (1991).

7. *World Employment* (1995), Table 15; also *World Economic and Social Survey* (1996), p. 115.

8. *World Economic and Social Survey* (1996), p. 123.

9. The registered unemployed does not count several important factors. For example, in Hungary in 1994 the official unemployment rate was about 10.9 percent but did not include those ineligible to register. As the policy at that time gave a limited period of time to register for unemployment and does not include in "unemployed" those women who have taken child-care leaves for up to three years or more, the figures (for all three countries) only provide an international comparison rather than "exact" figures. Korintus (in Evans, 1995) suggested that unemployment was growing rapidly in Hungary and that unemployment in January 1995 was 25 percent, for example.

10. *World Employment* 1995, Table 16, and United Nations Economic Commission for Europe: *Economic Bulletin for Europe*.

11. *World Employment* (1995), Table 18.

12. See Evans (1995), vol. I, p. 17.

13. There are some indications that women are pushed toward "involuntary vacations" more often than men, but figures for the three countries are not only hard to find but generally believed to be inaccurate when cited.

14. See Funk and Mueller (1993), for example.

15. The underground economy had grown in all three countries and there are some indications of women taking child-care leave and then working within this sector of the economy, too.

16. These numbers in this section are from the *Social Indicators of Development* (1996), pp. 52 (Bulgaria), 152 (Hungary), and 275 (Poland). We want to emphasize they are only one way of understanding "poverty."

17. Interview with Associate Director, National Institute of Nursery Schools, July, 1995.

18. In 1995, average monthly wages for one family member were reported to be (in U.S. dollars) $200 per month in Poland, $325 per month in Hungary, and $100 per

month in Bulgaria. These figures, of course, are not adjusted for inflation, cost differentials, etc. Whereas real income has increased in Poland and Hungary, it has continued to decrease in Bulgaria according to 1997 figures. However, even in Poland and Hungary, cost increases have escalated such that real income is still extremely low for the majority in each country.

19. Sources for 1993: Bulgaria-National Statistics Institute 1991 Annual Report, Ministries of Education and Health; Poland-Central Statistics Office and UNICEF, Interviews Ministries of Education and Social Welfare; Cornia and Sipos (1991); Hungary-Central Office of Statistics, Interviews in Ministry of Education and Social Welfare; Fernandez and Bloch (1993).

20. *Statistical Handbook of Hungary* (1996), p. 83. Interview with Marte Korintus of the National Day Care Institute who suggested that 1995 enrollments in nurseries was down to 8 percent, when the Bokros Proposal recommended reducing maternity leave from three years to one year.

21. *Statistical Handbook of Hungary* (1995, 1996), p. 108.

22. The division of care for 0–3s and 3–6s between Health and Education Ministries, and the differences in provision (less for nursery or creche care) because of the maternity leaves and allowances is also prevalent in Western and Nordic European countries. What one can assume, therefore, is that this is a family-wage-oriented policy that supports a parent to stay home with the youngest children; however, the fact that it is virtually always aimed at mothers supports this as a gendered discourse that positions most women in the home and as the natural child caretakers.

23. See Fernandez and Bloch (1993) for further detailed discussion of this history.

24. See Popkewitz (1996).

25. Vice Mayor District in Budapest, 1/15/95.

26. Interview with privatization consultant in Sofia (June, 1995).

27. Einhorn (1993), p. 6.

28. Funk and Mueller (1993), p. 14.

29. Sen (1993), p. 237.

30. Ibid.

References

Barry, A., T. Osborne & N. Rose. *Foucault and Political Reason.* Chicago: University of Chicago Press, 1996.

Burchell, G., C. Gordon & P. Miller. *The Foucault Effect: Studies in Governmentality.* Chicago: University of Chicago Press, 1991.

Cornia, G. A. & S. Sipos (eds.). *Children and the Transition to the Market Economy: Safety Nets and Social Policies in Central and Eastern Europe.* Aldershot, England: Avebury, 1991.

Einhorn, B. *Cinderella Goes to Market.* Boston: Verso Press, 1993.

Evans, J. *Who Is Caring for the Children? An Exploratory Survey Conducted in Hungary, Poland, Bulgaria, and Romania.* Report to the World Bank, Part I and II. Washington, D.C. The World Bank, 1995.

Fernandez, M. & M. Bloch. *Child Care during the Transition to a Market Economy: Focus on Bulgaria, Hungary, and Poland.* Washington, D.C.: Price Waterhouse International, 1993.

Foucault, M. "Governmentality." In *The Foucault Effect: Studies in Governmentality*, ed. G. Burchell, C. Gordon, and P. Miller. Chicago: University of Chicago Press, 1991, pp. 87–104.

Fraser, N. *Unruly Practices.* Minneapolis: University of Minnesota Press, 1989.

Fraser, N. & L. Gordon. "A Genealogy of 'Dependency': Tracing a Keyword of the U.S. Welfare State." *Signs* 19 (1994): 309–36.

Fraser, N. & L. Gordon. "Dependency Demystified: Inscriptions of Power in a Keyword of the Welfare State." *Social Politics* 1, 1 (1994): 4–31.

Funk, N. & M. Mueller. *Gender Politics and Post-Communism.* New York: Routledge, 1993.

Hacking, I. "How Should We Do the History of Statistics?" In G. Burchell, G. Gordon, and R. Miller (eds.). *The Foucault Effect: Studies in Governmentality.* Chicago: University of Chicago Press, 1991, pp. 181–96.

Haney, L. " 'But We Are Still Mothers': Gender and the Construction of Need in Post-Socialist Hungary." *Social Politics* 4, 2 (1997).

Hindess, B. "Liberalism, Socialism and Democracy: Variations on a Governmental Theme." In A. Barry, T. Osborne, and N. Rose, *Foucault and Political Reason: Liberalism, Neo-Liberalism and Rationalities of Government.* Chicago: University of Chicago Press, 1996, pp. 65–80.

Hungary. *Statistical Handbook of Hungary 1995.* Budapest: Hungarian Central Statistical Office, 1996.

National Statistics Institute, *Annual Reports 1991–1994.* Bulgaria: National Statistics Institute.

Orloff, A. S. "Gender and the Welfare State." *American Review of Sociology,* (1996): 22. Poland. Annual Reports. Central Office of Statistics.

Popkewitz, T. S. "Rethinking Decentralization and State/Civil Society Distinctions: The State as a Problematic of Governing." *Journal of Educational Policy* 11, 2 (1996): 27–51.

Rose, N. *Governing the Soul.* London: Routledge, 1990.

Sen, S. "Motherhood and Mothercraft: Gender and Nationalism in Bengal." *Gender and History* 5, 2 (1993): 231–43.

Skocpol, T. *Social Policy in the United States.* Princeton, N.J.: Princeton University Press, 1995.

Social Indicators of Development, 1996. Washington, D.C.: The World Bank.

United Nations Economic Commission for Europe. *Economic Bulletin for Europe* 46, 1994.

Wittrock, B. & P. Wagner. "Social Science and the Building of the Early Welfare State: Toward a Comparison of Statist and Non-Statist Western Societies." In D. Rueschemeyer and T. Skocpol, *States, Social Knowledge, and Origins of Modern Social Policies.* Princeton: Princeton University, 1996.

World Economic and Social Survey 1996. New York: United Nations.

World Education Report 1995. New York: UNESCO and Oxford Publishing Co.

World Employment 1995. Geneva: International Labour Organization.

CHAPTER 4

Public Education, Teachers' Organizations, and the State in Latin America

CARLOS ALBERTO TORRES

School reform agendas have been launched in the United States and in many Latin American countries, focusing on "restructuring" rather than merely transforming the efficiency of existing systems. Restructuring attempts the transformation of purposes, assumptions, and methods of schools systems (Darling-Hammond, 1993). Not surprisingly, this reform agenda is being implemented at times of serious financial retrenchment in public education everywhere. Because much of the "schools-are-failing" literature blames the teachers for the ills of education, the relationships between teachers and educational authorities are also being reconsidered. Even where there is less focus on blame, there is considerable attention to competency testing, certification, national standards—in short, diverse attempts to improve excellence in instruction and learning. Trying to reduce expenses of financially overburdened school districts and attempting to make the systems more cost effective often involves layoffs and substitution of lower-paid instructional personal for fully trained, more expensive teachers. This situation, along with recent initiatives for alternative school finance, such as vouchers, have placed teachers' organization at the center of disputes on educational policy and practice.[1]

Teachers, as State employees, are important actors who fulfill a leading role in the welfare State.[2] As such, many of them think of themselves as the main public employees responsible for the transmission of a nation's collective values to its children. This self-perceived mission, coupled with similar roles attributed by the State in Latin America, created a mystique of spiritual satisfaction, self-esteem, and professional status, and gave their professional organizations an opportunity to participate in the formulation of educational policy and curricula (see Lomnitz & Melnick, 1991). It is this unstable consensus between teachers and State and the perception of the mission of teachers

83

that is being eroded by changes in the role of the State and by drastic changes in the living and working conditions of teachers in Latin America. As a result, new areas of conflict in the interaction between teachers, teachers' organizations, and the State are developing.

Of particular relevance is the role of women teachers, and women leaders, their lives, views, and political actions in the context of educational restructuring. For instance, for the first time in Mexico's labor union history, a woman, Elba Esther Gordillo, was elected general secretary of the powerful national teachers' union (or SNTE, its Spanish acronym). In Argentina, many female teachers constitute the top leadership of the confederation of teachers (or CTERA, its Spanish acronym), including Mary Sánchez, former CTERA general secretary, and a prominent political leader in the country.

This chapter explores the patterns of behavior of teachers' organizations and the State's educational policies in Latin America. Examples and illustrations of these patterns will be drawn from the changing political and economic environments of Argentina, Brazil, Costa Rica, and Mexico during the last two decades. The rationale for choosing these four particular countries is based on demographic, economic, and sociopolitical factors. These four countries together represent two-thirds of the Latin American population. Costa Rica and Mexico represent two of the most stable democratic regimes in the region, while Argentina and Brazil have experienced authoritarian military dictatorships from the 1960s until the early 1980s. Early in their history as independent nations, Argentina, Mexico, and Costa Rica, were relatively successful in providing universal public elementary education for their populations. In contrast, Brazil, despite its significant economic development in the past four decades, has failed to provide a basic education for vast sectors of its population.[3] A premise of the analysis is that the State is an arena displaying the interaction of domestic and international institutions and actors.[4] Therefore the State reflects the microcosmic condensation of power relations in civil society, and to some extent the implications of trends of globalization of the economy and culture. A focus on tensions, contradictions, and conflict will offer a privileged vantage point from which to observe changes in educational policies in the context of renewed international and domestic efforts to modernize schools and societies. These changes have many implications for economic growth, social welfare, and political democracy.

The State, Education, and Society

The State as a Political Actor in Public Education

Latin America has been marked by patterns of conflict and concertation between the State and organized labor. Collier and Collier point to the introduction of corporatism as the distinctive characteristic of Latin American capitalism and politics in this century (Collier & Collier, 1991; Torres & Puiggros, 1995). Corporatism involves a set of structures which integrate society in a vertical manner, thus leading to the legalization and institutionalization of a workers' movement that is formed and largely controlled by the State.

In Latin America, the State itself is redefining its role in economic development and educational expansion. Historically, the State in Latin America has actively intervened in the development of national economies by means of redistributionist policies. During the second half of the nineteenth century and the first three decades of this century, the predominant State model in Latin America was a liberal State controlled by rural landowners or oligarchy (Boron, 1976). This form of the State consolidated the nation and generated relative political stability. In this political model, the oligarchy maintained tight control over the political process, at times by means of direct control over the State, and at other times through control of the parliament and important political parties. In order to implement this control, occasional electoral fraud or open repression were employed (Collier & Collier, 1991).

Public education played a major role in the legitimation of the political systems and the integration and modernization of the countries of Latin America (Puiggros, 1990).[5] Public education systems in the region were all developed as part of the project of liberal States seeking to establish the foundations of the nation and the citizenship. The role and function of public education in the creation of a disciplined citizen; the role, mission, ideology, and training of teachers; and the prevailing notions of curriculum and school knowledge were all deeply marked by the prevailing philosophy of the liberal State (Puiggros, 1992).

Furthermore, as part of its development project, the State extended social benefits to vast sectors of the population, as is evident in Argentina, Brazil, Costa Rica, and Mexico. Education played a key role in these social programs because mass schooling was viewed as a means of building a national citizenry, a productive labor base, and increasing social mobility. Ultimately, mass schooling was seen as a prerequisite for liberal democracy. This contributed to educational expansion and increased investment in public education.

The Latin American educational expansion during the early phase of industrialization in the 1960s represents the highest rates of educational growth in the world (UNESCO, 1974). Between 1960 and 1970, the indices of growth for higher education and secondary education were 247.9 percent and 258.3 percent respectively. However, the enrollment in primary basic education grew only 167.6 percent, while the illiteracy rate remained more or less constant in most countries of the area (UNESCO, 1971). One study of the late 1970s shows a fundamental continuity in this pattern of educational development (UNESCO/PNUD, 1981). Ernesto Schiefelbein argued that in the last four decades Latin America made significant progress toward democracy by "(i) expanding access to education for most children reaching school age; (ii) extending the years of schooling; (iii) improving timely entrance to school, (iv) providing early care to an increasing number of deprived children, and (v) increasing the provision of minimum inputs and eliminating tracks for social levels" (Schiefelbein, 1991).

In contrast to previous achievements in the expansion of public education, the past two decades have witnessed a decline in quantity and quality of schooling in the region (Avalos, 1986; Lockheed & Verspoor, 1991). Reimers argues that ministries of education in the region have been forced to sacrifice equity and efficiency in order to reduce educational expenditures under the constraints imposed by internationally mandated structural adjustment policies. These cuts have disproportionately affected primary education and are reflected in the limited resources available for teaching materials and school facilities, as well as in falling school enrollment rates (Reimers, 1991). They have also alienated teachers' organizations, forcing them to develop defensive actions and, occasionally, to come into conflict with the State in the formulation of educational policies.

The argument, of course, is not that conflict was not part and parcel of an uneasy, limited, and fragile consensus in the operation of public education systems in the region. Conflict in educational policy making has always permeated public education, more so in the latter part of this century. What I am arguing here is that the new economic and political reality of policy making, the structural constraints imposed by structural adjustment, and the policy preferences advanced by neoliberal governments have created a set of circumstances and behavior that make consensus even more remote and conflict more likely.

Economic and Sociopolitical Background: Crisis, Austerity, and Structural Adjustment in Contemporary Latin America

The 1980s have been labeled as the "lost decade" in Latin America.[6] It was during this decade that the region witnessed a cycle of high inflation—even hyperinflation—and recession never before experienced. The oil crises of 1973 and 1982, coupled with the 1980s' debt crisis left the region in a State of economic disarray. Faced with rising international interest rates, Latin American countries found it increasingly difficult to meet their debt repayment schedules. International financial organizations (for instance, the International Monetary Fund and the World Bank) required governments in the region to adopt structural adjustment policies to address balance-of-payment difficulties and fiscal deficits.

This model of stabilization and adjustment involves a number of policy recommendations, including the reduction of government expenditures, currency devaluations to promote exports, reduction in import tariffs, and an increase in public and private savings. Key aims of this model are a drastic reduction in the State sector, the liberalization of salaries and prices, and the reorientation of industrial and agricultural production toward exports. The overall purpose of this policy package is, in the short run, to reduce the size of fiscal deficits and public expenditures, to drastically reduce inflation, and to reduce exchange rates and tariffs. In the medium term, structural adjustment relies on exports as the engine of growth. To that extent, structural adjustment and subsequent policies of economic stabilization seek to liberalize trade, to reduce distortions in the price structures, to end "protectionist" policies, and therefore to facilitate the rule of the market in the Latin American economies (Bitar, 1988).

These changes are taking place in the context of redemocratization of political structures. Latin American societies have a long tradition of political authoritarianism, which has, to some extent, permeated many different policy arenas, including education. The historical irony is that the return to democracy in the eighties and the overall project of redemocratization was marked by unusual economic constraints.

Trends toward economic globalization, deteriorating political economic conditions—particularly hyperinflation in countries like Argentina and Brazil—the upsurging of neoliberal governments, the political debacle of the region's left, the failure of a socialist revolution in Central America in the 1980s (i.e., Nicaragua, El Salvador, Guatemala), and the collapse of the socialist economies, created the "right conditions" for structural adjustment policies to be fully implemented regionwide, despite past populist experiences of governance and the strength of unions.

Economic stabilization came about in Latin America as a response to debt crisis, fiscal crisis, industrial recession, and inflation (in some contexts hyperinflation). This happened, however, only after key social actors in the distributional conflict (the working class, campesinos, and even sectors of the middle classes) relinquished, consciously or by default, their ability to challenge cuts in public expenditures. There was a deadlock between the programs of the lower-class sectors (particularly trade unions) and the economic and political preferences of elites, which was finally broken with the onset of this period of adjustment (Laban & Sturzenegger, 1992).

While the extent of the social consequences of the crisis and stabilization policies are still a matter of debate, it is evident that for a number of international agencies, the overall welfare of the people in the region is worse, in many respects, than it was twenty years ago (see, e.g., United Nations Development Program, 1992a & 1992b). For instance, according to the Economic Commission of Latin America (ECLA), approximately 44 percent of the continent's population (183 million people) in 1990 were living below the poverty line—an increase of 112 million over 1970. ECLA attributed this growing impoverishment to "the dramatic fall in average income, which marked a tremendous step backward in the material standard of living of the Latin American and Caribbean population" (Rosenthal, 1989). Similar analyses are presented in a recent report by the Inter-American Dialogue (Aspen Institute, 1992).

To address the economic and fiscal crisis and its social and political consequences, stabilization and structural adjustment programs have been carried out under different names—by regimes with diverse ideological orientations—within the context of a general and deep crisis. The State's reform reduced its interventionist role in society and facilitated, through privatization and diminishing welfare policies, the rule of market forces in Latin American societies. This, of course, has implications for State legitimacy and for the role of public education in the region.

Latin American Economy, Politics, and Education in the Context of Globalization

It is imperative to situate the national and regional reality of Latin America within the context of global economic, political, and social changes of the past twenty-five years. The current regional situation is affected by innumerable changes including the rise of the newly industrialized countries in Asia and the Pacific Rim (and its impact on the models of economic development in Latin America); the promise of consolidation of regional economic markets (European Economic Community, NAFTA, and MERCOSUR); the intensification of competition among the major industrial powers of Germany, Japan, and the United States; the opening of Eastern Europe; and the resurgence of regional ethnic and religious conflicts.[7]

For better or worse, these changes show the emergence of a new global economy that operates in very different ways from the former industrial economy.[8] This new global economy is more fluid and flexible, with multiple lines of power and decision making analogous to a spider web, as opposed to the static pyramidal organization of the traditional capitalist system. The old economy was based on high volume and highly standardized production with a few managers controlling the production process from above and a great number of workers following orders. This economy of mass production was stable as long as it could reduce its costs of production (including the price of labor) and retool quickly enough to stay competitive. Because of advancements in transportation and communications technology and the growth of service industries, production has become fragmented around the world. Production now moves to locations where there is either cheaper or more highly trained productive labor, favorable political conditions, access to better infrastructure and national resources, larger markets and/or tax incentives.

The growing globalization of the world is not a novel process. It began with colonization and imperialism in the late nineteenth century, but with recent changes in technology, trade, and communications, has acquired new dimensions. Secondly, to emphasize globalization does not mean that it is complete or that it has the same impact in developing and developed countries. Finally, to argue of the existence of a growing globalization of technology, trade, communication, capital, and labor does not suggest that the nation-State has lost importance and that it is totally unable to control its own dynamics. Still the dependent State continues to be subject to domestic and international pressures that condition its actions to a greater degree than, say, industrially advanced States. While the rhetoric of neoconservatism and neoliberalism calls for a diminishing role of the State and the de facto (destatization) of civil societies, the role of the State has remained key in the articulation of social interests and the representation of groups and classes that benefit or suffer from the process of modernization and public policy formation.

In terms of education, the public education system in the old capitalist order was oriented toward the production of a disciplined and reliable workforce. The new global economy seems to have redefined labor relations, challenging the perception of teachers' organizations and the role of education in development (Reich, 1991).

In summary, I have argued thus far that the history of the State and public education systems and the degree of incorporation of teachers' unions into the corporatist framework are fundamental elements in explaining public policy in Latin America. Thus, there is the need for a political sociology of education informed by a political economy of education.[9] From a political economy of education perspective, the performance of the economy is a major issue underscoring educational policies, and questions related to how uneven rates of growth and skyrocketing inflation rates contributed to the fiscal debt and economic crises in the region are central. Likewise, it is important to question the extent to which the prescribed recipes of structural adjustment as a cure to the economic malaise are the bedrock for the current political behavior of the main actors concerned with educational services in Latin America today, particularly teachers' organizations. Despite the fact that teaching and the teaching profession are generally protected from international competition, changes in educational policies are not only totally dependent on the domestic context. These changes and the contradictions they create are increasingly related to the process of globalization of economies, cultures, and societies, and they exemplify the power of structural forces involved in education, especially during periods of severe crisis and restructuring of policy priorities and systems.

Public Education, Teachers, and the State in Latin America

Given the previous discussion, it is now useful to explore teachers' behavior in the context of changing State structures and especially neoliberal governments,[10] globalizing economies, and changing public policies. Two working hypotheses will help to explain teachers' behavior in the context of changing State structures and public policies.

Teachers Have Subsidized Educational Development in Latin America

Teachers have been subsidizing educational expansion in Latin America. This subsidy has been achieved through the continuous deterioration of teachers' salaries simultaneous with substantial increases in elementary and secondary enrollments. This was the case in Argentina, Brazil, Costa Rica, and Mexico. For example, table 4.1 shows that enrollments in elementary education have grown steadily in these countries. While enrollments continue to grow, the rate of growth of educational expenditures, adjusted for inflation, diminished in the 1980s. Fernando Reimers shows that between 1975 and 1980, total expenditures on education increased in all countries in the region. However, between 1980 and 1985, total expenditures in real terms diminished in twelve of the eighteen countries he studied.[11] Table 4.2 presents Reimers's data for Argentina, Brazil, Costa Rica, and Mexico, showing the deceleration

TABLE 4.1
Enrollments, Elementary Education (selected years)

	1960	1970	1980	1981	1982	1985
Argentina	2,849,071	3,648,057	4,110,821	4,217,992	4,382,351	4,589,291
Brazil	8,369,285	15,904,627	22,598,524	22,116,723	23,455,789	24,769,736
Costa Rica[a]	198,049	349,378	354,657	353,676	346,199	366,071
Mexico	4,884,988	9,248,290	14,666,257	14,981,028	15,222,916	15,124,160

Source: ECLAC-UNESCO. Changing production patterns with social equity. March 18, 1992, mimeographed.
[a]public education only.

TABLE 4.2
Changes in Public Expenditures in Education in Latin America Before and After 1980

	Million of Dollars			Annual Growth		
	1975	1980	1985	75–80	80–85	75–85
Argentina	1,651	2,643	1,201	9.87	–14.6	–3.13
Brazil	4,480	7,168	7,987	9.86	2.19	5.95
Costa Rica	130	278	162	16.50	–10.23	2.26
Mexico	4,246	4,702	4,424	2.06	–1.21	0.41

Source: Fernando Reimers. "Educación para todos en América Latina," 1990, p. 5, and based on M. Lockheed and A. Verspoor, 1989. "Improving Primary Education in Developing Countries: A Review of Policy Options." World Bank, manuscript, statistical appendix.

of rates of growth after 1980. Another way to look at changes in educational expenditures is to consider their evolution as a percentage of the GNP. Table 4.3 shows that, as a proportion of the GNP, educational expenditures declined in Argentina, Costa Rica, and Mexico in the 1980s.[12]

In Mexico, the expansion of the education system between 1940 and 1970 was facilitated by, among other things, a regressive income distribution policy (Morales-Gomez & Torres, 1990). Hugo Aboites (1984) estimates that real salaries for teachers dropped by approximately 60 percent in that period. It took 35 years between 1925 and 1960, for Mexican educators to reach the salary levels they had in 1921 (Aboites, 1984; 1986). Morales-Gomez and Torres have argued that "considering the level that teachers' salaries could have reached if they had normal growth, the value of the salary of one teacher allowed the government to hire three teachers during 1950–1965. . . . During the second half of the 1970s, teachers saw a rapid improvement in their economic condition as a result of the effects of the oil boom and the increase in international borrowing. In real terms, the government was able to raise teachers' salaries to levels well above those in the 1920s. This, however, drastically changed after 1982. By 1985, the value of teachers' salaries was only two and a half times the value of the minimum salary in the country, and between 1982 and 1986, real salaries in the education sector lost 55 percent of their value" (Morales-Gomez & Torres, 1990, p. 80).

The experience of teachers salaries in Costa Rica is similar. Fernando Reimers (1990) argues that after the economic and fiscal crisis of 1980 and

TABLE 4.3
Total Educational Expenditure as Percentage of GNP

	Argentina[c]	Brazil[d]	Costa Rica[e]	Mexico
1973	4.0[a]	3.6	4.6	3.2
1976	—	2.3	5.3	—
1977	2.4	3.2	5.0	—
1979	2.7[b]	3.3	5.9	4.4
1980	3.9	3.4	5.6	3.9
1982	2.5	4.3	5.2	3.4
1984	4.2	2.9	4.2	—
1985	2.8	3.3	4.9	2.6
1986	1.8	4.6	5.2	2.1
1987	1.9	—	4.1	—
1989	1.5	3.7	4.0	—

Source: UCLA Statistical Abstract of Latin America, volumes 19–28.
[a]1974
[b]1978
[c]For 1985–1989, *Unesco Statistical Yearbook,* 1992.
[d]For 1980 onwards, *Unesco Statistical Yearbook,* 1992.
[e]Carnoy and Torres, 1992, p. 61, table 2.

1981, primary and secondary school teacher salaries fell substantially between 1980 and 1986, much more than real wages in the economy as a whole. Whereas primary school teachers' real salaries increased by almost 67 percent between 1975 and 1980 and secondary school salaries by more than 25 percent, they fell back to 1975 levels for primary school teachers and far below 1975 levels for secondary school teachers. Real wages in the private sector, on the other hand, after falling 30 percent in 1981 and 1982, had recovered by 1987 to 1980 levels. See table 4.4 showing the decline over time in teachers' salaries.

In Argentina a similar process of teachers' salaries subsidizing school expansion took place. With few exceptions, between 1970 and 1986 nominal teachers' salaries (elementary and secondary) at 1987 consumer prices (which accounts for inflation) lost value.[13] This loss is more pronounced in years of acute economic crises (1981, 1982, 1985, 1989), but on average, in real

TABLE 4.4
Teacher Base Salaries Compared to All
Government Workers and Industrial Workers 1975–1990 (1985 colones per month)

Year	Primary Aspirante[a]	Primary Teacher	Secondary Teacher	Average Government	Worker Mkt. Wage
1975	7,220	9,180	13,780	11,710	
1976	8,240	10,140	14,580	—	
1977	9,424	11,250	15,200	—	
1978	11,480	13,200	17,790	—	
1979	11,550	13,120	17,325	—	
1980	11,125	12,460	16,020	17,633	n.a.
1981	9,750	10,725	13,325	14,025	n.a.
1982	8,660	9,180	10,545	10,634	n.a.
1983	8,800	9,190	10,220	11,322	5,605
1984	8,570	8,910	9,830	11,965	5,628
1985	8,380	8,950	9,850	12,306	6,955
1986	8,550	9,570	10,550	13,245	7,580
1987	8,020	9,260	10,150	13,240	7,515
1988	7,770	9,340	10,030	12,903	7,360
1989	9,390	11,125	11,930	13,828	7,755
1990	10,100	11,900	12,760	—	7,945

Source: Ministry of Education, Salary Indices. Industrial wages from Maurilio Aguilar Rojas, *Evolución de los Salarios Industriales. 1980–1990.* Camara de Industrias de Costa Rica, April, 1990, Tables A-4 and A-6. Presented in Martin Carnoy and Carlos Alberto Torres, *Educational Change and Structural Adjustment: A Case Study of Costa Rica.* UNESCO, Bureau for the Co-Ordination of Operational Activities (BA0). Paris: September 1992, p. 70.

Notes: Primary teacher taken as Pt-3, a middle-level primary teacher salary. Secondary teacher taken as Mt-3, a middle-level secondary teacher salary. Most secondary teachers are at Mt-4, with a base salary of 13,450 1985 colones in 1990—about 700 colones per month high.

[a]Teacher without a teaching certificate.

terms, elementary school teachers lost 12 percent of their salaries between 1975 and 1988 (Petrei, Montero & Maraviglia, 1989). (See table 4.1.) Moreover, comparing teachers salaries with salaries in the private sector and with their own historical levels, it is clear that teachers' salaries by 1988 were below those of ten years before. Compared to salaries in the private (noneducational) sector of the economy, the salary of a teacher with fifteen years of seniority was, on average, only 64 percent of a secretary employed in the private sector, and only 75 percent of the salary of a chauffeur. At the top of the scale, an elementary school teacher with twenty-four years of seniority received a salary that, on average, represented only 11 percent of the salary of a manager in the private sector, and 76 percent of the salary of a secretary in the private sector (Petrei, Montero & Maraviglia, 1989, p. 180).

Furthermore, the deterioration of teachers' salaries is by no means homogeneous across categories. Salaries of elementary school teachers and university professors in Argentina between 1975 and 1988 deteriorated more sharply than salaries of part-time and full-time secondary school teachers in the same period (Petrei, Montero & Maraviglia, 1989, p. 183). Differentials in salary performance is one of the reasons why teachers' unions in Argentina have been unable to develop a common political strategy in the defense of salaries and working conditions. Salary differentials affecting primary, secondary, and university employees, based on seniority and administrative function in the system (e.g., school principals), have widened substantially between 1975 and 1986. This has further eroded the ability of teachers' unions to develop a unified policy for teachers who have no seniority and/or hierarchical function in the system and for those who have seniority and/or hierarchical function. Furthermore, the diversity of teachers' union representation in Argentina makes unified political action on the part of teachers' unions highly unlikely.[14]

In short, this hypothesis suggests that declining remuneration for teachers has provided funds to permit educational expansion. However, there is also evidence that in general the educational sector, including teachers' salaries, has had declining resources or resources that did not keep up with inflation during the 1980s. Hence, what needs to be explained is educational expansion in a period of declining resources. A shift of resources within a declining sector, say from teachers' salaries to other educational expenditures, cannot itself fund the expansion since what is needed is a net increment of resources. There are a number of additional empirical questions: Is it possible that declining average wages (measured as mean wages, median wages, and modal wages) reflect a change in the composition of the instructional workforce rather than a clear reduction of (real) wages of current teachers? It is generally noted that real wages declined in the economy as a whole in the eighties. What happened to teachers in elementary and secondary public education? While many people's wages declined in real terms, did teachers' wages decline in real terms even more?

*Teachers' Organizations Have Played Major Roles under Corporatist
Arrangements and Welfare States*

While teachers have played major roles in Latin America, particularly in
corporatist States, this relationship of consensus and cooperation between
State and teachers' organizations is turning into conflict under neoliberal
governments. Women teachers in particular are playing new roles in the context of changes in their labor conditions and their roles within teachers'
organizations.

Previous research indicates that teachers behave politically like any other
corporation in defense of their working conditions and salaries. Teachers'
unions remain mostly corporatist unions. There is growing conflict with the
State, however, because reduction in public spending, low wage increases if
any, and control of labor are key components of structural adjustment programs. Health care and elementary and secondary education systems are labor intensive industries. They are the largest employer of labor in the public
sector, with salary expenditures representing more than 90 percent of their
budgets. Not surprisingly, policies of decentralization and privatization are
perceived by teachers' organizations as threatening cost-cutting measures
affecting the lives of teachers, their symbolic role in society, their self-esteem,
and even the future of public education. These perceptions and political views
deeply affect corporatist arrangements and lead to conflict and confrontation,
rather than consensus and cooperation, in educational policies.

In this scenario of conflict, female teachers seem to play new leadership
roles in labor unions. Many authors have persuasively argued that teaching is
a gendered profession and that, in the context of commodification of knowledge, teachers are deskilled (see Acker, 1988; Connell, 1985; Apple, 1982,
1988, 1993). For instance, in his study of educational reform in industrialized
societies, Thomas Popkewitz (1991) argues that "[t]he unionization of teachers after the 1890s spawned organizations created specifically to articulate
women's interests in teaching, and some women union leaders did define the
problems of teaching as related to larger social movements and gender relations" (p. 75). In a similar vein, Michael Apple (1993) explores the question
of how "[w]omen teachers, like all workers, may overtly resist intensification
and the loss of their autonomy and skills" (p. 141).

What is really happening to female teachers in the context of teachers'
labor unions in Latin America? A focus on female teachers and syndicalism
will offer a meaningful framework for this analysis. Any systematic study of
the teaching profession in Latin America should also explore teachers' resistance to outside (State) control in the context of deskilling, standardization,
and rationalization of the teaching profession, and particularly how women
teachers react to the new measures prompted by structural adjustment policies
and austerity. In the context of the changes brought about by structural ad-

justment, the lack of detailed and reliable data, and the fast pace of changes in teachers' organizations, this chapter can only outline the contours of the interactions between teachers and the State and pose a number of relevant questions and queries—questions that perhaps cannot be answered at the present time with the available empirical evidence.

Departing from the Norm? The São Paulo Experience

A premise of our analysis is that teachers behave politically like any other corporation in defense of their own working conditions and salaries. Teachers' unions remain mostly corporatist unions, although their behavior in specific communities depends on historical traditions and political junctures. That is to say, unions may have a cozy, consensual or a conflictive, uneasy relationship with State agencies.

Corporatism, in principle, does not always help in substantially improving democratic conditions in the countries, the democratization of the educational system, or quality of education but, facing reduction of public spending and the constraints of structural adjustment, corporatist organizations could oppose, quite fiercely, public policy. Since health and education systems are labor intensive "industries," to speak the lingua of economists, they are the largest employers of labor force in the public sectors, with salary expenditures representing more than 90 percent of their budgets. Not surprisingly, policies of decentralization and privatization are seen as cost-cutting measures impinging upon the lives of teachers.

Without a new political will implemented by the State, few initiatives linking teachers' lives and struggles for better and more democratic schooling can be successful. If the history of educational reform in the region offers any firm ground for speculation, without State interventionism, no substantial gains can be achieved in educational reform and democratization. However, even if a new political will is found by the State, no matter how much teachers' organizations agree with that political will expressed in a particular regime, when the status quo of their labor conditions and salaries is jeopardized, teachers will continue to behave in corporatist terms. The experience of São Paulo, Brazil, is a case in point.

When the Worker's Party (or PT) won the municipal elections of November 15, 1988, in São Paulo, Paulo Freire (a member of the party since it was founded in 1979 and president of the Wilson Pinheiro Foundation, an educational foundation sponsored by the PT), was a natural choice for secretary of education of the city of São Paulo. Appointed by Mayor Luiza Erundina de Sousa, Paulo Freire worked as secretary of education from January 3, 1989, until May 27, 1991, when he resigned to resume his academic activities, lecturing, and writing.

The new policies implemented during Freire's administration included a comprehensive curriculum reform of the level of education provided by the municipality of São Paulo (from kindergarten to grade eight); a movement of literacy training (MOVA-São Paulo), built as a partnership between social movements and the State; and school governance reform with the implementation of school councils at the school level (Torres, 1994). In advancing the reform of school governance, the Freirean administration drafted a teacher statute, the *estatuto do magisterio municipal* (Statute of the Municipal Teaching Profession),[15] which proposed that school principals, vice-principals, and pedagogical directors be elected by the school community. People with the appropriate qualifications could be elected to these positions for a period of two years,[16] and they could be reelected for an additional two years. However, after concluding this second period, they could not run for office again until a two-year period had elapsed; thus in practice forcing school administrators to return to classroom teaching every four years. All parents,[17] all children of ten years of age and older, administrative staff (including janitors and maintenance and security personnel), and faculty would be eligible to vote. Combined parent and student votes would account proportionately for 50 percent of the total of votes, while combined staff and faculty votes would account for the remaining 50 percent. To remove any school official from the school council before the end of his or her mandate would require a petition signed by 50 percent of the total eligible electors in the school community.

After lengthy discussions with union officials, teachers, and administrators, the draft of the Statute of the Municipal Teaching Professional was overwhelmingly rejected. Teachers and school administrators, as well as union officials, were vehemently opposed to elected positions in the schools. They were also opposed to new provisions regarding working conditions that would have forced teachers working in both the State of São Paulo system of education and the municipal system of education of the city of São Paulo to accept full-time employment in only one of them. A new statute was drafted and decreed as Municipal Law 11.229 of June 26, 1992.[18] Freire recognizes that his first proposal was flatly defeated. However, he argues that this defeat "does not show that we were politically mistaken, but that the municipal educational system is politically backward."[19] Freire attributes the rejection of the statute to Brazilian corporatism.[20]

Notwithstanding, during the PT municipal administration, teachers saw a substantial improvement in their working conditions with the implementation of a teachers statute, and changes in their salary scales, in terms of dedication (full/part-time), night/day schools, and real salaries. Teachers in the municipal system now make substantially more than their counterparts in the State of São Paulo school system. Not only have teachers teaching at night seen an increase in their paychecks, but also a salary differential between teaching positions at central (more desirable) regions, intermediary regions, and peripheral (less desirable) areas has been instituted, with the explicit goal of attracting the best and most experienced teachers to teach in the poorest areas of the city. By international standards, however, the best paid part-time teachers in the system earn $364.75 a month (Torres, 1994).

Would teachers embedded in corporatist relationships of power, and with a tradition of corporatist behavior, endorse democratic reforms in curriculum and governance such as the one advanced by the PT/Freirean administration in São Paulo? To answer this question, it will be necessary to investigate in the context of a new right-wing municipal administration sworn in January 1993. Teachers' behavior patterns, for instance their strikes for better salaries, indicate whether teachers will simply defend their own corporatist interests, or instead, whether they will also defend the democratic measures such as a new school curriculum, a new model of governance, and new models of in-service teachers training that many of them may have supported during the Freirean administration.

The State and Public Education in Neoliberal Times

How can we assess the commitment of the State toward educational expansion and educational quality in the region? A concern of teachers and teachers' unions is whether increasing user fees, decentralization, privatization, and municipalization policies are affecting, and eventually excluding, growing numbers of children from public schooling. A similar concern is the dissatisfaction of rank-and-file teachers with the economic implications of the new agendas for educational reform.

Changes in the relationships among *economy* (i.e., trends toward deindustrialization and export-oriented models in the context of globalization), *politics* (i.e., a growing neoconserative rhetoric regarding diminishing the welfare roles of the State, a withdrawal of public investment, and shrinking public employment) and *education* (i.e., the a new impetus toward privatization and user fees, decentralization, and vouchers), challenge previous notions about the role of education in development. These changes also question the role of the State in promoting educational expansion. They may also sharply redefine the ideas of an educational system created to provide equality of educational opportunity and citizenship building to all citizens.

In the context of these changes, it is reasonable to ask if the measures resulting from structural adjustment are hindering the development of compulsory schooling, both at the primary and secondary levels. In the same vein, it is important to examine the role granted to education in the construction of the modern citizen in Latin America. Is there a retreat in the commitment of the State to deliver free and compulsory public education to the population at large, or is this simply a "pause" in educational development caused by drastic economic conditions and the conditionalities of structural adjustment? In short, is this a short-term retrenchment or rather a drastic (and eventually lasting) change in the orientation and political commitment of the State to public education? These questions include an interrogation of the possible changes of educational purposes in the region. Under the logic of a welfare State, educational policies pursued the twin aims of promoting, on the one hand—social integration and citizenship building—and, on the other hand, technical competence oriented to train human capital. Alternatively, educational policies developed by neoliberal governments that accept the rule of the market as the dominant principle for social organization may emphasize technical competence and school choice at the expense of social integration and the building of solidarity through welfare policies.

This issue is important for a number of reasons. If the process of globalization and the neoliberal programs assign to the State a less prominent role in the construction of citizenship and the provision of social services to large segments of the population, this implies a loss of solidarity implicitly embedded in welfare policies. If there is a loss of solidarity in the community attributed to the changing role of the State, this poses important problems for democratic theory.

From a political perspective, power is fragmented and diffused, as several versions of postmodernism argue (Morrow & Torres, 1995). Looking at the moral crisis of contemporary societies, a central element in the analysis is that the distinctions of *différénce*—to paraphrase Bourdieu—led people to construct the categories of *otherness*. By placing the blame and responsibility of the perceived economic, social, or moral crisis on "the other" as scapegoats, the ethical and political dilemmas emerging in the constitution of working and caring communities are diffused or ignored. Thus, shifting the blame to "others" (illegal immigrants, lazy workers, minorities, etc.) facilitates a pedagogical discourse that relocates the responsibility of providing high-quality education to all citizens from the hands of the State to the market. After all, the market, as a *deus ex machina*, will discriminate against less able individuals. Hence, the most rational means of resource allocation (i.e., the markets' supply-and-demand dynamics) will identify means and ends, making it possible for the most motivated, best educated, and "productive" individuals to succeed.

With the logic of the market prevailing, the argument goes, individuals will then be free from State intervention and from clientelist and patrimonialist State practices. They will be able to pursue their free will without outside intervention in the context of a freer exchange of goods and services regulated by market mechanisms. This position may be considered a philosophy of libertarianism with its exacerbation of individualism, and it does little to develop forms of solidarity beyond kinship and small groups. An unqualified total market orientation will pit individuals and the social representation of the notion of free individuals against socially constructed notions of community and collective attempts for social change. The construction of community in contemporary and fragmented capitalist societies, given the exclusionary nature of capitalist development, demands the creation of social inducements—beyond individual ethics—to foster generosity and solidarity. In addition, it requires notions of social contracts (or a social pact) that can be achieved even though operational notions of individual autonomy and freedom may be, following the Rousseauian dilemma, qualified and, occasionally, restricted, so the whole community could access convivial levels of freedom.

In the same vein, following the postmodern notion that the State is mostly social regulation, any crisis of social regulation refers to deep fractures in society—for instance what Habermas called "legitimacy deficit" in late capitalism—but also to typical problems of the State in late capitalism (Morrow & Torres, 1995). The paradox is that crises of social regulation, and by implication drastic changes in the role of the State, may explain the decline in solidarity. However, a reconstructed theory of the pedagogical subject suggests that the notion of *otherness* has multiple expressions calling for a notion of cultural diversity in schools.

There are several indications of serious dislocations in schools systems in Latin America. For instance, teachers may find students aloof, with no interest in learning cognitive skills or pursuing public deliberation. Students may find teachers (and the adult society in general) distant from their own interests and social construction of knowledge—a knowledge base that is the result of the appropriation of a global mass culture. Another example, closer to the experience of the United States, relates to debates on the politics of identity. Taken in one of its most extreme versions, the politics of identity and representation of minority groups in schools and universities may agree with the theory of a zero-sum society. With a zero-sum approach, the affirmation of rights of one group of underrepresented individuals, and the appropriation of resources to satisfy a historical grievance or modify an identifiable process of discrimination will imply, by definition, that resources are taken from one group at the expense of another group of underrepresented individuals. Thus, the result is the continuous conflict among diverse constituencies representing minority, women, class-based, ability, and other underrepresented groups, given the implicit (and widely accepted notion) that resources are fixed or inelastic.

What are the implications of dislocations of this magnitude for the relocation of the politics of identity and difference in Latin America? Is it possible to find a model or framework of solidarity that does not depend entirely on the performance of the welfare State or any reconstructed notion of State intervention which could be made sharply distinct from the neoliberal State? This question requires different levels of analysis. To begin with, the notion of social regulation set forth by Foucault is very useful to link the workings of structures and the process of reception, adaptation, resistance, and reelaboration of knowledge by individual actors. Can social regulation operate independently from competing ideologies? If this is the case, then the gap between generations, or the declining State intervention in sponsoring solidarity, should not be an issue. The rules of regulation and the instruments of regulation will simply have changed hands, giving a more prominent place to market exchanges. Knowledge will not only be fragmented but segmented by social hierarchies. Those who can afford to pay growing user fees will continue to send their children to schools, and their offspring will be able to access the "pool" of knowledge that society has to offer. Those who will be unable to pay the growing out-of-pocket expenses will simply become marginal to mainstream knowledge (and societal structures).

The same can be said regarding the socialization of children and youth who are introduced to new technologies, computers, or advanced communications devices. Technological literacy will become a central component in the context of social differentiation in the region. The best-endowed private and public schools will be able to take advantage of the reception of these new technologies in terms of both teaching and learning. This, in turn, increases the exposure of middle- and upper-class students to the most creative and productive—not to mention the most profitable—technologies. Public schools which do not have access to additional funding to modernize their technological structure, to hire specialized teachers and technicians, and to attract the best students in their areas of influence, will remain quite distant from the avant-garde training and socialization.

With these increasing processes of differentiation, the educational system will then be another form of exclusion rather than inclusion, reflecting the dualization of society. Dual societies reflect in dramatic ways how individuals differ in their access to wealth, power, influence, and political representation. There is no reason why, with the withdrawal of the State from its public mandate, society will provide free and compulsory education to its citizens. Schooling will become growingly dualized.

Latin American societies have become increasingly dual, with rich and poor sectors growing very much apart. This dualization of class structures is not exclusive of Latin America but a phenomenon of worldwide proportions (Aspen Institute, 1992; Boron, 1992; Marshall, 1965; Gorz, 1988; Phillips, 1990). Therefore, there are serious contradictions, tensions, and imbalances between the social citizenship and the political citizenship. The social citizenship is expressed by the effective access to a certain quantity of goods and services, both material and symbolic, which decisively condition the quality of life of individuals. The political citizenship is expressed by means of equal and universal suffrage and the exercise of rights and obligations. This schism between both types of citizenships, so insightful argued by T. H. Marshall, will propitiate the proliferation of attitudes, beliefs, and values antagonistic to the democratic stability and the legitimation formulae on which democratic regimes are founded. Needless to say, with teachers' perceptions that they need to transmit the collective values of the nation to children and youth, there is no surprise that teachers' leaders and rank and file are visibly upset with diminishing investment in public education, which is seen as one more trend in this process of dualization. In this context, it is legitimate to ask if the disequilibrium between these two citizenships may explain the withdrawal of State investment in education and compulsory schooling. This withdrawal, perhaps forced by structural adjustment conditionalities, is reflected in educational budgets and eventually in declining enrollments, particularly in public secondary education.

The dualization of schooling will result in, and be an example of, the constitution of at least two broad types of citizens: triple A citizens, to use a term in vogue in Latin America emulating or resembling the nomenclature to classify the quality of bonds and credit ratings of institutions, and "dispensable" citizens or class B citizens. Triple A citizens are those who can exercise any model of political representation and participation they wish, not only through their vote but also through political action, because they are connected to the networks of power. They can achieve information quickly through new cybernetic technologies—and the navigation of the growing "information super highway"—and their cliques, and can manipulate the symbols of the highbrow cultural capital. Dispensable citizens are those whose marginality is constructed through the process of representation of mass media coupled with their political isolation and fragmentation. They are also suffering serious economic pressures, many of them are already part of a poverty belt surrounding the metropolitan areas of Latin America, or located in deteriorating sectors of cities, particularly inner cities. Their strategies for survival in their everyday life takes precedence over any other activity, including politics. Both types of citizens are exposed simultaneously to the multiple messages of a growingly internationalized mass media committed to the construction of the "possessive individualism," to use the term popularized by MacPherson in his insightful critique of liberal theories of democracy (MacPherson, 1983, 1962; Carens, 1993). In Latin America this is is what a cultural critic called "the unilateral North Americanization of the symbolic markets" (Canclini, 1993, p. 10).

This issue of dual citizenships poses the perennial question of who is being included and who is being excluded from compulsory schooling. The inclusion and exclusion of social groups from schooling should be discussed in light of increasing user fees, decentralization, privatization, and municipalization policies. These policies are not restricted to Latin America, and therefore this discussion has an intellectual and political appeal that goes well beyond idiosyncratic or regional considerations. What remains to be studied in detail is to what extent the conditionalities of structural adjustment have increased the dualization of class structures and citizenship, or if this process of dualization has independent dynamics that structural adjustment may have been unable to slow down or, on the contrary, has simply accelerated.

Unfortunately it is difficult to assess what has really happened in the last years of educational systems undergoing structural adjustment given the quality and paucity of data available in the region. A careful analysis of disparities between and within national data sets, and in international educational statistics, should make us wary of the lack of precision in educational statistics. Data should not be taken at face value. There are serious questions about quality, scope, paucity, and reliability of data about Latin American educational systems. More often than not, crucial decisions in planning and policy are based on data that is shaky or even faulty. A careful exploration, analysis, and contrast of data—and data sources—will help clarify some of the fundamental issues regarding educational development under structural adjustment conditions.

In summary, looking specifically at teachers' collective action, this chapter has examined teachers' organizations in the context of corporatism and the demands for democracy in Latin America. While the hypotheses advanced need to be reexamined and refined, they may serve as a starting point for more in-depth analysis. Moreover, the available data do not facilitate an examination of issues of professionalization, skilling/deskilling, or standardization or its impact on teachers as workers, and particularly as women workers in the region. Any systematic study of the teaching profession undergoing structural adjustment in Latin America should also examine teachers' resistance in the context of deskilling, standardization, and rationalization of the teaching profession, and particularly how women teachers react to the new measures prompted by structural adjustment policies. This is particularly relevant in the case of Latin America because the growing impression that distorted views of liberation and shortcomings in the practice of the Left in the region have created a legacy which has shortchanged women and pushed aside women issues and the feminist agenda (Randall, 1992). However, paraphrasing the appropriate title of Jo Fisher's book (1992), women are out of the shadows in Latin American politics, and this will be reflected in any study of the teaching profession in the region.[21]

Implications and Suggestions for Further Research

It is with a view to the changing role of the State and to the current economic and sociopolitical repercussions of structural adjustment policies that we should study the educational systems and teachers' organizations in Latin America. How have teachers' organizations and trade unions—particularly women teachers and union women leaders—defined the role of public education in the overall process of democratization of their societies which are facing neoliberal structural adjustment policies?

This chapter has suggested a number of research dimensions and research questions that need to be addressed in further research. Let me quickly reState, in closing, several very important questions:

1. There is a debate in Latin America about whether the change from a type of welfare State to a neoliberal State more responsive to market demands has also altered the role and functions of public education. Given the requirements to decrease educational spending under structural adjustment programs, are the new national educational policies a temporary response to the crisis or has the State diminished its political commitment to educate all citizens? What are the views and policies of teachers' organizations?

2. What is the role that women teachers play in shaping new educational policies? Did teachers' unions with an increasing female leadership better articulate women's interests in teaching and educational policies? Did women union leaders define the problems of teaching as related to larger social movements and gender relations?

3. What actually happened in the last two decades in terms of educational expansion and financing? How have the debates surrounding educational expansion and financing been perceived by teachers' organizations and State officials? Are teachers' organizations concerned with deskilling, standardization, and rationalization of the teaching profession? What positions have teachers' organizations taken, particularly women leaders, on educational restructuring?

4. Are there shared "visions" among teachers' organizations and State agencies about the role public education should play in terms of equity, equality of educational opportunity, and quality of education. What are the views of the functionaries responsible for public education and teachers' unions leadership, particularly those representing primary and secondary education teachers, a great majority of them women?

These questions demand urgent analytical answers informed by empirical studies, but further research may be hampered by the proverbial fact that data is a political prisoner of governments. A key issue for research is the quality, reliability, and availability of statistical data informing policy decisions. Reviewing secondary data sources, and making a comparative analysis of international and domestic data on education in the region, it is relatively simple to identify trends and point to areas where more research is needed. However, a fundamental issue that researchers need to address here is the inconsistent nature of the data available on education, how such data irregularities might affect educational policy making, and how competing views on education may resort to disparate data sources to justify their claims and policy preferences (Chapman, 1991).

Finally, an important preoccupation of research on teachers' unions in Latin America is the need to understand the new role of women teachers as union leaders. Feminist scholars have argued that women are more nurturing than men, and that having been excluded from the networks of power, women leadership will be less compromising with the status quo and more prominent in the defense of the poor and the underclass, particularly children (Butler & Scott, 1992). In considering these arguments, a number of issues and questions emerge. Do female union leaders manage to specifically articulate women's interests in the practice of teaching and educational policies, defining the problems of teaching as related to larger social movements and gender relations? Is there a change of guard from an "old-boys" teachers trade-unionism, to a new facilitating female teachers' leadership? Do women leaders perceive their role as resisting work intensification? Do they perceive a loss in the autonomy and skills of teachers?

Considering these questions and the great degree of uncertainty regarding the implications of policies of structural adjustment and stabilization in public education, more research is needed. Particularly, it is necessary to understand what is really happening to women teachers and specifically to female teachers' leaders in the context of a growing conflict in the relationship between teachers' unions and the State; a relationship that may be drastically changing from historical patterns of an unstable consensual relationship into an abrasive political conflict, especially in the formulation of public educational policies.

Notes

1. It is no secret that teachers' unions in the United States were enthusiastic and energetic supporters and major contributors to President Clinton's campaign and its message for change. In 1993, California teachers invested heavily in defeating a Statewide voucher initiative.

2. The welfare State is considered a particular form of the democratic liberal State in industrialized societies. Its origins have been associated with the industrial and financial reconstitution of the postdepression era in the United States, which was based on a "social pact" (New Deal) and concertation policies between employers and labor. A striking feature of the welfare State is the interventionist role of the State in the economy and enlarged public spending in both productive and nonproductive sectors of the economy. Welfare policies are defined as government protection of minimum standards of income, nutrition, health, housing, and education. As Wilensky argued, these welfare benefits were assured to every citizen as a political right rather than as charity. See Wilensky, 1975, 1976; Popkewitz, 1991.

3. Although the adult illiteracy rate in Costa Rica and Argentina is as low as 5 percent and 6 percent, respectively, and 10 percent for Mexico, in Brazil it remains as high as 22 percent (World Bank, 1991; also Plank, 1987).

4. For a discussion on the relationship between the State and education, see Torres, 1995a.

5. For an alternative explanation using a world-systems framework, see the work of representatives of the institutionalist school. For example, Boli & Ramirez, 1992; Torres & Puiggros, 1995.

6. Of course, despite disparities in income distribution and the fall in the GNP in the region, this decade considered "lost" for economic growth was extremely prosperous for several sectors of the Latin American bourgeoisie, particularly the segments associated with the State that have enjoyed fiscal incentives and specific protectionism in certain areas of the economy. It is important to emphasize that not everybody lost during the "lost decade" and that some factions of the elites became even richer while several segments of the population grew poorer. That is the reason that Latin American societies are now, if not more than, at least as unequal as before but, as documented by a number of sociodemographic studies, poverty has increased dramatically (see Boron & Torres, 1994).

7. Many social scientists have analyzed these changes. See, for example, Przeworski, 1991; Ohmae, 1990; Reich, 1991.

8. *Fortune* (December 14, 1992): 52–66. For an argument suggesting the analysis of the State as a decisive analytical variable in the context of globalization and world-systems approaches, see Amin, 1991.

9. A fascinating work in this direction is Popkewitz, 1991; See Torres, 1990.

10. Neoliberalism, or the neoliberal State, are terms employed to designate a new type of State that emerged in the region in the last two decades. The first example of economic neoliberalism in Latin America is usually associated with the policies implemented in Chile after 1973. In many respects, neoliberal policies are for free trade and small public sectors and against excessive State intervenionism and tight regulation of markets. Lomnitz and Melnick (1991), among other scholars, argue that, historically and philosophically, neoliberalism has been associated with structural adjustment programs. Structural adjustment, in turn, is usually described as a broad range of policies recomended by the World Bank, the International Monetary Fund and other financial organizations. Although the World Bank differentiates among stabilization, structural adjustment, and adjustment policies, it acknowledges that the general use of these terms "is often imprecise and inconsistent" (Samoff, 1990; Reimers, 1990).

11. Fernando Reimers concludes that the educational sector was proportionally more affected by cuts in expenditures than the overall public sector expenditures (see Fernando Reimers, 1990, p 16).

12. International educational statistics must be used with great caution and, perhaps, skepticism. Let us take Brazil as a case in point. There is inconsistency in data reported for the same year in UNESCO Yearbooks for various years. For instance, a great discrepancy occurs in the percentage of GNP dedicated to education reported for 1965. The 1969 Yearbook reports 1.4 percent of GNP went to education in 1965, while the 1975 yearbook reports 2.9 percent for 1965. As another example, while the 1987 Yearbook reports 2.9 percent for 1984 in the following year, the 1988 Yearbook reports 2.8 percent for 1984. In the 1990 Yearbook, however, the GNP

dedicated to education in 1984 is estimated as 3.3 percent. Moreover, although trends are similar, the data reported in UNESCO does not correspond exactly to the data reported by the Ministry of Education and Culture in Brazil in several publications. For an example of a healthy skeptical analysis of the problems with data and comparisons in education, see Samoff 1991. From a very different theoretical vantage point, Stephen Heyneman (1993) also expresses reservations about quality and reliability of data in his presidential address to the Comparative and International Education Society (CIES): "Why is it that after 4 decades of international statistical efforts, the system remains so fragile and, in the minds of some, is regressing?"

13. Exceptions are the years between 1976 and 1980.

14. There are a variety of teacher's unions in Argentina, including a Confederation of Teacher Unions of the Argentine Republic (CTERA), unions representing sectoral interests (e.g., elementary education teachers, secondary education teachers, secondary technical education teachers, higher education professors), and unions representing private elementary education, private secondary education teachers, and teachers in the provinces and municipalities in the country.

15. After sixty years of operation of the municipal educational system, no statute of the teaching profession had been implemented until the Freirean administration. Freire told us that he considered it important to correct this omission.

16. Qualifications for school principals are three years of seniority in the municipal system of education and a proper teaching credential (Secretaria Municipal de Educação de São Paulo, 1991).

17. Whether parents have more than one child enrolled in the school, or whether they are also members of the staff or the faculty of the school, they will not alter the norm of "one parent one vote."

18. Among key principles of this statute, the first ever in the history of municipal education in the city of São Paulo, are the following: monthly salary adjustments for inflation (garantia de piso salarial profissional); changes in working conditions, including the creation of a Jornada de Trabajo Integral; full-time positions of thirty hours a week, including twenty contact hours and ten additional hours for extra-classroom activities; guaranteed part-time positions of twenty hours a week, with the possibility for those part-time teachers with tenure to opt for a full-time position; and implementation of a conselho de escola (school council) as a deliberative organ made up of the school principal, teachers, teachers' aids, students, and parents.

19. Conversation with Paulo Freire, São Paulo, Brazil, July 2, 1991.

20. Ibid. For a discussion on corporatism and education, see Morales-Gómez & Torres, 1990.

21. For a discussion of feminism and education in Latin America and the role of womens' movements, see for instance, Eckstein, 1989; Penaloza, 1992; Jaquette, 1989. For an analysis of teachers as an empoverished middle class, Lomnitz & Melnick, 1991.

References

Aboites, H. "El salario del educador en México: 1925–1982." Coyoacán. Revista Marxista Latinoamericana 8 (January–March 1984): 70–72.

Aboites, H. "Sesenta Años del salario del educador (1925–1985)." *Cuadernos Obreros,* 1986: 84–88.

Acker, S. "Teachers, Gender, and Resistance," *British Journal of Sociology of Education* 9, 3 (1988).

Amin, S. "The State and Development." In David Held (ed.) *Political Theory Today.* Stanford: Stanford University Press, 1991, pp. 305–29.

Apple, M. *Teachers and Texts: A Political Economy of Class and Gender Relations in Education.* New York and London: Routledge, 1988.

———. *Official Knowledge. Democratic Education in a Conservative Age.* New York and London: Routledge, 1993, p. 141.

Apple, M. (ed.) *Cultural and Economic Reproduction in Education.* London and Boston: Routledge and Kegan Paul, 1982.

Aspen Institute. *Convergence and Community: The Americas in 1993—A Report of the Inter-American Dialogue.* Washington, D.C.: Inter-American Dialogue of the Aspen Institute, 1992, p. vi.

Atilio, A., A. Boron, & C. Torres. "Pobreza, Educación y Ciudadanía." Paper presented to the Conference on Educación y Desigualdad Social en America Latina, Toluca, Mexico, Colegio Mexiquense, October 26, 1994.

Avalos, B. "Moving Where? Educational Issues in Latin American Contexts." *International Journal of Educational Development,* 1986.

Bitar, S. "Neo-Conservatism versus Neo-Structuralism in Latin America." *CEPAL Review* 34 (1988): 45.

Boli, J. & F. Ramirez. "Compulsory Schooling in the Western Cultural Context." In Robert F. Arnove, Philip G. Altbach, and Gail P. Kelly (eds.) *Emergent Issues in Education. Comparative Perspectives.* Albany: State University of New York Press, 1992, pp. 25–38.

Boron, A. The Formation and Crisis of the Oligarchical State in Argentina, 1880–1930. Ph. D. dissertation, Harvard University, 1976.

———. "La pobreza de las naciones. La economía política del neo-liberalismo en la Argentina." Buenos Aires: EURAL Working Paper 43, 1992.

Butler, J. & J. Scott. *Feminists Theorize the Political.* New York and London: Routledge, 1992.

Canclini, N. "Una modernización que atrasa. La cultura bajo la regresión neoconservadora." *Revista Casa de las Americas* 193 (October–December 1993): 10.

Carens, J. (ed.). *Democracy and Possessive Individualism: The Intellectual Legacy of C. B. Macpherson.* Albany: State University of New York Press, 1993.

Chapman, D. "Education Data Quality in the Third World: A Five Country Study." *International Review of Education* 37(3): 365–79.

Collier, R. & D. Collier. October 1, 1997. *Shaping the Political Arena: Critical Junctures, the Labor Movement, and Regime Dynamics in Latin America.* Princeton, N.J.: Princeton University Press, 1991.

Connell, R. *Teachers' Work.* Boston: Allen and Unwin, 1985.

Darling-Hammond, L. "Introduction" to *Review of Research in Education.* Washington, D.C.: American Educational Research Association, 19, 1993: xi.

Eckstein, S. (ed.) *Power and Popular Protest: Latin American Social Movements.* Berkeley and Los Angeles: University of California Press, 1989.

Estatuto do magistério municipal. Minuta do anteprojeto de lei. São Paulo: Secretaria Municipal de Educação de São Paulo, March 1991, p. 44.

Fisher, Jo. *Out of the Shadows: Women, Resistance, and Politics in South America.* New York and London: Monthly Review Press, 1992.

Fortune (December 14, 1992): 52–66.

Gorz, A. *Métamorphose du Travail.* Paris: Galilée, 1988.

Heyneman, S. "Quantity, Quality, and Source." *Comparative Education Review* 37 (November 1993): 381.

Jaquette, J. (ed.) *The Women's Movement in Latin America.* London: Unwin Hyman, 1989.

Laban, R. & F. Sturzenegger. "Fiscal Conservatism as a Response to the Debt Crisis." Los Angeles and Santiago de Chile, manuscript, 1992.

Lockheed, M. & A. Verspoor. *Improving Primary Education in Developing Countries: A Review of Policy Options.* Washington D.C.: World Bank and Oxford University Press, 1991.

Lomnitz, L. & A. Melnick. *Chile's Middle Class: A Struggle for Survival in the Face of Neoliberalism.* Boulder, Colo.: L. Rienner, 1991.

MacPherson, C. *The Political Theory of Possessive Individualism: Hobbes to Locke.* Oxford and New York: Oxford University Press, 1983, c1962.

———. *Democracy in Alberta: Social Credit and the Party System.* Toronto, University of Toronto Press, 1962, c1953.

Marshall, T. *Class, Citizenship, and Social Development.* Garden City, N.Y.: Anchor Books, 1965, pp. 71–134.

Morales-Gómez, D. & C. Torres. *The State, Corporatist Politics, and Educational Policy Making.* New York: Praeger, 1990, p. 80.

O'Cadiz, M. & C. Torres. "Literacy, Social Movements, and Class Consciousness: Paths from Freire and the São Paulo Experience." *Anthropology and Education Quarterly* 25, 3 (September 1994): 1–18.

Ohmae, K. *The Borderless World: Power and Strategy in the Interlinked World Economy.* New York: Harper Buisness, 1990.

———. *Triad Power: The Coming Shape of Global Competition.* New York: Free Press, 1985.

Petrei, A., M. Montero & A. Maraviglia. "Estudio comparativo de las remuneraciones en el sector educación." In A. Humberto Petrei (ed.) *Ensayos en economía de la educación.* Buenos Aires: Ministerio de Educación y Justicia/Banco Mundial/ Programa de las Naciones Unidas para el Desarrollo, 1989, p. 165.

Phillips, K. *The Politics of Rich and Poor: Wealth and the American Electorate in the Reagan Aftermath.* New York: Random House, 1990.

Plank, D. "The Expansion of Education: A Brazilian Case Study." *Comparative Education Review* 31 (1987).

Popkewitz, T. *A Political Sociology of Educational Reform: Power/Knowledge in Teaching, Teachers Education, and Research.* New York and London: Teachers College, Columbia University, 1991.

Przeworski, A. *Democracy and the Market: Political and Economic Reforms in Eastern Europe and Latin America.* New York: Cambridge University Press, 1991.

Puiggrós, A. *Sujetos, disciplina y curriculum en los orígenes del sistema educativo argentino.* Buenos Aires: Galerna, 1990.

————. *Democracia y autoritarismo en la pedagogía argentina y latinoamericana.* Buenos Aires: Galerna, 1986.

————. et al., *Escuela, democracia y orden (1916–1943).* Buenos Aires: Galerna, 1992.

Randall, M. *Gathering Rage: The Failure of Twentieth-Century Revolutions to Develop a Feminist Agenda.* New York and London: Monthly Review Press, 1992.

Raymond Allen Morrow, R. & C. Torres. *Social Theory and Education: A Critique of Theories of Social and Cultural Reproduction.* Albany: State University of New York Press, 1995.

Reich, R. *The Work of Nations.* New York: Vintage Books, 1991.

Reimers, F. "Educación para todos en América Latina en el Siglo XXI: Los desafíos de la estabilización, el ajuste y los mandatos de Jomtien." Paper presented to the workshop on Poverty, Adjustment, and Infant Survival, organized by UNESCO in Peru, December 3–6, 1990, p. 16.

Reimers, F. *A New Scenario for Educational Planning and Management in Latin America.* Paris: International Institute of Educational Planning, 1990.

————. "The Impact of Economic Stabilization and Adjustment on Education in Latin America." *Comparative Education Review* 35 (May 1991): 325–38.

Rosenthal, G. "Latin America and Caribbean Development in the 1980s and the Outlook for the Future." *CEPAL Review* 39 (1989): 1.

Samoff, J. "The Façade of Precision in Education Data and Statistics: A Troubling Example from Tanzania." *Journal of Modern African Studies* 29, 4 (1991): 669–89.

————. "More, Less, None? Human Resource Development: Responses to Economic Constraint." Palo Alto, June 1990, mimeographed, p. 21 (unpublished ms.).

Schiefelbein, E. *Financing Education for Democracy in Latin America Santiago de Chile: Unesco-OREALC,* January 1991, mimeographed: 4.

Stromquist, N. (ed.). *Women and Education in Latin America: Knowledge, Power, and Change.* Boulder, Colo.: Lynne Riemmer, 1992.

Torres, C. *Politics of Nonformal Education in Latin America.* New York: Praeger, 1990.

————. "Paulo Freire as Secretary of Education in the Municipality of São Paulo." *Comparative Education Review* 38, 2 (May 1994): 181–214.

————. "The State and Public Education in Latin America." *Comparative Education Review* 39, 1 (February 1995).

————. "The State and Education Revisited; Or, Why Educational Researchers Should Think Politically about Education." *Review of Research in Education* 21 (1995a): 255–331.

————. "Fictional Dialogues on Teachers, Politics, and Power in Latin America." In Mark Ginsburg (ed.) *The Politics of Teachers' Work and Lives.* New York: Garland, 1995b.

UNESCO. Conferencia de ministros de educación y ministros encargados de ciencia y tecnología en relación con el desarrollo de América Latina y el Caribe. Venezuela, December 6–15, Caracas, Venezuela: UNESCO, 1971, mimeographed.

————. *Evolución reciente de la educación en América Latina.* Santiago de Chile: UNESCO, 1974, mimeographed: pp. 167, 227.

UNESCO/CEPAL/PNUD, Desarrollo y Educación en América Latina: Síntesis General. Buenos Aires: Proyecto DEALC, 4 vols, 1981.

United Nations Development Program. Mitigación de la pobreza y desarrollo social. Montevideo, Uruguay: UNDP project RLA/92/009/1/01/31, 1992, mimeographed.

————. Desarrollo Humano y Gobernabilidad. Montevideo, Uruguay: UNDP project RLA/92/030/I/01/31, 1992, mimeographed.

Wilensky, H. *The Welfare State and Equality:Structural and Ideological Roots of Public Expenditures.* Berkeley and Los Angeles: University of California Press, 1975.

Wilensky, H. *The New Corporatism: Centralization and the Welfare State.* Beverly Hills, Calif.: Sage, 1976.

World Development Report, 1991: The Challenge of Development. Washington, D.C.: World Bank and Oxford University Press, 1991, pp. 204–205.

New Schools for New Times? Notes toward a
Sociology of Recent Education Reform

GEOFF WHITTY, SHARON GEWIRTZ,
AND TONY EDWARDS

The rhetoric of the approach to education reform of the recent Conservative government in Britain was summed up in what is called its "five great themes"—quality, diversity, parental choice, school autonomy, and accountability (DFE, 1992). One institutional manifestation of these themes could be seen in the creation of a "new choice of school"—City Technology Colleges (CTCs), which were launched at the 1986 Conservative party conference (DES, 1986). These were intended to be new secondary schools for eleven to eighteen year olds, located in inner-city areas and with a curriculum emphasis on science and technology. All or a substantial part of their capital funding was to be met by business sponsors, while their recurrent costs were to be met by central government. These schools were intended to "break the mold" of English secondary education by introducing a greater element of specialization and choice into the system and encouraging business sponsors to take a more active role in the funding and provision of education. Being entirely outside the local education authority (or school district) system, they would operate as autonomous units free to experiment with new forms of curriculum and pedagogy and new approaches to school management. They were also encouraged to experiment with a longer school day and a longer school year (Whitty et al., 1993).

The CTC program itself was blighted by funding difficulties and produced only fifteen schools to the original blueprint. However, many of the ideas embodied in the CTC experiment have since been spread much more widely—if thinly—throughout the education system. It therefore makes sense to see CTCs in the context of a changing approach to the provision and governance of education. The 1988 Education Reform Act and the 1993 Education Act have brought about local (or site-based) management and per-capita funding for virtually all schools. In addition, they have given most schools the opportunity to opt out of their local education authorities and become grant-maintained schools, run as autonomous units receiving their funding directly from central government. These acts have also included measures to extend parental choice through open enrollment to most state schools and the encouragement of greater specialization and diversity of provision.

We want to argue that such developments are not of purely local interest. Despite considerable variation in the detailed nature of reforms, even within different parts of the United Kingdom, the same themes are echoed in the rhetoric of reform in many other countries (Whitty & Edwards, 1992). For example, the policy initiatives and debates associated with the *America 2000* program and the British Education Reform Act have many similarities (Apple, 1992). Even at the level of detail, there are some striking similarities with initiatives being launched elsewhere. In 1991, President George Bush launched the New American Schools initiative, which seemed remarkably similar to the British government's CTC program. New American Schools were to be based upon a unique partnership among "communities, inventors, educators, and entrepreneurs . . . a new partnership between the private sector and government." They would help "break the mold" of American education by challenging "assumptions commonly held about schooling" (New American Schools Development Corporation, 1991). These include the prevailing adherence to blackboard and chalk, a curriculum organized into subjects and class periods, the six-hour day and the 180-day school year, technology located only in the computer lab and the principal's office and policies that discouraged risk taking and offered few rewards for improved learning. Breaking the school district monopoly in the provision of state education was also seen to be a feature of the policy by some of its advocates.

Although, like the British CTC program, the New American Schools initiative itself has encountered funding problems, the general thrust of the *America 2000* program has been carried into *Goals 2000* under the Clinton administration, while similar concerns underlie a multitude of restructuring programs in individual states and school districts. Choice programs, site-based management, charter schools, the debates about vouchers and about the desirability of a national curriculum and national testing all have parallels with developments in Britain (Apple, 1993, 1996). Yet, despite the obvious similarities, a White House official we interviewed during the Bush era denied any specific relationship between CTCs and the New American Schools initiative and judged CTCs to have been at most a very minor influence. Saturn schools, Nabisco's "Next Century Schools" and the activities of Whittle Communications seem to have been much more influential. The relevance of the British CTCs was recognized but, rather like magnet schools in relation to CTCs, as a source of confirmation rather than as a direct model. Much the same seems to be the case with choice policies, charter schools, and withdrawing school districts' exclusive franchise to provide public education. Such proposals are being legitimated by reference to British experiments, thereby making the "unthinkable" appear more reasonable, but the process is less a matter of direct "policy exchange" than of mutually reinforcing versions of reality. John Chubb, who has now become closely associated with the American reform agenda, visited Britain briefly during the debate over the 1988 Education Reform Act. He claims that that visit had "very little impact" on his initial work with Terry Moe (Chubb & Moe, 1990), but he has now written up a subsequent visit as "a lesson in school reform from Great Britain" (Chubb & Moe, 1992).

Policy makers in many other countries also seem to have been working within similar frames of reference and producing parallel policy initiatives (Whitty et al., 1998). Although in the case of the British and American central governments of the 1980s and early 1990s this process may have been facilitated by the existence of a common policy community with a shared political philosophy (Whitty & Edwards, 1992), this "New Right" network factor is less convincing as an explanation of developments elsewhere. It is clear that support is being given to the diversification and specialization of educational provision and to local control of schools from a variety of political perspectives, as well as in countries with different political regimes. Indeed, although school choice policies in the United States received particular encouragement from Republican presidents Reagan and Bush, the growth in site-based management policies, magnet schools, and other schools of choice has received much broader support within all parties in the United States. While some of the specific elements of the *America 2000* strategy were downgraded during the first Clinton administration, other aspects have remained firmly in place and renewed emphasis has recently been placed upon charter schools.

Apparently similar policies have been pursued by governments of various political hues in other parts of the world. In New Zealand, where advocates of community empowerment united with exponents of consumer choice against the old bureaucratic order, a Labor government's moves in the direction of devolution and school autonomy prepared the ground for the market-oriented policies now being pursued by a right-wing government (Gordon, 1992; Grace, 1991). Much the same has happened in Victoria, Australia. Meanwhile, for rather different reasons, the centrally planned education systems of the Communist regimes of Eastern Europe have often been replaced with experiments in educational markets (Glenn, 1992). More surprisingly, both Communist China and the highly standardized Japanese system of education have been experimenting with policies to encourage greater devolution and diversity. Finally, international organizations are now encouraging the introduction of similar policies into some of the less developed countries (Arnove, 1996).

These tendencies have certainly not yet penetrated all countries that economists regard as the "center" let alone the "periphery." Even in Europe, the picture remains uneven and, even where broadly similar themes are identifiable, the immediate provenance of the specific reforms and the manner of their implementation vary considerably according to the traditions of different nation-states and different political parties.

Despite the rather ill-defined phenomenon of "globalization," the specific relations between local, national, and international influences are highly variable and historically contingent. Furthermore, much of the literature on globalization tends to understate the continuing significance of the nation-State, particularly in the field of internal regulation, including education policy (Green, 1997).

Yet, the trend toward a similar constellation of policies in various countries does suggest a prima facie case that they may reflect broader and deeper changes emerging in the nature of modern societies. We now explore that case in more detail by considering how far it is useful to draw upon various concepts of contemporary social theory to make sense of all these individual reforms as part of what one observer has called the "bigger picture" (Ozga, 1990). We consider in turn the extent to which recent education reforms may be considered an aspect of the "new public management," a response to those deeper shifts in patterns of production and consumption that are often termed "post-Fordism," or an expression of that rather ill-defined constellation of changes that is sometimes taken to signal that we are living in a "postmodern" age. While accepting that such concepts can provide some useful insights into the broader significance of recent education reforms, we shall conclude that, at least in the case of Britain, it is equally important to recognize some strong continuities at the level of outcomes between current trends and traditional patterns of social and educational inequality.

The "New Public Management"

Evidence of the broader significance of the changes might be drawn from the fact that the move away from the "one best system" of providing mass education has parallels in changes in other aspects of social policy. In Britain, the most obvious parallels are in reforms in the housing, health, and welfare services, where there was a general thrust toward the creation of "quasi markets" during Mrs. Thatcher's third term of office and under the Major government. Particularly significant from the quasi-markets perspective was "the gradual but accelerating phenomenon of the expansion of the housing association movement to supplant local authorities as the main new providers of social housing" (Le Grand, 1992, p. 6), notably as the result of the 1988 Housing Act, which allowed for the transfer of public housing to private

landlords, housing associations, or tenants' cooperatives. Although these housing policies undoubtedly brought choice and self-determination for some
tenants, choice for others was curtailed. Forrest and Murie, writing in 1988,
predicted that "the public housing sector is well on the way to becoming an
unambiguously residual, second class form of housing provision, serving the
poorest sections of the population" (Forrest & Murie, 1988, p. 83) and the
parallels with the fears expressed by critics of market policies in education
were clear.

At one level the restructuring of state welfare can be seen as part of a
retrenchment in public expenditure, but what has actually changed has been
the pattern rather than the level of public expenditure. This has particular
relevance in the case of education, where privatization, in the strictly economic sense of the term, has been of limited significance. What has been
more in evidence has been a shift in the ways in which State-funded education has been provided and consumed. Equally significant has been a shift in
the way education is administered. Alongside, and potentially in place of,
collective provision by elected bodies with a responsibility to cater to the
needs of the citizenry, there are increasing numbers of quasi-autonomous
institutions operating with devolved budgets and competing for clients in the
marketplace.

Along with changes in the way the state regulates other areas of social
activity, such as housing and health, the new administrative arrangements for
managing education can be seen as new ways of resolving the problems of
accumulation and legitimation facing the State. They are a response to a
situation where the traditional welfare State cannot deliver what it promises
or resolve the contradictions between different functions of the state (Dale,
1989). With the removal of tiers of government between the central State and
individual institutions, conventional political and bureaucratic control by elected
bodies is replaced or supplemented by market accountability assisted by a
series of directly appointed agencies, trusts, and regulators. This involves
different forms of devolution in different contexts, partly because the advocates of such new institutional arrangements are drawn from a wider constitu-
ency than neoliberal market fanatics. Although such developments are a move
in the direction of a market-based pluralism, thoroughgoing neoliberals often
believe they do not go far enough.

Chubb and Moe (1990, 1992) are among a growing number of commentators of various political persuasions who argue that the combination of
democratic control by elected bodies and the powerful bureaucracies they
generate is a major cause of the poor performance of modern mass-education
systems. The new institutional arrangements that they propose make it appear
that education has been removed from this political arena. Quasi-autonomous
institutions with private and voluntary involvement in their operation, even
when they are largely state funded, blur the boundary between the state and

civil society and appear to make education less of a political issue. Manfred Weiss (1992) has suggested that calls in Germany for a shift of responsibility for education down to individual schools and an increased emphasis on parental empowerment are a response to a legitimation crisis of the state. In other words, they constitute an attempt to reposition education in relation to the state and civil society and, in doing so, they also call into question conventional understandings of the state/civil society relationship. Just as Andy Green (1990) has suggested that education policy has often been an important aspect of state formation in the past, so the current repositioning of education can be seen as related to the changing role and, indeed, nature of the state in contemporary societies.

The rhetoric accompanying the reforms seeks to suggest that education has been taken out of politics as normally understood. This was made explicit by British Education Secretary John Patten when he argued, in launching the 1992 *White Paper* which preceded the 1993 Education Act (DFE, 1992), that one of its aims was to "depoliticize" education by removing it from the local political arena and giving power to parents and school governors. The changes brought about by earlier acts had already destroyed the quasi-corporatist approach to educational policy making that had emerged in the period following World War II. Of central government's traditional partners in education policy making, organized teachers were no longer a significant partner in the initiation of educational policy, and local education authorities (LEAs) had already been consigned to a distinctly subordinate role in its implementation. Charles Raab (quoted in Whitty, 1989) has suggested that the new arrangements may constitute a form of dispersed pluralism, the ideal version of which is the atomized market.

Weiss (1992) doubts that the state will be successful in deflecting responsibility for educational decision making to market forces and atomized individuals and units operating within civil society. In practice, anyway, the education reforms in Britain have as much to do with transferring power from the local State to the central State as with giving autonomy to the schools. Indeed, Peter Riddell (1992) has suggested that the likely outcome is that criticism of education that has hitherto been conveniently directed at LEAs will now fall squarely on central government. Yet it is just as likely to fall on individual schools and their managements. In effect, the reforms will enable central government to make cuts in expenditure and blame the consequences on poor management practices.

Another interpretation of current trends offered by Raab is that the government may still be engaging in special-interest group politics by identifying new partners in the form of parents and industry—partners who are less coherent and identifiable than its traditional partners in education policy making (the LEAs and the teacher trade unions) and hence more open to manipulation by central government. On the other hand, the reforms have also produced an increase in the number of potentially significant arenas for educational politics in its widest sense, and some of these may be highly susceptible to the influence of other vested interests—including the liberal educational establishment. Indeed, some research has indicated that, on the newly powerful governing bodies of schools, professionals and parents tend to act together (Golby & Brigley, 1989). This is particularly ironic in that one of the main targets of reform has often been the perceived notion of "producer capture" of the education system by professional educators.

Nevertheless, at the level of policy formation and initiation in education, the role of central government has clearly been strengthened by recent legislation. McKenzie (1995) argues that British governments have actually increased their claims to knowledge and authority over the education system while promoting an apparent movement toward devolved decision making by institutions and individual consumers. The notion that decentralization and centralization are straightforward alternatives is thus called into question. The new arrangements might also be seen in terms of a reworking of the dual polity approach to contemporary politics rather than as a straightforward abandonment of corporatist planning in favor of market forces (Saunders, 1987). But these observations on the effects of the policies do not detract from our earlier claim that, at least in terms of the rhetoric, many of the reforms are broadly consistent with new ways of understanding and managing public institutions that are fast becoming an orthodoxy in many parts of the world (Rhodes, 1991; Dale, 1992).

Post-Fordism

If these changes are a response to crises of accumulation and legitimation, it may be too simplistic to dismiss them as merely a passing aberration of Thatcherism or Reagonomics. Some observers suggest that we are witnessing the transportation of changing modes regulation from the sphere of production into other arenas, such as schooling and welfare services, and that these changes in turn relate to deeper changes in the mode of accumulation. They point to a correspondence between the establishment of markets in welfare and a shift in the economy away from Fordism toward a post-Fordist mode of accumulation that "places a lower value on mass individual and collective consumption and creates pressures for a more differentiated production and distribution of health, education, transport and housing" (Jessop et al., 1987, 109).

Various writers have claimed to see in CTCs and other recent education policies a shift from the "Fordist" school of the era of mass production to what Stephen Ball has termed the "post-Fordist school" (Ball, 1990). The emergence of new types of schools may therefore be the educational equivalent of the rise of flexible specialization in place of the old assembly-line world of mass production. According to Kenway et al., these educational institutions are designed "not only to produce the post-Fordist, multi-skilled, innovative worker but to behave in post-Fordist ways themselves. . . . [This] post-Fordist mind-set is currently having implications in schools for management styles, curriculum, pedagogy and assessment" (Kenway et al., 1993, p. 115).

CTCs would appear to be in the vanguard of such a shift, with their shopping-mall or business-park architecture, their "flat" management structures, and their emphasis on "niche marketing," all apparently offering support for what appears to be an updated version of the Bowles and Gintis "correspondence thesis" (Bowles & Gintis, 1976). There are also potential parallels to be drawn between the management strategies of post-Fordist industries and those of CTCs. So-called post-Fordist business entrepreneurs typically achieve maximum flexibility by abandoning the old industrial sites in favor of green-field locations, with planning deregulation and nonunion labor. In a similar way the CTC initiative, at least as initially conceived, facilitated a similar flexibility for educational entrepreneurs. By virtue of direct State funding and green-field locations beyond the control of local authorities, they sought to avoid what they saw as "restrictive practices" on the part of teacher unions and local bureaucrats.

There are, however, many problems with the underlying notion of post-Fordism and the term itself signals too much coherence to both Fordist and post-Fordist regimes of accumulation and a discontinuity between them that is difficult to sustain empirically. As Rustin (1989) comments: "It is dubious in principle and possibly misleading in fact to make linear extrapolations from what might seem to be 'leading instances,' or current trends, to the shape of a whole system" (p. 58). This is a salutary warning in relation to the concerns of this chapter and, unlike Brown and Lauder (1992), we would actually prefer to acknowledge these difficulties by using the term *neo-Fordism* to characterize those shifts that have taken place in the prevailing mode of regulation. This term treats the changes more as an adjustment to the problems of Fordism than as a qualitatively new economic direction or a "step beyond" Fordism into a new era (Allen, 1992).

Just as there are problems with the notion of post-Fordism as an entirely new regime of accumulation, we need to be cautious in concluding from any parallels that may exist between economic and social modes of organization that we are experiencing a wholesale move away from a mass-produced welfare system toward a flexible, individualized, and customized post-Fordist one. In the field of education, too, it is difficult to establish a sharp distinction between mass and market systems. In Britain, the so-called comprehensive system of education was never as homogeneous as the concept of mass-produced welfare suggests. Indeed, it was always a system differentiated by class and ability. What may be different in the new era is an intensification of these differences and a celebration of them in a new rhetoric of legitimation involving choice, specialization, and diversity to replace the previous language of common and comprehensive schooling (see also Brown & Lauder, 1992).

Postmodernity

Jane Kenway and colleagues (1993) have brought together a number of the theories underlying the idea of "new times" to argue that, in education as elsewhere, modern societies *are* now entering a qualitatively new era. They suggest that accounts that concentrate solely on institutional changes pay insufficient attention to other cultural shifts that help to explain why markets in education have found such a receptive audience. For these authors, "the rapid rise of the market form in education is best understood as a postmodern phenomenon" (Kenway et al., 1993, p. 105). In postmodernity, the significant nexus is that between the global and the local, limiting even the scope of the individual national state. But notions of "difference," far from being eradicated by the "globalization of culture," are assembled, displayed, celebrated, commodified, and exploited (Robins, 1991). Diversity is regulated into a commodity form.

Kenway and colleagues see the new technology as a key element in the development of new and commodified cultural forms. What they call "the markets/education/technology triad" is a crucial feature of postmodernity, a triad in which CTCs and New American Schools can clearly be located. They argue that "transnational corporations and their myriad subsidiaries . . . shape and reshape our individual and collective identities as we plug in . . . to their cultural and economic communications networks" (Kenway et al., 1993, p. 119). Whittle's Channel One in the United States would be a good example of this process (Apple, 1993), though it should be noted that most of the large information technology and media corporations declined to become involved in the British CTC program.

Kenway and colleagues' account of postmodernity is essentially a negative and pessimistic one. Yet there are other accounts of postmodernity where the rhetoric of "new times" offers *positive* images of choice and diversity. In this context, recent reforms might be regarded as part of a wider retreat from modern, bureaucratized state education systems that are perceived as having failed to fulfil their promise and now seem inappropriate to the heterogeneous societies of the late twentieth century. Thus, part of the appeal of recent education policies lies in the claim that different types of schools will be responsive to the needs of particular communities and interest groups that exist as a result of complex patterns of political, economic, and cultural differentiation in contemporary societies that have replaced the traditional class divisions upon which common or comprehensive education was predicated. While this process of differentiation is partly about creating new markets for new products, the multiplicity of lines of social fissure that are emerging may also be associated with deeper changes in modes of social solidarity. Insofar as these divisions and associated identities are experienced as real, they are likely to generate aspirations that will differ from traditional ones.

This has contributed to more optimistic readings of postmodernity than the one to which Kenway and colleagues subscribe. Compared with the oppressive uniformity of much modernist thinking, it is possible to regard postmodernism as "a form of liberation in which the fragmentation and plurality of cultures and social groups allow a hundred flowers to bloom" (Thompson, 1922, pp. 225–26). Thus, many feminists have seen attractions in the shift toward the pluralist models of society and culture associated with postmodernism and postmodernity (Flax, 1987). The possibilities for community, rather than bureaucratic, control of welfare are also sometimes viewed positively by some minority ethnic groups. In the United States, the reforms of the school system in Chicago were originally enacted as a result of a curious alliance between New Right advocates of school choice and Black groups seeking to establish community control of their local schools, together with disillusioned White liberals and some former student radicals of the 1960s (Hess, 1990).

Support for schools run on a variety of principles other than those of the "one best system" might then be seen as recognizing a widespread collapse of a commitment to modernity. Or, put another way, it may be viewed as a rejection of the totalizing narratives of the Enlightenment Project and their replacement by "a set of cultural projects united [only] by a self-proclaimed commitment to heterogeneity, fragmentation and difference"; social development is no longer seen as "fulfilment of some grand historical narrative" but as a "pragmatic matter of inventing new rules whose validity will reside in their effectivity rather than in their compatibility with some legitimating discourse" (Boyne & Rattansi, 1990). The notion of "unprincipled alliances," which at one time might have prevented such a political configuration as emerged in Chicago, may be less appropriate in a context of postmodernity, which is seen by Lyotard (1986), its leading philosopher, as a pluralist, pragmatic, and restless set of partially differentiated social orders. If large-scale attempts at social engineering have been perceived as failing, less ambitious aspirations may now be in order.

In Britain, the Labour Party's traditional social democratic policies have also been perceived as unduly bureaucratic and alienating by many Black parents, who, it is sometimes claimed, welcomed the new opportunities offered by the 1988 Education Reform Act to be closer to their children's schools (Phillips, 1988). While they did not necessarily endorse the Thatcherite dream, some aspects of it did seem to connect to the aspirations of groups who found little to identify with in the grand master narratives associated with class-based politics. Policies that seem to emphasize heterogeneity, fragmentation, and difference may thus represent more than a passing fashion among neoliberal politicians and resonate with changing notions of an open, democratic society as well as with a market ideology. Put in those terms, it is understandable that recent policies have had a potential appeal far beyond the coteries of the New Right. Indeed, this is now recognized in the British Labour Party's newly found support for more specialized and diverse forms of secondary schooling.

Whether any of this is sufficient to argue that recent reforms are a postmodern phenomenon is doubtful, although the evidently "slippery" and imprecise nature of the concept *postmodern* makes it difficult to arrive at a judgment. To some extent new and restructured schools can be seen as "new schools for new times." Thus, if we equate curriculum specialization with niche marketing, they appear to display some of the characteristics of what is usually termed post-Fordism. Their changing institutional relationship to government is broadly consistent with emergent forms of public administration more generally. The emphasis on specialization and diversity in their legitimating rhetoric can be seen to parallel broader cultural changes. But there is also another side to it. For example, notwithstanding conscious attempts to make CTCs look more like business organizations than schools (BBC Radio 4, 6 June 1989), they are still readily identifiable as secondary schools, with more similarities to nearby conventional comprehensive schools than differences. Though some of the sponsors of CTCs may have wanted their schools to prepare workers and citizens with new forms of subjectivity, the classroom realities we encountered in our own fieldwork in these new schools were much more conventional (Whitty et al., 1993).

None of this suggests a radical break with the concerns of modernity. Just as changes in ways of managing production might be better characterized as neo-Fordism—and new institutional forms as merely a new way of managing the modernist project—so much of contemporary thinking about education can also be seen as a variation on a familiar theme. There are certainly serious problems in trying to see the sort of diversity sponsored by recent reforms as a postmodern phenomenon in the strong sense of reflecting deep-seated changes in the nature of society.

Reworking Old Themes

Some aspects of the reforms are the very epitome of the modernist project. This was apparent, for example, in the manner in which the high-tech image of CTCs was invoked in the early publicity. At least as much as conventional comprehensive schools, CTCs seemed to express an underlying faith in technical rationality as the basis for solving social, economic, and educational problems. Even in the Major government's *White Paper* devoted to "Choice and Diversity," this modernist project predominated. It was "specialization" rather than "diversity" that was given prominence. And, although the subsequent 1993 legislation was "drawn widely enough to encourage more schools to specialise in other fields too," the main emphasis throughout was to be on technology, which would help to "break down the divide between academic and vocational studies" and "equip young people with the technological skills essential to a successful economy" (DFE, 1992, p. 45). Indeed, the justification for specialization was that "other leading industrialized nations combine the attainment of high standards with a degree of specialisation" (DFE, 1992, p. 43).

Furthermore, although CTCs may have particular attractions for some members of the minority ethnic population, the ethos of CTCs is often assimilationist rather than one that actively fosters cultural pluralism. Indeed, one of the publicly made criticisms from students at one of the London CTCs was that "they're leaving out the black people—in [our old school] they taught us about Rastas, black history and culture" (*Daily Telegraph*, 4 July 1991). And, although Muslim leaders welcomed the 1992 *White Paper* for heralding State-funded Islamic schools through the "opting-in" of existing private schools (*Observer*, 2 August 1992), the subsequent opportunities for this have proved decidedly limited in practice. Overall, the notion of curriculum specialization, at least in technology, is much more clearly spelled out than that of diversity. Indeed, the chapter of the 1992 *White Paper* entitled "Specialisation and Diversity in Schools" is almost entirely about specialization.

Nevertheless, this rhetoric of specialization and diversity is given an added popular appeal by the suggestion that it would not entail selection and hierarchy. The Major government stressed specialization rather than selection and said that it wanted "to ensure that there are no tiers of schools within the maintained [State] system but rather parity of esteem between different schools, in order to offer parents a wealth of choice" (DFE, 1992, p. 10). Interestingly, it did not seem to be committed to parity of esteem between the public and private sectors. The emphasis was on encouraging parental choice rather than selection, but this failed to recognize the reality of what happens, either overtly or covertly, when schools are massively oversubscribed. In those circumstances, it is schools rather than parents that do the choosing.

The impression was also given that each school was to be judged on its specific character and on its merits, rather than as embodying the characteristics of a hierarchically arranged series of "types." Yet we found that parents choosing CTCs were frequently concerned, not with specialized excellence in technology, but with the extent to which this "new choice of school" was *similar* to academically selective private and grammar schools and *different* from mainstream comprehensive schools. In other words, they were seeking positional advantage for their children. Furthermore, Walford and Miller claim that, while comprehensive schools attempted to overcome the historic links between diversity of provision and inequalities of class and gender, CTCs "have played a major part in re-legitimizing inequality of provision for different pupils." Indeed, they argue that the "inevitable result" of the concept of CTCs, especially when coupled with Grant Maintained Schools and local management of other schools, is a "hierarchy of schools with the private sector at the head, the CTCs and GMSs next, and the various locally managed LEA schools following" (Walford & Miller, 1991, p. 165). While we have a few doubts about where exactly different types of schools will eventually settle in this hierarchy, the idea that there will be no hierarchy of school types at all is difficult to sustain in the light of past experience.

However, the Major government rejected any idea that a new hierarchy of school types would develop and dismissed the relevance of the experience of the tripartite system of the 1950s and the 1960s by arguing that we now live in "a different educational world" with the National Curriculum ensuring equality of opportunity (DFE, 1992, p. 10). Yet, the highly traditional and elitist form of National Curriculum introduced by the Thatcher government has restricted the amount of cultural diversity officially sanctioned in schools and, through its limited conception of what counts as school knowledge, effectively imposed a master narrative that differentiates cultures on a hierarchical basis. Epistemologically, it involves a reassertion of foundationalism and inscribes an exclusive and authoritarian version of rationality in the officially prescribed curriculum and its associated testing practices. The combined effect of competition among schools for pupils and the publication of assessment scores is to arrange schools and pupils in a hierarchy, which leaves the most disadvantaged and demotivated pupils concentrated in schools with low aggregate test scores, declining resources, and low teacher morale (Gewirtz et al., 1995).

Ball suggests that, below the various types of schools of choice that are being fostered by current policies, there is already developing a third tier of "sink" schools—those which are unpopular and under subscribed (Ball, 1990, p. 91). One of the results of the "deregulation" of schooling is that the onus is increasingly on parents to make separate applications to each school. The CTC policy also introduced a new mode of selection for schools, based on the criteria of motivation, commitment, and aptitude. Gewirtz, Ball, and Bowe (1992) argue that these new modes of application and selection privilege those with the system know-how, time, and energy to make applications and mount a good case. At the same time, they discriminate against those who have more pressing immediate concerns than being an educational "consumer." Members of this group are also less likely to have the appropriate cultural resources to exercise choice, whether it be in education, housing, or health care.

However, the distinction between those who are privileged and those who are disadvantaged by the CTC policy and parallel "market" initiatives would *not* appear to be a straightforward middle-class/working-class or White/Black one. While detrimental to large sections of the working class, the reforms are also likely to benefit some working-class families as well as lower middle-class ones. For example, our own research findings suggest the CTC policy may have attracted certain fractions of the minority ethnic population. But, while such policies may reflect changes in the nature of class reproduction, they do not significantly interrupt it. Indeed, in some respects, they intensify it.

Thus, whatever the intentions of their sponsors, recent policies are as likely to increase structural inequalities as to challenge them, while fostering the belief that the championing of choice provides genuinely equal opportunities for all those individuals who wish to benefit from them. There is little evidence yet that, taken as a whole, the reforms are helping to provide a structure that will encompass diversity and ensure equality of opportunity for all pupils. They seem more likely to produce greater differentiation between schools on a linear scale of quality and esteem than the positive diversity that some of their supporters hoped for. For those members of disadvantage groups who are not sponsored out of schools at the bottom of the status hierarchy, either on grounds of exceptional academic ability or alternative official definitions of merit, the new arrangements may just be a more sophisticated way of reproducing traditional distinctions between different types of school and between the people who attend them. This could have disastrous consequences for some sections of the predominantly working class and Black populations who inhabit the inner cities.

Continuity and Change

In this sense, the recent reforms maintain continuity with a long history of educational inequality in English education (Banks, 1955). Although current education policies may seem to be a response to changing economic, political, and cultural priorities in modern societies, it would be difficult to argue—at least in the case of England—that they should be read as indicating that we have entered into a qualitatively new phase of social development. Despite the development of new forms of accumulation and changes in the state's mode of regulation, together with some limited changes in patterns of social and cultural differentiation in contemporary societies, the continuities seem just as striking as the discontinuities. Similarly, although it is easy to see why commentators such as Green (1991) regard recent policies as a first stage toward total atomization and privatization, most restructured systems still conform to Archer's definition of a modern State education system as "a nation-wide and differentiated collection of institutions devoted to formal education, whose overall control and supervision is at least partly governmental, and whose component parts and processes are related to one another" (Archer, 1984, p. 19).

Visions of our moving toward a postmodern education system in a postmodern society may thus be premature or a reflection of surface appearances. To regard the current espousal of heterogeneity, pluralism, and local narratives as indicative of a new social order may be to mistake phenomenal forms for structural relations. Marxist critics of theories of postmodernism and postmodernity, such as Callinicos (1989), certainly take this view and reassert the primacy of class struggle. Even Harvey (1989), who accepts that significant changes are taking place within capitalism, suggests that it may be more appropriate to see postmodernist cultural forms and more flexible modes of capital accumulation more as shifts in surface appearance than as signs of the emergence of some entirely new postcapitalist or even postindustrial society. At the very most, the current reforms in education would seem to relate to a version of postmodernity that emphasizes "distinction" and "hierarchy" within a fragmented social order, rather than one that positively celebrates "difference" and "heterogeneity" (Lash, 1990).

Furthermore, the reforms embody many apparent contradictions. At most, they lie at a point of tension between competing conceptions of contemporary social policy, as symbolized in an ongoing debate within the CTC movement about the desirability of social engineered catchment areas in the context of markets and parental choice. Thus, neoconservative and neoliberal policies vie with each other and with the residue of traditional liberal and social democratic approaches to educational reform. Roger Dale (1990) argues that a policy of "conservative modernization," which entails "freeing individuals for economic purposes while controlling them for social purposes," was a key feature of the Thatcher government's education policy and that it is a particularly useful concept for making sense of CTCs. It certainly seems more helpful to see recent education reforms in those terms than as a straightforward expression of postmodernity.

Nevertheless, CTCs and other new types of schools are developing a significant market appeal. While much of this can be explained in terms of their financial advantages and perceived position in a developing "pecking order" of schools, it would be inappropriate to interpret it all in this way. Despite the absence of a clear postmodern break within either schooling or society, the recent reforms may have been more responsive than their critics usually concede to those subtle but nonetheless tangible, social and cultural shifts that have been taking place in modern societies. In working through the implications of this, a straightforward return to the old order of things would be neither feasible nor sensible. While recent policies constitute a social text that helps to create new subject positions which serve to undermine traditional modes of social solidarity, the forms of collectivism associated with the welfare state often failed to include many members of society, especially women and minority ethnic groups. Liberal and social democratic approaches to education that have favored the idea of a common school are faced with this fact, as well as with a need to respond to those social changes that have taken place. This has been clearly recognized by the British Labour Party under Tony Blair.

Just as current discussions on the Left about citizenship are seeking ways of "creating unity without denying specificity" (Mouffe, quoted in Giroux, 1990), so is an appropriate response to greater specialization and diversity in society a challenge for education policy in the context of what Anthony Giddens (1990) terms "high" or" radicalized" modernity. In the United States, Charles Glenn believes it is possible to accommodate diversity and choice without abandoning the idea of public education (Glenn, 1992). In Britain, James Donald (1990) has called for policies that are based on "participation and distributive justice rather than simple egalitarianism—and on cultural heterogeneity rather than a shared humanity." Such views indicate a willingness on the part of educationists to "think the unthinkable," which belies the Major government's charge, echoed by Chubb and Moe (1992), that their opponents all favored a "uniformity in educational provision" that "presupposes that children are all basically the same and that local communities have essentially the same educational needs' (DFE, 1992, p. 3). But, in considering alternatives to past practice, it remains important to recognize that the questioning of old orthodoxies does not necessarily involve adopting the political agenda of the Right or abandoning the notion that education is a public responsibility rather than merely a private good.

Finally, we must acknowledge how our own discursive practices as sociologists have structured the analysis offered here. Our attempt to explore recent education reform through a variety of conceptual lenses might conceivably be read by some as a playful espousal of multiple perspectives in preference to a search for an overarching grand narrative—and thus as indicative of a slide into an acceptance on our own part of the postmodernist critique of traditional social science. However, while we would not claim that we could ever generate anything as coherent as *the* "bigger picture," we would not wish to abandon the essentially modernist project of the social sciences any more than we would want to argue that current educational reforms are a distinctively postmodern phenomenon. This, in turn, will clearly have contributed to the particular "readings" of recent education reform offered in this chapter.

Note

This paper arose out of work on an Economic and Social Research Council Project "City Technology Colleges: A New Choice of School?" (Project C00232462.)

It is based on chapter 9 of G. Whitty, T. Edwards, and S. Gewirtz *Specialisation and Choice in Urban Education: The City Technology College Experiment* (Routledge, 1993) and an earlier version of it was presented to a conference at the University of Wisconsin–Madison in June 1993.

References

Allen, J. "Postindustrialism and Post-Fordism." In *Modernity and Its Futures*, ed. S. Hall, D. Held, and T. McGrew. Cambridge: Polity Press, 1992.

Apple, M. "The Politics of Official Knowledge: Does a National Curriculum Make Sense?" John Dewey Lecture presented at the American Educational Research Association annual meeting, San Francisco, 20–24 April 1992.

———. *Official Knowledge: Democratic Education in a Conservative Age.* New York: Routledge, 1993.

———. *Cultural Politics and Education.* New York: Teachers College Press, 1996.

Archer, M. *Social Origins of Educational Systems.* London: Sage, 1984.

Arnove, R. "Neoliberal Policies in Latin America: Arguments in Favor and Against." Paper presented at the Comparative and International Education Society Conference, Williamsburg, Va., 6–10 March 1996.

Ball, S. *Politics and Policy Making in Education: Explorations in Policy Sociology.* London: Routledge, 1990.

Banks, O. *Parity and Prestige in English Secondary Education.* London: Routledge, 1955.

Bowles, S. & H. Gintis. *Schooling in Capitalist America.* New York: Basic Books, 1976.

Boyne, R. & A. Rattansi (eds.). *Postmodernism and Society.* London: Macmillan, 1990.

Brown, P. & H. Lauder. *Education for Economic Survival: From Fordism to Post-Fordism?* London: Routledge, 1992.

Callinicos, A. *Against Postmodernism: A Marxist Critique.* Cambridge: Polity Press, 1989.

Chubb, J. & T. Moe. *A Lesson in School Reform from Great Britain.* Washington D.C.: Brookings Institution, 1992a.

———. *Politics, Markets and America's Schools.* Washington D.C.: Brookings Institution, 1992b.

Cooper, B. *Magnet Schools.* Warlingham: IEA Education Unit, 1987.

Dale, R. *The State and Education Policy.* Milton Keynes: Open University Press, 1989.

———. "The Thatcherite Project in Education: The Case of the City Technology Colleges." *Critical Social Policy* 9 (1990): 4–19.

———. "National Reform, Economic Crisis and 'New Right' Theory: A New Zealand Perspective." Paper presented at the American Educational Research Association annual meeting, San Francisco, 20–24 April 1992.

Department for Education. *Choice and Diversity: A New Framework for Schools.* London: HMSO, 1992.

Department of Education and Science. *A New Choice of School*. London: DES, 1986.

Donald, J. "Interesting Times." *Critical Social Policy* 9 (1990): 39–55.

Edwards, T., S. Gewirtz, & G. Whitty. "Whose Choice of Schools?" In *Voicing Concerns: Sociological Perspectives on Contemporary Educational Reforms*, ed. by M. Arnot and L. Barton. Wallingford: Triangle Books, 1992.

Flax, J. "Postmodernism and Gender Relations in Feminist Theory." *Signs: Journal of Women in Culture and Society* 12 (1987): 621–43.

Forrest, R., & A. Murie. "The Social Division of Housing Subsidies." *Critical Social Policy* 8 (1988): 83–93.

Gewirtz, S., S. Ball, & R. Bowe. "Parents, Privilege and the Educational Marketplace." Paper presented at the British Educational Research Association annual conference, Stirling University, 31 August 1992.

———. *Markets, Choice and Equity in Education*. Buckingham: Open University Press, 1995.

Giddens, A. *The Consequences of Modernity*. Cambridge: Polity Press, 1990.

Giroux, H. (ed.). *Postmodernity, Feminism and Cultural Politics*. Albany: State University of New York Press, 1990.

Glenn, C. *The Myth of the Common School*. Amherst: University of Massachusetts Press, 1988.

———. "School Choice and Educational Freedom in Eastern Europe." Paper presented at the American Educational Research Association annual meeting, San Francisco, 20–24 April 1992.

Golby, M. & S. Brigley. *Parents as School Governors*. Tiverton: Fairway Publications, 1989.

Gordon, L. "The New Zealand State and Educational Reforms: 'Competing' Interests." Paper presented at the American Educational Research Association annual meeting, San Francisco, 20–24 April, 1995.

Grace, G. "Welfare Labourism versus the New Right." *International Studies in the Sociology of Education* 1 (1991): 37–48.

Green, A. *Education and State Formation*. London: Macmillan, 1990.

———. "The Peculiarities of English Education." In *Education Group II, Education Limited*. London: Unwin Hyman, 1991.

Green, A. *Education, Globalization and the Nation State*. London: Macmillan, 1997.

Harvey, D. *The Condition of Postmodernity: An Enquiry into the Origins of Cultural Change*. Oxford: Basil Blackwell, 1989.

Hess, A. *Chicago School Reform: How It Is and How It Came To Be*. Chicago: Panel on Public School Policy and Finance, 1990.

Jessop, B., K. Bonnett, S. Bromley & T. Ling. "Popular Capitalism, Flexible Accumulation and Left Strategy." *New Left Review* 165 (1987): 104–23.

Kenway, J. et al. "Marketing Education in the Postmodern Age." *Journal of Educational Policy* 8 (1993): 105–22.

Lash, S. *Sociology of Postmodernism*. London: Routledge, 1991.

Le Grand, J. "Quasi Markets and Social Policy." *Economic Journal* 101 (1991): 1256–67.

———. "Paying for or Providing Welfare?" Paper presented at the Social Policy Association annual conference, Nottingham University, July 1992.

Lyotard, J. F. *The Postmodern Condition*. Manchester: Manchester University Press, 1986.

McKenzie, J. "Education as a Private Problem or a Public Issue? The Process of Excluding 'Education' from the 'Public Sphere.' " In S. Edgell and S. Walklate (eds.) *Debating the Public Sphere*. Aldershot: Avebury Press, 1995.

New American Schools Development Corporation. Publicity brochure. No date.

Ozga, J. "Policy Research and Policy Theory." *Journal of Educational Policy* 5 (1990): 359–63.

Phillips, M. "Why Black People Are Backing Baker." *Guardian* 9 (September 1988).

Rhodes, R. "The New Public Management." Special Issue of *Public Administration* 69 (1991).

Riddell, P. "Is It the End of Politics?" *The Times* 3 (August 1992).

Robins, K. "Tradition and Translation: National Culture in its Global Context." In *Enterprise and Heritage: Crosscurrents of National Culture*, ed. J. Corner and S. Harvey. London: Routledge, 1991.

Rustin, M. "The Politics of Post-Fordism; Or, the Trouble with 'New Times.' " *New Left Review* 175 (1989): 54–79.

Saunders, P. *Social Theory and the Urban Question*. 2d ed. London: Hutchinson, 1987.

Thompson, K. "Social Pluralism and Post-Modernity." In *Modernity and Its Futures*, ed. S. Hall, D. Held & T. McGrew. Cambridge: Polity Press, 1992.

Walford, G. & H. Miller. *City Technology College*. Milton Keynes: Open University Press, 1991.

Weiss, M. "Changing Paradigms and Patterns of Education Policy in Germany." Paper presented at the American Educational Research Association annual meeting, San Francisco, 20–24 April 1992.

Whitty, G. "The Politics of the Education Reform Act." In *Developments in British Politics*. 3d ed., ed. P. Dunleavy, A. Gamble, and G. Peel. London: Macmillan, 1990.

Whitty, G. & T. Edwards. "School Choice in Britain and the USA: Their Origins and Significance." Paper presented at the American Educational Research Association annual meeting, San Francisco, 20–24 April 1992.

Whitty, G., T. Edwards, & S. Gewirtz. *Specialisation and Choice in Urban Education: The City Technology College Experiment*. London: Routledge, 1993.

Whitty, G., S. Power & D. Halpin. *Devolution and Choice in Education: The School, the State and the Market*. Buckingham: Open University Press, 1998.

When the Center Cannot Hold

The Devolution and Evolution of Power, Authority, and Responsibility in Russian Education

STEPHEN T. KERR

Turning and turning in the widening gyre
The falcon cannot hear the falconer;
Things fall apart; the center cannot hold;
Mere anarchy is loosed upon the world,
The blood-dimmed tide is loosed, and everywhere
The ceremony of innocence is drowned;
The best lack all conviction, while the worst
Are full of passionate intensity.
                    —Yeats, *The Second Coming*

Cataclysmic changes have shaken political and social life in Eastern Europe and the former USSR since 1989. Many aspects of these changes have been widely reported in Western news media—the discrediting and then dismantling of formerly unassailable political systems, rapid shifts in the forms of economic activity, dissemination of literature and popular culture formerly viewed as heretical, quick destruction of powerful political symbols (the Berlin Wall, statues of Lenin), and struggles to create new forms of social and political life to match the new possibilities.

In Russia, these changes have been perhaps even more troubling than in Eastern Europe—the Russian experience of living under a totalitarian regime was of longer duration, the habits of democracy were never well established, and the forms of authoritarian control were home-grown rather than imposed from without. In Russia, the fundamental orientation over nearly seventy-five years toward an omnipotent and supposedly omnicompetent Communist Party cannot be overestimated. Even among those least inclined to accept the myths of the Party's wisdom and infallibility, the Party's doctrines, images, ways of portraying the world, and definitions of social relationships exerted a powerful influence. Those affected included the ones most likely to play a role in social reconstruction—the intellectuals, the dissidents, the writers, the repressed social activists, and the very many more who merely accepted the Party Card so as to permit them to live a "normal" professional life. Consequently, the challenges faced by those attempting to build a new social order out of the chaos that now exists in Russia are faced with a set of problems almost unimaginable to a Western observer—how to construct an entirely new social and philosophical "center" for relationships among the state, individuals, and the wider world. In education, this question has become especially critical over the past few years, and it is this question we shall explore here.

Background: The Party as Social Center

In order to understand why the disappearance of the Communist Party has raised such serious problems for intellectuals, social activists, teachers, and other educators in Russia, we must first review the nature of Soviet Communism, of State-Party relationships in Russia prior to 1991, and the consequences of these patterns as they affected the mental landscapes of individuals. For in Russia as nowhere else (with the possible exception of Nazi Germany, a social order that had far less time to develop), the Party defined all. Or at least it tried to. And while not everyone accepted its definitions of how the world worked, the Party did define basic categories and fixed these firmly in peoples' thinking.

The Communist Party of the Soviet Union (CPSU) was the party of Lenin and Stalin, the party that was repressed under the Czars, that seized power in 1918, carried out collectivization, purged the country of dissent in the 1930s, organized the defense of the nation during World War II, and eventually managed the gradual transition to a less repressive but no less totalitarian form of control during the 1960s and 1970s. What is essential to understand about the period of Russian-Soviet history from 1918 through 1991 is that the Party was the center of Russian society in various senses. The Party was in fact the state, although there was a separate state structure that existed during all this time (the soviets, or councils, that defined civic life throughout the country, up to the Supreme Soviet, the various ministries, and so forth). In all state organs, a non-Party person could not attain any significant position, and all state functions, at all levels, were mirrored by a Party organizational structure that in fact made (or closely monitored and approved) all state decisions (see, e.g., DeGeorge, 1966; Hough & Fainsod, 1979; Kenez, 1985).

The Party did more than simply govern; it also defined the nature of social discourse. Through the all-pervasive ideology of Marxism-Leninism, basic relationships were defined, and the nature and categories of social life identified and described. Since the ideology was based on a comprehensive philosophical worldview (the Hegelian dialectic and its interpretation by Karl Marx), and claimed to be fundamentally "scientific," it in fact formed a kind of seamless whole which was very difficult to attack, and which only some intellectuals were able to critique in a way that did not expose them to immediate personal danger (loss of life under Stalin; merely loss of position or privilege under later leaders).

None of this is to say that people liked the ideology or found it attractive; on the contrary, from the early 1970s through the mid-1980s (what came during the Gorbachev era to be called the "period of prolonged stagnation"), there was a kind of pervasive malaise on all social levels, a covert realization that the goals that had long been touted for Socialist and Communist society were not only not being reached, but were fundamentally flawed in their original conception. Nonetheless, in spite of this, there remained a sense that the ideological center of society was in some way unchangeable, that the Party would always be there, and that all important discussions about social life would need to account for the presence, influence, and role of the CPSU and its accompanying ideological baggage.

This influence was not only social, but also individual and personal. Even those who later strongly dissented from the Soviet system often acknowledged that, in their early years, they considered themselves among the world's fortunates because they had had the luck to be born in the Soviet Union. Today, the uneasiness over rank privatization of the economy and the new radical economic stratification of society bring troubled reactions from many prominent Russian intellectuals. It is clear that the Party and its ideology provided a point of reference, a central intellectual framework on which all one's later consciousness somehow depended.

The CPSU and its ideology thus provided in some sense the "center" for the whole society, even for those who found it anathema. It was what there was to be railed against, to be angrily or laughingly dismissed, to which antidotes would need to be sought in Western or pre-Revolutionary Russian thought, or, more typically, what would need to be acknowledged, however routinely or unenthusiastically, in the initial pages of one's book or article, almost regardless of the subject. It was also the organization that became for almost all serious intellectuals, including those working in the field of education, a kind of unpleasant but necessary employment agency *cum* employer for virtually all work that involved contact with others, especially young people, and even more particularly in any administrative capacity. While a school teacher did not necessarily have to be a Party member, all those working in administrative positions (principals, as well as city, regional, and national education managers) were typically members of the CPSU, and became accustomed to orienting their decisions toward what they knew the hierarchy would approve.

In education, the Party's influence was not confined merely to control over employment, but also reached into decisions regarding the choice of content, the shaping of school programs, and the form for extracurricular activities with children. The concern for these spheres of educational life was not merely Soviet—it was mirrored in language used by pre-Revolutionary Russian educators, and that was adopted by their Soviet successors. The agency principally responsible for education first under the czars, then under the Commissars, was the Ministry (or People's Commissariat) of Enlightenment (*prosveshchenie*), a word with much broader connotations of civic improvement than *education* has in English. Similarly, the Russian concern for how young people are brought up, encouraged to develop socially in and out of school, and socialized into the adult world, was and is the subject in Russia of a large discipline, *vospitanie* (variously translated as "upbringing" or "nurturing"), which has no real parallel in English.[1] (On *vospitanie*, see Bronfenbrenner, 1970; Eklof, 1993; Mathews, 1982.)

Given this history—and the obvious concern with the formation of the rising generation that the new Communist leaders brought with them when they assumed power in 1918—it should come as little surprise that there was a great deal of attention in the early years of the USSR paid to education, and especially to its ideological content. The notion of *vospitanie* was quickly redefined so as to focus it more concretely on the formation of qualities needed by the new regime—devotion to the Motherland, commitment to the new economic structure socialism demanded, selfless identification with collective, rather than with individual, interests.

These qualities were highlighted through general curricula and specific examples held up as worthy of imitation (Pavlik Morozov, the child who informed on his parents during the period of collectivization; the Stakhanovs and other seemingly endless heroes and heroines of socialist construction). The "Moral Code of the Builder of Communism," a short litany most of which would not sound out of place at a meeting of a scout troop, Sunday school, or football team in the United States, became a required part of the curriculum in social studies at all levels.[2] The school curricula in history, literature, and the arts and humanities generally became infused with discipline-specific forms of the ideology (class conflict in history; "socialist realism" in literature and art; and, for a disastrous period in the 1930s and 1940s, Lysenkoism and Michurinism in Biology). Some subjects, such as cybernetics, were eliminated on ideological grounds from the curriculum altogether (see Fisher, 1967).

It is little wonder that most aspiring Russian children decided that academic preparation in the social sciences or humanities was simply a waste of time, and that they would have less need to deal with uninspired teaching and stultifying curricula if they focused their efforts on the natural sciences and mathematics, or on such arts as music and ballet, all fields where the ideological content was more difficult to define and, hence, controls were harder to impose and enforce.

This heritage and its corrosive (if often unrecognized) influence is what Russian educators and intellectuals were forced to confront beginning in the mid-1980s when Gorbachev's rise to power first made it possible to discuss and consider a range of alternatives that was far wider than anything imagined before. This seemingly beneficial step led to a crisis of confidence among Russian educators that it is heard for a Western observer to describe, much less appreciate on a deep personal, psychological level. It is this set of problems that we will address further below.

The Collapse of the Communist Center: Educators Respond

Education and the Collapse of the Communist State

The changes in the educational system wrought by Gorbachev's *perestroika* (restructuring) movement of the 1980s were both substantial and illusory. The final large-scale educational reform of the Soviet era (1984–85) was an attempt to link schools more directly to the ailing economy and bring other new approaches such as computers into the stodgy school system. It was met with general disdain by serious educators, and little came of it, primarily because there was finally freedom to discuss the proposed changes more openly than had been the case in the past.

But this did not automatically mean that educators were able to define new approaches of their own to the problems the schools faced. Communist ideology did not simply disappear one night; it lost its control gradually over a period of some six years (1985–91), experiencing during that time significant ups and downs in influence. Even as late as 1990, it still seemed that the Party might somehow retain much of its former level of control over social life and discourse.[3]

A large part of the crisis of confidence educators felt when facing the changes of the 1980s may be attributable to the fact that the stated ultimate educational goal from the 1950s of creating a "New Soviet Man" had never been challenged; official pedagogical theory had become heavily ideologized, and there were no strong alternative models for what educational practice might look like. By the early 1980s, there was increasing, if still restricted, discussion among specialists about the problems brought by this lack of diversity. The contributions of such pioneering psychologists of the 1930s as Vygotsky and Luria, officially anathematized during much of the Soviet period because of their focus on the individual in a social and cultural context, again gained currency among scholars.[4] The humanistic approaches of educators such as Sukhomlinsky and Ivanov were once again the subjects of study and experiment (see Soloveichik, 1989; Sukhonlinksii, 1979).

In 1986, these efforts provided the basis for a widely published new approach, the "Pedagogy of Cooperation" between students and teachers, a mode of teaching that would put the student's personality and human needs back at the center of attention. Shalva Amonashvili, the architect of the approach, gained wide popularity and was elected as a national deputy to the first Congress of People's Deputies in 1989. Those associated with the educational "movement" of the 1980s—Matveev, Soloveichik, Dneprov, Adamsky, Khiltunen, Shatalov, Lysenkova, and others—organized themselves into a loose federation, and promulgated their radical views through Matveev's *Uchitel'skaia gazeta* [*Teachers Gazette*] until 1989, when a resurgent CPSU forcefully removed Matveev as editor and replaced him with a Party hack (Amonashvili, Shatalov & Lysenkova, 1989; Kerr, 1994; Matveeva, 1992; Petrovskii, 1989).

While these new ideas and the possibility for more open discussion of educational philosophy and issues were heady for many teachers, the majority seemed confused and unsure about how to make use of them. If schools could now be organized differently, and if classroom practice might be built on different models than previously, then teachers and principals did not rush to make use of these new possibilities. Leaders of teacher-training institutions (pedagogical institutes, institutes for teacher retraining and "qualification raising") also seemed unsure how to proceed. There were a good many discussions in the press and elsewhere about how new approaches to education might be tried, but little of a concrete nature seemed to come from these. By 1991, when the August coup finally signaled the death knell for Communist ideology generally, only a few schools had taken the steps needed to become truly independent of the State and, only a few teachers were really able to work in new ways.[5]

The reasons for this lack of initiative on the part of educators may be found at least partially in their lack of experience with more open and participatory forms of civic life in general, and in the sphere of education in particular. Americans (and others from developed democratic countries) have typically had a childhood filled with exposure to countless open meetings, settings in which something like *Robert's Rules of Order* governed the assemblage and in which contrary opinions were at least acknowledged, if not always listened to. The experiences of participation in local government, of working for political parties or candidates in local elections, of participating in church, charitable, or civic groups, or working through problems in the workplace via quasi-open mechanisms for bureaucratic and administrative control—all these provide a distinctive mindset for one raised in the democratic tradition.

For Westerners working in education, these perspectives and skills have been honed through participation in local PTAs/PTSAs, civic and professional groups (including teacher unions, curriculum and textbook selection committees, strike and grievance committees, and perhaps more recently in local school or site councils). Additionally, teachers or administrators with strong professional interests have likely been active in one or more professional associations, may have presented papers or joined in symposia at these events, and perhaps have written or edited papers for professional journals.

These experiences—their presence in the developed democratic world and their absence in Russia—help to explain why the reform of Russian education has proceeded so slowly, even under conditions that suggest it might have been able to move more rapidly. For not only were these formative experiences lacking, but the CPSU, which formerly provided countervailing meaning and a way to organize civic and school life, had lost its capacity to provide moral leadership by the mid-1980s and had been removed from any pretense of power by 1991. In this sense, the collapse of the Soviet State was more than a mere political shift, it was a collapse that created a moral and social vacuum for those whose professional lives were directly touched and guided by the previously existing system. What resulted was a "Stateless" society where old institutions (structures of schools, systems for supplying texts, training teachers, etc.) continued to exist after they had largely lost their core rationale and basis for action—the ideology of Marxism-Leninism, as communicated and interpreted by the CPSU.

The Party not only disappeared, it left little in its wake. While in Eastern Europe and the Baltic countries the imposition of Soviet rule (and concomitant ideological forms) was of relatively recent origin and had been typically preceded by at least some period of acquaintance with democratic traditions in government and civic life, in the Russian case any such democratic experience was both much farther in the past (seventy-five years, as compared to forty to forty-five in Eastern Europe) and had been preceded by virtually no exposure to democracy as a form for civil life. If Eastern Europeans could return to something like the structures they had lived with before, Russians had no such support. The result was both a dearth of attractive alternative images for how to build a democratic civil life and a propensity to search out too quickly and uncritically possible alternative models from the West.

Education without a Center

In the complexity and passion of the moments immediately following the dissolution of the USSR in 1991 and immediately prior to that, there was a kind of exuberant groping for alternative models of pedagogical practice, alternative methods for organizing schools, and different approaches to the definition of school curricula. Many of these new models came from the West, with the result that all manner of Rogerian, Waldorf, and Montessori schools appeared on the Russian scene. Additionally, there were a number of approaches that rapidly gained wider currency in Russia than they had at home—Accelerated Christian Education, for example, attracted a surprisingly large number of adherents in Russia, as did various other approaches from the West.

The initial interest in these alternatives was intense, even if the Russian educators involved often appeared to have little capacity to deal with the underlying assumptions and postulates of these methods. The mental infrastructure needed to make sense of Steiner's Waldorf approach, for example, demands the kinds of experience with democratic forms and an appreciation for the inherent value of the individual. Indeed, the connections between aesthetic and other spheres of human activity featured in the Waldorf approach are complex even for many Western educators to address adequately. The hope that typical Russian teachers might be able to simply step in and start using such models in a deep way is rather naive.

A further consequence of the removal of the Party-oriented "center" from state—individual—institution relations has been the rapid flowering of a variety of new economic enterprises. While most private business activities were literally illegal under the old regime, there are now relatively few bounds to the scope of possible business affairs. In the economy in general, this has led to what some are calling economic chaos—a very rapid growth in unregulated capitalist (or at least commercial) activity, combined with swift "marketization" of the society generally. The latter phenomenon, seen in endless television ads touting various privatization schemes, mutual funds for investment in privatized enterprises, to say nothing of a flood of less-than-essential Western commercial products, has also spilled over into education.

On the surface, the marketization of education has led to the founding of a large number of private schools.[6] Some of these are simply commercial ventures—schools to prepare those who will work in the expanding financial and service spheres supporting Western (and occasionally native) business ventures (clerks, managers), or to teach English or other Western languages in an intensive way. Others are privatized versions of traditional schools, operating at different levels, in which pupil-teacher ratios have been reduced to something like fifteen to one instead of thirty or thirty-five to one, as is common in state schools (see Resolution of II the All Union Meeting).

Still other private schools are truly experimental in their approach, offering unusual curricula, new subjects, different pedagogical approaches. An example is the "Eureka Development" school in Tomsk, a school of nearly two hundred students in grades one through eight, together with two different kindergartens (one following the Montessori method and the other Waldorf), as well as a separate track for the primary grades that follows the pedagogical principles laid out by Leo Tolstoy. Such private institutions also operate on the postsecondary level, as in the Russian Open University, a Moscow institution with a number of departments (*fakul'tety*) in both traditional disciplines and those that are new for most Russian institutions of higher education, such as (religious studies, computer technology, and the like.

When the marketization of a society proceeds rapidly, there are bound to be some dislocations and problems. The freebooting style of capitalism that has appeared in Russia has promoted in some sectors a crude economic rationality as applied to education, a measuring of the educational value of a particular approach, discipline, or level of schooling by its possible economic outcomes or value. This is partly reflected in the arguments advanced in some quarters for the privatization of *all* schools, or at least for the issuance of government vouchers that would allow parents to pay part of the tuition at private schools (the parallels to the debate in the United States over voucher plans is direct and unashamed; the Russian word, *vaucher*, is also a direct borrowing). A similarly crude economic pluto-meritocracy is seen in the tuition plans now in use at a number of Russian postsecondary institutions: the best students are offered admission and a stipend, while those in the middle are admitted, but without stipends. The least capable are offered admission, but only on condition that they pay a steep tuition fee.

Another aspect of the sudden withdrawal of the ideological center for Russian education has been the quick collapse of child- and youth-oriented programs such as the former Pioneers, Octoberists, and Komsomol. It is indeed true that some of what these groups did was ideological, coercive, or generally supportive of the Soviet state—endless songs to Lenin, "contributions" of "socially valuable labor" to help harvest potatoes and cabbage, learning of the tenets of Marxism-Leninism in order to advance to higher levels, all inspired by the promise of easier access to good careers if one excelled as a supporter of the status quo.

But along with these negative aspects of the Communist youth organizations were other, more valuable features—the young people's camps during the summer where genuinely dedicated and talented teachers worked with children to foster a high level of social concern and the ability to function successfully as adults, the formation of character through widespread after-school programs. The best of these programs offered well-organized children's activities that supported the development of children as future citizens and moral social actors.

In the disintegration of the Soviet State, these organizations lost their political necessity, and so what the state regarded as their primary reason for existence. While many parents had tolerated the ideological loading of the Communist youth programs as the price to pay for an economic advantage for their offspring, they often didn't recognize the other values that the programs conveyed and so did not protest loudly when the programs were rapidly disassembled in the wake of the collapse of the Soviet Union in 1991. While some local groups have survived under other names, and while scouts and church groups have stepped in to fill some of the void, the departure of the Komsomol and affiliated groups from the scene has created a large gap in the net of children's programs.

Supporters without a Voice

If programs, approaches, and organizational forms for education have been thrown into turmoil by the removal of the former ideological "center," then individuals and groups who might rally to support schools and more generally programs for young people have also been left at a loss as to what to do. During the mid-1980s, at the onset and then during Gorbachev's *perestroika*, there was an outpouring of interest in the schools from quarters where there had been only silence before. Intellectuals of all varieties suddenly found significant what was happening—or could happen—in the schools. Artists, film directors, writers, and scientists all began to speak out on the problems of the schools and to propose alternative solutions. Members of the intelligentsia who had for years shunned the schools as places that only the least capable adult would want to work now found it meaningful once again to join in discussion of what might be, of how the schools might help in the large tasks of social and economic reconstruction that lay ahead. There was widespread interest in what some called "the pedagogization of society."

It was not by chance that many of those who joined in these discussions were those whose careers were rooted in the natural sciences, mathematics, or the arts, and who had earlier forsworn any involvement with the official social institutions of Communist society. It was as if they decided, with Gorbachev's encouragement, that collaboration with core social institutions was a game once again worth the candle, that there was something to be gained by it.

But their attempts were not always productive. While intellectuals were eager to join in discussions and participate in published debates about possible futures for education and schooling, they were often less than effective when they tried to organize themselves in new ways to work toward significant changes in policies or practice. The Creative Union of Teachers (CUT), for example, founded with considerable fanfare in 1988 by a group of educators but with strong support from many well-known intellectuals from science and the arts, foundered due to a lack of management expertise by the autumn of 1991. While growing chaos in the Russian economy was at least partly to blame, the principal difficulty lay in the founders' inability to create a structure for the continued operation of a voluntary organization. Such rudimentary activities as the collection of dues, publication of a newsletter in sufficient copies to reach the membership, staging regular meetings, and producing a coherent platform of organizational purposes were beyond the experience of those who so hopefully created the new organization just a few years before. The CUT, at the end of the Soviet era, fell into an entirely predictable Soviet pattern, with the departure in disgust of the best of the original founders while the remaining members squabbled among themselves for positions, access to cars and telephones, and other minor perks.[7]

This scenario was not an isolated one. In other cases where promising new groups have appeared (the Eureka Open University, the Center for Cultural Policy), the leaders of those groups have found it difficult to expand their operations. Part of the difficulty is the lack of infrastructure that Westerners take for granted—phones, faxes, electronic mail, as well as more basic things such as reliable postal service, mailing lists, newsletters, dependable facilities for printing and distribution of materials, access to computers, paper supplies, printers and binders, and so forth. There is also a deeper difficulty in conceptualizing how one might organize a group so that it might become self-perpetuating—how, for example, to provide for a system of governance and leadership, how to train and encourage new recruits so that they might reliably run an organization's branch office in a distant city without the need for constant oversight, how concretely to explain the purposes and aims of an organization to an audience of those unacquainted with its work. All these things, which make up the warp and woof of an open and democratic society, were either unknown in the Soviet era or were so much within the domain of the Party and the "apparat" that the practical skills involved were never widely disseminated.

Perhaps it was also the case that the Party apparatchiks themselves never really had to learn how to organize and manage groups; rather they relied on personal contacts, influence, corruption, and naked power to get done what had to be done. The skills of organization, influence, training (*trening*, another loan word from English), and politics in the best sense of that term were never widespread in Russia. Now, they are having to develop in an atmosphere not very hospitable to them.

A further instance of this difficulty Russian educators have in finding a voice and expressing it is seen in the preparations for the national political elections of December, 1993. While the background to the elections was troubled (Yeltsin's arguments with the Supreme Soviet through 1993, the mutual acrimony leading to dissolution of Parliament and dismissal of the president of September, 1993, and the bloodshed of October, 1993), the campaigns themselves revolved around basic issues of national economic survival. In these debates, however, there was almost no note taken of education as an issue affecting regional or national life; in the few cases where education did figure in the campaigns, it was noted only in passing as a minor part of a larger political platform. None of the parties made education a central feature of its campaign, nor was there concerted effort to discuss what might be required in the way of an education law that would provide a reasonable basis for further development.

Education was long politically disenfranchised by a system that officially honored it but relegated it in practice to the role of an economic strut in the building of totalitarian control. Now, the education system must cope with a newly open political structure that still ignores questions of education, perhaps because so many practicing politicians are themselves holdovers from the old regime.

Administrators without Resources

It is a truism in developed democracies that a principal function of educational administrators is to help determine how financial resources may best be distributed within a system to meet the most pressing needs of that system, and how other resources (human, legal, etc.) can best be brought to bear to deal with emerging problems. In the Russian case, the collapse of the previous structure, along with the rapid economic dislocations accompanying the breakup of the Soviet Union, have left administrators on all levels without resources to draw on. The rise of the Impoverished State has meant that serious attempts at educational restructuring have had to go begging, underfunded or unfunded in the general scramble to save institutions perceived to be more central to national survival.

The common image used in the Russian press to discuss this situation has contrasted the state norms for construction of new pigsties with those for schools (cost per square meter, for example); unfortunately, the schools come up short. Other recent discussions have focused on the need for new school construction (mirrored in the increasing numbers of schools that teach children in two or even three shifts per day, keeping school buildings busy until the middle hours of the evening), the difficulty in locating moneys for any sort of novel program (including those for national minority groups, publishing innovative textbooks), and the catastrophic state of children's health.[8]

Other resources are equally difficult to find and apply. The lack of a new code of laws pertaining to education, for example, has been a serious hindrance for those seeking to renew Russian schools. Previously, while there were laws that described how schools would operate, under whose control they would fall, and so forth, these were always secondary in practice to whatever the CPSU decreed or desired. The absence of a "rule of law" in the USSR was a major theme of Gorbachev's intended reforms of the 1980s, and the idea of a *pravovoe gosudarstvo* (government of law) has been a recurring topic of discussion among intellectuals and government officials. Unfortunately, while there has been much discussion, and considerable legislation actually passed, the confusion and uncertainty over just which laws are (or, more importantly, ought to be) in force makes it almost impossible for educational administrators on national, regional, or local levels to know what applies, or on what legal foundation to base their actions.

Part of this problem stems from disputes between the government of Boris Yeltsin and the nationally elected parliament (the Duma). Tensions between Yeltsin's government and the Duma came to a head when Yeltsin dissolved the parliament in September, 1993. The armed uprising among the parliamentarians, a consequent shoot-out on the streets of Moscow in October, 1993, and elections in 1993 and again in 1996 provided Yeltsin with a seeming popular mandate, but it has left the country with a fractious and divided system of governance, leading in turn to widespread flouting of laws and regulations.

Further uncertainty is added in many parts of the country by the factionalism, ethnic separatism, and irredentism that has come to characterize Russian political life: local and regional elective bodies pass their own laws, sometimes contradicting those passed at other levels, and often leaving educators completely at a loss as to which set of orders to follow. While laws regarding matters of school finance may be largely moot at the present, since so little money is available, they ultimately will be significant; likewise, laws regarding teachers' salaries and benefits, provision of children with meals and health services via the schools, the development and distribution of educational materials, and so forth, all have either immediate or long-term significance. Under the Soviet regime educators were burdened with a large bureaucracy that duplicated virtually all functions and control mechanisms at union, republic, regional, and city levels. Now, they face the remnants of that large bureaucracy, reduced in authority and resources, but with an indeterminate residuum of power and a confusing welter of conflicting laws, rules, and regulations.

The result of these uncertainties is that administrators, at least those on the national level, have lost much of their reason for being. Without financial resources to distribute, there is little purpose for a bureaucratic superstructure; without generally agreed upon laws and administrative structures to guide their actions, educators on any level above that of the individual school cannot provide teachers and principals with general guidelines for action.

Overall, the consequence of these difficulties is a kind of throwing back to the local level of all major decisions that affect a school's operation and future course of action. School principals increasingly find themselves called on not merely to implement policies decided upon at some far-removed level; rather, they need to make for themselves and their schools real decisions about the best course to follow. Many respond by not responding—that is, they continue to work according to laws and rules that now lack any legal or moral basis. Others see in the new freedom possibilities to recreate their schools in dramatically new ways. Unfortunately, the muddiness and difficulty in interpreting the laws and administrative procedures leaves them very uncertain about their ability to sustain particular decisions, especially if those should be arbitrarily questioned by those still ostensibly in positions of control.

Devolution and Evolution in Russian Education

If all of the above suggests turmoil in Russian schools, and in the relationships between the State, the educational system, the wider world community, and the individual, then I have been successful in describing the state of affairs in Russian education today. It may make sense here to try to list more concretely the immediate consequences and some possible future developments that may emerge from this confusing landscape.

The System Devolves, or the Continuing Saga of Count Potemkin's Villages

It is a famous (if largely apocryphal) anecdote from Russian history: Catherine the Great is planning a tour of her recently acquired southern provinces, and commands her trusted advisor, Count Grigory Potemkin, to prepare an itinerary for the journey. She is especially interested in seeing the many new villages that were to have been constructed to forward the settlement of ethnic Russians in the region and therefore the colonization and economic integration of the area into the Russian Empire. Potemkin, whose work on this score has not been as rapid as hoped or as promised, immediately improvises: "villages" (mostly facades and empty huts) are quickly constructed and hapless peasants moved into the region from other districts. When the Empress appears, all look diligently busy, and cheer appropriately as Catherine's caravan passes. For his obviously successful efforts, Potemkin is suitably rewarded.

Although the story itself is largely untrue, it nonetheless contains a deeper truth about Russian life, for such events have been repeated many times in Russian and in Soviet history. The word *pokazukha* (literally "stuff for show") describes such situations perfectly—the factory that is opened on time, then immediately closed for several months to allow the real finish work to be completed; the giant airplanes, dams, limousines, and other technical ephemera of Communist power that were supposedly mass produced but were in fact virtually hand made in very limited quantities; the *spetsshkoly* (special schools) that were for years shown to foreigners as "typical" examples of the Soviet educational system at work.

Unfortunately, the approach seems now to be well ensconced in the Russian worldview, for it keeps reappearing. The old habit of establishing institutions on the basis of *pokazukha* is now curiously mixed with the tendency to adopt and adapt all things Western, as if they would by themselves lift the country out of economic and social doldrums. (While Westernization is slowing somewhat at the present, perhaps due to the unhappy experiences of some Russians in encountering Western confidence-persons, it is still a very real part of the local scene.) The result includes new schools that are established on the basis of tenuous contacts with some Western partner, models borrowed and put into practice with grave pronouncements but with little real understanding of the underlying purpose or rationale for the model, proposals and projects developed to "democratize" a school or a system without any experience in democratic process, new books and curricula that are rapidly developed and rushed to press to capitalize on new markets but with no conception of how the product may be used or what circumstances will be needed to assure its success.

All of these are in some sense evidence of the devolution of the education system from one of closely controlled centralism to one of rampant localism, with few central controls or standards. They are the consequences of the disappearance of the centralized structure's rationale, its *raison d'etre*, the Communist Party. The Party provided the universal truth, the single model, the image of how things must and should be. By so doing, it assured a certain uniformity of external appearance while also allowing the ancient tradition of *pokazukha* to continue unabated; for as long as the forms and appearances were kept up, it mattered little what was actually happening behind the scenes. That what did happen there was often perverse, corrupt, inhumane, capricious, pointless, or brutal was a secret, a matter whispered among Party managers only at the highest levels (if typically also known or deeply suspected at many or all levels elsewhere in the hierarchy).

With the collapse of the Soviet State and the Communist Party, power increasingly devolved to local regions and cities, and the old images, the old standards, the old authorities lost much of their power. But unlike other revolutionary situations in which there is a clear victor and clear loser, and in which the victor can simply abolish or radically reconfigure old institutions, the Russian case was different. The old structures, deprived of moral and much real political authority, nonetheless continued to exist alongside new structures. Moreover, the old structures, inefficient and corrupt as they were, knew how to get things done—they could make the system work: school buildings (however badly constructed) would be built; textbooks (however shoddy) would be printed and distributed; food (of however poor quality and meager quantity) would be delivered to the schools; teachers (however incompetent and uncaring) would be trained and moved (however unwillingly) into job slots in the schools; students (however mechanistically and inhumanely) would be prepared to take the jobs (however unsatisfying) that the economic system provided. Schools (however inefficiently) worked.

The new, upstart educational organizations and institutions of Russia as a free-market economy have not had the experience of power, and so their progress has been slowed by the need to learn where the levers are, and what it takes to pull them. Thus, the devolution of Russian education has resulted partly in confusion and rapid development of institutions "for show," as power structures shift and new groups appear on the scene with considerable interest and enthusiasm, but often meager understanding of fundamental principles and little in the way of organizational ability.

The System Evolves: Rediscovering a Worthy Past

While there is a good deal of pokazukha involved in the current attempts to define new models of educational organization and practice in Russia, there are also examples of change that are well grounded, carefully organized, and thoughtfully executed. While it would be tempting in some quarters to claim that these are united by a common orientation toward Western democratic liberalism, that would not be accurate: there are a number of classical gymnasia, religious academies, and educational research and development centers that are deeply rooted in traditionally conservative traditions of Slavic culture, as well as others which, while democratic in form and values, do not borrow only from the West. What seems to bind them is a search for a distinctively Russian approach to the fundamental issues and problems of education. The desire is to take from the West what is appropriate, but also to maintain—or more accurately, resurrect—approaches, ideas, and traditions that were parts of the Russian intellectual heritage but which were repressed or ignored during the era of Soviet power.

In this case, the departure from the scene of the Communist Party has allowed some approaches to flourish. The new newspaper for teachers, *Pervoe sentiabria* (*September First*), edited by the well-respected journalist Simon Soloveichik until his death in 1996, has consciously focused on creating and recreating a new and appropriate Russian educational philosophy. The paper prints extracts from both Western and Russian philosophers who have written on education or related topics, purposely avoiding such currently popular (in Russia) Western authors as Dale Carnegie in favor of Eric Fromm, Mortimer Adler, and Richard Rorty. The Russian models include nineteenth-century philosophers such as Berdyaev, educators from the recent and far past such as Sukhomlinskii (1979) and Makarenko, as well as current intellectuals from literature and the arts. The paper aims to provide teachers with material that is "a bit beyond their grasp," according to Soloveichik, "for that is what they need in order to develop." While the approach may sound paternalistic to Western ears, the paper apparently is seen by teachers as offering something useful and otherwise unavailable: in its first fourteen months, it garnered

317,000 subscriptions, at a time when many other, established papers fell on hard times and even closed.

The new interest in the works of Lev Semenovich Vygotsky offers another glimpse into how educational theory and practice can evolve in new ways, parallel to and linked to Western ideas, yet still distinctively Russian. Vygotsky, who lived and worked in the Soviet Union of Stalin's time, was a Marxist psychologist who nonetheless saw individual and collective psychological development as being inextricably linked with historical and cultural patterns that were ultimately larger than those suggested by Marx himself. Vygotsky's approaches were too humanistic for Stalin, and for his too-close identification with the "pedology" movement of the late 1930s (a kind of "child-centered" approach that would not look out of place in many American schools), Vygotsky's ideas were banned and he became after his death in the mid-1930s a kind of nonperson on the Soviet educational scene. Nonetheless, his ideas were sufficiently interesting and popular that they were kept alive by his students, and in the 1950s a third generation of Soviet psychologists and educators, freed from the most repressive Stalinist policies, began to explore Vygotsky's work once again.

By the end of the Soviet period, although there had been a number of reverses and problems along the way, there were also a number of laboratories and schools that were operating according to Vygotskian principles. Foremost among the followers of Vygotsky was Vasily Vasil'evich Davydov, a key figure in the formation and governance of the new Russian Academy of Education. His "developmental teaching" approach, which borrowed much from Vygotsky, became widely recognized in the West and drew adherents from a variety of educational institutions and directions. If there was one thing that these diverse programs shared, it was an interest in creating a distinctively Russian model for pedagogy, one that recognized both the contribution and importance of the individual, but also stressed the role of the group, the social "collective" in forming personality and developing cognitive capacities. Far from being a simplistic revamping of the earlier Soviet emphasis on "Communist upbringing," which ruthlessly subjugated the place of the individual to that of the group and the State, this new "developmental" approach viewed the group and the individual as actors in a mutually beneficial symbiotic relationship.[9]

Further examples of the ways in which traditional models of education from the Russian past are seen in the various schools affiliated with the Association of Directors of Innovative Schools and Centers. These include public schools with special emphases or unusual approaches to education (such as Isak Frumin's School No. 106—the "Universe" school—in Krasnoiarsk and Alexander Tubel'sky's School No. 734—the "School of Self-Definition"—in Moscow), as well as private schools (such as Tatiana Kovaleva's

"Eureka Development" school in Tomsk, described earlier). All of these schools strive to keep their patterns of organization open and their curricula flexible; all consciously style themselves as "innovative" schools. Also affiliated with the association are several consulting and training organizations such as Alexander Adamsky's Eureka Open University (which has provided in-service education opportunities for some thousands of Russian teachers over the past ten years) and the International Training Center under Viacheslav Pogrebensky.

One distinguishing characteristic of these schools is that they have all accepted the overall model of improved teacher-pupil relations outlined and supported in the position papers published in the late 1980s under the general rubric of "the pedagogy of cooperation." Teachers are hired and evaluated on the basis of their abilities not only to instill academic knowledge in their charges, but also to pay attention to their psychic and emotional well-being. There is also a conscious search for alternative models that are in some cases Western, but increasingly homegrown: the fascination with Vygotsky as not only an academic exemplar but also a model for practical classroom work, the rediscovery of Tolstoy as an educational thinker, the value newly discerned in the works of such educators as Sukhomlinsky—all point to the desire to create a new educational practice that recognizes international experience but that is at the same time founded on important national models.

Evolution in Social Interaction: The Diversification of Discourse

What emerges clearly from this survey of recent changes in Russian education is a sense of growing willingness to deal with new thinking about how schools are organized, what and how pupils are taught, and what schools are for. What is less clear is the extent to which this ongoing discussion, admittedly present in a minority of schools at the moment, can spread and affect what goes on in the many thousands of ordinary Russian schools. To a large extent, the success of the new educational entrepreneurs must depend on their ability not only to get their message out, but also to engage with their less progressive colleagues in ways that differ from what was typical past practice. The heritage left by the Communist system included a number of patterns, some referred to above, that are ultimately pernicious to the creation of a more open, democratic, diverse system of education. Assumptions common in the West about how a social system best operates—established laws, expression of personal and group interests, channels through which one can express and defend those interests, ways of dealing with adversaries and handling disagreements, and techniques for achieving a social consensus around difficult issues—all these are essentially lacking or under strong pressure in Russia due to the collapse of the old system and lack of any commonly accepted replacement to it.

As noted above, the lack of local experience with democratic forms and models contributes to these problems. Other difficulties include the continued existence of past forms (forms of administrative and fiscal control in particular) even when the legal and moral bases of those forms have disappeared, resulting in confusion as progressive educators seek to deal with two sets of constituencies at once—the hold-over institutions of the past, to which in many cases they must still legally answer, and the progressive groups who provide much of the support for the very activities that have moved them into positions of prominence.

Previously, the social contract between citizen and State in the Soviet Union provided for a kind of officially sanctioned dualism in thought and action: there was what was officially demanded—obeisance to Party dictates, citation of Marx and Lenin as the authors of all important ideas, minimal participation in Party functions—and there was what was privately done and officially tolerated. The latter included negative aspects (corruption, lack of attention to individuals' humanity, crude standards for interpersonal behavior) as well as positive ones (maintenance of personal moral standards within many families, attempts on the parts of some educators to define a "school world" that was supportive of both teachers and pupils in spite of what happened in the world outside). The difficulty of making a transition, of uniting these two spheres of public life, should not be overestimated.

Part of what requires adjustment here is our own non-Russian perceptions of how Russia (as the Soviet Union) worked. There was a widespread assumption that the USSR was a monolithic state in which there was little diversity of opinion or practice even on the lowest levels. This image, a product of Stalin-era cold war political analysis, was accurate only as it applied to the surface levels of Soviet reality. It never described very accurately what happened within institutions, where personalities and local bureaucratic politics tempered the otherwise universal influence of the ideology. The uniformity of social institutions in the USSR lessened startlingly as the system developed in the 1960s and 1970s. While development was not always in a positive direction, by the start of the 1980s and the advent of Gorbachev to power, the system was much less uniform in style if not in structure.

Diversity began to creep into the system willy nilly with the advent of de facto interest groups among employers, teachers, directors, parents, and so on. Also, the official structure of education-related institutions—the Academy of Pedagogical Sciences and the various pedagogical institutes—had grown to allow somewhat more diversity in what was permitted to be studied, discussed, and written about. Even the Communist Party itself was increasingly prone to factionalism, as witnessed in the arguments during the early years of Gorbachev's reforms over the fate of *Uchitel'skaia gazeta* (*Teachers Gazette*), the formerly quiet paper that had become a muck-raking proponent of reforms under its then-new editor, Vladimir Matveev. Although Matveev rapidly became anathema to the Party bureaucrats in charge of education, his paper was under the auspices not of the Party Secretariat for Education, but rather of that for the press, and so remained relatively untouchable for several important years, long enough to further diversify the educational scene.

The legacy here, however, was very corrosive. The Party constantly preached that there was a single model for appropriate theory, appropriate practice, in any sphere of social life, including education. There was, simply put, a "right way" to do things, even if that way made no sense and had obvious faults. The lack of reference to alternatives was a pattern stretching back to the Tsarist era, but it increasingly polluted social discourse by leaving people without a way to deal with differences and diversity. This also produced a characteristic pattern of response to proposed innovations in social life, a pattern of passivity, inertness, carelessness, and insensitivity, a constant deference to the hegemony of what in Gorbachev's time came to be called the "command-administrative system."

Breaking out of these patterns is obviously not easy, and doing so may take far longer than Westerners are accustomed to allow when approaching changes in social life. The devolution of authority in education away from centralized Russian political control is one positive and necessary precondition for needed diversity to appear. But the evolution of diverse, locally based practice and, more importantly, new, democratic modes for social discourse are even more critical components of the process of change. The challenge now is to try to preserve some semblance of the existing structure of Russian schools while at the same time encouraging the changes that are so desperately needed.

Notes

1. On *vospitanie*, see U. Bronfenbrenner, *Two Worlds of Childhood: US and USSR*. New York: Basic Books, 1970; B. Eklof (ed.), *School and Society in Tsarist and Soviet Russia*. New York: St. Martin's Press, 1993; and M. Matthews, *Education in the Soviet Union*. Winchester, Mass.: Allen & Unwin, 1982.

2. A version of the "Moral Code" may be found in *Obshchestvovedenie* (*Social Studies*). Moscow: Izd-vo politicheskoi literatury, 1968, pp. 321–22.

3. For more complete descriptions of the educational changes of this era, see Dunston, 1992; Eklof & Dneprov, 1984; Kerr, 1989, 1990, 1991, 1992; Long, 1990. J. Dunstan (ed.) *Soviet Education under Perestroika*. London: Routledge, 1992; B. Eklof & E. Dneprov, *Democracy and the Russian School: The Reform Movement in Education Since 1984*. Boulder, Colo.: Westview, 1993; S. T. Kerr, "Reform in Soviet and American Education: Parallels and Contrasts." *Phi Delta Kappa* 71, 1 (1989): 19–28; S. T. Kerr, "Will 'Glasnost' Lead to 'Perestroika'? Directions for Educational Reform in the USSR." *Educational Researcher* 19, 7 (1990): 26–31; S. T. Kerr, "Educational Reform and Technological Change: Computer Literacy in the Soviet Union."

Comparative Education Review 35, 2 (1991): 222–54; S. T. Kerr, "USSR." In *International Handbook of Educational Reform*, ed. P. W. Cookson, Jr., A. R. Sadovnik, and S. F. Semel, 473–93. Westport, Conn.: Greenwood Press, 1992; and D. H. Long, "Continuity and Change in Soviet Education under Gorbachev. *"American Educational Research Journal*, 27, 3 (1990): 403–23.

4. On the rediscovery and reinterpretation of the psychological heritage of Russian education, see Shchedrovitskii, 1993; Sdoveichik, 1989; Vygotskiiy Luriia, 1993. See G. P. Shchedrovitskki, *Pedagogika i logika* (*Pedagogy and Logic*). Moscow: Detskaia literatura, 1989; and L. Vygotskii & A. Luriia, *Etiudy po istorii povedeniia* (*Studies in the History of Behavior*). Moscow: Pedagogika-Press, 1993.

On Ivanov's "Communard movement" see S. Soloveichik, *Vospitanie po Ivanovu* (*Upbringing Ivanov Style*). Moscow: Pedagogika, 1989; and A. Sidorkin "The Communard Movement." *East-West Education* 16, 2 (1995). Not much of Sukhomlinskii's work is available in English; in Russian, see V. Sukhomlinskii, *Rozhdenie grazhdanina* (*Birth of a Citizen*). Moscow: Molodaia gvardiia, 1979.

On the ideas of the "movement" and its work, see Sh. Amonashvili, *Edinstvo tseli* (*Unity of Purpose*). Moscow: Prosveshchenie, 1987; Sh. Amonashvili, V. Shatalov, & S. Lysenkova, *Pedagogika nashikh dnei* (*Pedagogy for Our Days*). Krasnodar: Krasnodarskoe knizhnoe izdatel'stvo, 1989; S. T. Kerr, "The Alternative Pedagogical Press." *Russian Education and Society* 36, 1 (1994a): 4–8; T. Matveeva (ed.), *Vladimir Fedorovich Matveev*. Moscow: Russian Open University, 1992; and A. V. Petrovskii, *Novoe pedagogicheskoe myshleni* (*New Pedagogical Thought*). Moscow: Pedagogika, 1989.

5. The attempts of the remaining "innovators" to coalesce and further the movement's work are detailed in Kerr, 1994. S. T. Kerr, "Diversification in Russian Education." In *Education and Society in the New Russia*, ed. A. Jones, 45–74. New York: M. E. Sharpe, 1994.

6. Vasily Davydov, vice president of the Russian Academy of Education and a noted psychologist, estimated that over five hundred such schools existed in Russia by spring, 1993; see V. Davydov, 1995. "The Influence of L. S. Vygotsky on Education Theory, Research, and Practice." *Educational Researcher* 24, 3 (1995): 12–21.

7. The breakup of the CUT as an effective counterforce is documented in L. Borisova, V. Nikolaev & A. Trukhacheva. "Soiuz umer: Da zdravstvuet soiuz!" ("The Union Is Dead: Long Live the Union!") *Uchitel'skaia gazeta*, 8–15 October 1991, p. 1, and in "Igra vs'edz, ili 'parlamentskii kretinizm' " ("Playing at a Congress; or, 'Parliamentary Cretinism' "). *Uchitel'skaia gazeta*, 22–29 October 1991, p. 3.

8. The horrid state of Russia's schools and educational programs generally is chronicled in the annual reports of the Ministry of Education (1995), e.g., Ministry of Education, *Ob itogakh raboty Ministerstva obrazovaniia Rossiiskoi Federatsii v 1994 godu i osnovnykh zadachakh razvitiia obrazovaniia na 1995 god* (A Summary of the Work of the Ministry of Education of the Russian Federation in 1994 and Basic Tasks for the Development of Education during 1995). *Vestnik obrazovaniia* 6 (1995): 4–82.

9. Vasily Davydov and his colleagues have been the principal architects of "development instruction" ("razvivaiushchee obuchenie"); see Davydov, 1986, *Problemy razviavaiushchego obucheniia* (*Problems of Developmental Instruction*). Moscow. Pedagogika, 1986.

References

Amonashvili, Sh., V. Shatalov, & S. Lysenkova. *Pedagogika Nashikh Dnei (Pedagogy for Our Days)*. Krasnodar: Krasnodarskoe knizhnoe izdatel'stvo, 1989.

Borisova, L., V. Nikolaev, & A. Trukhacheva. "Souiz Umer. Da Zdravstvuet Soiuz!" ("The Union is Dead, Long Live the Union!"). *Uchitel'skaia gazeta* 41(1991): 1.

Bronfenbrenner, U. *Two Worlds of Childhood: US and USSR*. New York: Basic Books, 1970.

Davydov, V. *Problemy Razvivaiushchego Obucheniia (Problems of Developmental Teaching)*. Moscow, 1986.

Davydov, V. *The Influence of L. S. Vygotsky on Education Theory, Research, and Practice*. Presentation at the annual meeting of the American Educational Research Association, Atlanta, Georgia, 1993.

DeGeorge, R. T. *Patterns of Soviet Thought*. Ann Arbor, MI: University of Michigan Press, 1966.

Dunstan, J. (ed.). *Soviet Education Under Perestroika*. London: Routledge, 1992.

Eklof, B. (ed.). *School and Society in Tsarist and Soviet Russia*. New York: St. Martin's, 1993.

Fisher, G. *Science and Ideology in Soviet Society*. New York: Atherton, 1967

Hough, J., & Fainsod, M. *How the Soviet Union is Governed*. Cambridge: Harvard, 1979.

Kenez, P. *The Birth of the Propanganda State*. London: Cambridge, 1985.

Kerr, S. T. "Diversification in Russian Education." *Education and Society in the New Russia*. T. Jones, Armonk, NY: ME Sharpe: 47–74, 1994.

Mathew, M. *Education in the Soviet Union*. Winchester, MA: Allen & Unwin, 1982.

Matveeva, T. (ed.). *Vladimir Fedorovich Matveev*. Moscow: Russian Open University, 1992.

Petrovskii, A. V. *Novoe Pedagogicheskoe Myshlenie (New Pedagogical Thinking)*. Moscow: Pedagogika, 1989.

Sidorkin, A. "The Communard Movement." *East-West Education* 16 (2), 1995.

Soloveichik, S. *Pedagogika Dlia Vsekh* (Pedagogy for Everyone). Moscow: Detskaia literatura, 1989.

Sukhonlinksii, V. *Rozhdenie Grazhdanina (Birth of a Citizen)*. Moscow, Molodaia gvardiia, 1979.

Part III

Governing, Governmentality, and Educational Change

CHAPTER 7

Decentralization and Recentralization in the Argentine Educational Reform

Reshaping Educational Policies in the 1990s

INÉS DUSSEL, GUILLERMINA TIRAMONTI,
AND ALEJANDRA BIRGIN

A New Cartography for Educational Reform

Educational reform is a paramount issue today in Argentina and in the rest of Latin America. If the 1980s were once called the "lost decade" for the area, the nineties have been rich in major structural transformations that have made the educational systems one of their prime targets. The need to reform education has been put at the top of the social agenda, and consistently deep changes in the organization of the system and in the daily life of schools have been effected.

In this chapter, we would like to approach these transformations as contingent, strategic moves involved in power relations. From our standpoint, the reforms can be productively analyzed through some spatial metaphors that can help us destabilize their "naturality" and "inevitability," reinscribing them in the history of power/knowledge relations. We have grounded our analysis in two different corpora of literature. One includes Foucault's notions of power and history, Bourdieu's notion of field, and particularly Popkewitz' creative use of them in educational theory (1991, 1998). The second comprises the efforts by Latin American intellectuals to provide a new cartography of the social space that is emerging in our peripheral postmodernities (Garcia Canclini, 1990; Sarlo, 1994; Beverley, Oviedo & Aronna, 1995).[1] In both cases, space is not conceived as empty or homogeneous, but as a set of relations saturated with qualities and temporalities (Foucault, 1985/86). Thus, its representation, or cartography, is also a science that exerts power relations, settling boundaries and establishing the visible and invisible. The new cartography, then, is not located outside power relations but as another strategic movement as well. We, as intellectuals-cartographers, are not neutral observers of social reality but part of the power game ourselves.

Trying to think through these spatial metaphors, we will talk about current educational reforms in terms of reterritorialization. Garcia Canclini (1990), focusing on the production of culture, has used this concept to remark that Latin American postmodernism has implied the loss of traditional relations of culture to geographical and social territories while at the same time has brought partial relocalizations of the old and the new.[2] To speak about reterritorialization, thus, seems to be appropriate to grasp the reshaping of boundaries and relations that is taking place in the educational reform in contemporary Argentina.

In this change, the decentralization policies have taken a privileged place. As in many countries, the notion of "school autonomy," site-based curriculum, and teacher training have been central to the rhetoric of change. However, powerful movements of recentralization are visible in the policies that are being implemented in Argentina. Together with their tensions and frictions, they constitute what we will call the "reterritorialization of the educational field," which will be traced in this article through two interrelated movements: the hybridization of discourses and the design of new maps of relations between the center and the periphery of the system. Although different in scope and magnitude, these movements provide us with tools to analyze the multifarious ways in which the reform is transforming our educational experiences. We will conclude the article by pointing to the contradictions and displacements produced by the reterritorialization, hybrid products themselves whose direction cannot be predicted.

Decentralization: Hybrid Discourses

Hybridity is a fad term today in social theory. Originating in biology, the notion of hybridity is used currently to denote the blurring, confusing, intermixing phenomena of contemporary culture (Garcia Canclini, 1990; Bhabha, 1994). However, we would not like to repeat the postmodern confidence that this is the first time in history that human beings can enjoy a complex, blurred, and more fragmented world (Stoler & Cooper, 1997). In some respects, one can find hybrid discourses in education since the emergence of public schooling. The notion of curriculum itself can be considered as a hybrid, if we think of it as the result of an alchemy that proceeds from the selection of culture and translates it to a particular institutional setting and to a particular audience (Bernstein, 1990; Popkewitz, 1991 and in this book). The curricular discourses have also been studied as a hybrid which combined different traditions and disciplinary movements, building coalitions that gave way to peculiar consensus (see Kliebard, 1986, for the U.S.; Dussel, 1997, for Argentina).

Although it is difficult to claim it as a "new" phenomenon, nevertheless a peculiar feature can be noted. What is striking in contemporary hybridization is the rapidity with which it moves to include diverse discourses and thus the rapidity with which the original markers of the discourses are lost. In its first years, the Argentine educational reform was proposed as a reflection of the Spanish reform held by the Socialist government of Felipe Gonzalez in the 1980s. In its turn, the Spanish had adopted many of the U.S. reforms to produce their own, a move that was not acknowledged by Argentine authorities. (See the notion of the *indigenous foreigner* in Popkewitz' introduction to this book.) But later on, as the Spanish reform was increasingly presented as a failure, the official rhetoric moved to other European and Latin American countries to find some legitimacy. In every step, the traces of the original context, its own systematicity and historicity, were effaced and blurred in a mixture of policies whose emergence was no longer recognizable.

Hybridization operates through mobilizing diverse discourses within a particular setting. It articulates not only external models, repeating one of the traditional movements done in the periphery toward the center—that is, an impossible, always failed copy/imitation of the original (Richards, 1995)—but also different traditions and discourses. In this new staging of concepts and figures, it creates new meanings. In that respect, we would like to stress the fact that, although we certainly agree with the idea that there are no essential significations for a concept ("concepts have wings," as Wittgenstein said), nonetheless these "wings" are opened within particular horizons defined by history. For example, the Spanish general education reform, or the Colombian New School experience, are being mobilized within a discourse that acknowledges directly or indirectly national and local traditions and experiences. Hybridization implies a translation process that puts these new experiences and directions in relation to the ones that were available previously, and even if it erases and blurs the original markers, they remain as part of its texture, as when we find traces of previous writings in the palimpsest.

The hybridization produced by this reterritorialization is constructed through recognition and sanction as well as through forgetfulness and repression (Shapiro, 1997). In this respect, we would like to distance ourselves from the mere celebration of pluralism that believes that the multiplicity or "magma" of discourses eliminates hierarchies and binaries. Hybridization definitely disrupts the established hierarchy of discourses, but it constructs a new one, not necessarily a more democratic one.[3]

This is particularly evident in the construction of "decentralization" as a central issue in educational reform. Although we cannot trace the emergence of this problematic in Argentine educational history in this chapter, let us say that the centralization of educational services was the dominant drive until the late 1950s, despite the nineteenth-century constitutional mandate of federal organization of primary schooling. Successive waves of decentralization took place in the 1960s, the 1970s, and the 1980s, associated in each case with the privately oriented progressive education movement, the military dictatorship, and the return of democratically elected governments, respectively. By the 1980s, the concept of decentralization had shifted profoundly to articulate antiauthoritarian, antimilitarist, and projuvenile struggles (Birgin, 1994; Puiggros, 1997; Tiramonti, 1994).

Decentralization in the Current Reform: The "Needy" and the Construction of a New Center

The current wave that started in 1992 has introduced new ingredients in relation to the different discourses that have shaped decentralization policies in Argentina, and has combined them with different, even contradictory traditions in the field. The democratic and federalist rhetoric is being mobilized, but it coexists with utterances that can be linked to economicism and efficientism. The emergence of the latter is related to the hyperinflation crises suffered in the late 1980s, which gave way to a deep economic crisis and a fear of political instability. The "excesses" of the welfare state were identified as the cause of the mishaps of the economy, and the presidential strength and the market forces were highly prized as the redeemers, even if in a different context they would appear to be opposing forces. The centrality of democratic citizenship was displaced by notions of the productive worker. The current decentralization policies that finally transferred all the educational institutions that were still dependent on the National Ministry of Education to the provincial administrations were posed as responding both to a historical claim for democracy and to an adjustment to a decreased budget.

Even though the antiauthoritarian statements continue to be present in the laws and parliamentary debates, there are important shifts in the meanings they articulate at present. To make this point, we argue that the democratic value or effect of a particular statement cannot be judged apart from the conditions in which it is uttered, and particularly from the series of discourses in which it is included. In Judith Butler's words, "it is important to distinguish the utterances themselves from the sites of utterance, which provide the enunciation with a particular efficacy" (Butler, 1997). Thus, the notion of "democratic" has come to be equated in the official rhetoric to "local," "private" endeavors, a shift that will be dealt with extensively in the following section and that takes place mainly at the level of school organization and finance. On the other hand, in the official discourses on decentralization democratic statements are mainly articulated in terms of a populist philanthropism. In this context, a new figure, that of the "needy," is being produced.

The needy is the individual subject who is identified by the welfare offices as the recipient of their policies, due to her/his placement on a scale of welfare. Democracy's duty is, first and foremost, to take care of the basic needs of the population; rules and debates are not as important. The needy is thought of as an individual "voice" whose representation should no longer be assumed by articulated ways of representation, but through her/his individual negotiation with the State agencies. In that respect, current reforms involve significant changes in the social organization, as these voices emerge as an alternative to organized, unionized, and traditionally more collective ways of representation. It should be kept in mind that, unlike in the United States, where the urban myths of the self-made man fed the growth of the State, in Argentina social action was always conceived of in terms of groups or classes, be they in support of the State in opposition to it, as with trade unions, mass demonstrations, and multitudinous demands (Rama, 1997, p. 55).

In the case of the National Ministry of Education, the needy has become the privileged subject/recipient of educational policies. This remapping displaces the traditional agencies involved in the mediation of demands, and constructs a direct, radial connection between the central State and the individual. This is visible in the ambitious compensatory program called the "Social Plan." Initially, this program ranked all the schools in the nation according to their buildings, the social backgrounds of their population, and their drop out rates, and took the one thousand schools that ranked the lowest on the scale to provide them with special supplies (books, new buildings, in-service teacher education). In 1997, the program had grown so much as to include more than ten thousand schools. Another example in the same line is the national system of evaluation that included the social background of the school population within the "independent variables" to be taken into account. In 1996, the schools that ranked higher and whose population was low income, were rewarded with special resources. In all these operations, a whole set of meanings is being attached to "democratic": redistribution, poverty, equality of conditions.

At the same time, other associated meanings such as the challenge to authoritarianism, discussion of procedures, and public accountability of expenses, are excluded. Although claims from NGOs and civilian associations have been pushing toward their inclusion in the social agenda, they remain secondary to the emphasis on social redistribution.

In different provincial settings, the discourse of the needy is linked to an "ethics of caring" more related to the social doctrine of the Catholic Church than to laïc modernization theories and efficientist discourses, as has been the case in the national government. The notion of the needy is central to these policies but in this case assumes a broader scope. In the province of Buenos Aires, the administration has implemented dozens of compensatory programs that range from nutritional supplies to vacations at the beach. Its slogan has been to make available for everybody (especially, the "needy") not only the basic goods but also the pleasure—as is the case in the organization of soccer tournaments and school-end trips paid for by the government.

Another discourse overlaps with the ethics of caring and the national emphasis on redistribution, and that is the discourse on gender. In Buenos Aires, most of the compensatory programs have been organized by the Woman's Council (in singular in Spanish)—formerly the Secretary for Social Welfare. This council is conceived of as one of the main ways for decentralizing the system. The council gives money to the parents' associations for lunch and snack, and directly distributes school uniforms, supplies, and sport shoes free of cost, whenever the condition of "needy" is established. All the intermediate bureaucracy is left aside in this new structure of power, with a centralized agency that relates radially to each school and parents' association.

Assigning the social welfare to women is justified on particular conceptions of womanhood, as naturally taking care of nurturing their children and families. The Woman's Council is in charge of distributing food to the needy and looking after the population. The council is structured in district committees that promote an organization by blocks. Each block is represented by a woman who is in charge of transmitting information and local demands to the district leaders. Most of these demands are presented by the women in the families who manifestly feel more comfortable talking to other women about their problems.

All this involves a sort of "invasion" of the public sphere by women which has few antecedents in Argentine history (the most famous probably being Evita Perón's centrality in the 1940s and 1950s). However, this act of "giving" and "chatting" is conceived of as independent of politics; politics involves negotiation and dirty issues that supposedly are not at stake in assisting the needy. Assisting others has become "a women's issue," while "politics" is masculinized (Auyero, 1997).

Thus, decentralization has involved the construction of the poor people as needy, a shift that embodies a whole set of new values and hierarchies, as well as new definitions of gender and politics. Whereas before, the poor would be described with certain characteristics (as decent, working people), later on they were classified as "dangerous people" (Gonzalez, 1993) or "at-risk populations" (Castel, 1991). The present administration has produced a new figure, the needy, naturalizing the demands and abstracting them from the realm of daily politics. The needy receive "gifts" and "donations" from "those who care," in actions that efface the long-standing struggles that have shaped these conditions and demands.

Also, the imbrication of the needy in the discourse of decentralization shows how hybridization operates to construct new languages for social and individual experiences. There are particular histories and traditions embedded in the struggles for decentralizing the educational system that are mobilized in different ways in the present context. The federalist rhetoric and the democratic statements are inscribed in strategies that produce new significations, as in the case of the needy and the philanthropic woman. The remapping has produced a "structure of forgetfulness" (Shapiro, 1997) that represses antiauthoritarian statements and recognizes the subject of welfare only outside the realm of politics. In the following section, we will deal with its effects more directly.

New Maps for the Center and the Periphery

The remapping of the educational field is nowhere as visible as in the organizational reform that has been held in the educational system. As has been said, in Argentina the educational system was traditionally homogeneous and centralized. As in France, whose model was followed, it constructed a particular notion of "equity" that was defined as a common morality, a common dignity pertaining to a grand nation with unlimited possibilities (Nique & Lelièvre, 1993). Rich and poor should sit together in the school's desks; talents would emerge clearly out of this common education, effacing the traces of social origins. Gender, race, and class differences would be left outside the school building, wherein everyone would be "just a teacher or a pupil."

Religion was to be left aside as well. The common morality was grounded on a powerful laïc myth in which the state and the nation took the place of God. The expression "God is Argentine" was coined at that time, symbolizing the exceptionalism of the national experience and the rosy future that the twentieth century seemed to promise (Dijkink, 1996). The national identity that was forged in those years was based on the territory governed by the State.[4] In this constitution of citizens "from the top," the state monopolized the space of "the public" (Hilb, 1994; Téllez, 1996). "The private" was equated to backwardness, religious sectarianism, and traditionalism, while "the public" represented the republican ideals of homogeneity and equity. The experience of modernization and industrialization was galvanized through these collective myths. Public instruction was thought as the "vital condition of the Republic," the best guarantee that the sovereign would exercise its duties in the right way.

The current reforms have represented an abrupt interruption on these identities and long-held imaginaries, although they may still be current as we will show in the final section. This break has not implied, as some critics have argued, that the National State has abandoned the center of the field; it implies a complete redefinition of what "being in the center" means, its functions and regulatory power. Also, the territory that is intended to be the site of regulation is changing, populated by new discourses and subjects, as we have argued previously.

The reforms were built on some mid-1980s diagnoses that remarked that the centralized structure kept the National State as the mediator between particular interests that struggled for resources and contents. This mediating role, far from increasing its power, consumed all its energies and reduced its possibilities to conduct the system effectively (Tedesco, 1987). Thus, the current administration assumed that a shift in the power relations had to be effected. The mediating role should be assumed by the provincial govern- ments, and the intermediate bureaucracies should disappear or be reduced to a minimum. Some Interamerican Development Bank loans were assigned to study a new organizational structure for the National Ministry of Education. By 1990 they had produced a slogan, "A Ministry Without Schools," that represented this new shape of the educational landscape.[5] The National State should no longer take charge of direct school administration or bargaining processes; its role was to set the objectives and the contents of education, and to evaluate them. In this new diagram the National Ministry has kept for itself the intervention in four major areas: a set of common contents, evaluation of outcomes, compensatory programs, and in-service teacher training. Also, it would coordinate the action of the provincial administration through a special council and monopolize the negotiation and administration of external loans. Through all these measures, the National Ministry has effected a powerful recentralization of the system, perhaps even greater than when it directly administered the schools themselves.

On the side of the provincial governments, there has been a similar move to decentralize the administration of education, which has also effected deep changes in the structure of their fields, although in different directions. Some of them, as in the province of Mendoza, have focused on the production of professionalized bureaucracies (Mintzberg, 1990). District seats and councils of supervisors and principals are now in charge of the administration of the system. The external control is focused on the inputs and outputs, and the peer groups seem to decide autonomously about the procedures.

However, these horizontal liaisons are crisscrossed by other dynamics that configure the territory of education in other directions as well. On the one hand, there is a strong drive toward competitiveness among schools that prevents the construction of solidarity links and fragments the system into small pieces. The introduction of standardized tests and the publicity of each school's performance have produced tough competition among institutions. On the other hand, there is a recentralization that operates at many levels, determining not only the objectives but also the way people think and reason about schooling and change. The introduction of remedial programs that re- ward educational innovations along the lines of quantitative and statistical formulation of the problems have shaped the uses that schools can make of the autonomy they are supposedly given, as they configure "problems," "tech- niques," and "solutions" in peculiar ways.[6]

The remedial programs themselves have implied a major transformation in the ways in which the "periphery" of the system was organized, a transformation that is also at the base of the discursive construction of the needy. They have been based on the strategy of "reverse discrimination." As Charles Taylor has characterized it, their argument goes as follows: Populations and institutions that share an unequal differentiation are recognized, and they receive a temporary "reverse discrimination" that intends to gradually "level the playing field and allow the old 'blind' rules to come back into force in a way that doesn't disadvantage anyone" (Taylor, 1994, p. 40). Differences should be stressed temporarily so that equality can be possible in the long run. Focusing the programs on particular "target populations" has been a major change in a system that, since the old republican ethics, has always stressed that homogeneous policies are the most democratic ones. In the new territory, students are placed on a scale that goes from normal to deviant, and are measured according to these patterns. The appearance of the "at-risk" language is pervading the way educators think about "learning problems," and the notion of "danger" is increasingly occupying a place in teachers' relations to children and teenagers. As we will see in the final section, this has caused new tensions to arise.

In the case of Buenos Aires, the restructuring of the relations between the center and the periphery of the system has gone along different lines, related to the political party system. The notion of "autonomy" assumes a different meaning; it should not be associated with an isolated institution but with the dismantling of the bureaucratic apparatus and the construction of tight links with the local political structures. One of the ways in which this transformation takes place is in the distribution of resources through a special fund called the Fund for the Historical Reparation of the Great Buenos Aires, which must be used for the construction of infrastructure—namely, public buildings and highways. In the case of the construction of new school buildings or the repair of old ones, the budgetary approval process is long. It should start in a local group, generally the parents' association, that must present a plan and budget for the construction. The school board analyzes it and approves it or not. If approved, the plan goes to the provincial special committee. There, another study of feasibility and costs is done, and if it is congruent with the local one, the project can be developed. The money is given directly to the parents or local association, which becomes responsible for its execution.

Decentralization thus involves complex negotiations and shifts in power relations. Besides the steps up and down the organizational structure, the allocation of resources has changed dramatically and has no universal logic. Every step in the ladder is highly arbitrary, and having the adequate political contacts with the neighborhood's broker or *puntero* becomes the central key to success, guaranteeing that a local demand can turn into a State priority. Another important feature is the community's capacity to get expert advice to design the plans and budgets. It goes without saying that the availability of this expert advice is extremely variable according to urban/rural settings or high/low income populations. But again, political affiliations can help in the process or can hinder it even when cultural capital is at hand.

Purportedly, these changes have been effected to relieve the overload of work of teachers and supervisors and to let them focus on the task of teaching. Also, there are legal issues involved in the administration of money, as the accountability of a civil association is supposed to be greater than the bureaucracy's. But these changes can be productively analyzed as well through the framework we have been using in this chapter. These shifts are constructing a new field of relations, with an increased power of the central administration and of these local associations, intertwined in a complicated system of loyalties and perquisites, and a clear cut back of the independence of the bureaucratic power.

The remapping, thus, operates by assigning new functions and regulative power to different agencies. The central supply centers establish a direct relationship to parents' and communitarian associations, that are presented as the best representatives of the needy. Beyond the populist rhetoric, the families are called to become central agents of control and discipline of the traditional culture of teachers and bureaucrats (Hunter, 1994). But the families themselves are also being disciplined by this process, being configured by a particular relation to the State that places them as recipients of its favors.

The restructuring of the educational landscape embodies a complex chain of meanings and mutual dependencies that still locates the provincial state as the distributional center of the net. The difference of this approach to former analysis in educational policies is that they assumed the state as the already-defined and stable center, and as an entity independent of social relations; whereas the important issue for us, following Rose and Miller, is to trace "how, in relation to what mentalities and devices, by means of what intrigues, alliances and flows, is this locale or that able to act *as* a center." (Rose & Miller, 1992, p. 185.) The state that emerges out of the remedial programs, the allocation of spending, and the act of giving as a perquisite, constructs particular social relations and subject positions that are not the ones assumed by the official rhetoric. Far from a retreat of the state that leaves other forces free to develop their own fate—be it glorious or tragic—the transformation of the educational system we are witnessing, with all its traumatic effects, should be regarded as profoundly productive of new subjects, boundaries, and knowledge, even of a new center whose rules and agents are transformed.

Displacements and Contradictions

Up to this point, we have been focusing on the effects that these shifts are having in the educational field. But we would not like to depict an overwhelming efficacy of these changes, a total reversion of structures, or a complete victory of the language of reform. In this final section, we would like to focus on the contradictions and tensions produced by this reconfiguration of the field. Of course, there are oppositions all throughout the system. Teachers express that they are being deskilled by the changes, and that the compensatory projects imply an increasing power for the principal at the expense of their own. Also, in 1997, teachers' unions had been quite successful in speaking out their claims through new forms—having placed a tent in front of the National Congress and having held a prolonged hunger strike that received a wide support from society.

However, we would not like to present these contradictions as external, successive movements. Educational reform is not a "zero-sum" game whose players increase their power at the expense of some others', but a collection of strategies that operate at many levels and reshape all the players in the field, through the production of new relations, rules, and knowledge (Popkewitz, 1996). Contradictions are part of the game and are implied in the setting-to-work of the structures and designs because, as was said in the introduction, space is saturated with multiple qualities and temporalities. The remapping reorganizes people's experience, and this reorganization inscribes past experiences and future expectations in a complex way. As we have tried to emphasize through the discussion of hybridity as a palimpsest, traces of old formations and feelings may be found in today's practices. Changes are not imposed on a vacuum, but have to negotiate with traditions and institutional cultures and practices that may cause frictions and new hybrids to occur.

One of the changes that has faced the biggest opposition is related to the restructuration of the public expenditure. Until 1995, in the province of Buenos Aires, the so-called rational allocation of resources mandated that each classroom and school fulfilled a minimum quantity of students (thirty-five in the case of most classrooms.) This meant that, if a classroom had fifty students, another section could not be opened until a total of seventy was reached (two groups of thirty-five). In some cases, the rationalization caused several teachers and administrative employees to lose their jobs as their schools did not reach the fixed ratios. In others, many schools rounded up their numbers in order to keep their personnel. Numbers became the central site for struggles. The results were both a policelike control of the statistics by the central administration, with sudden inspections of schools, and generalized chaos in the quantitative data.[7] Although it is not clear how widespread this action is, its emergence nonetheless undermines the claims of validity of statistics as the objective representation of reality.

Another point of friction can be pointed out in the introduction of statistical and "at-risk" language that has attempted to break down how schools think and deal with social difference, and specifically with class issues— which, as we have said before, was the traditional way in which collective representation was articulated in Argentina. We can trace here one of the more powerful challenges to current reforms that confronts the "structures of forgetfulness" imposed by the present remapping.

We illustrate this point by reference to a remedial program being implemented in the province of Mendoza. It is a nutritional program that is centered again on the notion of the needy, and which shows to what extent this construction is a hybrid product of diverse traditions. The needy who will receive nutritional supplies is determined by classification of the school population following anthropometric measurements: those who measure below average in the scale of weight, height, and head circumference are supposed to be underfed and receive a dietary supplement.

Although nobody in schools denies the need for nutritional supplements for poor children, problems arise in the face of the operationalization of the act of feeding some children and not all. The nutritional supplies are distributed by a central agency to the schools, but the institutions have to define for themselves how they will give them to the needy children. Some schools ring a bell, and the children who receive the supplement leave the classroom to have lunch while their classmates continue doing their work, in what most teachers describe as a traumatic experience for all. In some other schools, the food is rationed so that everybody can receive it, but this strategy does not work well with all types of food. Some principals save the food of one day and add it to the following day's supply, so that they can also feed everybody without enacting an overt differentiation. Efforts to dismantle the program have been made by teachers and principals without success so far.

The problematic implementation of the nutritional program intends to show that, although the new languages have pervasive effects in the daily life of schools, still, as in the palimpsest, marks of the old formations are visible, particularly in the ways in which social difference is to be performed and constructed in schools. Principals and teachers react to this classification with their old ethics of the republican school that purportedly brought the rich and the poor to the same school desk. Within this ethics, while differentiation according to achievement is highly valued, social and class differentiation should remain invisible. Poverty has always been thought of as "deficit," but this deficit was to be supplemented by the equalization provided by the school. When mandated to perform overt differentiation, one of the "unspeakables" of the old formation is thrown into the light, and it creates tensions and distinctions that produce disquiet. As one disquieted principal puts it, scientific criteria that distinguish the needy do not replace the feelings of their hearts that go in a different direction—that of nurturing everybody. We can find no better words to describe the clash of a persistent, entrenched ethos with the new trends in educational policies.[8]

Where do these displacements and contradictions leave us? We hope that they have helped us point to some theoretical and political arguments. First, we have attempted to show that, although power is ubiquitous, domination is not overwhelming and complete. There are always frictions, tensions, and blindspots on which to base not only the critique but also different actions in the future. On the other hand, we would like to stress the fact that these strategies are multiple and combine diverse elements, not necessarily "progressive" ones. Moreover, they are neither "pure" nor "uncontaminated" by the current process, but are themselves an effect of the power relations brought into play by the reterritorialization. Thus, our view is not intended to romanticize these resistances as examples to follow, or to adopt them as generalized strategies to counteract the reforms. On the contrary, it seeks to illustrate the impossibility of predicting a particular direction in which change will be effected, and if that seems true for the official efforts to reform the system, it is also valid for oppositional responses as well. This does not mean abandoning politics, but rather reinstalling it as contingent and open-ended strategies (Laclau & Mouffe, 1985).

Reforming a Field of Relations

Throughout this chapter, we have been trying to provide a new framework for analyzing contemporary educational reforms in Latin America, and particularly in Argentina. In that respect, we intend to have made both a theoretical and a political point. The restructuring of the educational field that is taking place in Argentina as well as in the rest of Latin America should not be considered as a "zero-sum" game in a fixed field, in which some agents increase their power at the expense of some others'. We looked at current efforts as strategies to reform a field of relations. These strategies are plural, not because they are derivations of but rather they imply *translations* from the space of political rationalities to the modality of techniques and proposals that are used in particular locales (Rose & Miller, 1992). In order to reconstruct the educational territories, the reform programs have to interact with particular knowledges and images, and with particular constructions of authority and power. The results are hybrid discourses that mobilize historical traditions, actual policies, and external models in specific, productive ways. We have analyzed the notion of the needy as a new figure constructed through these hybridizations.

The strategies of reform have also implied a wide restructuring of the field, of the character and relations between the center and the periphery of the educational system. In this process, the players in the field are repositioned and reshaped. Central authorities, bureaucrats, teachers, children, and parents are given new functions, and their knowledge and the structure of their power have been radically altered. This shift in power/knowledge relations, in the language and the knowledge that is sanctioned and made available in educational policies and practices, reorganizes in a profound, dramatic way the spatial and experiential scopes of the educational agents. It assigns new qualities and opens up new temporalities to them. Some perceive these changes as pure loss, and some others as pure gain, but these perceptions are also molded on these displacements. The inclusion in our map of the emergent displacements and contradictions is intended to argue that the aforementioned translations are not uniform, smooth processes but quite turbulent, conflictive ones, whose direction is not guaranteed.

Finally, throughout this chapter we have intended to contribute to this new cartography of the educational landscape through posing ourselves as intellectuals in a place different from the statist prophet or the technocrat—roles that Latin American intellectuals have traditionally played (Rama, 1997). No effective system for the mastery of change is prescribed here. Neither are prophetic interpellations subscribed. However, this does not imply an indifference to the wounds and pains provoked by this reterritorialization, or to the uneven and unequal effects that these power relations have on particular people. In that respect, we are also caught in the displacements and contradictions we have been talking about, as is the rest of the field. Latin American intellectuals have a strong tradition of social criticism and responsibility that many times leads them to believe that they are the prophets of the yet-to-come. If we would like any conclusion to be drawn from our writing, it is that the traces of this tradition may still help us to avoid hopelessness and engage creatively in new struggles, more modestly but not less passionately.

Notes

The authors would like to thank Tom Popkewitz for his comments and suggestions in the writing of this chapter. Also, Lynn Fendler helped us both with the content and English version. Silvia Duschatzky was part of our research team in Buenos Aires, and some of the ideas we develop here emerged out of our daily interchange. Patricia Redondo and Sofia Thisted were privileged interlocutors when thinking about schooling in low-income populations and the effects of populist philantropism. Of course, as it is usually said, the responsibility for what has been written is only ours.

1. The notion of peripheral postmodernities is taken from some Latin American intellectuals, as Beatriz Sarlo, Nelly Richards, Nestor Garcia Canclini, and Silvano Santiago, who stress the fact that the reception of postmodernism in this region should be read in relation to their uneven and unequal experience of modernization, modernism, or modernity. As Nelly Richards puts it, the cultural critic has to look at the uneven "dispositions of . . . these countries to postmodernity, considered as the critical balance of the achievements and frustrations of a modernity encrusted according to regionally specific dynamics of forces and resistances" (Richards, 1995, p. 218). This movement is not only "endogenous," if such a thing exists, but occurs in tension with the decentering of the center, the new defense of the margins that is produced by the

very center of Western culture, a rediagramming of the world that challenges the axis of the identities and politics constructed in the Latin American marginality.

2. Although it will not be followed in this chapter, we acknowledge that Deleuze and Guattari use this term in a different way. For them, even if the space we inhabit is defined for us, we "never stop moving our furniture around." Reterritorialization implies for them a side of contestation, change, and growth, a challenge to the boundaries. Reterritorialization is the opposite of deterritorialization, that is, taking the territory as an object, as a material to stratify, to make resonate (Deleuze & Guattari, 1997; also, Hebdige, 1988).

3. The notion of democracy stands as one of the most controversial ones in social theory, and it is not without problems that we adopt it here as a criteria on which to judge some statements. We adopt William Connolly's definition of democracy as both a form of governance and a cultural medium that denaturalizes settled identities and conventions. Democracy should be thought of as spaces, energies, and allegiances that interrupt territorial configurations, but, Connolly argues, "even that may not be enough" (Connolly, 1995, p. 161). Always escaping fixation, democracy should be thought of more as an impulse to destabilize power relations than as a particular set of values.

4. Gertjan Dijkink, in a suggestive analysis of the geopolitical visions in different countries, quotes a study done on the political geographical socialization of children from Argentina and England in the 1990s. According to this study, the English boys gave much more importance to the people and the principles that hold their nation together than they did to their national territory. Argentine boys, on the contrary, seemed to be more prepared to look at their geography in political terms (cf. Dijkink, 1996, ch. 1).

5. This idea is developed in C. Wilkinson et al., 1990. The reader should keep in mind that the "educational transformation" that has been the slogan of the present administration is based on reorganizing the educational system. One of the major innovations has been the change of its structure from seven elementary school years plus five secondary school years, to a ten-year general compulsory education plus three-year postgeneral education. This is being accompanied by broader transformations in the organization and content of schooling: new curricular designs, restructuring of teacher education, restructuring of school administration, and reorganization of the bureaucratic apparatus.

6. We have analyzed these remedial programs elsewhere (see Birgin et al., 1995). We would like to emphasize that statistics embody certain assumptions about the social world, i.e., that it can be represented "objectively," and that the numbers are neutral. Following Ian Hacking's genealogical approach, statistics appear as a technology of power that construct arbitrary classifications of people and social experiences and configure identities that are embedded in power/knowledge relations (I. Hacking, 1991). As has been noted in the past twenty years, to talk about "sex" or "gender" is not neutral or power free; also it is the case of "race" or "ethnic origins." Each categorization embodies assumptions about the social world, the subject positions, the nature of experience, etc.

7. The enforcement of this regulation has weakened in past years, and supervisors are more flexible when inspecting the size of classes. This shift can be productively read from a Foucauldian framework. Foucault said in 1975, in relation to the

history of sexuality: "The coherence of such a history does not derive from the revelation of a project but from a logic of opposing strategies." The struggle is indefinite, and for each move of the adversary there is an answering one by the other. Power can retreat here, but to "reorganize its forces, invest itself elsewhere . . . and so the battle continues" (Foucault, 1977, p. 56).

8. On the complexity and centrality of the problem of giving/nurturing, both in its Kantian versions and the postmodern critique, see Coles, 1997.

References

Auyero, J. "Evita como performance: Mediacion y resolucion de problemas entre los pobres urbanos del Gran Buenos Aires." In *Favores por votos? Estudios sobre el clientelismo politico contemporaneo,* ed. by J. Auyero, Buenos Aires: Ed. Losada, 1997, pp. 167–233.

Bernstein, B. *The Structuring of Pedagogic Discourse,* New York and London: Routledge, 1990.

Beverley, J., J. Oviedo & M. Aronna (eds.). *The Postmodernism Debate in Latin America.* Durham and London: Duke University Press, 1995.

Bhabha, H. *The Location of Culture.* London and New York: Routledge, 1994.

Birgin, A. *Panorama de la educación básica en Argentina.* Buenos Aires: Serie Documentos e Informes de Investigación/FLACSO, 1994.

Birgin, A., I. Dussel & G. Tiramonti. "Programas y proyectos en las escuelas: Los alcances de la reforma escolar." In *Contexto e Educaçao/Universidade de Ijuí* 40 (1995): 26–48.

Butler, J. *Excitable Speech: A Politics of the Performative.* New York and London: Routledge, 1997.

Castel, R. "From Dangerousness to Risk" In *The Foucault Effect: Studies in Governmentality,* ed. G. Burchell, C. Gordon, and P. Miller. Chicago: University of Chicago Press, 1991, pp. 281–98.

Coles, R. *Rethinking Generosity: Critical Theory and the Politics of Caritas.* Ithaca, N.Y.: Cornell University Press, 1997.

Connolly, W. *The Ethos of Pluralization.* Minneapolis and London: University of Minnesota Press, 1995.

Deleuze, G. & F. Guattari. "City/State." In *Rethinking Architecture: A Reader in Cultural Theory,* ed. Neil Leach. London and New York: Routledge, 1997, pp. 313–16.

Dijkink, G. *National Identity and Geopolitical Visions: Maps of Pride and Pain.* London and New York: Routledge, 1996.

Dussel, I. *Curriculum, humanismo y democracia en la escuela media argentina (1863–1920).* Buenos Aires: Oficina de Publicaciones del CBC/FLACSO, 1997.

Foucault, M. *Power/Knowledge: Selected Interviews and Other Writings, 1972–1977,* ed. C. Gordon. New York: Pantheon Books, 1980.

———. "Of Other Spaces: Utopias and Heterotopias." *Lotus* 48, 9 (1985/1986): 9–17. (Also included in *Rethinking Architecture: A Reader in Cultural Theory,* ed. Neil Leach. London and New York: Routledge, 1997, pp. 350–56.)

García Canclini, N. *Culturas híbridas: Estrategias para entrar y salir de la modernidad.* Mexico: Grijalbo, 1990. English version: *Hybrid Cultures: Strategies for Entering and Leaving Modernity,* trans. Ch. Chiappari and Silvia Lopez. Minneapolis and London: University of Minnesota Press, 1996.

Gonzalez, H. "El sujeto de la pobreza: Un problema de la teoría social." In *Cuesta abajo: Los nuevos pobres y los efectos de la crisis en la sociedad argentina,* ed. A. Minujin et al. Buenos Aires: Losada/UNICEF, 1993.

Hacking, I. "How Should We Do the History of Statistics?" In *The Foucault Effect: Studies in Governmentality,* ed. G. Burchell, C. Gordon, and P. Miller. Chicago: University of Chicago Press, 1991, pp. 181–95.

Hebdige, D. *Hiding in the Light: On Images and Things.* London and New York: Routledge, 1988.

Hilb, C. "Notas para repensar lo publico." Paper submitted to the Conference on Local Experiences in Decentralization. Buenos Aires, May 1995.

Hunter, I. *Rethinking the School: Subjectivity, Bureaucracy, Criticism.* New York: St. Martin's Press, 1994.

Kliebard, H. *The Struggle for the American Curriculum (1893–1958).* New York and London: Routledge, 1986.

Laclau, E. and C. Mouffe. *Hegemony and Socialist Strategy: Towards a Radical Democratic Politics,* trans. W. Moore and P. Cammack. London: Verso, 1985.

Mintzberg, H. *La estructura de las organizaciones.* Barcelona: Ed. Ariel, 1990.

Nique, C. & C. Lelièvre. *La République n'éduquera plus: La fin du mythe Ferry.* Paris: Librairie Plon, 1993.

Popkewitz, T. S. *A Political Sociology of Educational Reform.* New York: Teachers College Press, 1991.

———. "El Estado y la administracion de la libertad a finales del siglo XX: Descentralizacion y distinciones Estado/sociedad civil." In M.A. Pereyra y otros, *Globalizacion y descentralizacion de los sistemas educativos.* Barcelona: Ed. Pomares-Corregidor, 1996.

———. *Struggling for the Soul: The Politics of Education and the Construction of the Teacher.* New York: Teachers College Press, 1998.

Puiggrós, A. (ed.). *Dictaduras y utopías en la historia reciente de la educación argentina (1955–1983).* Buenos Aires: Ed. Galerna, 1997.

Rama, A. *The Lettered City.* Durham, N.C.: Duke University Press, 1997.

Richards, N. "Cultural Peripheries: Latin America and Postmodernist Decentering." In *The Postmodernism Debate in Latin America,* ed. J. Beverley, J. Oviedo, and M. Aronna. Durhman and London: Duke University Press, 1995, pp. 217–22.

Rose, N. & P. Miller. "Political Power beyond the State: Problematics of Government." *The British Journal of Sociology* 43, 2 (June 1992): 173–205.

Sarlo, B. *Escenas de la vida posmoderna.* Buenos Aires: Ariel, 1994.

Shapiro, M. *Violent Cartographies: Mapping Cultures of War.* Minneapolis and London: University of Minnesota Press, 1997.

Stoler, A. L. & F. Cooper. "Between Metropole and Colony: Rethinking a Research Agenda." In *Tensions of Empire: Colonial Cultures in a Bourgeois World,* ed. F. Cooper & A. L. Stoler. Berkeley/Los Angeles/London: University of California Press, 1997.

Taylor, Ch. "The Politics of Recognition." In *Multiculturalism: Examining the Politics of Recognition*. Princeton, N.J.: Princeton University Press, 1994.

Tedesco, J. C. *Desafío educacional, calidad y democracia*. Buenos Aires: Grupo Editor Latinoamericano, 1987.

Téllez, M. *El declive de la educacion como cuestion publica: Notas para una resignificacion sin nostalgias*. Caracas: Universidad Central de Venezuela, 1996 (mimeo).

Tiramonti, G. *Panorama de la educación secundaria en la Argentina*. Buenos Aires: Serie Documentos e Informes de Investigación/FLACSO, 1994.

Wilkinson, C. et al. *Redefinicion del rol del Ministerio de Cultura y Educacion: Modelos, alternativas e implicancias organizativas y juridico-institucionales*. Buenos Aires: PRONATASS, 1990.

CHAPTER 8

Rethinking Decentralization and the State/Civil Society Distinctions

The State as a Problematic of Governing

THOMAS S. POPKEWITZ

In a variety of national contexts, there have been discussions about the changing relations of the State to the educational arena.[1] Often, these discussions center on issues concerning the centralization and decentralization of the State or the devolution of power, the latter referring to shifts in the loci of power to geographically local contexts, for example, through community governance of education. The State is treated as an "object" that produces, and in some cases, mitigates against the modernization of educational systems. These discussions posit the state as a "real" entity in opposition to civil society (public vs. private, government vs. economy). At a different level are discussions about the "privatization" and "marketization" of social policy, concepts which indicate a major change in the relation of the state to civil society. These sets of distinctions accept political rhetoric as the presuppositions of analysis rather than making that rhetoric itself the focus of what is to be understood and explained.

The purpose of this chapter is to locate the problem of the state in the problematic of regulation. I use the concept of "arena" to think of two related layers. One is the State as the patterns of relations in which certain actors are authorized to organize, classify, and administer school practices.[2] A second layer of regulation involves the governing systems that organize and classify the objects for scrutiny and action in the arena. In the nineteenth century, Foucault (1979) argues, there occurred a new relationship between state governing practices and individual behaviors and dispositions. If the state was to be responsible for the welfare of its citizens, he argues, the identity of individuals had to be linked to the administrative patterns found in the larger society. This embodied a power/knowledge relation. New institutions of health, labor, and education tied the new social welfare goals of the state to the self-reflective and self-governing principles of individuality (Donald, 1992; Hunter, 1994; Rose & Miller, 1992; Shapiro, 1992). Governing, then, is used to focus on historically specific practices through which the individuals can think of, conduct, and evaluate themselves as productive individuals. This "socialization," as in Bourdieu's (1984) (and before him Durkheim's and Weber's) *habitus*, is not part of the anthropological universe of functional sociology but the outcome of specific social practices through which subjectivities are constructed. It also entails a change from a sovereignty notion of governing to one of governing people and things.

I explore the problem of the state as a system of regulation in three ways. First, I look at the relation of actors and discourses in the educational reforms of four apparently different countries—Russia, South Africa, Sweden, and the United States. I draw maps of similarities and differences in the constructions/reconstructions in the educational arenas. My concern is how the subjectivities of various actors are historically constituted through the patterns of relation produced. *I argue that the effects in the governing patterns are not only related to the child and teacher but also to the field of actors in the educational arena.* Second, I look at homologies between the construction of the teacher and the child in the educational arena and changes occurring in politics, the arts, and economics. My purpose at this level of analysis is to explore an amalgamation of noncausal intersections in patterns of governing. Third, I consider pedagogy as a specific site which relates political rationalities to the capabilities of the individual. That governing, however, does not occur on a level playing field in the sense that there is an uneven distribution of eligibility for participation and action. The systems of distinctions and differentiation in pedagogy, I argue, produce systems of inclusion/exclusion as local, and partial knowledges are inscribed as universal and global. "Constructivist" pedagogy, given prominence in the United States and international reforms, is an exemplar of the production of such differentiations.

While public discussions about school reform are populist and sometimes evangelical—reforms ostensibly promote local, individual choice, empowerment, and democracy—I argue that reforms are governing technologies that problematize the possibilities of action and self-reflection. Such governing is not linear but a story of fluctuation, uneven movements, and unpredictable transformations as political rationalities are brought into the pedagogical discourses through multiple capillaries, capillaries that traverse distinctions between state and civil society.

Constructing the Problem-Solving Citizen Changing Patterns of Regulation

The past two decades involve important changes in the governing of the educational arena in Sweden and the United States, two industrialized countries which on the surface are historically different. In this section, I compare the educational arenas of these two countries to explore the transformations. My discussion problematizes a discussion that begins with Hegelian to post-Kantian moral and political philosophy and continues into the present. Its underlying premise is the idea that the State is not only the regulation of the legitimated forms of political and economic action, but the modes of action that act on the dispositions, sensibilities, and awarenesses that enable individuals to be productive and autonomous actors. The subjectivity of the person, then, becomes "not only *subject to* the play of forces in the apparatus of the social but also act as author and *subject of* its own conduct" (Donald, 1992, p. 14).

In focusing on the state as patterns of regulation, I engage a notion of power that has been prominent in postmodern discussions about the politics of knowledge. This concern is to understand how power is deployed through multiple capillaries that produce and constitute the "self" as an agent of change (Barrett & Phillips, 1992; Butler, 1993; Shapiro, 1992; Young, 1990). My use of the concept of the educational arena is to interpret power relationally and historically as an amalgamation of institutional and discursive practices that function as "a collective assemblage of disparate parts on a single social surface" (Crary, 1990, p. 6).

The discussion refocuses the notion of power from that of *sovereignty,* which seeks to identify the "origins" or roots of power through classifying those groups that are structurally dominant and those that are repressed. While the notion of sovereignty provided certain insights, it also ignores or misrecognizes the disciplining and productive qualities of power in the construction of the autonomous and self-reflective person. I have discussed the problems of the *sovereignty* notion of power in the study of schooling elsewhere (Popkewitz, 1991; Popkewitz & Brennan, 1998). For now, suffice it to say that the sovereign notion of power as a historical narrative posits unified, often evolutionary processes and structures. I argue, however, that power tends to be constructed, envisioned, and deployed in a manner that is historically contingent, with multiple and fluid boundaries. In a prominent category of traditional analysis, while one can posit a generalized condition of capitalism as a background to the organization of power, this positing does not provide an adequate theoretical grounding for understanding how the capillaries of power work in contemporary societies. There is no one "model" of capitalism; neither is its history one of a single, unified development (for different discussions related to this, see, e.g., Boyer, 1995, Crary, 1990; Sousa Santos, 1995).

Governing at a Distance: Reconstituting the Swedish Arena

The construction of the modern Swedish welfare state in the 1920s and 1930s transformed a network of diverse and often antagonistic voluntary associations, trade unions, political parties, and local municipal bureaucracies into the centralized professional and administrative apparatus of the "welfare state."[3] This type of governing embodied certain principles and ideals of social engineering, that is, the application of a universal rational knowledge and apparently "neutral" professional expertise that would calculate and regulate social, economic, and moral affairs. That welfare state would ensure high levels of employment, economic progress, social security, health, and housing (education as a governmental activity came much earlier in Sweden).

The major responsibility for planning and evaluation belonged to the central state ministry and bureaucracies, not to the teacher. Detailed parliamentary instructions to teachers were legislated. The Swedish Board of Education, for example, was constructed with this bureaucratic, social engineering approach to social progress. Further, the educational sciences were mobilized, particularly in the post–World War II period, in the administrative development of schooling, and in the production of a self that brought the extension of processes of rationalization to a disciplined, autonomous, self-reliant, and morally inner-directed individual.[4]

The past two decades have seen important shifts in the governing patterns that constitute the Swedish educational arena. By the 1970s, the centralized school system produced a number of unsolved problems and developed a great deal of "inertia." Demands emerged for more flexible local responses to education, such as those provided historically by parish and later municipal schools (see, e.g., Kallós, 1995). In fact, there was a common move to increase the scope of action of municipal school boards during the 1970s, the consequences of which are "visible" in the reforms of the 1980s and 1990s. By 1991, the Board of Education was replaced with a new agency, the Swedish National Agency for Education (Skolverket). The latter is a smaller entity that has both regional and central concerns in the administration of schools. In one sense, the construction of the Swedish educational agency, Skolverket, is a Parliamentary effort to undo the strongly centralized and uniform school bureaucracy. At the same time, Skolverket is located within historically contingent changes in the educational arena that are neither evolutionary nor reducible to the conscious intentions of Parliament.

I explore the changes in the educational arena by recognizing that the revisioning of the "welfare" state is less the beginning of a new form of state than the construction of a new mode of inscribing political rationalities in the self-government of the individual. The changing patterns of regulation are examined through the repositioning of actors and problem solving produced in the educational arena.

The new problem solving embodies a revisioning of the Swedish State curriculum (*Läroplan*) that is reformulated as a goal-driven conception of the state vis-à-vis the educational arena (Carlgren, in press). General curriculum goals are set by the central government to provide local school districts with flexibility and a certain degree of autonomy in developing implementation plans. In return, the central state bureaucracy monitors outcomes and content through psychometric measurements rather than processes. If we view the current situation from one view of the state, the Swedish National Agency for Education establishes what is legitimate and reasonable for the conduct of education, but localities and teachers have the responsibility for evaluating and, in same cases, choosing from the many goals.

While the word stayed the same, the Läroplan embodies a restructuring of the problem-solving capabilities of the teacher and local administrative authorities. The new teacher who participates in the modern state is one who is flexible, responsive to changes, and acts with greater autonomy in finding solutions to social problems.

Although there is debate about the reforms, the categories that are used to construct the teacher are generally not made problematic. The governing practices of the new Läroplan embody sets of assumptions related to the importation of two Anglo-American words—*curriculum* and *professionalism* (see, e.g., Kallós & Lundahl-Kallós, 1995; Kallós & Nilsson, 1995). The word *curriculum* brings into focus distinctions about teaching, and helps to construct a teacher who has autonomy and capabilities in local planning, organizing, managing, and evaluating school knowledge. The call for professionalism relates to a revisioning of occupational identity. It gives value to school work that includes greater teacher responsibility and flexibility in implementing goal-governed approaches of the state.[5]

The importation of the words *curriculum* and *professionalism* represents more than a simple process of borrowing words to express desired "states" of the future teacher. Instead these words embody "rules of reasoning" about the self-examination and capabilities of teachers, educational researchers, bureaucrats, and teacher educators. "Curriculum" and "professionalism" are concepts drawn from Anglo-American governing traditions in education where a "weak" central bureaucracy historically interacts with civil organizations, local school districts, and professional groups to produce pedagogical practice. These traditions provide a stark contrast to previous continental European practices. However, they have relevance in the current reconstitution of the Swedish educational arena (Popkewitz, 1993a).

The Swedish reception of notions of "curriculum" and "professionalism" are not "merely" brought into its educational arena as "fixed entities." They are given interpretation within the patterns of relations in the educational arena that have a specific historical horizon. For example, the words *curriculum* and *professionalism* are nuances through continental European (Danish and German) educational traditions associated with Herbart, and an outlook about an educated class that is different from, but intermixes with, the Anglo-American notions of expert knowledge.

These changes in the problematic of regulation are not only of the rules regarding teachers and students; they effect the subjectivities of the various actors in that arena. For example there is a self-problematization of the bureaucracy.[6] The former governmental official who monitored the school operated with the assumption that the rules of schooling were clearly defined within a hierarchical authority. This is no longer so, and the bureaucratic official needs to operate in a more fluid, pragmatic, and locally defined problem-solving context. In this sense, the bureaucrat who "administers" the school is defined and understood in the reconstitution of the governing principles of the educational arena.

Contemporary Swedish university and teacher education also involve a visioning/revisioning of the production of knowledge and expertise. At one level, there has been a disbanding or weakening of governmental agencies that had previously coordinated and monitored the universities. In this new schema, universities occupy a changed relationship relative to other actors in the educational arena as there is greater internal control over faculty positions and budget. Contemporary political rhetoric speaks (either positively or negatively, depending on the ideological position of the speaker) about the "new" Swedish university as responsible to some mythical notion of "market" that is flexible to changing conditions, although the nature of faculty involvement is often prescribed through the rationalities of "self-government" and financial strategies of the central government that govern organizational matters.

Epistemologically, the State as centralized governmental structures has been challenged by a more pragmatic outlook that focuses on problems of teachers and didactics, with a greater use of "qualitative methods" to assess local implementations of reforms and on teachers' problem-solving abilities. At the same time, centralized statistical information about children's achievement, school resources, and reform implementation has been authorized as the central government finds itself with different requirements for information about school outcomes. The production of the latter type of information has become a recognizable industry within the university as new national tests are being constructed to monitor governmental programs.

Epistemological shifts in this arena involve the appearance of two new sets of authorized actors. One of these is the psychometricans who have been present in the educational arena since the early 1950s but are given a new credibility in the current restructuring.

A different grouping of actors is teacher educators who had previously had little authority in the research community. I will call them the "local" researchers. They focus on knowledge that is deemed "useable" to regional authorities, the "decentralized" teacher education programs, and local parents. The local evaluators see themselves as "practically" oriented to respond to "demands" about the use of reform programs. With an emphasis on "qualitative" methods, the new evaluation practices focus on teacher practices related to goal-governed educational steering.

The local researchers are themselves positioned in relation to a reemergence of didactics in the study and training of teachers. The didactics brought into current programs, however, are different from those of the German idealism of earlier professional educational schemas. The new didactics give importance to relations between the teachers, the learners, and the academic content of school subjects through constructivist psychologies (the latter are called "progressivist" in Sweden). The emphasis is on a teacher who is a problem solver and who works in a flexible environment of constant flux.[7]

The changes in the construction of the teachers do not occur through formal governmental directives but instead through changes in program and discourses, as certain strategies are brought into play as "professional education." These include notions such as "the reflective teacher" and "action research" (Kallós & Selander, 1993). The latter emerges through an increased emphasis on instruction in classroom evaluation; strategies that govern at a distance through the art of self-examination. Without arguing a correspondence, it can be seen that strategies described here as didactics and the "autonomous" professional teacher who is self-reflective are related to the teaching dispositions inscribed in the state goal-steering practices discussed earlier.

The discourses about curriculum, professionalization, didactics, and action research, among others, are positioned within a set of relations whose governing patterns comprise the state. The resulting patterns of relations, however, cannot be adequately understood as a reconstruction of what was dismantled by the 1920s, but instead as a reconstitution of power whose relations comprise the educational arena. The new governing practices are themselves being debated and the outcome is not clear.

Governing at a Distance: The United States

Similar reform discourses can be seen in the United States. However, the reform discourses are embodied in different historical sets of relations in the educational arena.[8] From the nineteenth century, the governing of the school was organized through complex patterns that included commercial textbook publishers, municipal financing of and hiring in schools, and a strong local school district administration. In some discussions, the role of the state in the United States has been viewed as "weak" in comparison to Sweden's "strong" state tradition. The U.S. Department of Education had little if any role in the construction of schooling until after World War II and the reform movements beginning in the late 1950s. In fact, most educational histories and research accept implicitly the idea of a weak state through various categories of interpretation, such as descriptions of the U.S. system as decentralized and localized, school outcomes through psychological "learning" theories, micro-ethnographies of the classroom culture, and the principal as the key to school reform.

The notions of "weak" and "strong" states, however, have little analytic value when considering the problematic of governing. In fact, such language tends to be more misleading than helpful. One needs to look no further than current U.S. policy discourses about "virtuous" subjectivities to understand that the United States embodies a strong set of institutional relations and discourses that govern subjectivities. Current debates about the regulation of smoking and the labeling of foods to discipline the dietary habits of individuals, for example, point to strong rules that relate governmental legislation to the moral deportment of citizens. This inscription of the harmonizing of administrative patterns and individual self-government transcends ideologies. National discourses about abortion and child's rights, women's abuse, teenage pregnancies, and welfare reform, constructed with different ideological agendas, converge through the acceptance of the harmonization of political rationalities with the moral deportment and behaviors of individual subjects.

The differences between Sweden and the United States are seen in how governing patterns are constructed rather than in such labels as weak or strong. The linking of political rationalities with subjectivities in U.S. schools during the nineteenth and early twentieth centuries, for example, involved different trajectories than those described previously in Sweden. Certain discourses about the pedagogy of the child, childhood, school administration, and measurement of achievement, for example, circulated nationally to construct the object and subject of schooling. The rules of curriculum and childhood inscribed notions of progress that tied social engineering approaches to child development with the construction of self. At the same time, an academized knowledge of the "teacher" in teacher education and the development of management techniques to hire, organize, and assess teacher performance were woven together with other practices to govern the teacher and child. The amalgamation of ideas, technologies, and institutions that formed the governing systems were not weak, decentralized, or evolutionary.

The current reforms can be understood as a reconstitution of the patterns that have governed the school arena. Captured in the recently used phrase "systemic school reform," new sets of relations among governmental agencies, professional teaching groups in the various school subjects, research communities, and regional authorities have emerged. As in Sweden, the new governing strategies move among multiple sets of actors whose patterns of governing constitute the state in education. The discourses of standards and professionalism appear within a context of building strong U.S. government monitoring and steering systems, such as national curriculum goals, assessment techniques (e.g., portfolio assessments), and a national teacher certification test. The discourses about national standards and teacher professionalism emerge from coalitions among groups within State agencies, professional groups, foundations, and teacher unions. The national discourses about standards are joined with discussions about site-based management, shared decision making, teacher education reforms about a "reflective teacher," and a constructivist pedagogy. A consequence, I will argue in the last section, is a revision of the problematic of the governing of the self through the applied reasoning.

The sets of actors being mobilized and the relations established in the educational arena of Sweden and the United States involve a reconstitution of the problem-solving field for the possibilities of action, but in different historical, national conditions. In neither instance can we assume that educational change involves a linear and evolutionary process in which a stable and consistent group of actors is suddenly challenged by a newly emerging group. Such an account of the reform process implies an illusion of stability that ignores the assemblage of techniques and images that intersect to create subject positions and to position and reposition actors. The bureaucratic actor who practices social engineering in Sweden is a different bureaucratic actor in the current problem-solving context. In an important sense, actors who might appear on some level to be the same are, in fact, transformed as they compete in different patterns and through different epistemological rules of engagement. Concepts such as "markets" and "privatization" that are offered in both countries to explain changes leave unscrutinized the field of relations being produced in the educational arena.

Changing Regimes and the Patterns of Regulation: Russia and South Africa

Whereas changes in Sweden and the U.S. government relate to party policies, Russia and South Africa involve changes in the rationalities and rules of politics and citizenship associated with their regimes.[9] Yet both countries are engaged in educational reform programs that have certain similarities to those of Sweden and the United States. The historical conditions in each country involve different sets of relations in order to consider the meaning of the state in education. My focus on those relations here is twofold: to historicize the notion of state through exploring the intersection of changing actors and epistemologies in changes of political regimes; and to locate the production of problem solving to govern social practices. That letter requires attention given to expert mediate knowledge in the construction of governing patterns. The tying together of actors and discourses, again, is to offer a multilayered, relational, and historical notion of the state.

Russia and South Africa are both witnessing a change in the political regimes. In both countries discussions are emerging about constructing a "civil society" (through nongovernmental organizations—NGOs), an ideological focus within international agencies and policy discussion. Civil society, it is believed, provides intermediary social institutions between the individual and State that can democratize society and reduce or eliminate the authoritarian practices of the previous regimes (see, e,g., Fukuyama, 1995; Zakaria, 1995). Further, Russia and South Africa have policies that point to a decentralization that coincides with a centralization (nation building) that, on the surface, seems similar to that discussed earlier in regard to Sweden and the United States. The former countries, for example, have developed a rhetoric of decentralization, site-based management, and reforms that focuses on didactics through the incorporation of a psychological constructivism.

In Russia, a potentially liberal political and capitalist economic regime is replacing the system of centralization organized by the Communist Party. The previous Soviet regime, for example, had no governing actors outside of the infrastructure of the formal governmental agencies and the Party from which strong hierarchical systems of regulation were constructed and monitored. The rapid emergence of the Soviet system after the revolution resulted in a combination of Czarist and Communist policies that had prevented a viable civil society or public associations from forming. In all respects, the Party dominated the political, social, and cultural activities. (In the language of international funding agencies, there were no viable NGOs in the former Soviet Union.)

We can contrast the transformations currently taking place in Russia with those in South Africa as the apartheid system is politically dismantled. Although it was authoritarian in its technologies that suppressed dissent, South Africa's apartheid system had a strong capitalist economic system and relatively strong social, academic, and labor movements. Even during the worst moments of apartheid, Black labor unions were strong, and certain community groups functioned even though the economic consequences of racial discrimination often destroyed the fabric of family life. Furthermore, groups in exile challenged South Africa from outside. Although the educational system was segregated, there was an educated Black elite, which came mainly from missionary schools. Academics could contribute to the social sciences through study abroad and domestically (sometimes they could read books considered as "subversive" in special sections of libraries). The academic situation of South African intellectuals, then, presents a stark contrast to Soviet social and educational scientists for whom theoretical and methodological development were severely restrained. In South Africa a consequence of the functioning of these different groups outside and inside the country was developed administrative capabilities that could be brought into the restructuring of governing patterns once apartheid ended.

It is within this political context that we can think historically about a mobilization of a social engineering that "slept" during the apartheid years— some intellectuals were exiled, or lived in fear of reprisals if they acted out of concert with governmental policy. As apartheid began to be officially dismantled, the "sleepers" in South African civil society could be awakened. They had the necessary skills (mentalities) to work as "planning groups" alongside official governmental bodies.

With the Soviet Union's collapse, there were no sleepers except those from the old party system. The Communist Party was so encompassing in its control (and fear) mechanisms that there was no developed civil society to interrelate with the formal governmental agencies in the construction of governing patterns.[10] Equally important was the fact that people did not have the dispositions and "civilizing rules" of capitalistic modernity in which to negotiate the complexities of their new situation. It is no accident that many of the people who make decisions in Russia are the same people who were Party bureaucrats in the old system, but now act within the "new" epistemic spaces of institutional reforms that emphasize "choice" and individuality (Kerr, this volume).

Both instances of changes in regimes entailed a production of expertise to govern reason and "reasonable" people. The struggles about the new citizen and polity are most dramatically illustrated in the conflict between the Russian parliament and the Russian president. However, these struggles are just as profoundly embodied in the reshaping of the educational arena. The Russian educational problem is, among other things, the need to develop an "expertise" necessary for managing a more fluid and less bureaucratically centralized administration of schools. This expertise is not, however, merely technical competence. It also involves a reconstitution of the teacher—how one feel, thinks, sees, and acts as a competent subject in schooling.

As in Sweden and the United States, the governing of teachers and children is central to the construction of the educational arena. On the surface, the new regimes in Russia and South Africa need to produce more teachers, retrain existing teachers, and construct a new content in the curriculum.[11] But the reform practices are more than recruitment practices or changes in curriculum foci; the map of the educational arena is also being reordered through the relations established.

Let me explore this through the work of the SOROS Foundation, a New York philanthropic agency investing large sums of money in Eastern Europe to facilitate changes toward a market economy. This foundation has been working with the Russian Ministry of Education to produce new high school textbooks about the new "imagined communities" of nationhood and the citizen inscribed with Western liberal philosophies and histories of ideas.

Previously Soviet teachers worked from well-scripted lesson plans that chronologically detailed an exact sequence for each lesson. The styles of presentation for materials were ritualized—everyone in the country was to use them in a standardized manner. The SOROS textbooks, in contrast, were intended to construct mentalities that combined different Russian approaches to pedagogy with Western liberal and progressive notions of child-centered education. While the discursive constructions are not monolithic, the "new teacher" was one who could act autonomously, using problem-solving capabilities. In other words, this teacher is the embodiment of the problem-solving teacher discussed in a previous section.

However, the task of constructing a new, imagined community is more than merely writing textbooks. It involves reconstituting the "author" as a subject and object of scrutiny. When SOROS located authors to write such textbooks, the project planners realized that the authors did not have the requisite skills. A statist mentality associated with the previous Communist regime was embodied in the textbook authors. To produce the textbooks, the SOROS Foundation held workshops to teach the authors how to think about, and organize, curriculum content, didactics, and assessments. The teacher's guides provided teachers with a choice of activities and had visual and psychological appeal for children-things that are taken for granted in Western countries. Less explicit but on the horizon of the curriculum construction were Russian views about spirituality and specific religious outlooks that have become part of the discourses of schooling.

The practices of the SOROS Foundation provide one point of entry into the changing relations of different actors and the struggles over the production of reason. The rewritten textbooks occupy a problematic position in relation to other school and teacher practices that center on the mastery of school content embodied in the examination systems provided by the Russian Ministry of Education in Moscow. A more geographically localized context of school management with regional authorities and finances also redefines the planning and the production of knowledge embodied in the Russian Academy of Education and Teacher Education. At present neither of these agencies has a monopoly in the production of teachers or of the epistemological systems that construct the curricula, the didactics, and the teacher. As in Sweden, there is a new local researcher/evaluator.

The map of the South African arena has a different historical construction. As the South African negotiations for a change-over in regimes came closer, the African National Congress, with private internal and external foundation assistance, set up policy-making units to rival those functioning within the formal government controlled by the Afrikaaner National Party.

One such academic group in education produced the NEP (National Educational Plan). Whereas previously, policy was dominated by Afrikaan academics and a "Fundamental Pedagogics" that legimated apartheid, the NEP was intended to appraise and develop goals for a new multicultural system of education. Implementation of this plan resulted in the production of a series of polished booklets that outlined the purposes and directions of a multicultural curriculum, administration, and economics of a new educational system. The NEP assumed a strong role of the state in steering South Africa toward national goals. This process, as was found in Sweden, was coupled with developments in local government and a teacher autonomy, expressed as professionalization.

If one expunges a particular rhetoric related to South Africa from the NEP documents, (such as references to apartheid and equity and democracy), the texts embody universalized discourses about calculating and managing change that are also found in other countries, such as the United States and Britain.[12] The NEP also inscribes many of the priorities of inter-state agencies, such as the World Bank, through its definition of problems and options for problem solving.[13]

The NEP documents were produced by a new group of academic experts drawn from previously marginalized groups within the English and Indian universities as well as from colored and black South Africans trained in postgraduate education outside the country (these distinctions are themselves the effects of power in the apartheid system that are still productive in its dismantling). Less visible and rarely acknowledged are foundations and interstate agencies. These consist of not only SOROS in Russia, but also other institutions such as the World Bank, US AID, Swedish SIDA, and OECD, as well as nongovernmental institutions such as the Ford, Rockefeller, and McArthur Foundations, which operate within Russia, South Africa, Sweden, and the United States (see, e.g., Fisher, 1993; Lagemann, 1989).

My argument to this point is that if we narrowly view the State as only confined to governmental agencies in the current historical conjuncture, we misrecognize the power relation through which the governing practices are forming. While similar reform practices about decentralization circulate among the four countries, there are historical distinctions in the constituting of relations and power in the educational arena. Various actors within civil society and government have no essential, unchanging attributes but are defined through the systems of relations established. The reforms emerge through multiple trajectories and are given authority through different sets of actors that are located both in the state and civil society. My focus on Russia and South Africa, however, was also to bring the position of academic scientific actors into sharper relief in the governing principles to construct the teacher and the child in schooling and teacher education. But even here, we cannot assume the academic actors are a single unified group. Only certain groupings of academics are authorized to speak. Understanding the patterns of regulation requires that we consider the notion of actor as problematic; to understand empirically the relations among groupings in their arena of practice and to consider the knowledge systems that give direction and interpretation to those practices. The latter bring the problem of governmentality to the fore to understand how epistemological rules of problem solving position and are positioned by the various actors in the educational arena.

Global Systems, the Capabilities of the Individual and Educational Reforms

The restructuring of the patterns of regulation in education, as my previous comments indicate, needs to be understood historically and globally. At one dimension, these discourses are elements of an international circulation of ideas about appropriate practices and interpretations of school change. The circulation of international discourses occurs not only through formal institutions concerned with policy, but through professional associations, journals, conferences, and the mobility of academics around the globe.[14] Globalization is not restricted to particular hegemonic groups of nations as postcolonial literatures have illustrated the hybridity of discourses (see, e.g., Appiah, 1992; Young, 1990).

We can think about globalization through homologies between the regulatory patterns of education and those of other arenas.[15] I use the term *homologies* to consider relations of education to other social practices in a manner that is neither causal nor suggests a single origin of the changes. This second dimension of globalization enables me to extend the discussion of the regulatory norms of constructivism through situating the "sensibilities" of the teacher to other transformations in the patterns of politics, culture, and economy which schooling both expresses and influences.

The shift from bureaucratic centralism (rule governing) to "goal steering" is occurring not only in Sweden but also in many European countries. The changes can be related to a tendency for political projects to become more local and less class focused, such as in the Green movements and the politics of feminism in the past decade. Several years ago a member of the Swedish Parliament, for example, talked about the feminist movement as too important to be left to women; today that view of the state is no longer prevalent. Localized practices are also found in academic discourse, with an emphasis on pragmatic knowledge, local social histories, and rejections of universal histories and generalization (Lloyd, 1991).

The administrative-legal reorganization of the government is also related to changes in the relation of global and regional economies whose patterns of regulation are homologous to the educational arena. The new corporate structure is less hierarchical and pyramidal than it was in the past, and it has eliminated many middle layers of management. The language of the business pages of major newspapers is similar to that of the professionalization literature in teaching; the new business organization, for example, is "the law of the microcosm," which postulates that the most agile and flexible companies are those most likely to survive. The new business entails a work condition that involves problem solving—where highly variable customer demands, new technologies, multicentered business structures, and horizontal structures organize workers into groups concerned with specific projects that do not have the older layers of management. The smaller units are utilized to empower workers and to develop flexible, responsive environments that can respond quickly to customer (read "corporate") demands.

This corporate restructuring embodies changing patterns of governance toward work and productivity. In examining efforts to increase production, Donzelot (1991) argues that there are increasing efforts to break previous psychological ties that define individual identity according to fixed notions of work and production. The new approaches accent the relation of the individual's autonomy and the capacity to adapt and be an agent of change in a changing world as integral to one's self-fulfillment. "Instead of defining the individual by the work he [*sic*] is assigned to, [the new psychology] regards productive activity as the site of deployment of the person's personal skills" (p. 252).

There is a particular set of epistemological rules around which the teacher is defined in current reform practices.[16] These rules often evolve around a label of "constructivism" which draws on psychology and social-interactional perspectives. Constructivist strategies are intended to enable teachers to have the "correct" dispositions and capabilities for effecting school reform. Knowledge and subjectivities are viewed as contingent and plural. They can be represented through the following equation:

"I understand it" + "I can do it" + "I care about it" = "capacity"[17]

But constructivist pedagogies are not neutral strategies to teach problem solving; they politicize the body through connecting power/knowledge. There is a shift from the individual defined by having particular sets of competencies, skills, and knowledge (such as those for cognitive mastery) to the individual who embodies pragmatic capabilities and dispositions. The capabilities of the teacher are self-confidence, self-discipline, problem solving, and a willingness to learn.

If we examine the Holmes Group (1986, 1990), organized by deans of leading schools of education in the United States to produce change in teacher education, a constructivist psychology is offered as a template for improving the quality of teaching in professional development schools. Constructivism is brought to bear on the formation of teachers when it is asserted that "the generic task of education" consists of "teaching students how to make knowledge and meaning—to *enact culture*"—or when it is argued that it is necessary for institutional networks to develop multiple models of reform "rather than a template for a single conception" (Holmes Group, 1990, pp. 6,10).

In certain crucial ways, the dispositions of the person that Donzelot identifies are homologous to the constructivism we have seen in the Holmes Reports and the National Curriculum Standards, as well as in the conceptual change literature associated with constructivist teaching of school subjects. Individual goals are now tied more closely and directly than before to institutional and corporate goals.

The individualism of constructivism is homologous to the changing conceptions of "individuality" that Donzelot describes and which exist as well in culture practices, philosophy, and politics. It is a world of instabilities, pluralities, and a need for pragmatic actions as individuals interact with communication systems. It is a world of contingent qualities in contexts that quickly change. The pedagogical changes in how a teacher sees, appreciates, and acts in the world are related to other social changes, but not in correspondence to other social arenas.

The significance of the strategies of reform in the problem of governing are in their intrusive qualities. The potential of constructivist discourses result from their linking people's knowledge of the world with institutional goals in a manner that enables them to feel satisfied that the process will effectively reap personal as well as social ends. Inscribed in the concrete technologies of pedagogy are the *dispositions* and capabilities that regulate and police the teacher who, in the discourse of reform literature, is not only "able" but also "inclined" (see, e.g., Barth, 1986; Cazden, 1986; Newmann et al., 1989). But the intrusive, regulatory quality is not a reflexive element of the discourse. The sense of "doing" and "wanting" are uncritically accepted as a prescription for action. Thus, when we consider the shift in educational discourses from the individual defined as having particular sets of competencies, skills, and knowledge (such as those for cognitive mastery) to the individual who embodies pragmatic capabilities and dispositions, these changes in the loci of regulation are related to changes in arenas other than those in education.

Knowledge as Governing Systems of Inclusion/Exclusion

Early in this chapter, I suggested that the construction of governing systems does not occur in level playing fields. The same subjectivities are not constructed for all through the governing patterns that constitute the state. The governing constitutes an economy that enables and disenables subjectivities through the inscription of different rules of participation and action. Here, then, I pursue briefly how the rules of reason in psychological constructivism in pedagogy normalize and inscribe subjectivities that exclude as well as include.

We can think of the principles of pedagogy as constructing an imagined community. Its systems of classification draw boundaries about what is included on the "map" through its ordering and dividing practices. This can be thought of as analogous to a map of a country that identifies citizens within its territory. The inclusions not only define but have historically redefined identities (e.g., calling Ibos "Nigerians"), excluded through not being given representation.

In pedagogy, the "maps" are of reason, achievement, competence, and capabilities drawn through the rules of classification. The rules classify "reason" that normalizes particular dispositions and sensitivities of the individual who is in school. The normativity does not appear directly but through the rules of the normal, which seem universal and applicable to all. Thus, we can look at contemporary ideas about educational reform in the United States as constructing distinctions that separate the normal from the not-normal through the distinctions. Distinctions about inner-city youth, learning styles, remediation, and cultural diversity, implemented ostensibly to give value and to help children who have not succeeded in schooling, involve such normalization.[18] The reasoning establishes a silent set of norms that positions the child named as an Other. Relations of sameness/difference are established. The at-risk and diverse child is interned and enclosed as different, not having the competence, achievement, and capabilities of those classified as normal.

It is in this context of normalization that we can explore how pedagogy includes/excludes through the classifications of problem solving. The constructivist pedagogy presumes, as do the systems of ideas that define the inner-city child, a silent normativity which is obscured, as problem solving is seen as universal and natural for all groups of children who come to school. Where diversity is assumed, it is a populational notion in which groups are defined in opposition to universalized unspoken norms. The problem of instruction is how to provide efficient lessons so that all children can solve problems in flexible ways; or so that teachers can be reflective about their practices, with "reflection" seeming to have a logic to it that is independent of historical time or social location. The rules are assumed to be natural and universal.

However, the reflections, thinking, and problem solving, presumed by constructivism to be universal, are not global characteristics but local. A variety of research, for example, enables us to understand that the notions of problem solving that we take as universal emerge from groups within a society that have "cultural capital," to borrow from a term from Bourdieu, to insert their sensitivities, tastes, and cognitive ordering as authoritative (see, e.g., Bourdieu, 1984; Hertfeld, 1992; Zerubavel, 1993).[19] The universalizing of reason is an inscription of power through taking what is locally produced and making it appear global, natural, and essential.

Why is the change from local to global important to the notion of the State? The distinctions represented as universal, to continue with the example of constructivism, are partial and exclude those whose capabilities and disposition inscribe a normativity in the construction of subjectivities. The processes of inclusion/exclusion can be likened to a broader discussion called "the two-thirds solution." Commentaries about social policies in Europe have suggested that the social policies in Europe may produce divisions in societies (see, e.g, Wagner, 1994). Two-thirds of the society consists of those people whose subjectivities embody the sentiments and dispositions to create "opportunities," where the Other/others embody different habitus that exclude them from "the main spheres of society in which social identities can be formed" (Wagner, 1994, p. 167).

The inclusions/exclusions are not in the categorical constructions that are associated with labeling theories, such as calling a child "socially disadvantaged," "at-risk," or from "the inner city." Rather, the inclusions/exclusions are embedded in the systems of recognition, divisions, and distinctions that construct identities. The systems of recognitions generate the normalcies by which individuals are to see, conduct, and evaluate themselves as normal and reasonable people. The production of subjectivism is historically specific and inscribed within the subject relations of the arenas of social practices.

I argue by analogy that systems that are intended to include are never universal; they produce simultaneous exclusions. The universalizing of reason in constructivism has a duality: its governing systems are intended to open possibilities for those who have the appropriate dispositions and sensitivities to capitalize on the new curriculum, while those who do not are excluded. Thus, instead of opening up spaces for those who are different, the reform systems may instead place them in an oppositional or marginal space. This occurs as constructivism names the children who need remediation or special assistance while, at the same time, asserting a universalism to its systems for classifying how thinking occurs. As Dumm argues in a different context, the discourses of the social sciences are normalizing practices that classify marginalized groups, such as people of color, as different from the norm and who, at best, can be "like the normal person." Particular groupings of people are enclosed and interned (Dumm, 1993). Thus, the production of governing principles and actors also involves systems of inclusion/exclusion through the subjectivities produced.

But this issue is not only one of internal differentiation. As Badie and Birnbaum (1994) suggest in a recent paper on the state, the rise of transnational relations and the crisis in the machinery for regulating inter-nation-state relations have imposed new regulatory patterns. I want to suggest here that the distinctions in the reconstruction of inter-state-nations may not be at the national-territory level but through the production of distinctions and differentiations related to subjectivities. In a recent review of the policies of international lending agencies toward the restructuring of teacher education, distinctions were produced among the teachers in first-world and second/third-world countries (Carnoy et al., 1994). Whereas first-world countries emphasized university education and scientific cultures in the education of teachers, international funding agency policies toward nonindustrialized countries gave preference to the practical, school-based training of teachers.

These differences in approaches in teacher education are ostensibly to save money in the educational sector, but the financial rules also intertwine the deployment of power with the production of distinctions. However, if we focus not on the World Bank as a sovereign actor but on "the rules of reasoning" about educational practices, the educational practices can be understood as part of a broad set of discourses and practices intended to reconstruct the way teachers think about and assess their performance. The differences among countries are not only in what is overtly learned, but in the distinctions, dispositions, and sensitibilities produced in social practices. My earlier discussion of the linking of work and leisure, the homologies between the dispositions associated with "constructivist" didactics and other transformations in industrialized societies, together with national differentiations all point to the deployment of power through the construction of particular styles of thinking and acting. Thus, while we may talk about a universalized school, as do Meyer and his associates (1992), we must historicize the constructions of pedagogy to understand how distinctions and differentiations are the effects of power.[20]

At a different layer of discussions about the state, it has been popular to label the changes as a "conservative restoration," labels that I believe miss the long-term historical processes that underlie these changes—some occurring as early as the 1940s and 1950s—well before Thatcher in Britain or Reagan in the United States (see, e.g., discussion in Popkewitz, 1991; Whitty, this volume). If we examine current rhetoric about neoliberal slogans of "markets" and "privatization" that emerged as political slogans and that have been brought into social scientific concepts, we realize that the changes do not start with recent policies but are part of more profound social changes that have been moving in uneven ways during at least the past four decades. At one level is the breakdown of the Fordist compromise in postwar Europe and the United States, a compromise among workers, industrialists, and the state which produced a division of labor and mechanization in exchange for a favorable wage formula and the implementation of a state welfare system, as Fordism lost its efficiency with technologies and markets. The organizations of work that we are now witnessing is in part a response to the lack of efficiency of Fordist mass production.

The changes in governing have no single origin that can be reducible to "ideology," economy, or hegemony; but they embody multiple historical trajectories. There are

> a range of other challenges to the mechanism of social government that emerged during these same decades from civil libertarians, feminists, radicals, socialists, sociologists and others. These reorganized programmes of government utilise

and instrumentalise the multitude of experts of management, of family life, of lifestyle who have proliferated at the points of intersection of socio-political aspirations and private desires for self-advancement. (Rose & Miller, 1992, p. 201)

If I pursue Rose and Miller's argument, the problem of the state is the constitution of governing practices. This position transposes much contemporary analyses that define the State as an "object" that dispenses power rather than as a set of relations through which governing and government are produced. It is interesting to note here that contemporary discussions about "bringing back the State" in social and educational theories tend to incorporate nineteenth-century historicist and structural distinctions in the theoretical deliberations. The distinctions evoke images of the past that, I have argued, are inadequate for understanding the changing patterns of governing discussed above. (For a general discussion of nineteenth-century epistemologies and contemporary social theory, see Wallerstein, 1991; in education, Popkewitz, in press.)

Some Concluding Notes

My interest in the state has been to consider the problem of governing in education through sets of concepts that are relational, historical, and comparative. Two different but related intellectual strategies guided the chapter. One is related to the concept of an educational arena. The idea of an arena directed attention to the position of different actors as analogous to players in a game; it is also important to recognize that some players have more resources and capital, in Bourdieu's sense, than do others. Embedded in the notion of an arena was a second move, the exploration of the relation of actors to the construction of systems of regulation. This concept drew on Foucault's notion of "governmentality" to direct attention to the rules of the game that discipline reason and the self-governing of "reasonable" people. While the disciplining is never totally coercive, the production of knowledge positions and produces power through the regulatory principles applied as "reason" and "truth."

The meaning of the state lies, then, in the relation of these two sets of empirical problems as they change over time and at its multiple levels. Russia, South Africa, Sweden, and the United States provided examples of changes in the relations that constitute their educational arenas. My examples focused on the actors who are authorized to "speak" about the object and subject of education and the social relations where intelligibility for speaking takes place. Attention was focused on the proximity among different groupings of actors in the production of the categories and distinctions. The state, then, was treated as an epistemological category to consider empirically the patterns of governing.

My concern, however, was not only with patterns of relations but also practices of governing as producing systems of inclusion/exclusion. Governing to include/exclude occurs through the reasoning applied rather than in any "overt" systems of exclusion. Here, attention to reason as an effect of power is, I believe, an important contribution of postmodern feminist theory and political analyses to our understanding of the micropractices of schooling.

Different dimensions in the study of policy, power, and schooling can now be addressed. We cannot assume that the actors and their positions in the educational arena are stable and fixed categories. The categories of actors are at times the effects of power themselves. Further, the "actors" in the educational arena are not monolithic and universalized groups but are instead historically formed and reformed groupings. In fact, the grouping and position of actors does change over time even as their labels may stay the same. As an example, while we can say that educational researchers are positioned in the production of power, their groupings and position change as the regualtory patterns are reconstituted. In this sense, there are neither old nor new actors who hold power, just patterns of relations.

The production of power, then, can be understood as relational to the patterns in which the actor is constructed and constituted. While most analyses of the politics of reform apply structural concepts of power (i.e., questions about who rules and are ruled), the subjectivities in the educational arena are formed through an amalgamation of ideas, technologies, and relations that are historically contigent. In other words, the "reasonable" governmental bureaucrats who "monitor" the reforms, the educational research community which produces systems of reflection and self-reflection, as well as the teacher and children who classify their practices are not, as they might appear to be, universal and neutral categories, but are instead situated in time and space. The refusal to make the subject problematic is one of the major difficulties of policy and studies of education.

Another dimension is pedagogy as a technology of power. Pedagogy links political rationalities to autonomous self-examination, self-reflection, and self-care of the individual. But its importance in the problem of governing is not only that of production. It also inscribes systems of differences and distinctions that include and exclude. This occurs, I argued, through practices of normalization that applied local dispositions and sensitivities as universal and natural to all. The normalizations and practices of inclusion/exclusion in pedagogy should not be viewed as an epi-phenomenon of other, more primary "causes." The exploration of homologies in politics, art, economics, and the educational arenas, as well as the governing technologies of constructivist pedagogy, suggest relations that are not of correspondence or evolutionary, but of multiple historical trajectories in which the technologies that govern subjectivities are constructed that have no single origin.

I thus return to a point where I started. Discussions about conservative restorations, privatization, marketization, and the dichotomy between State and civil society obscure the changes occurring through their systems of reasoning. These categories are often constructed within a field of political rhetoric and brought into social and educational sciences as the phenomena to explain. The reasoning applied, however, assumes the State as a "real entity" with stable actors. Further, such analyses assume what has to be made problematic—that is, the subject of the state as government. The assemblage of actors, techniques, and images that intersect in the construction of governing are left unscrutinized. This assemblage is neither evolutionary nor structural, but historically contingent. I argued that there are long-term shifts in the problems of governing that require different analytic distinctions to interpret the alternatives offered than those of the State as an sovereign entity related to its territory. While it is clear that the moral and political rhetoric of educational struggles has shifted, such analyses beg the question of the changes in the historical conditions through which power is constructed and deployed. Again, if the comparative discussions about homologies among politics, arts, science, economics, and education *and* the constructions of differences among national educational arenas are historically appropriate, then the changes that we now witness in the school arena are changes involving uneven movements over a long duration in multiple arenas, beginning before Reagan and Thatcher took office.

Notes

This chapter was originally prepared and presented as a lecture at the University of Granada, Spain. I wish to thank the following people for their comments as I wrote and rewrote drafts. Some agreed, others disagreed with the directions taken, but I appreciated all the conversations: Lynn Fendler, Dory Lightfoot, Fran Vavrus, Miguel Pereyra, Lizbeth Lundahl-Kallós, Daniel Kallós, Michael Shapiro, Ingrid Carlgren, Eva Aström, Ulla Johannson, Christina Segerholm, Bob Tabachnick, Geoff Whitty, and the seminar group at Pedagogik Institutionen, Umeå University, Sweden, and the Wednesday Group at Madison.
    1. I use *arena* to think of educational practices as occurring as in a field of changing relations. These relations entail one of positions among actors and discursive practices. I use *arena*, therefore, as a historical concept to consider the changing social positions and power within education. The concept is discussed in Popkewitz and Pereyra, 1993. The notion of arena borrows from Bourdieu's (1984), view of "field; and the notion of discourse is related to both Foucault's (1979) arguments about science as a normalizing and disciplining practice. My particular way of relating these two concepts is discussed as a social epistemology in Popkewitz, 1991.
    2. I use the notion of actor to speak about social grouping in the arena. I am not concerned with actors in the individual sense nor from the perspective of structural

theory. When *State* is capitalized, it refers to an essentialized entity; when *state* is not capitalized, it indicates a problematic of governing.

3. To cite a few statistics in education to illustrate (Kallós, 1995). There were 2700 municipalities as late as 1957, and in 1995 there were only 286. The Ministry of Education in 1967 had a staff of 90 persons, the National Board of Education had 550, and the Office of the Chancellor of the Universities about 100. The National Board of Education in 1977 allocated approximately 60 percent of all educational financing.

4. In the United States, for example, educational sciences received institutional "pushes" through its ties to normal (teacher training) schools during the rapid expansion period of mass schooling at the turn of the century and during World War I, in which there was a great demand for military discipline. Psychologists were deeply involved in the problems of recruitment and training; as well as in the search for ways to develop peaceful, democratic dispositions after the war. (For the later, see Freedman, 1987; also see O'Donnell, 1985.)

5. It is interesting to note that many Scandinavian countries have a Germanic tradition in which the word *profession* tended not to be used in talking about an educated occupation such as law or medicine. Also the strong State-centered tradition tended to make the educated occupations tied more closely to the government with a less autonomous civil society. It is also important to note that hidden in discourses of professions is a relation of the state, the development of capitalism, and issues of gender (see, e.g., Popkewitz, 1993a).

6. My assumption, borrowed from Giddens (1990), is that professional knowledge plays an important role in mediating between social changes and those in which the person interprets and acts in modernity. Further, I also view the concept of professionalism as a particular one associated with state developments (see T. Popkewitz, 1993a).

7. For a discussion of distinctions in traditions of didactics in the United States, Germany, and Sweden, see Hopmann & Riquarts (1995).

8. This discussion is drawn from Popkewitz, 1991, 1993b.

9. My involvement in Russian education started in 1976, while I attended a U.S.-Soviet seminar in Washington, and continued with a Fulbright in 1981 where I spent a semester with the Soviet Academy of Pedagogical Sciences, and continuing into the present. My observations about South Africa is related to an Oppenheimer fellowship given to me to lecture in universities and meet with its academic communities in May–June 1993. I provide this "credentialing" with great hesitation as I recognize the situations within these countries are far more complex that I can grasp here.

10. Russians have had to construct laws in areas about which they had no experience since the first decades of the century: on private property, banking, finance, bankruptcy, private schools, and so on.

11. For insightful discussions of the changes in South Africa, see Cloete (1993); and in Russia, see Kerr (this volume).

12. The rationalizing involving various sets of actors in the construction of regulation may have been necessary, if only to prevent a civil war, which, to this point, has been successful.

13. During the political negotiations among the South African parties, a member of a teacher's union commented to me that much of the discussion about restructuring the educational system existed with categories related to the priorities set by the World Bank. Even though the bank would not be involved in South African reforms until the transitional period, the bank, the unionist thought, was part of the horizon of negotiation. The two major parties wanted to be able to say to the electorate that they had access to World Bank money in the restructuring.

14. The mobilization of intellectuals is evident if we consider the movement historically. Whereas previously only the elites of intellectual life moved in international circles, today it is commonplace; the European Community's ERASMUS program is an official recognition of such mobility. One can also examine the increased use of English as the lingua franca of scientific communities, as well as the increased and quick translations of social scientific texts occurring from English and into English.

15. I use the word *homology* to suggest a historical relation among events and discourses. It is not meant as a causal relation.

16. While we can understand "constructivist" as having many different views about teaching and learning, there are particular epistemological standards and rules from which the diversity occurs. My use of "constructivist," therefore, is to focus on the general standards and rules, paying only partial attention to its inner distinctions. In certain ways, my focus on constructivism can be likened to Thomas Kuhn's (1970) discussion of the problem solving within a paradigm of "normal science."

17. I draw this distinction from an International Labour Organization discussion about the changing characteristics of metal-working skills and the labor of metal working. They compare the new conditions of work with that of a Fordist model that focused on the competencies of the worker rather than on the capabilities. While I use this formulation, my intent is to signal changes that are cultural and social as well as economic. Many of these changes, as Wagner argues, occur within social movements that cannot be reduced to economic changes (Wagner, 1994).

18. I recognize that the calls for multicultural curriculum and education that appreciates cultural diversity have multiple agendas in reorganizing the governing patterns of the subjectivities produced in schooling. My argument is that the discursive practices are located within rules of pedagogical reasoning that position children as "the other" within a sameness. See, e.g., Young, 1990, for a discussion of this notion of colonialization as it crosses liberal and oppositional left discourses.

19. These differences are in the production of different "habitus," and occur through distinctions and manners available to different groups, from tastes in what is eaten, read, watched, bought, talked about, and seen as valuable and useful. They are found in the tastes that we have in the reading of newspapers, the movies that we see, the books that we buy, as well as the food we eat and our manners of eating. These sensitivities. distinctions, and differentiations construct power.

20. J. Meyer, J. Ramirez, and Y. Soysal. (1992). "World Expansion of Mass Education, 1870–1980." *Sociology of Education* 65: 128–49.

References

Appiah, K. *In My Father's House: Africa in the Philosophy of Culture.* New York: Oxford University, 1992.

Badie, B. & P. Birnbaum."Sociology of the State Revisited." *International Social Science Journal* 139 (1994): 153–67.

Barrett, M. & A. Phillips. *Destablizing Theory: Contemporary Feminist Debates.* Stanford, Calif.: Stanford University Press, 1992.

Barth, R. "The Principal and the Profession of Teaching." *The Elementary School Journal* 86 (1986): 471–92.

Bourdieu, P. *Distinction: A Social Critique of the Judgment of Taste.* Cambridge: Harvard University Press, 1984.

Boyer, R. "The Capital Labour Relations in OECD Countries: From the Fordist 'Golden Age' to Contrasted National Trajectories." In J. Schor and J. I. You (eds.), *Capital, the State, and Labour: A Global Perspective,* Aldershot, UK: United Nations University Press, 1995.

Butler, J. *Bodies That Matter: On the Discourse Limits of "Sex."* New York: Routledge, 1993.

Carlgren, I. "Professional Cultures in Swedish Teacher Education." In *Professional Lives,* ed. A. Goodson and A. Hargreaves. London: Falmer Press, in press.

————. (1995) "National Curriculum as Social Compromise or Discursive Politics: Some Reflections on a Curriculum-Making Process." In *Journal of Curriculum Studies*: 27 (1995 Jul/Aug): 411–30.

Carnoy, M., L. Fendler, T. Popkewitz, B. Tabachnick & K. Zeichner. *Teacher Restructuring: Some Trends and Implications.* Geneva: International Labour Organization, 1994.

Cazden, C. "Classroom Discourse." In *Handbook of Research on Teaching,* 3d ed., ed. M. Wittrock. New York: Macmillan, 1986, pp. 432–63.

Cloete, J. J. N. *Democracy: Prospects for South Africa.* Pretoria: J. L. van Schaik, 1993.

Crary, J. *Techniques of the Observer: On Vision and Modernity in the Nineteenth Century.* Cambridge: MIT Press, 1990.

Donald, J. *Sentimental Education: Schooling, Popular Culture and the Regulation of Liberty.* London: Verso, 1992.

Donzelot, J. "Pleasure in Work." In *The Foucault Effect, Studies in Governmentality,* ed. G. Burchell, C. Gordon, and P. Miller. Chicago: University of Chicago Press, 1991, pp. 251–80.

Dumm, T. "The New Enclosures: Racism in the Normalized Community." In *Reading Rodney King: Reading Urban Uprising,* ed. R. Gooding-Williams. New York: Routlege, 1993, pp. 178–95.

Fisher, D. *Fundamental Development of the Social Sciences: Rockefeller Philanthropy and the United States Social Science Research Council.* Ann Arbor, Mich.: University of Michigan Press, 1993.

Foucault, M. "Governmentality." *Ideology and Consciousness* 6 (1979): 5–22.

Freedman, K. "Art Education as Social Production: Culture, Society and Politics in the Formation of Curriculum." In T. Popkewitz (ed.), *The formation of the School Subjects: The Struggle for Creating an American Institution.* New York: Falmer, 1987.

Fukuyama, F. (1995) *Trust: The Social Virtues and the Creation of Prosperity.* New York: Free Press, 1995.

Hertfeld, M. *The Social Production of Indifference: Exploring the Symbolic Roots of Western Bureaucracy.* Chicago: University of Chicago Press, 1992.

Holmes Group. *Tomorrow's Teachers*. East Lansing, Mich.: Holmes Group, 1986.
———. *Tomorrow's Schools*. East Lansing, Mich.: Holmes Group, 1990.
Hopmann, S. and K. Riquarts. "Didactics and/or Curriculum: Basic Problems of an Internationally Comparative Science of Education." *Z. Pädagogik,* supplement 33 (1995): 9–34.
Hunter, I. *Rethinking the School: Subjectivity, Bureaucracy, Criticism.* New York: St. Martin's Press, 1994.
Kallós, D. "Reflections on Decentralization as a Concept in Education Policy Analyses." Paper presented at the Second Comparative Education Policy Seminar: New Policy Contexts for Education: Sweden and the United Kingdom: Centre for Educational Studies, King's College, London, April 27–29, 1995.
Kallós, D. & Lundahl-Kallós, L. "Recent Changes in Teachers' Work in Sweden: Professionalization or What?" In *New Policy Contexts for Education: Sweden and United Kingdom,* ed. D. Kallós and S. Lindblad. Umea, Sweden: Pedagogiska institutionen, Umea universitet, 1994, pp. 140–68.
Kallós, D. & I. Nilsson. "Defining and Redefining the Teacher in the Swedish Comprehensive School." *Educational Review* 47 (1995): 173–88.
Kallós, D. & S. Selander. "Teacher Education and Teachers' Work in Sweden: Reform Strategies and Professional Reorientation." In *Changing Patterns of Power: Social Regulation and Teacher Education Reform,* ed. T. Popkewitz. Albany: State University of New York Press, 1993, pp. 211–62.
Kuhn, T. *The Structure of Scientific Revolutions.* Chicago: University of Chicago Press, 1970.
Lagemann, E. *The Politics of Knowledge: The Carnegie Corporation, Philanthrophy, and Public Policy.* Middletown, Conn.: Wesleyan University Press, 1989.
Lloyd, C. "The Methodologies of Social History: A Critical Survey and Defense of Structurism." *History and Theory: Studies in the Philosophy of History* 30 (1991): 180–219.
Meyer, J., J. Ramirez & Y. Soysal. "World Expansion of Mass Education, 1870–1980." *Sociology of Education* 65 (1992): 128–49.
Newmann, F., D. Griffin & M. Cole. *The Construction Zone: Working for Cognitive Change in Schools.* Cambridge: Cambridge University Press, 1989.
O'Donnell, J. M. *The Origins of Behaviorism: American Psychology, 1870–1920.* New York: New York University Press, 1985.
Popkewitz, T. *A Political Sociology of Educational Reform: Power/Knowledge in Teaching, Teacher Education, and Research.* New York: Teachers College Press, 1991.
———. "Professionalization in Teaching and Teacher Education: Some Notes on Its History, Ideology and Potential." *Teaching and Teacher Education* 10 (1993a): 1–14.
———. "U. S. Teacher Education Reforms: Regulatory Practices of the State, University, and Research." In *Changing Patterns of Power: Social Regulation and Teacher Education Reform,* ed. T. Popkewitz. Albany: State University of New York Press, 1993b, pp. 263–302.
———. *The Denial of Change in the Process of Change: Systems of Ideas and the Construction of National Evaluations.* Oslo, Norway: Norwegian Royal Ministry of Church, Education and Research, in press.

Popkewitz, T. & M. Brennan. "Restructuring Social and Political Theory: Foucault, the Linguistic Turn and Education." In *Foucault's Challenge: Discourse, Knowledge and Power in Education*, ed. T. Popkewitz and M. Brennan. New York: Teachers College Press, 1998, pp. 3–35.

Rose, N. & P. Miller. "Political Power beyond the State: Problematics of Government." *British Journal of Sociology* 43 (1992): 173–205.

Shapiro, M. *Reading the Postmodern Polity: Political Theory as Textual Practice*. Minneapolis: University of Minnesota Press, 1992.

Sousa Santos, B. *Toward a New Common Sense: Law, Science and Politics in the Paradigmatic Transition*. New York: Routledge, 1995.

Wagner, P. *Sociology of Modernity: Liberty and Discipline*. New York: Routlege, 1994.

Wallerstein, I. *Unthinking Social Science: The Limits of Nineteenth-Century Paradigms*. Cambridge, UK: Polity Press. 1991.

Young, R. *White Mythologies: Writing History and the West*. New York: Routledge, 1990.

Zakaria, F. "Bigger Than the Family, Smaller Than the State: Are Voluntary Groups What Make Countries Work?" *The New York Times' Book Review*, August 13, 1995. Section 7, pp. 1 & 25.

Zerubavel, E. *The Fine Line: Making Distinctions in Everyday Life*. Chicago: University of Chicago Press, 1993.

CHAPTER 9

From the "People's Home"—*Folkhemmet*—to the Enterprise

Reflections on the Constitution and Reconstitution of the Field of Early Childhood Pedagogy in Sweden

GUNILLA DAHLBERG

From the 1930s until the late 1970s, one can observe how the picture of an embodied modernity in the Swedish context has contained *a political rationality*, which was exhibited by a language of a *centralized* and *rule-governed* welfare state, and which was explicitly or implicitly supported by the metaphor of *Folkhemmet*—the "People's Home." During the late 1970s a rupture took place, in which this political rationality was exchanged for a rationality dominated by a terminology such as *decentralization* and *goal governing*, and explicitly or implicitly supported by the metaphors of the *market* and the *enterprise* (Dahlberg, et al., 1991).[1]

By moving from the political and pedagogical discourses of the 1930s to the present, the following analysis illustrates how this rupture can be identified in the field of early childhood pedagogy—in its institutions and in the ways specific identities of the Swedish preschool child and preschool teacher have been constituted and reconstituted throughout this period. Generally speaking, the analysis shows how the rupture meant a major shift from an understanding of the field as a central part of the construction of a *spirit of community*—a common good—to an understanding of the field as a *market*—and as a matter of freedom of choice and as a service for the customers.

The analysis draws on several studies, and it is placed within a theoretical context which Foucault called *governmentality*. In Foucault's thinking (1988, 1991a), governmentality is a type of *political rationality,* and according to him the concept of government can provide a way to analyze the shifting ambitions of all social authorities that have sought to administer and govern our minds and lives. Foucault and other researchers drawing on the perspective of governmentality have been interested in studying technologies of power that aim at integrating individuals into a political totality, resulting in an increasing individualization and the reinforcement of this totality. Thereby, each individual becomes, on the one hand, both a subject and an object to her/himself and, on the other hand, she/he becomes a significant element of the State and an object of state concern.[2]

Modernist Visions of Building a Progressively Better Society

A central question in the analysis is how the field of early childhood pedagogy became an object of State concern and intervention and thus subjected to a certain kind of political rationality. This question can be placed in the context of the process of modernization and in relation to modernist visions and revisions of building a progressively better society, an improved human race, and freer individuals. In this project the child was given a key role, and many researchers have shown how the metanarrative of progress coincides with the vison of "the child as futurity" (see, e.g., Hultqvist, 1990; Jencks, 1994). On the basis of Rousseau's ideas, during the nineteenth century the child became a project and a symbol for the future in the endeavor of creating a better society and a new societal community. The child became "the seed of our future," as Fröbel put it.[3] This also applied in the Swedish context.[4] Ellen Key, the influential and controversial Swedish thinker who was driven by a strong developmental optimism based on Darwin's evolutionary theory, envisioned in *The Century of the Child* the twentieth century as the century when the child, through methods of self-regulation and self-discipline, would be liberated from the external constraints of tradition and prescriptions of religious authorities (Key, 1927).

The kindergarten movement can be seen as emerging from this liberal ambition of relieving the child from old boundaries and reembedding her/him in a new social world. However, the movement must also be understood in relation to the moral crisis, which followed the processes of industrialization and urbanization at the end of the nineteenth and early twentieth century. In this process of social transformation the family was seen as an institution on the verge of a breakdown, and a concern for children in relation to the demoralizing effects and disintegrative tendencies of the street arose. As this transformation was seen as a threat to the moral order of the society and to the spirit of community, the child and childhood also became a social problem for the modern State (Hultqvist, 1990; Sandin, 1986). The State now saw a possibility to reestablish the moral order and the spirit of community, through the upbringing of the next generation in some form of institution—the kindergarten—an upbringing which obviously was related to a reorganization of the working-class family.

In light of the above, the development of *Folkbarnträdgården*—kindergarten for the children of the people—can be seen. *Folkbarnträdgården* was the form of institution that later came to be at the center of interest for the State, and the first institution was opened in 1904 in the city of Norrköping by two sisters: Ellen and Maria Moberg. The Moberg sisters had an explicit social perspective, with a strong class-compensational and class-educational view. In their view the poor child would be compensated within the framework of the kindergarten, and the kindergarten would function as the educational link to the working-class home. "Bourgeois happiness for working-class children" was the idea behind their kindergarten, states Hatje (1990). The working-class child was to be exposed to middle-class ideals and values. Backed up with home visits and educational meetings for mothers, the working-class family would also would be transformed into a more morally superior unit of society.

Despite Ellen Key's strong deprecation of kindergartens, the pioneers of the kindergarten movement, such as the Moberg sisters, made use of her contemporary notions of women's distinctive character in their construction of the field of early childhood pedagogy. On the basis of biology and evolutionary theory, Key stressed the idea that women should have the same value as men, but with separate and different duties. In this context the social and pedagogical field opened up a new arena for bourgois women, as they were seen as morally superior, which made them especially suitable to be central figures in the kindergartens and in the project of turning the home of the poor into a clean and moralized home. In this moral project children were to be taught good habits, cleanliness, honesty, helpfulness, and the love of God, nature, and patriotism, with mild authority. Backed up with home visits and educational meetings for mothers, the influence of the children would also transform the working-class family, and through this the working-class family would be relinked into the community (Hatje, 1990; Rose, 1996).

The pioneers of the kindergarten made up only one group that engaged themselves in trying to find new strategies for governing the poor family into the moral family. Philantropists, doctors, and others were also engaged in the project of maintaining morality, public health, and hygiene. Together these people also became central bearers of a scientific discourse built on medicine, psychology, antropology, and sociology, which developed around the child, and especially around the poor child, in Sweden and in other countries (Ohrlander, 1992; Rose, 1996). In this sense, the endeavors of the pioneers of the kindergarten movement to build an early childhood pedagogy *for the sake of the child* also became part of a political rationality that would construct a field of pedagogical and social work around a scientifically objectified and classified child. Through measuring, weighing, and diagnosing huge groups of children and judging the results in relation to scientific knowledge, norms could be set for the best way of bringing children up, and those children that did not meet the standards could be identified.

Foucault (1990) has called this a *process of normalization,* and he sees it as an important historical outcome of *bio-power,* or the power over life. He argues that in the development of bio-power we can see the growing importance of a power to quantify, measure, appraise, and hierarchize according to the norm. This scientific construction of the child through a discourse of development "is not a matter of uncovering a set of empirical facts of epistemological truths which stand outside, or prior to, the conditions of their production. In this sense developmental (as other) psychology is productive; its positive effects lie in its production of practices of science and pedagogy" (Walkerdine, 1984, p. 163). Besides producing an abstract and universal child, this produced a mentality where children's behavior was interpreted in terms of a norm. Even if the intention was not to divide children into categories such as normal and unnormal, the objectively "normal child" set the standard within the early childhood pedagogy context and the "unnormal" child became an object of intervention by professionals. Accordingly the empirical sciences helped to demonstrate how social institutions could function in an objective and nonnormative way. The objectively "normal child and normal teacher" was the child and teacher in accordance with the normal distribution, a normal distribution that could set the standard within early childhood education.

The Birth of a Discourse of a Comprehensive Early Childhood Pedagogy

The 1930s opened up a discourse of a comprehensive early childhood pedagogy—a discourse that became an important part of the choreography of a political rationality holding modernist visions and revisions of a better society. Through a policy of redistribution of income combined with general welfare services, the aim was to establish freedom and emancipation as well as solidarity between different social groups. To turn Sweden into a modern welfare state major sociopolitical reforms were needed in which a reconstruction of the traditional communal structures could be made and new institutions could be built. The state as an organizer, which could express and transmit the objectively proper life, or *police life,* as Hirdman (1990) has expressed it, thenceforth acquired a very decisive meaning for the development of all public institutions in Sweden.

To represent society as a large community and to construct a spirit of community, Per Albin Hansson, the Social Democratic prime minister at that time, used the metaphor of the "People's Home" (*Folkhemmet*).[5] The metaphor or representation of the People's Home, became the leading metaphor for many different projects in Sweden during this period and until the late 1970s. The representation must be seen as highly relational and contextual. The People's Home was a society marked by solidarity and equality, as well as one in which decisions and plans were based on reason and science. The symbolic practice of Folkhemmet could be incorporated into the discourse of a comprehensive early childhood pedagogy system, as the kindergarten movement was strongly supported by many people in the government policy arena. In this context Alva Myrdal's writings were important.[6] As a reaction against philantropic, moral, and essentialistic notions, and by building on an idea of *gender equality* as an organizing principle of the field, Alva Myrdal argued for women doing their share in public life during child-bearing years. In *City Children* (*Stadsbarn*), she visualized the preschool or the *"enlarged nursery of the home"* (*Storbarnkammaren*), as she termed it, as a model for the home. In her thoughts, *enlarged* implied the enlargement of society with a new institution in the very heart of community.

Although only a few enlarged nurseries of the home were actually built in Sweden during this period, the ideas behind them have been important for the construction of the child and the field of early childhood pedagogy during the twentieth century. The enlarged nursery of the home emerged as a symbol of a new social and cultural space—a link and a meeting place between the child, home, and society (Dahlberg & Lenz Taguchi, 1994; Hatje, 1990; Hultqvist, 1990). In this process the God, King, and the Country were replaced by Science, Social Policy, and the People's Home. Albeit simplified, one can argue that Alva Myrdal broke with God, morals, and authoritarian duty and allied herself with social policy and the social sciences. Tallberg Broman (1991, 1994) comments that the thoughts and the actions were no longer to be directed by faith and traditionalism, but by reason and scientific knowledge.

Developmental psychology was an important instrument in this strategy, in which the child is supposed to bring her/himself in agreement with social normativity, universality, and the principle of reason. To use a concept from Foucault (1980), one could say that from then on developmental psychology and a child-centered pedagogy became a form of *discursive regime of truth,* which governed what was seen as important to do in practice, but also what could be thought and said or not thought and said about children.

We can now focus on the central aspect of *governmentality* as revealing the *missionary* role of science in society as a whole (Popkewitz, 1990; see also, Kliebard, 1986). In Folkhemmet, the field of early childhood pedagogy and the preschool teachers formed a symbiosis with the State, science, and technology. To legitimize their endeavors, the advocates of Folkhemmmet referred to natural laws of science, statistical mean values, and psychological, objective truths about human development—a strategy that was later manifested in the notion of social engineering (Hirdman, 1990).

We here find the close relation of the knowledge of social engineering and the constitution of politics. In this process the professions, for example the kindergarten teachers, have played a significant role by rendering the complexities of modern social life knowable and amenable to governing. According to Johnson (1993, p. 151), by the identification of new social problems with the construction of the means for solving them, and staffing the organizations created to cope with these problems, teachers have become "socio-technical devices through which the means and even the ends of government are articulated."

We have also seen how a changing discourse and practice of government coupled with new metaphors opened up a new space—a social room in which the child would be liberated from the moral discourse and introduced into the more social discourse of developmental and social psychology (Hultqvist, 1990). This change in the strategies of governing also changed the image of the child and the preschool teacher from morally obedient individuals equipped with a moral agency into socially responsible individuals equipped with a social agency (see also Rose, 1996).

However, it is important to note that the field of early childhood pedagogy was only one brick in this wider societal construction, where the political rationality was based on a form of power Foucault (1990) has named "bio-power," or the power over life. Foucault (1980) states that the true object of this form of power is the *population* and the care of people as a population. An illustrative example of bio-power is the form of State policy that followed after the publication of Alva and Gunnar Myrdals's *Crisis in the Population Question* (*Kris i befolkningsfrågan*) (Myrdal & Myrdal, 1934). In this book one can see how falling birthrates in the whole population could be tied to Alva Myrdal's vision of building enough nurseries that every working mother could make use of them, and a rising birthrate could follow. This vision contributed both to a rising birthrate, a rate which still is very high compared to many other European countries, and to the birth of a discourse of a comprehensive early childhood pedagogy.[7]

The Field of Early Childhood Pedagogy as an Encounter Between the Private and the Public

In retrospective, the Folkbarnträdgården and the enlarged nursery of the home, and their later counterparts, can be understood as an important first step in the construction of what Hultqvist (1990) calls *gemenskapsbygget* (the building of a spirit of community). In this construction, Folkbarnträdgården and the enlarged nursery of the home became components of a rapidly developing social network of institutions and social relations, which incorporated everything from the woman and the family to the system of modern institutions and the State.

This rapidly growing network of institutions and social relations can be said to form the "Social," to use a concept coined by Donzelot (1979). From Donzelot's point of view the Social cannot be seen as a result of a private or a public initiative, but constitutes a hybrid between the private and the public.[8] According to this concept, the field of early childhood pedagogy came to constitute an important arena for the building of a spirit of community— *gemenskapsbygget*—symbolized in the metaphor of Folkhemmet.

From our presentation we have seen how the link between the public and the private is embodied in the discourse about the home (Dahlberg & Lenz Taguchi, 1994). Lenz Taguchi (1996) has argued that the discourse of the home marks a preschool setting that can be comprehended as a "professional home." In her view it symbolizes the important link between the individual and the State and can be seen as an active incorporation and blending of discourses connecting the family and the private into discourses concerning the Social and the public. This is also reflected in the way these institutions are named: *storbarnkammaren* (the enlarged nursery of the home), *daghem* (day homes), and *barnstugor* (children houses), with *syskongrupper* (sibling groups).

Hultqvist (1990) has interpreted this process as a new *social paradigm*, understood from the viewpoint of methods of regulation and intervention concerning the life of individuals, social groups, and classes. What Hultqvist is referring to is the art of government—governmentality—which implies a constant correlation between an increasing individualization and totalization.

In this process, the child was seen more and more as an individual with different needs. At the same time, the child became a societal investment for the future. The child became both *individualized* and *socialized* at the same time.

In this context the metaphor of Folkhemmet—the People's Home—together with concepts such as the enlarged nursery of the home, day homes, children houses, and sibling groups, became important representations and mechanisms of translation between the general and the particular, between the national and the social, and between the economic and personal life of the individual. In this respect, binding symbols and representations of the people, the interest of the nation and the home together, was a technique that made the world, on the one hand, intelligible and, on the other hand, manageable as an object for intervention. The role of language, as we have seen, has been important in this process. I agree with Miller and Rose when they argue:

For it is in language that *programmes of government* are elaborated, and through which consonance is established between the broadly specified ethical, epistemological and ontological appeals of political discourse—to the nation, to virtue, to what is or is not possible or desireable—and the plans, schemes and objectives that seek to adress specific problematizations within social, economic or personal existence. (1993, p. 8)

From the above we can see how the pioneers of the field constructed a field of pedagogical and social work around discourses of the *essential gender equality*. These discourses bear upon strong conceptions of female emancipation and, as Donzelot (1979) has argued in relation to the emergence of the Social, the increase in women's domestic power would give her access to public life. Thereby the field also became the springboard that women needed for the recognition of their political rights. Although women in this process gained political access, we have to observe that the discourses of *gender difference* and *equality*—which were used by the pioneers in the field of early childhood education in their struggle—share a dualistic and bipolar conception of human life. This implies that a choice between equality of the sexes or the maintenance of gender difference remain in the same paradigm. This is a paradigm entrenched in the thought of a dualistic philosophy, where mind is opposed to body and culture to nature (Gatens, 1991; Lenz Taguchi, 1996).

A Period of Centralization and Rule Governing

By the mid 1960s there was a broad consensus among political parties around the idea of building a national preschool system governed by ideological, economical, and juridical rules effectuated by an effective bureaucracy, creating national uniformity (Dahlberg, et al., 1991; Gustafson, 1994; Uddhammar, 1993).[9] This consensus was still supported via the representation of the nation as Folkhemmet and the metaphor of Folkhemmet was, during this period, taken almost as a social given, as a natural order, as it by now had become part of the cultural construction of bureaucratic practices.

A number of economic motives can be traced in this consensus. The growing requisites for labor and the related increase in women's gainful employment had brought about an increasing demand for child care, and in 1968 the government appointed a Child Care Committee (see, e.g., SOU, 1972:26 and 27), which had as its purpose to fuse the more pedagogically oriented part-time preschool, which had developed out of the kindergarten tradition, and the crèches, which had developed from the more socially oriented institutions. The *preschool*, the concept used for this fusion, should, thence forward, be a sociopolitical resource for equalizing differences in children's living conditions and should give "the families and the children economical security" (SOU, 1972:27, s. 13).

The Abstracted and Decontextualized Child

From the start, the Child Care Committee concentrated their efforts on questions related both to the fact that children from all social classes were supposed to be integrated in the same preschool and to the awareness that a modern society had to transgress traditional authority. The shift into a comprehensive and nontraditional preschool, with its rhetoric of democracy and equality, can also be traced in changing discourses of the child and pedagogy. In the committee report a traditional, adult-governed pedagogy, as well as a more adult-passive Gesellian-influenced pedagogy, were dismissed, and an idea of a *dialogue pedagogy* as a construction for the relationship between children and adults, and between the child and the surrounding world, was introduced (SOU, 1972:26, p. 43). Accordingly, the idea of integration and the problematic between freedom and coercion, and between autonomy and *gemeinshaft*, could be choreographed by a discourse of a human dialogue. Hultqvist (1990) has argued that the dialogue pedagogy is a construction for interpersonal relations, a social-psychological construction, for the human encounter in the Social, to use Donzelot's idea of the fusion between the home, the private, and the State. Accordingly the *preschool child* and the *preschool teacher* of the Child Care Committee were fellow beings, who were supposed to embody both private and national considerations.

By introducing Piaget's constructivist theoretical approach and Homburger Erikson's theory to administer this new institution and pedagogy of the State, it was possible to deal with the political consensus that had been gained for this large-scale reform strategy and implementation. By focusing on, for example, Piaget's stage theory with its universal structures and operation, social institutions could be demonstrated to function in an objective way. These theories were also strategically seen as radical and progressive and as functioning with legitimate ideas and actions for expanding freedom and liberty (Dahlberg, 1985).

Although these theories presuppose an active interaction between the individual and the surrounding world, by rendering children's social and cultural experiences and position in society to psychological theories, the preschool child became abstracted and decontextualized (Dahlberg, 1985). Instead of a pedagogy viewing the child as constituted in a cultural and social context, the dialogue pedagogy was still adapted to processes of development that were supposed to be inherent in the nature of the child—as universal laws. Selander writes:

> As an ideology the dialogue pedagogy was rather free floating in relation to actual conditions in economy, different social classes in the educational system etc. Seldom was the dialogue pedagogy related to existing framefactors or to prevailing traditions, with the present transformations in society or to the expansion of the educational system. The dialogue pedagogy was an idea concerning the relation between human beings and an ideology concerning change. What should be changed was rather diffuse. (1984, p. 170, my translation)

However, as seen above, the committee had an ambition to break the normalizing discourse of developmental psychology and its accompanying normalized child and teacher and to construct a more socially capable child and teacher who could embody both private and national considerations. There are also discourses in the committee reports that are in opposition to the universal and abstract discourse that was formalized through science and then, especially, psychology. Instead of practices constituting the universal and abstract child, there have been practices that have competed with this dominant discourse by placing the child into a social context. Such discourses are obvious in the Child Care Committee reports. In one of the reports (see, e.g., SOU, 1975:67, p. 340), there is a strong recognition of how the growth of child psychology can be interconnected with the growth of scientific classifications and, as such, result in "the statistically average child" produced by behaviorism.

A Process of Reconstruction

The political rationality that took shape in the first half of this century is now being displaced. As in many other countries during the late 1970s and early 1980s, it became obvious that the reform strategy toward unity through rational planning from above, also contained programs and technologies characterized by standardization and normalization of human activities. When these strategies were no longer defined as appropriate, the idea of the State as an organizer that could govern and regulate the life and behavior of individuals and groups—*policing the lives of individuals* toward a better society for all—began to dissolve. Sweden now entered a period of cognitive uncertainty in relation both to the role of the State and to public intervention from above, as well as in relation to the belief in social progress that had been at the core of modernity.

This rupture is exemplified in the arena of early childhood pedagogy through an official program that was adopted in 1987 (Allmänna Råd, 1987, p. 3). Compared to the reports from the 1968 Child Care Committee, which consisted of several extensive reports followed by governmental implementations, this new program was a very "thin" product and was not followed up by governmental implementation.

The political rationality related to a discourse of centralization and rule governing was now exchanged for a discourse of *decentralization* and *goal governing,* and hence promoting a new distribution of responsibilites between the individual, society, and the State (Dahlberg et al., 1991). In the goal-governing strategy the former rules and the relatively detailed plans are replaced by clear goals and strategies for evaluation of goal attainment. To support such a strategy of governing, the program is worked out as an administrative program with the purpose of regulating the responsibilities between different levels of the political and the administrative system.

A Political Rationality Supported by the Metaphors of the Market and the Enterprise

It is obvious that the discursive practices of this new reform, implying changing patterns of regulation, meant a deplacement of the historically constructed ways of reasoning that took shape in the first half of this century and culminated in the sixties. This discourse has been supported by new representations and metaphors. In the same way that Folkhemmet functioned as a valid symbolic practice for the relationship between the individual and the society, the *market* and the *enterprise* now seem to have come to function as valid symbolic metaphors and practices.[10] This has challenged existing categories and classifications and opened up a new space. The language of the market and the enterprise signals a shift in early childhood pedagogy from a common good to a service for the customers. Citizenship no longer seems to be construed in the language of solidarity, welfare, and security, but in the language of free personal choice and self realization, something which earlier would have disturbed the symbolic order and been interpreted as politically inappropriate.

To establish efficiency and productivity and to regulate supply and demand, a totally new form of organization has been established at the local level. The local authorities have now constructed an order and executed organization and, in the field of early childhood pedagogy, most preschools had been relabeled "production units" and heads of preschools have been relabeled "preschool managers." In relation to the above one can here argue that the representations of the market and the enterprise have rendered the field of early childhood pedagogy to be conceptualized and manageable in a new way. These representations have come to function as a form of intellectual technology by constituting new sectors of reality and making new fields practicable.

Freedom of Choice and the Shaping of Distinctive Profiles

In relation to these changes, Sweden is facing profound reconstructions. The preschool is seen as sucessful if it can promote *freedom of choice* while also promoting proliferation and differentiation. Efficiency is now increasingly related to the number of different profiles of preschools the local authorities can offer, as well as to how large a percentage are turned into private preschools during a fixed time interval.

This opens up a new space—a space building on the idea of creating a rationality of autonomy by marketing and image construction. For example, before the mid-eighties, very few preschools had brochures for their programs. Today, many preschools have lavish brochures and are producing exhibitions to explain and legitimize why their pedagogical approach should be chosen over other programs available on the market.[11] As a consequence, the "traditional Swedish preshool model" is getting true competition from other approaches, such as the Montessori, the Reggio Emilia, the Waldorf, and environmental preschools. The market idea also implies competition, and preschools that do not have sufficient *customers* have to close down. The old idea of building the system on solidarity between preschools in the area, where staff connected to local authorities would support centers that were not functioning well, is in dissolution. The preschool is no longer an enterprise of moral and social commitment as the exercise of the market becomes the moral domain of public and private choice.

The Entrepreneural Teacher and the Entrepreneural Child

The reshaping of the field of early childhood pedagogy into a market and the preschool into an enterprise has been followed by a reshaping of the identities of the preschool teacher and the preschool child—for example, what it means to be a preschool teacher and a preschool child in these institutions. Preschool teachers are now seen as *enterprising individuals* running their own businesses, as a result of being seen as freed from the regulations and constraints of the former centralized system. In this view, to be productive is symbolized and understood as being goal oriented, not following fixed rules, being self-reliant—and of choosing a distinctive pedagogical approach. It is also obvious that the preschool teachers are seen as active, not only in the shaping of their own identities but also as shapers of the prerequisities for children's self-realization. That is, the self-realizing preschool teacher is to become the facilitator for the creation of the self-governing and self-realizing child—a child who is supposed to manage her/himself by constructing her/his own biography and identity outside the binding codes of religion and legal authorities.

Children's parents are also involved in these processes. By choosing a preschool with a special meaning for themselves, parents show that they have chosen something specific, something which can tell them who they are or who they want their children to become. Providing choice with a personal meaning is to promote an image of construction, while at the same time symbolizing that one is preparing one's child for a career.

The entrepreneurial teacher is also a teacher who likes and is committed to her/his work and is guided, as Wagner (1994, p. 99) has expressed it, "by the phantasies of efficiency and dreams of pleasure."

These new identities of the child and the teacher correspond to changes occuring in the business field. As in many other countries, Sweden in the eighties reformed the corporate structure by doing away with middle mangement in an attempt to reduce the hierachical structure. Today, a decade later, this change is further developed into managing work as an element in a personal project of self-fulfillment and self-actualization.

One can wonder, Why has the language of the enterprise become so significant in recent years? Drawing on Gordon's work, Miller and Rose (1993) give a reasonable answer that is in agreement with the current analysis. They argue that the language of enterprise enables a translatability between the most general, a priori assumptions of political thought and a range of specific programs for administering the national economy, the internal world of the firm, and a whole host of other organizations from the school to the hospital. They also argue that these programs bestow a new priority to the self-regulating capacities of individuals by forming new relations between the economic health of the nation and the private choice of the individual.

New Regulative Devices

At one level, there seems to be an expanding space that is opened for teachers and children through this new political rationality. The strategy of goal governing and freedom of choice, however, also pushes forward new modes of regulation and new modes of administering the population. The form of manageability that had been developed in the postwar period—was administered mainly through rules and strong administrative departments—is now displaced by governing through goals and through an institutionalization of different practices such as management consultation, guidance, and evaluation (Dahlberg and Åsén, 1992). In relation to this, the role of the expert has also changed into more of a counselor and tutor, a person who can pose new questions and open up new explorations.

In order to create new conditions for an organization built on "demand and supply" and on teachers and children's self-realizing and self-governing capacities, educational leaders in the early childhood pedagogy system at the local level and in preschools have been involved in leadership and management courses. Since parents are given responsibility for their choice of preschools, to a greater extent evaluations of *the consumer's* satisfaction have also been carried out by almost all local authorities.[12] In this process one could say that parents are transformed into consumers and inculcated with certain attitudes and values of enterprise (Rose, 1996).

Accordingly, evaluation strategies and management courses can be seen as organizing devices and interventions, functioning as a form of policy making (Dahlberg et. al., 1991; Dahlberg and Åsen, 1994). This is in agreement with Popkewitz's (1990) argument that evaluation in the modern state takes on a policing quality, whether we see it as part of the noble intent and desire of those who seek to improve schools or as part of a strategy of regulation.[13]

Practicing Freedom

A strong idea behind the Swedish welfare politics has been the endeavor to support children and women and to create a more modern and democratic life, while at the same time producing national wealth. However, it is obvious that this intention, or arts of government, has been inscribed in modernist and liberal ideas of progress, universality, and dualism. From the above presentation it is also obvious that the arts of government has been linked to the practice of freedom. The historical analysis has illustrated how the field of early childhood education and institutions, such as Folkbarnträdgården and its later counter-parts, can be seen as important sites, as a space in which the exercise of different ideas of freedom and civility has been brought into play. Freedom both as an ideal, as articulated in struggles of resistance against power, and also freedom in a Foucaultian sense, as a mode of organizing and regulation and as a certain way of administering a population that depends on the capacities of free individuals. Rose (1996) states that freedom in this Foucaultian sense is a form of power, which is articulated into norms and principles for organizing our experience of the world and of ourselves. This is a form of freedom other than freedom as a formula of resistance. From this perspective of freedom liberalism can be viewed as an art of government, and in a liberal society we have to act on ourselves as both free and responsible and as being part of liberty as well as members of a society. According to this, techniques for self-mastery can be seen simultaneously as techniques for instituting sociality.

The present analysis has shown how new rationalities and technologies of governing constitute new modes of administering how we have acted on ourselves, or been acted upon by others, and in the wish to be free (see further, Rose). Shifts in the art of government also imply shifts in identities and in the way we understand ourselves and the world. In the nineteenth century and in the beginning of this century—in a space that had become more and more unstable and complex and where the family had lost many of its former functions, the reformatory strategy, or formula of government— was to invent conditions that would enable the child and the preschool teacher to take responsibilities through a moral agency. In the 1930s, and after World War II, the technologies of government became more and more linked to the idea of a "spirit of community" symbolized by the representation of the People's Home. Through the recreation of a lost community and through ensuring equality and economic growth, the child became part of the project of handling the individual and the national together. The child and the teacher became social agents in a social room.

For a couple of decades it has seemed that we now live in a period of changing discourses and practices of government, a new choreography of political rationality. This rationality has challenged the welfare state through the reshaping of the field of early chidlhood education into a market and the preschool into an enterprise, followed by a reshaping of the child and the preschool teacher into self-governing and self-realizing individuals. The problem of freedom now comes to be understood in terms of the capacity of an autonomous individual to establish an identity through acts of choice, in the market of different pedagogical approaches and preschools. This transformation has led Foucaultian thinkers to argue that the postmodern individual is free not only to choose to be free, but also *obliged to be free*, and to understand and enact their lives in terms of choice (Rose, 1996). Hultqvist argues that today's children and adults become burdened with the *duty of freedom* (Hultqvist, 1995). Or with the words of Rose:

> The ethical regime that we call freedom is thus a double-edged achievement. We have been freed from the arbitrary prescriptions of religious and political authorities, thus allowing a range of different answers to the question of how we should live. On the other hand, we have been bound into relationship with new authorities, which are more profoundly subjectifying because they appear to emanate from our individual desires to fulfill ourselves in our everyday lives, to craft our personalities, to discover who we really are. (Rose, 1996, p. 20)

We have earlier described how science and the professionals have been key resources in modern forms of government and have contributed to the game of identity construction through placing universal norms over children's and parent's behavior according to the normal distribution and shaping of the "normal child" and the "normal preschool teacher." In a postmodern or neoliberalistic society, freedom, according to Rose (1996), is also enacted through the reliance on experts. However, the enactment of freedom requires another role of the expert. It requires an expert who is more of an adviser or a mentor, and who can enable people to be governed and to govern themselves, in terms of their identity (see also, Giddens, 1991).

A New Becoming?

As this new situation opens up totally new discourses, reclassifications, and reorganizations of the relation between power and knowledge, its political implications need to be scrutinized and problematized in relation to changing patterns of governing. As a consequence of this, we must formulate new questions concerning rules of inclusion and exclusion. Questions such as For whom will these new practices create a greater freedom and choice? Who will be authorized to speak and who will have the resources to practice them?[14] What kind of ethical relationship to ourselves and to the world does this change open up? Are there ways of organizing and practicing our relationship to ourselves and the world other than the ones at the same time described above? And are there other ways to understand ourselves?

The deconstruction outlined above may be helpful in the process of problematizing these new strategies and the practices that they entail in our present. As well as indicating the arbitrariness of different fields and institutions, it can show us other ways of practicing our relationship to ourselves and the world. This can open up a new space for reconstituting the field of early childhood pedagogy.[15] As Foucault expounds:

> It seems to me that the real political task in a society such as ours is to criticize the working of institutions which appear to be both neutral and independent; to criticize them in such a manner that the political violence which has always exercised itself obscurely through them will be unmasked so that one can fight them. (1991a, p. 6)

Notes

1. An interesting analysis of this development is also given by Hultqvist, 1995.

2. Recent research with a focus on governmentality has shown that over the last two centuries, complex procedures of representation and intervention have been developed to establish manageability and intelligibility of the social world. See, e.g., Gordon, 1991.

3. See, e.g., Johansson and Astedt, 1993.

4. For an analysis of how the idea of the child as a project for the future became a supporting discourse for the development of the Swedish preschool, see, e.g., Hultzvist, 1990.

5. The metaphor of the *Volksheim*, or the People's Home, was also used in programs in many other countries, but to a highly varying degree and with different meaning in different contexts. However, according to Wagner (1994), the programs, practices, and the metaphors used, all restricted the notion of individual liberty in the name of a collectivity.

6. Alva Myrdal was a well-known Swedish social democratic politician and in the thirties and forties she was head of a social-pedagogical seminar. She was also head of the U.N. department of social questions and head of UNESCO's department of social science in the fifties. She was married to Gunnar Myrdal, another well-known Swedish social democratic politician and national economist.

7. Between 1965 and 1990, the number of children in full-day preschool settings increased from 10,000 to 250,000 (Johansson, 1992, p. 17).

8. The network of institutions and social relations Donzelot called "the Social" sprung from an interaction between discourse of law and administration, wealth and poverty, the city and the countryside, medicine and science, the family and the school (Donzelot, 1979, pp. xxiii–xxiii).

9. The first decision to give State support to the preschools was handed down in 1943, but this decision did not result in any expansion of the early childhood education system.

10. Even though Sweden has not gone as far as Britain in respect to profit, this shift resembles much of what happened in England during the Thatcher era. Miller and Rose (1993) have argued that Britain became exemplary for the reorientations occurring in the Northern hemisphere.

11. In practice these preschools, in general, do not differ to any great extent from the pedagogical approach that can be called "a traditional Swedish model." However, their significance must be seen in relation to the new emerging rationality of government.

12. In relation to this process of change, the Board of Social Welfare and the National Agency for Education have new assignments, being changed into informative and evaluating authorities, with their own departments of evaluation.

13. From a perspective other than the one presented here, Weiler (1990) has argued that the control which the process of decentralization gives away with one hand, evaluation may take back. He discusses this phenomena as the paradox of decentralization.

14. For an interesting discussion in relation to this question, see further, Fraser (1989).

15. Handelman (in Herzfeld, 1992), in an argument derived largely from his reading of Foucault, has shown how new bureacratic classifications and taxonomies were not necessarily more logical than those that preceded them. According to his study they were calibrated to the need of certain institutional structures, and became instruments of power and surveillance that could be used quite variably by differently situated actors.

References

Allmänna råd från Socialstyrelsen (1987): 3. Pedagogiskt program för förskolan. (Public Advice from the Board of Social Welfare (1987): 3. Pedagogical Program for the Preschool). Stockholm: Allmänna Förlaget.

Dahlberg, G. "Context and the Child's Orientation to Meaning: A Study of the Child's Way of Organizing the Surrounding World in Relation to Public Institutionalized Socialization." Studies in Curriculum Theory and Cultural Reproduction/ 12. Stockholm Institute of Education. Department of Educational Research, 1985.

Dahlberg, G., U. P. Lundgren & G. Åsén. *Att utvärdera barnomsorg (Evaluating Early Childhood Education)*. Stockholm: HLS Förlag, 1991.

Dahlberg, G. & G. Åsén. "Mot vad leds barnomsorgen?" ("Toward What Is Early Childhood Education Headed?). *Locus* 2 (1992): 7–17.

————. "Evaluation and Regulation: A Question of Empowerment." In *Valuing Quality in Early Childhood Services*, ed. by P. Moss and A. Pence. London: Paul Chapman, 1994, pp. 157–71.

Dahlberg, G. & H. Lenz Taguchi. *Förskola och skola—om två skilda traditioner och om visionen om en mötesplats (Preschool and School—Two Different Traditions and a Vison of an Encounter)*. Stockholm: HLS Förlag, 1994.

Donzelot, J. *The Policing of Families*. London: Hutchinson, 1979.

Foucault, M. "The Subject and Power." In Michel Foucault, *Beyond Structuralism and Hermeneutics*, ed. H. L. Dreyfus and P. Rabinow. New York: Harvester Wheatsheaf, 1982, pp. 208–26.

——. *Technologies of the Self: A Seminar with Michel Foucault*. Amherst, MA: University of Massachusetts Press, 1988.

——. *The History of Sexuality*. Volume 1: *An Introduction*. New York: Penguin, 1990.

——. "Governmentality." In *The Foucault Effect: Studies in Governmentality*, ed. G. Burcell, C. Gordon, and P. Miller. Chicago: University of Chicago Press, 1991, pp. 87–104.

Fraser, N. *Unruly Practices: Power, Discourse and Gender in Contemporary Social Theory*. Minneapolis: University of Minnesota Press, 1989.

Gatens, M. *Feminism and Philosophy: Perspectives on Difference and Equality*. Cambridge: Polity Press, 1991.

Giddens, A. *Modernity and Self-Identity: Self and Society in the Late Modern Age*. Cambridge: Polity Press, 1991.

Gordon, C. "Governmental Rationality: An Introduction." In *The Foucault Effect: Studies in Governmentality*, ed. G. Burchell, C. Gordon, and P. Miller. Chicago: The University of Chicago Press, 1991, pp. 1–52.

Gustafson, S. "Childcare and Types of Welfare States." In *Gendering Welfare States*, ed. D. Sainsbury. London: Sage, 1994, pp. 45–61.

Hatje, A-K. "Borgerlig lycka åt arbetarbarn: Glimtar ur Ellen Keys och systrarna Mobergs tankevärld." ("Bourgeois Happiness for Working-Class Children: Glimpses from Ellen Key's and the Moberg Sister's World of Ideas"). In *Se barnet: Tankegångar från tre århundraden (See the Child: Ideas from Three Centuries)*, ed. G. Halldén. Stockholm: Rabén & Sjögren, 1990, pp. 115–145.

Herzfeld, M. *The Social Production of Indifference: Exploring the Symbolic Roots of Western Bureaucracy*. Chicago: University of Chicago Press, 1992.

Hirdman, Y. *Att lägga livet tillrätta—Studier i svensk folkhemspolitik (To Police Life—Studies In Swedish People's Home Policy)*. Stockholm: Carlssons, 1990.

Hultqvist, K. *Förskolebarnet: En konstruktion för gemenskapen och den individuella frigörelsen (The Swedish Preschool Child: A Construction for the Spirit of Community and Individual Freedom)*. Stockholm: Symposion, 1990.

——. "En nutidshistoria om barns välfärd" ("A History of the Present of Children's Welfare). In *Seendet och seendets villkor: En bok om barns och ungas väldfärd (The Seeing and the Conditions of Seeing: A Book of Children's and Youngsters' Welfare)*, ed. L. Dahlgren and K. Hultqvist. Stockholm: HLS Förlag, 1995, pp. 141–61.

Jenks, C. "Child Abuse in the Postmodern Context: An Issue of Social Identity." *Childhood* 3 (1994): 111–21.

Johansson, J-E. *Metodikämnet i förskollärarutbildningen: Bidrag till en traditionsbestämning*. ACTA Universitatis Gothoburgensis, 1992.

Johansson, G. & I-B. Åstedt. *Förskolans utveckling—Fakta och funderingar (The Development of the Preschool—Facts and Thoughts)*. Stockholm: HLS Förlag, 1993.

Johnson, T. "Expertise and the State." In Foucault's *New Domains*, ed. M. Gane and T. Johnson. London: Routledge, 1993, pp. 139–52.

Key, E. *Barnets århundrade (The Century of the Child)*. Stockholm: Albert Bonniers Förlag, 1927.

Kliebard, H. *Struggle for the American Curriculum*. London: Routledge and Kegan Paul, 1986.

Lenz Taguchi, H. "The Field of Early Childhood Pedagogy in Sweden: A Female Project of Emancipation." *Nordiske Udkast* 1 (1996): 41–57.

Miller, P. & N. Rose. "Governing Economic Life." In Foucault's *New Domains*, ed. M. Gane and T. Johnson. London: Routledge, 1993, pp. 75–105.

Myrdal, A. *Stadsbarn: En bok om deras fostran i storbarnkammare (City Children: A Book about Their Upbringing in the Enlarged Nursery)*. Stockholm: Kooperativa förbundet, 1935.

Myrdal, A. & G. Myrdal. *Kris i befolkningsfrågan (Crisis in the Population Question)*. Stockholm: Bonniers, 1934.

Ohrlander, K. "I barnens och nationens intresse: Socialliberal reformpolitik 1903–1930" ("In the Interest of the Child and the Nation: Social Liberal Reform Politics 1903–1930). *Studies of Psychology and Education* nr 39. Stockholm: Almqvist & Wiksell International, 1992.

Popkewitz, T. "Some Problems and Problematics in the Production of Evaluation." In *Evaluation as Policymaking: Introducing Evaluation into a National Decentralized System*, ed. M. Granheim, M. Kogan, and U. P. Lundgren. London: Jessica Kingsley Publishers, 1990, pp. 103–19.

Rose, N. "Towards a Critical Sociology of Freedom." *Nordiske udkast* 1 (1996): 3–21.

Sandin, B. *Hemmet, gatan, fabriken och skolan (The Home, the Street and the School)*. Lund: Arkiv, 1986.

Selander, S. *Textum institutionis: Den pedagogiska väven (The Pedagogical Web)*. Stockholm: Gleerup, 1984.

SOU, 1972:26, 27. Förskolan del 1 och del 2. Betänkande från 1968 års barnstugeutredning. Stockholm: Allmänna Förlaget.

SOU, 1975:67. Utbildning i samspel (*Education in Cooperation*). Betänkande från 1968 års barnstugeutredning.

Tallberg Broman, I. *När arbetet var lönen: En kvinnohistorisk studie av barnträdgårdsledarinnan som folkuppfostrare (When the Work was the Salary. A Women-Historical Study of the Kindergarten Teacher as "Folkupbringer")*. Malmö: Almqvist & Wiksell International, 1991.

———. "För barnets skull"—En studie av förskolan som ett kvinnligt professionaliseringsprojekt ("For the Sake of the Child"—A Study of the Preschool as a Professionalization Project for Women). Lärarhögskolan vid Lunds Universitet, rapport 593, 1994.

Thurer, S. *The Myths of Motherhood—How Culture Reinvents the Good Mother*. London: Penguin, 1994.

Uddhammar, E. En analys av statsteorier och svensk politik under 1900-talet. (*An Analysis of Theories of the State and Swedish Politics during the Nineteenth Century*). Stockholm: City University Press, 1993.

Wagner, P. *A Sociology of Modernity: Liberty and Discipline*. London and New York: Routledge, 1994.

Walkerdine, V. "Developmental Psychology and the Child-Centered Pedagogy: The Insertion of Piaget into Early Education." In *Changing the Subject*, ed. J. Henriques et. al. London: Methuen, 1984, pp. 153–202.

Weiler, H. "Decentralization in Educational Governance: An Exercise in Contradiction?" In *Evaluation as Policymaking: Introducing Evaluation into a National Decentralized System*, ed. M. Granheim., M. Kogan, and U.P. Lundgren. London: Jessica Kingsley, 1990, pp. 42–66.

Governmentality in an Era of "Empowerment"

The Case of Tanzania

FRANCES VAVRUS

> I don't think that we should consider the "modern state" as
> an entity which was developed above individuals, ignoring
> what they are and even their very existence, but on the
> contrary as a very sophisticated structure in which individu-
> als can be integrated, under one condition: that this indi-
> viduality would be shaped in a new form, and submitted to
> a set of very specific patterns.
>
> —Michel Foucault, *The Subject and Power*

Most studies of education in the Third World draw upon either modernization or dependency theory to explain the relationship between schooling
and the State.[1] Theories of modernization suggest that the State consists of a
number of discrete subsystems that function to maintain a stable society. An
increase in the quantity and quality of skilled "human capital" through education is assumed to trigger modernization in other sectors of the State (Haddad,
1981; Psacharopoulos & Loxley, 1985; Welsh, 1985; World Bank, 1988).
Dependency theories, on the other hand, treat education in the Third World
as a product of global rather than local forces. It is argued that schooling in
the Third World can be explained by the cultural and economic dependency
of these states in the periphery of the capitalist world system (Altbach, 1982;
Arnove, 1982; Ramirez & Boli-Bennett, 1982).

Despite the large amount of research these two bodies of theory have
stimulated, neither modernization nor dependency can account for the present
disjunctures in the economic, educational, and political arenas of countries
throughout the Third World. The boundaries of the education subsystem, like

the cultural and economic borders of peripheral states, are increasingly "fractal"; that is, lacking the regularity, stability, and predictability that modernization and dependency would suggest (Appadurai, 1994, p. 337). Recognizing the fluidity of civil/state boundaries, Popkewitz argues in this volume for a notion of the state as "patterns of regulation" rather than as an entity set apart from civil society. From this perspective, one can study the historical patterns of regulations specific to a particular region while also looking at global forms of regulation as they become embodied in the subjectivities of actors in different yet overlapping social arenas.

In this chapter, I consider changes in the subjectivities of actors in one Third-World country—Tanzania—by examining shifts in local and global patterns of regulation around the issue of girls' schooling. In terms I will explicate below, I examine how commonsense beliefs about gender, education, and tradition have functioned historically to construct subjectivities for "experts"— teachers, government administrators, aid officials—and for the youth upon whom the expert gaze falls. The first section of the chapter, following the definition of terminology below, explores the historical trajectories of colonialism, Tanzanian socialism (*ujamaa*), and structural adjustment as they coalesce in the particular patterns of governing today. I provide this historical context as a way of situating the subjectivities of contemporary actors in the specific time-and-space nexus in which Tanzania is located. Second, I look at the subjectivities of today's national and international experts in the educational, political, and economic arenas in Tanzania, and I consider homologies—noncausal relationships—among these three arenas. The third section of this chapter examines experts' commonsense beliefs about gender and tradition, and how common sense gets enacted through the schooling practices designed by experts to "empower" Tanzanian school girls. I analyze the semantics of "empowerment" in two educational programs for girls in Tanzania as a way to "defamiliarize taken-for-granted beliefs in order to render them susceptible to critique" (Fraser & Gordon, 1994, pp. 310–11). My specific purpose in this chapter is to show how commonsense beliefs about *power/empowerment* and *African tradition* have operated historically to construct the subjectivities of experts and the social worlds they set out to reform.

Subjectivities, Arenas, and the State

In this section, I expound on the theoretical notions of *subjectivities, arenas,* and the *state* as used in this chapter to examine patterns of regulation in Tanzania. *Subjectivities* incorporates the notion that governing occurs on two intersecting planes: that of the individual and that of institutions. The subjectivities of individuals are those patterns of tastes, preferences, and sensibilities referred to by Bourdieu as *habitus*—"a system of lasting and transposable dispositions which, integrating past experiences, functions at every moment as a matrix of perceptions, appreciations and actions and makes possible the achievement of infinitely diversified tasks" (Bourdieu & Wacquant, 1992, p. 18). Although *habitus* operates at the level of the individual, we can also consider the commonsense beliefs that govern the subjectivities of groups of actors with similar institutional locations.

By *arenas* of the state I mean the social spaces in which institutions and groups of individuals are located. One can think of institutional relations as governing both the subjectivities of administrators—upon whom expert status is conferred—and the subjectivities of those whose lives they seek to organize. *Governing the Soul*, as Rose (1989) calls his exegesis on psychotherapy and subjectivity, occurs as knowledge is enacted in the techniques of institutions that in turn affect the beliefs and behaviors of a population. Escobar suggests that the discursive techniques of an institution govern what institutional actors see as the problems they are supposed to be addressing: "A basic feature of this operation is its reliance on textual and documentary forms as a means of representing and preserving a given reality. Inevitably, texts are detached from the local historical context of the reality that they supposedly represent" (1995, p. 108). In the case of the *educational arena* in Tanzania, for example, institutions such as the Ministry of Education and Culture, the World Bank, and myriad nongovernmental organizations utilize similar discursive strategies in their classification of individuals as populations and in their construction of problems and solutions for schooling. The particular words chosen for these classificatory schemes reflect "taken-for-granted commonsense belief that escapes critical scrutiny" (Fraser & Gordon, 1994, p. 310). Throughout this chapter, I examine homologies among the representations of problems in the educational, economic, and political arenas in Tanzania today in order to foreground the linkages between institutional and self-governance.

Subjectivity and arenas are theoretical notions integral to the conception of *state* used in this chapter. As mentioned above, I share with Popkewitz a view of the state as "patterns of regulation" rather than as an entity set apart from civil society. The focus in this chapter is on the regulatory practices of institutions and of self during the colonial era, the early postcolonial period, and at the present moment in Tanzanian history. Considering the state as historically contingent patterns of regulation directs attention toward the spatially and temporally specific aspects of power, toward "the point[s] where power surmounts the rules of right which organise and delimit it and extends itself beyond them, invests itself in institutions [and] becomes embodied in techniques" (Foucault, 1980, p. 96). In the case of Tanzania, we will see how patterns of regulation have become embodied in institutions and in the subjectivities of institutional actors whose programs reorganize the techniques of schooling for girls at the most local level.

Regulating "Tradition" in Colonial and Postcolonial Tanzania

The changes occurring in the economic, political, and educational arenas in Tanzania today share certain similarities with other countries discussed in this volume. However, there are also historical circumstances that affect both the patterns of regulation and the subjectivities of state actors in ways specific to Tanzania. Instead of viewing the current climate in Tanzania as the product of an evolution from the colonial period to the present, I identify in this section the historical trajectories that are part of the present patterns of governing. These include changes in the discourses of governance within Tanzania, in the economic relations among African and Western nations, and in the international political and economic organizations whose social programs construct new ways of governing the self in Tanzania today.

To speak of Tanzanian history is to gloss over the markedly different pre- and postcolonial histories of the various regions and ethnic groups that make up present-day Tanzania. Yet despite the very distinct cultural, political, and economic practices of the coast and the inland plains, a unified country was imagined by the German and British administrations as they divided "East Africa" into their respective spheres of influence. German East Africa, the core of which consisted of present-day mainland Tanzania, was taken over by the British during World War I and remained under British authority until independence in 1961 (Coulson, 1982).

Colonial states are often seen as monolithic and omnipotent, yet colonial actors envisioned their roles quite differently depending on their social location. Cooper and Stoler argue that "although the agents of colonization— officials, missionaries, and entrepreneurs—possessed seemingly immense culture-defining capacity, more and more evidence is emerging of the anxiety of colonizers lest tensions among themselves over class, gender, and competing visions of the kind of colonialism they wished to build fracture the facade" (Cooper & Stoler, 1989, p. 609). Differences among mission societies abounded in colonial Tanzania, as did tensions between many missionary organizations and the colonial government over such issues as language policy and the financing of education for Tanzanians (Rogers, 1972; Wright, 1993). Yet despite differences in their vision of state and self, colonial actors shared a familiarity with fin-de-siecle racialism, nationalism, and morality. These systems of ideas coalesced in the construction of "traditional" African political and economic institutions through which British colonialism operated. Ranger argues that British actors' "own respect for 'tradition' disposed them to look with favour upon what they took to be traditional in Africa. They set about to codify and promulgate these traditions, thereby transforming flexible custom into hard prescription" (1983, p. 212). In the political and economic arenas, colonial actors established a vast network of "traditional" Native Authorities in the belief that the chiefs and elders whom they first encountered possessed "a rudimentary idea of kingship" (Ranger, 1983, p. 229). Furthermore, the Native Authority system was based on a notion of decentralized governance, yet it was a very hierarchical system intended to meet the needs of the centralized colonial administration to garner knowledge of and access to local communities.

Institutional discourses about tradition and social progress for Africa embodied multiple and often conflicting images for the colonial self; however, certain similarities can be discerned for the groups of actors who operated in the educational arenas of the British colonies. For instance, seeing one's self as a "guide" in the evolutionary adaptation of African societies was a leitmotif in colonial discourses from the 1920s to the early 1940s. Teachers and educational administrators played particularly important roles as guides in that their social practices were believed to be closely observed by African youth. Colonial actors in the educational arena were to "order their home activities so that the African youth may be guided aright in their ideas and habits relating to the home" (Jones, 1925, p. 28).

As guides, government and missionary teachers saw themselves as responsible for inscribing a certain set of dispositions in the sons of chiefs—the future Native Authorities—and in the young women who might someday be the chiefs' spouses. Schools for the sons of chiefs were established with great effort to maintain 'traditional' systems of authority, such as in the division of the students "into their blood tribes and selecting from among themselves their sultans and subordinate chiefs" (Mumford, 1929, p. 143). Girls who were selected for missionary or government schools were taught the skills considered necessary to maintain native traditions in the home, but also to improve upon them by "observing hygienic prescriptions" and disavowing polygamy (Jones, 1925; Thurnwald, 1935). These illustrations suggest that colonial power operated most effectively through the everyday practices of institutions like the school and home wherein new dispositions were constructed from the interplay of "tradition" and "progress." This was no less true for colonial actors than it was for the population of "traditional" African leaders they hoped to influence. In the arenas of education, economics, and politics, specific institutional practices affected how administrators saw themselves, the Tanzanian citizenry, and their role vis-à-vis the colonial apparatus.

By the late 1940s, the patterns of regulation of colonialism were under increasing attack as relations among British and Tanzanian actors shifted after World War II. The already meager colonial funds for educational and other social welfare projects were stretched thin during the war, while local governing councils of Tanzanians were becoming more vociferous in their demands for schooling and economic opportunities for their children (Lawuo, 1980; Rogers, 1972). Nationalist movements in other parts of the British Empire provided a political, economic, and moral discourse around which to organize an independence campaign in Tanzania, and in 1954 the Tanganyikan

African National Union (TANU) Party was formed with Julius Nyerere as the party leader. Drawing on the rhetoric of modernization, which had by now replaced evolutionary race theories as the system of ideas influencing colonial actors, TANU waged a successful bid for independence, and in 1961 Nyerere became the first president of independent Tanzania.

After a short-lived program of liberal economic modernization from the early to mid-1960s, Tanzania embarked on a socialist form of governance known as ujamaa ("Tanzanian socialism") that led to profound changes in the configuration of its political, economic, and educational arenas.[2] Ujamaa also embodied a new discourse of self-government through the construction of the "self-reliant," socialist citizen. In the political arena, the Native Authorities were abolished, British bureaucrats were replaced by Tanzanians, and new district, regional, and area councils were established to implement TANU Party policy (Coulson, 1982). The patterns of regulation shifted from local chiefs, who lost their official status, to party members drawn from both educated and less-educated social groups. In the economic arena, the nationalization of industries and tighter regulations on imports and foreign exchange opened up another space for TANU-affiliated actors to operate (Samoff, 1990). Local party leaders were also given the task of implementing the new policy of *ujamaa vijijini*, or planned communal villages, whereby farming would be done collectively.[3]

The new patterns of regulation in the economic and political arenas constructed new sets of disposition for state actors and for the targets of their policies in the educational arena. Headmasters at government schools were sent to Kivukoni Ideological College to do basic military training and "to learn to be a good TANU man."[4] Tanzanian headmasters were now part of the socialist state and were expected to inscribe in their students an appreciation for rural life through an expanded practical skills curriculum of agricultural and vocational projects. The Education for Self-Reliance policy of 1967, which inserted the philosophy of ujamaa into the educational arena, was intended to reduce regional, ethnic, and class inequalities in education through a revisioning of primary school education. Primary schooling was to become "a complete education in itself," teaching children the kind of practical skills and appreciation of collective activity that Nyerere believed characterized traditional life in rural Tanzania (Nyerere, 1968, p. 61). Primary schooling was also intended to instill a "former attitude of the mind" based on national unity and community at the local and national levels (pp. 6–12). "Self-reliance" at this historical juncture contained idealized notions of a precolonial mentality cleansed of foreign influences as well as an idealized, nonaligned, socialist state free from dependence on foreign donors for economic assistance:

> If every individual is self-reliant the ten-house cell will be self-reliant; if all the
> cells are self-reliant the whole ward will be self-reliant; and if the wards are

self-reliant the District will be self-reliant. If the Districts are self-reliant, then the Region is self-reliant, and if the Regions are self-reliant, then the whole nation is self-reliant and this is our aim. (Nyerere, 1968, p. 34)

In the educational arena, the efforts toward national self-reliance did achieve widespread primary school expansion, dramatic improvements in the literacy rate, and in some cases a reduction in regional educational inequalities (Samoff, 1994a). However, the goal of becoming less reliant on external sources of funding was never fully realized, for even during the late 1960s and 1970s, foreign financial assistance to the educational development budget was estimated at between 13.9 percent during 1967 and 1968 and 87.1 percent for 1976 and 1977. This funding came largely from the Scandinavian countries of Sweden, Denmark, and Norway, and from the World Bank and UNICEF (Samoff, 1990).

For a variety of reasons, the relatively prosperous conditions of the 1960s and early 1970s gave way to a severe economic crisis from the end of the 1970s through the mid 1980s.[5] Since the early 1980s, Tanzanian government budget allocations to the Ministry of Education and Culture (MOEC) in terms of recurrent expenditures have been steadily declining, from 13.3 percent in 1982 and 1983 to 3.3 percent in 1993 and 1994, thus increasing the need for private funding to keep the educational sector afloat (MOEC, 1995c). The MOEC now states that because of the decline in allocations for education in the national budget, there is a need "for a more effective financing plan in which emphasis is re-directed more at cost sharing and cost recovery measures with NGOs [nongovernmental organizations], private organizations, individuals, and communities" (1995a, p. 90).

Changing Patterns of Regulation in an Era of "Empowerment"

The changes Tanzania is currently experiencing in its economic, political, and educational arenas are not unlike changes in other countries, such as in Argentina, Russia, and South Africa, as discussed in this volume. However, the experiences of colonialism, ujamaa, and Tanzania's current location in the global economy affect the patterns of regulations of self and of institutions in ways that are *specific* but *not unique* to Tanzania.[6] In the following sections, I argue that (a) while the significance of expert knowledge has remained a constant in twentieth-century Tanzania, the groups of actors designated as expert is historically contingent, as are the commonsense beliefs they bring to their administrative tasks; and (b) empowerment is a keyword shaping the commonsense beliefs of present-day experts in the educational arena and their organization and administration of schooling practices for girls. However, the commonsense notion of empowerment assumes a universal system of reasoning about gender, power, and local control, thereby eliding the historical and cultural specificity of the representations that empowerment embodies. Let us examine each of these points in turn for the case of Tanzania.

The Changing Face of the Expert

The shift from socialism to economic liberalism affects both the rules by which actors and institutions operate and the ways state actors see themselves and the targets of their reforms. In the economic arena, party officials who once made policy decisions favoring small-scale peasant farmers and parastatal industries have found themselves largely replaced by free-market economists authorized to implement "economic recovery" or "structural adjustment" programs for economic development. Structural adjustment programs are designed to make a country eligible for loans from the International Monetary Fund and the World Bank by demonstrating its commitment to economic "reform." To qualify for such loans, a country must normally reduce government expenditures, control interest rates, allow private foreign investment, and devalue its currency. International institutions such as the International Monetary Fund and the World Bank are part of Tanzania's reconstituted economic arena, for it is their definitions of problems and solutions that largely govern how Tanzanian state economists envision economic reform. Knowledge of the economic situation in Tanzania is no longer "local" in the sense that it is produced by and for Tanzanians, but rather such knowledge is produced in the context of "postcolonial mobility—in the world of global contacts" (Behdad, 1993, p. 41).

International organizations also play a significant role in the political arena as Tanzania moves from a one-party system governed by the CCM (the successor to Nyerere's TANU party) to a multiparty civil society. In 1995, United Nations' monitors were sent to encourage and supervise the country's first multiparty presidential election, a contest between the CCM, "the party of the revolution," and its contender, CHADEMA, "the party of democracy." Nongovernmental organizations supported voter education programs before the election and continue to support research and small-scale projects on the role of these organizations in a civil society (Moshi, 1994). These transformations in the political arena provide a space for groups of experts affiliated with international organizations to define problems and solutions that reflect their institution's priorities. Their expertise goes beyond simply monitoring ballot boxes and teaching rural citizens how to vote; it embodies a change in self-government by proposing different political rationalities for state actors and rural citizens. For instance, political actors in the current multiparty climate are to eschew bribery and promote accountability for elected officials; concomitantly, rural citizens, once known for their unfailing support for the "party of the revolution," are now to espouse the virtues of political pluralism and economic liberalism.

Despite the enthusiasm for a reconstitution of the political arena among many local and international groups of actors, there are also countervailing opinions resulting from Tanzania's specific historical conditions. For example, discussions about the virtues of multiparty democracy are also discussions about the potential for ethnic conflict, as in neighboring Rwanda and Burundi. In some communities, people remain concerned that a future victory by the opposition party, CHADEMA, will lead to the domination of the country by the Chagga, the small but economically and politically powerful ethnic group from which the opposition party leader hails.[7] During the campaign, some CCM supporters reportedly drew parallels between the ethnic conflict in Rwanda and the fate that might befall Tanzania if the opposition were victorious. On the island of Zanzibar there was even greater confrontation between supporters of the CCM and of its rival party, leading some commentators to suggest that the island would split from mainland Tanzania and form its own nation. Other political discussions question the sincerity of the discourse of political pluralism because the same sorts of social institutions now touted as essential to a civil society were suppressed during ujamaa. In the Tanzanian journal *Change,* for example, a university professor concluded his article on the problems of multiparty democracy by stating: "In fact, given the realities of the 1970s and 1980s and the kind of questions posed then, one gets a feeling that multiparty democracy was initiated from above as means to hijack the debates and derail them" (Chachage, 1993, p. 11). These discussions suggest that reforms in the political arena do not generate predictable transformations in the subjectivities of government and civil actors.

The role of expert knowledge in the educational arena is perhaps even more influential than in the economic and political arenas because of the active role international organizations have taken in "cost sharing" with the Ministry of Education and Culture. Samoff argues that along with the increasing reliance on World Bank and International Monetary Fund financial assistance comes a greater dependency on the advice that foreign educational advisors bring:[8]

Education policy-making in Tanzania is not a solely Tanzanian activity. Like their colleagues elsewhere in Africa, Tanzanian education policy-makers look to the North Atlantic for models, analyses and diagnoses, and approval. Often subtle, this deference to external authority conditions policies—*from specifying what is problematic to designing intervention strategies to evaluating outcomes.* Even more important, most new projects in education and even a portion of recurrent expenditures rely on externally provided finance. (Samoff 1994b, p. 143, emphasis added)

Samoff's observations are particularly salient when one considers the 1995 *Education and Training Policy* (ETP) produced by the Ministry of Education

and Culture. This text reads very differently from documents produced only
a few decades earlier by groups of actors who, trained during ujamaa, espoused the philosophy of nonalignment and state control of all sectors of the
education system. While paying lip service to a socialist notion of self-reliance,
the ETP makes it clear that the macrolevel policies it endorses "revolve
around issues of rationalization of investment, liberalization, entrepreneur-
ship, self-reliance, enhancement and integration of development efforts"
(MOEC, 1995a, p. xi). The ETP also explicitly calls for a much greater role
for nongovernmental organizations, communities, parents, and students in the
financing of schooling at all levels. With nongovernmental organizations providing a good deal of the financing and expertise in the educational arena, we
now turn to an examination of how the projects of two such organizations
construct the problem of girls' education in Tanzania today.[9]

Empowerment and the Local Production of Knowledge

With this background on educational expertise in mind, we now focus on
the second theme of this chapter: expert knowledge and the discourse of
"empowerment." In contrast to the socialist vision of self as inseparable from
one's self-reliant ujamaa community, today's economic, political, and educational discourses draw upon neoclassical economic metaphors of the market
in their construction of self and community in Tanzania. The subjectivities for
experts and nonexperts alike, as embodied in these discourses, suggest a new
type of "economic 'rationality' and a purely material, individualistic, self-
interested orientation toward economic decision making" (Todaro, 1989, p.
8). From this neoclassical perspective, "rational" macrolevel decision making
means decentralizing, liberalizing, and privatizing, while at a microlevel
neoclassicalism promotes "empowering" individuals to act on the basis of
economic self-interest. Yet this way of seeing the problem and solution simultaneously excludes other foci and options that were heretofore a part of discourses about self and community. In this section I argue that "empowerment"
has become part of commonsense belief about the problems of women in the
Third World such that alternative interpretations of local power relations are
obscured. To illustrate this claim, I examine the usage of "empowerment" in
two educational programs for girls in Tanzania and explore how this usage
forces a dualism between tradition and power by eliding the nonlocal genesis
of putatively "empowering" dispositions.

In the educational reform materials prepared by the nongovernmental
organization CARE Tanzania and a joint World Bank-Ministry of Education
and Culture (MOEC) project, *empowerment* is the name given to the set of
dispositions rendered capable of solving the problem of girls' education. The
CARE program, entitled the *Community Mobilization for Girls' Education
Project*, plans to use "high impact interventions that will set the stage for *long*

term attitudinal changes and the empowerment of girls and women in the communities they live in" (1996, p. 3, emphasis added). Similarly, the *Girls' Secondary Education Support* program of the World Bank/MOEC constructs empowerment as a psychological disposition whereby girls and their parents can simply "change their attitudes" from the traditional (disempowering) to the modern (empowering) ones. Despite differences in the scope and scale of these two projects, I will consider the programs alongside one another because of their cognate usage of *empowerment*.

The World Bank/MOEC program for Tanzanian secondary school girls identifies five "supply-side constraints" it believes are responsible for girls' poor secondary school enrollment: (1) the lack of secondary school places for primary school graduates, especially for girls who want to attend boarding school; (2) girls' limited access to Tanzania's best schools in the country, the top ten of which are all-male schools; (3) the gender bias in the vocational tracking system, especially in the home economics track; (4) the "traditional stereo type [*sic*] oriented teaching methods" and teachers' "low expectations of women with respect to performance"; and (5) the observation that "most parents still hold the traditional attitudes that girls are born to become wives and mothers as the first and foremost responsibility" (MOEC, 1995b, pp. 13–14). While each of these points is worthy of a study unto itself, I will focus my attention on the latter two points because this is what the programs themselves address. That is to say, neither the World Bank/MOEC nor the CARE program proposes ways to increase the number of girls' boarding schools, desegregate the top all-male schools, or restructure the vocational tracking system. Rather, both programs are designed to change attitudes about gender in the school and home, which illustrates how educational policy constructs subjectivities for those in its purview.

The World Bank/MOEC and CARE documents include descriptions of the research methods they used to determine the problems their programs should address. Using data-collection methods often associated with activism and intervention—interviews, focus groups, participatory appraisal—as well as surveys and tests in the World Bank/MOEC case, the programs conclude that the problems facing girls' education can be resolved through the "sensitisation" of local communities on gender and education issues to overcome the "nonfinancial constraints" on girls' participation in schooling. To solve the problem of teachers using traditional "stereo type" teaching methods, the World Bank/MOEC program proposes to bring in "gender and education specialists" to develop gender-awareness seminars for school staff and gender-sensitive teaching materials for classroom use. The CARE program is even more specific about who will do the gender sensitization planning, stating that non-Tanzanians will handle the workshops: "International technical assistance will be required for the development of gender sensitive teaching and learning practices, teacher training and teacher-generated material development" (1996, p. 7). The CARE and the

World Bank/MOEC projects will also address the "traditional attitudes" of "most parents" by sending out "marketing consultants" to publicize the scholarship program. Once girls are selected to receive scholarships, they "enter into contracts," along with their households, promising adequate time at home to study and attendance at "gender awareness meetings to be organized by [a] gender specialist" (MOEC, 1995b, p. 14).

We can think about the relationship between "empowerment" and the production of expert knowledge by considering the modes of rationality inscribed in the World Bank/MOEC and CARE programs. The "rational" subject in the World Bank/MOEC program bears a striking resemblance to the "rational" self-interested subject of neoclassical economics and to the "rational" advocate of multiparty reforms in the political arena. For instance, one of the purposes of the World Bank/MOEC program is to "encourage girls to come up/out and talk, participate, perform, win, inculcate positive/proper role models, to speak out their minds and be ready to seek counseling" (MOEC, 1995b, p. 45). Through school practices designed to help girls "participate, perform, [and] win," the "rational" subject is constructed as one who is competitive and individualistic rather than deferential and collaborative. The program constructs a "proper" and "positive" subjectivity for young women that is self-interested and receptive to the counsel of the new educational experts.

The significance of this universal construction of the "empowered" female can be explored in two ways. First, we can consider how NGO-sponsored programs, which appear to be motivated by a genuine concern to include more girls in the educational system, concomitantly create new social divisions that lead to the exclusion of those who have not relinquished the dispositions that were heretofore considered appropriate. In some Tanzanian communities, such as among the Chagga in the Kilimanjaro Region, there appears to be a growing rift between youth who attend secondary school and the members of their age-group who do not. Chagga girls in secondary school often speak disparagingly of the girls in their communities who get married instead of going on to secondary school, a situation common to the vast majority of youth since less than 15 percent of primary school graduates matriculate into public or private secondary school (MOEC, 1995c). Despite high unemployment rates for secondary school leavers, secondary school girls speak confidently of how they, unlike primary school leavers, will use their knowledge of English and commerce to gain employment and raise their children without relying on the financial support of a husband or parents. Male secondary school students in this area tend to reject the idea of marrying a girl who hasn't attended secondary school and to eschew the notion of relying on one's parents in farming collectively with them or with members of one's extended family. In discussions about their future plans, male students often described a future of self-sufficiency, arguing that their academic credentials will allow them to be "self-reliant" and beholden to neither parents nor community. Thus, the expansion of secondary schooling increases the number of young people who identify with the "positive/proper role models" of the World Bank, yet these changes in the dispositions of school-educated youth also create new divisions in kin and coetaneous relationships.

A second aspect of the universal representation of the "empowered" woman concerns the relationship between data collection and problem construction. In the design documents of the World Bank/MOEC program, there is repeated reference to "the message" or "appropriate messages" that will be conveyed through the marketing program, messages which appear to address problems identified by local participants during the data-collection phase of the program. The use of interviews, observations, and focus groups to gather information for the design of the project makes it seem as though the solutions embodied in this message are "for girls themselves" (World Bank/MOEC program) or, in the case of CARE, the solutions are "initiated by girls." However, upon closer scrutiny, the priorities of the World Bank are inscribed in the messages of its program for girls' education, suggesting social change that extends far beyond the educational arena:

> Messages will underscore the benefits of such education for the girls' own personal development, ability to contribute to Tanzania [*sic*] society, and the accrued social returns as enumerated in the GSES pilot document. On the basis of anticipated roles of parents in this program, promotional messages to households will emphasize responsibilities families have in choosing schools based on quality and bursar award. . . . The message for schools (with appropriate sense of humor) will inspire participating low secondary schools to recruit girls from among those identified as disadvantaged, adopt gender-sensitive approaches to teaching and learning, provide supplementary or remedial instructions to all low performers, improve their schools, and manage the bursar funds in a manner acceptable to GSES pilot. . . . Appropriate messages will urge the village council to ensure that transparency in the selection process prevails. National and local leaders, civil servants, key education policy makers and donors will be targeted with the message on the importance of shared responsibility for the education of the female population. (1995b, p. 43)

Thus, the use of phrases such as "accrued social returns," "transparency in the selection process," and "family responsibility for school choice" belie the claim that the solutions embodied in "the message" originate with Tanzanian girls or with rural village councils; instead, "empowerment" is externally conferred on girls, schools, and communities by actors located in institutions like the World Bank and the Ministry of Education and Culture.

The CARE program also relies on data collection methods that appear to encourage "local" participation in the identification of school-related problems for girls. According to program documents, parents, teachers, and "traditional authorities from village chief to ngoma [drum and dance] organizers" will identify local problems and recommend solutions during participatory appraisal sessions (1996, p. 3). However, the range of possible recommendations seems limited to the problems and solutions identified in advance by CARE project staff: "The recommendations will be components of a village 'action plan' or commitment to improve quality, access and equity in their school. Project staff will facilitate the self assessment process, sensitise on education and gender issues, and identify subsequent areas of project intervention with the communities" (1996, p. 4). As in the case of the World Bank/ MOEC program, empowerment in the CARE project has more to do with the construction of gender-sensitive subjectivities than with local determination of school-related problems and solutions.

In sum, data-collection methods such as focus groups and participatory appraisal sessions may appear to be "empowering" regardless of the context in which they are used because they utilize a familiar discourse of democratic participation in the research process. This commonsense belief about the virtue of local participation affects the way development institutions conduct the practices of school reform, from the collection of data about educational problems to the administration of school-based solutions. It also affects the construction of subjectivities of educational experts by allowing them to see themselves as individuals sensitive to local concerns rather than as employees of international development institutions with their own agendas.

How does the discourse of empowerment achieve its universalizing effects given that empowerment is constructed as a local endeavor? We might consider for a moment the semantics of the term *empowerment* and the notion of power it embodies. First, while empowerment as it is constructed in the World Bank/MOEC and CARE programs assumes a local genesis for change, empowerment is an exogenously performed act. The denotative meaning of *empower* is to invest or authorize; additionally, *empower* is a transitive verb which requires that it take an object; that is, someone or some thing must receive authorization or investment *from* an external source. By definition, then, empower means to confer authority rather than to acknowledge local transformation, a point often deliberately reinterpreted in the empowerment discourse.

Second, often embedded in the notion of empowerment in institutional discourses is what Popkewitz refers to as the "universalizing of reason." In this volume, he argues that although constructivist pedagogy is part of a particular set of historical configurations, the modes of problem solving embedded in it are treated as universal. The systems of reasoning produced locally in late twentieth-century United States, for example, now appear "global," natural and essential. If one applies Popkewitz's analysis to the discourse of empowerment, one can also identify a universalizing of reason that is in fact part of a particular sociohistorical set of circumstances. For instance, the use of interviews, observations, and focus groups to know the problems of a local community is part of a historically specific movement to democratize the research process. While the use of these techniques may alter the way program administrators think of themselves, I argue that their use is not necessarily democratizing. These programs construct a particular subjectivity *for* girls and generate new oppositionalities between "empowered" school girls and the putatively traditional and dependent girls who have not attended secondary schooling. Therefore, what is "local" about "empowerment" is perhaps thousands of miles away from the African villages where "empowerment" is presumed to originate.

We can explore further the history of "the local" in the "empowerment" discourses of the World Bank/MOEC and CARE by considering another aspect of the subjectivities of experts authorized to organize development programs. The responsibility for imagining empowering alternatives for "local" women in the Third World is a role often assumed by groups of actors in the political, economic, and especially in the educational arenas (Bove, 1986). What are the dispositions of State actors in the Tanzanian case that privilege a particular construction of the "empowered" Tanzanian girl? We should remind ourselves that given the way knowledge circulates today both intra- and internationally, there are few actors in Tanzania or elsewhere in the Third World who can speak from a position of alterity by virtue of their authentic "native" status untainted by "Western" intellectual practices (Behdad, 1993; Narayan, 1993; Spivak, 1989). Therefore, we can posit an answer to the question of how Tanzanian girls are constructed in the empowerment discourses by considering two systems of knowledge—feminism and developmentalism—that in many respects govern how "native" and "nonnative" experts see the problem of girls' education in the Third World.

Looking first at discourses about gender, we can examine the prevalence of the notion of empowerment in two influential strands of Western feminism: liberal feminism and Marxist/socialist feminism. Liberal feminists often support the notion that equality is possible within the existing political and economic system so long as these systems are made more receptive to women. "Empowerment" from this perspective is part of a "value system" which "addresses women's experiences of subordination to men and women's need for equity" (Hall, 1992, p. 5). Marxist/socialist feminists, in contrast, make connections between women's disempowerment and class oppression rather than looking at individual women's values and attitudes. "Empowerment" has multiple meanings for Marxist/socialist feminists, but it is a term often used today in conjunction with participatory action techniques similar to those described above whereby "people become enabled to govern themselves effectively" (Bystydzienski, 1992, p. 3). Without minimizing the distinctions between these two frameworks, liberal and Marxist/socialist feminisms treat power as an entity that can be "given, provided, controlled, held, conferred, taken away" through the process of empowerment or disempowerment (Gore, 1992, p. 57). From my reading of the authors and citations in the World Bank/MOEC and CARE programs, I suggest that these two feminisms govern the way actors in many nongovernmental organizations see themselves as feminists and see Tanzanian girls as lacking the agency that "empowerment" would provide for them.

Turning now to geographic representations, we can think about Tanzania as part of a broader discourse about development in the Third World. If we recall that subjectivities (in Bourdieu's sense of *habitus*) are the relatively stable dispositions of an individual, we can explore why, when actors move between different institutions and arenas, they draw upon similar constructions of problems and solutions. Said's work on Orientalism reminds us that views of self and Other are retained as one moves across institutional boundaries because our views are part of a broader body of common sense, of what we believe we know about the social world (1978). Therefore, when experts define problems and solutions for Tanzanian girls, their definitions refer to other discourses about Tanzania, Africa, and the Third World.

Mohanty argues cogently that embedded in discourses on women and development is a dichotomy based on commonsense beliefs about women in the First World and Third World. She describes this as a dichotomy between "ignorant, poor, uneducated, tradition-bound, domestic, family-oriented, victimized" women in the Third World and Western women, who are seen "as educated, as modern, as having control over their own bodies and sexualities, and [having] the freedom to make their own decisions" (1991, p. 56). Given these commonsense assumptions, development experts tend to view tradition as that which renders girls powerless in their natal communities and keeps them in a disempowered state of poverty. Disregarding historical specificities, the discourse of empowerment constructs education as the only way out of the state of tradition, which supposedly governs girls' lives throughout the Third World:

> When girls are not educated, their labor has little economic value outside the home. They are forced to marry young and unable to stand up to their husbands. They have more children than they really want and are unable to invest heavily in each child. Poverty is perpetuated. (Summers [speaking to a group of World Bank economists], 1994, p. 5)

Through educational programs like those sponsored by CARE and the World Bank, it is assumed that girls' labor will have greater economic value outside the home, they will marry later and stand up to their husbands, they will have as many children as they *really* want, and they will be able to stop the perpetuation of poverty by investing heavily in the few children they *choose* to bear. This is "the message" that is assumed to be universally applicable yet one that has been constructed in the local context of development institutions staffed by Western-educated administrators. In sum, the discourse of empowerment embodied in the programs of the World Bank/MOEC and

CARE identifies the root cause of girls' educational problems as something beyond the programs' culpability—that is, African tradition—and ignores the local effects of international economic and political relations that cannot be remedied by scholarships and seminars alone.

Concluding Remarks

In this chapter, I have focused on two different yet interrelated aspects of the state and education in Tanzania that are often overlooked in studies of modernization or dependency. First, I provided examples from several critical moments in Tanzanian colonial and postcolonial history to illustrate how patterns of regulation change over time depending on which groups of actors are constructed as experts in different social arenas. This is not an evolutionary or functional sense of change; rather, I have argued for an understanding of change as shifts in authoritative systems of knowledge that define educational problems and solutions. The notion of change as historically contingent was illustrated by considering homologies between the economic, political, and educational arenas at different points in time in twentieth-century Tanzanian history. A second theme in this chapter concerned the subjectivities of those actors authorized to make decisions in the economic, political, and educational arenas in Tanzania today. I argued that the empowerment discourses exemplified by the World Bank/MOEC and CARE programs assume a local, Tanzanian genesis for the "empowerment" message, yet what is local about these discourses lies in their historical specificity within Western developmentalism.

My decision to highlight the example of the World Bank-Ministry of Education and Culture program underscores one of the central points of this chapter: Patterns of relations are historically contingent and are implicated in the practices of governing among the economic, political, and educational arenas. The groups of actors currently authorized to make decisions in the educational arena in Tanzania have changed from the ujamaa period to the present even though some of the individuals involved have remained the same. To say that these changes have led to greater modernization or to increased dependency begs the question as to how the relations of governing are produced in national and global contexts. My point is that relations between institutions such as the World Bank and the Ministry of Education and Culture have shifted over time for a variety of historical reasons such that today one cannot always draw a clear distinction between Tanzanian and non-Tanzanian organizations in the economic, political, and educational arenas. Institutional actors in both the "center'" and the "periphery" operate increasingly in a context where ideas about "reform" and "empowerment" circulate internationally, thus affecting the dispositions and sensibilities of "rational" educational planners around the globe. It would be wise to heed Appadurai's call for a recognition of the overlaps in the global circulation of cultural and economic forms lest we "remain enmired in comparative work which relies on the clear separation of entities to be compared, before serious comparison can begin" (Appadurai, 1994, p. 337).

The global circulation of commonsense beliefs about empowerment, for example, has profound implications for the subjectivities of educational planners as well as for the targets of their reforms. Girls' education in Tanzania and elsewhere in the Third World has recently become visible through international conferences on education and population, and through the discovery of women's integral role in rural economic development (Escobar, 1995). Through programs designed to increase the number of girls in school and to alter the gendered climate of schooling in Tanzania, subjectivities for girls are constructed that emphasize a particular form of assertiveness and self-interest. These dispositions are assumed to be universally appropriate even though they have emerged from social movements with specific histories. If we are to understand the state as patterns of relations that are historically contingent, then the study of shifting subjectivities is an integral part of comparative studies in education and beyond.

Notes

I would like to thank the following people for their comments on earlier drafts of this chapter: Lynn Fendler, Tim Leinbach, Richard Peterson, Tom Popkewitz, and Debra Rothenberg. I owe special thanks to Stacie Colwell for her insights on the semantics of "empowerment."

1. I use the term *Third World* throughout this chapter despite its current usage as a synonym for *underdeveloped*. Third World was first used by representatives at the 1955 Bandung Conference in Indonesia to designate their countries' alignment with neither capitalist nor socialist world powers. Robert Young suggests using Third World "as a positive term of radical critique even if it also necessarily signals its negative sense of economic dependency and exploitation" (1990, p. 12). With this dual sense of Third World in mind, I will use the term to designate those countries in Africa, Asia, and Latin America that share certain historical, social, and economic features with Tanzania, the focus of this chapter.

2. The Three Year Development Plan of 1961–1964 was based largely on two reports prepared shortly before independence, one by the World Bank and one by the U.S. consulting firm Arthur D. Little for the Agency for International Development (USAID) (Coulson, 1982).

3. According to official statistics, the number of ujamaa villages rose from 809 in 1969 to 7684 in 1977 (Coulson, 1982).

4. This information comes from an interview with a former headmaster of several government secondary schools during my fieldwork in the Kilimanjaro Region of Tanzania from January to December, 1996.

5. These reasons include the war between Tanzania and Uganda, which led to a marked decline in Tanzania's foreign exchange holdings, drought, and the high cost of importing petroleum (Samoff, 1990; Shao, 1992).

6. I use the phrase "global economy" instead of "capitalist world economy" (Wallerstein, 1982, p. 41) to avoid assigning structural positions to nation-states. While Tanzania would fall into the category of "periphery" from a world-systems perspective, this label elides the significant role certain groups of Tanzanian actors play in the global economic arena. Thus, in this chapter I make reference to the "global" or "international" circulation of economic and cultural capital to emphasize that relations of power do not necessarily correspond to the boundaries of the nation-state.

7. The information in this paragraph is based on fieldwork conducted in Tanzania from January to December, 1996. I also spent seven months in Tanzania in 1993, during which time there were several instances of violence triggered by the formation of opposition parties. In two instances, it was believed that supporters of the ruling CCM party in the Kilimanjaro Region attacked pork butcheries at a large outdoor market to suggest a consolidation of Muslim rule by the CCM, whose leader at the time was Muslim. This was interpreted as a threat by the mainly Christian Chagga, who supported the formation of an opposition party under the leadership of Augustine Mrema, a Chagga who had been a high-ranking official in the national government.

8. While I concur with Samoff's analysis in the chapter cited here, I would argue that the distinction between "Tanzanian" and "non-Tanzanian" policy makers is blurry when one considers the similar subjectivities of State actors around the world. Many of the officials in the MOEC and consultants from the University of Dar es Salaam have received their training in Western countries and are as much a part of the production of knowledge *about* the Third World as they are *of* the Third World. I agree with Behdad when he writes that "notions such as coherent communities and unified identities have become inadequate, for no longer can the boundaries of center and periphery, home and abroad, self and other be drawn so distinctly" (1993, p. 41).

9. Although I discuss only two educational projects in this chapter, there are numerous other educational programs being funded primarily by European aid programs such as DANIDA (Denmark), SIDA (Sweden), Irish Aid, and the European Union (CARE, 1996). There are also British programs, such as School Partnership Worldwide and World Challenge, that bring recent A-level graduates to Tanzania to teach for six to nine months in Tanzanian high schools. The Peace Corp and several American church organizations also participate in providing "expert" knowledge through volunteer teachers or teacher-training programs.

References

Altbach, P. G. "Servitude of the Mind? Education, Dependency, and Neocolonialism." In *Comparative Education*, ed. P. G. Altbach, R. F. Arnove, and G. P. Kelly. New York: Macmillan, 1982, pp. 469–84.

Appadurai, A. "Disjuncture and Difference in the Global Cultural Economy." In *Colonial Discourse and Post-Colonial Theory: A Reader*, ed. P. Williams and L. Christman. New York: Columbia University Press, 1994, pp. 324–39.

Arnove, R. F. "Comparative Education and World-Systems Analysis." In *Comparative Education*, ed. P. Altbach, R. F. Arnove, and G. P. Kelly. New York: Macmillan, 1982, pp. 453–68.

Behdad, A. "Traveling to Teach: Postcolonial Critics in the American Academy." In *Race, Identity and Representation in Education*, ed. C. McCarthy and W. Crichlow. New York and London: Routledge, 1993, pp. 40–49.

Bourdieu, P. & L. J. D. Wacquant. *An Invitation to Reflexive Sociology*. Chicago and London: University of Chicago Press, 1992.

Bove, P. A. *Intellectuals in Power: A Genealogy of Critical Humanism*. New York: Columbia University Press, 1986.

Bystydzienski, J. M. (ed.). *Women Transforming Politics: Worldwide Strategies for Empowerment*. Bloomington and Indianapolis: Indiana University Press, 1992.

CARE Tanzania. *Community Mobilization for Girls' Education Project: Concept Paper*. Dar es Salaam: CARE Tanzania, June 1996.

Chachage, C. S. L. "Some Reflections on the Limits of Multi-Party Democracy in Africa." *Change* 3 (1993): 10–11.

Cooper, F. & A. L. Stoler. "Tensions of Empire: Colonial Control and Visions of Rule." *American Ethnologist* 16 (1989): 609–21.

Coulson, A. *Tanzania: A Political Economy*. Oxford: Clarendon Press, 1982.

Escobar, A. *Encountering Development: The Making and Unmaking of the Third World*. Princeton, N. J.: Princeton University Press, 1995.

Foucault, M. *Power/Knowledge: Selected Interviews and Other Writings 1972–1977*. New York: Pantheon, 1980.

———. *The Subject and Power*, Afterword to H. Dreyfus and P. Rabinow, *Michel Foucault: Beyond Structuralism and Hermeneutics*. Chicago: University of Chicago Press.

Fraser, N. & L. Gordon. "A Genealogy of *Dependency*: Tracing a Keyword of the U.S. Welfare State." *Signs* 19 (1994): 309–36.

Gore, J. "What We Can Do for You! What *Can* 'We' Do for 'You'?: Struggling over Empowerment in Critical and Feminist Pedagogy." In *Feminisms and Critical Pedagogy*, ed. C. Luke and J. Gore. New York and London: Routledge, 1992, pp. 54–73.

Haddad, W. D. "The World Bank's Education Sector Policy Paper: A Summary." *Comparative Education* 17 (1981): 127–39.

Hall, C. M. *Women and Empowerment: Strategies for Increasing Autonomy*. Washington, D.C.: Hemisphere Publishing, 1992.

Jones, T. J. *Education in East Africa*. London: Edinburgh House Press, 1925.

Lawuo, Z. E. *Education and Social Change in a Rural Community*. Dar es Salaam: Dar es Salaam University Press, 1980.

Ministry of Education and Culture (MOEC). *Basic Education Statistics in Tanzania (BEST) 1990–1994*. Dar es Salaam: Ministry of Education and Culture, 1995c.

———. *Education and Training Policy*. Dar es Salaam: Ministry of Education and Culture, 1995a.

———. *Girls' Secondary Education Support Pilot: Design*. Dar es Salaam: Ministry of Education and Culture, 1995b.

Mohanty, C. "Under Western Eyes: Feminist Scholarship and Colonial Discourses." In *Third World Women and the Politics of Feminism,* ed. by C. T. Mohanty, A. Russo, and L. Torres. Bloomington and Indianapolis: Indiana University Press, 1991, pp. 51-80.

Moshi, C. A. (1994). *A Comprehensive Report on a Local Government Elections Study Done in Old Moshi East Ward—Moshi Rural District in September/ October, 1994.* Ms [photocopy].

Mumford, W. B. "Education and the Social Adjustment of the Primitive People of Africa to European Culture." *Africa* II (1929): 138–59.

Narayan, K. "How Native Is a 'Native' Anthropologist?" *American Anthropologist* 95 (1993): 671–86.

Nyerere, J. K. *Ujamaa: Essays on Socialism.* Dar es Salaam: Oxford University Press, 1968.

Popkewitz, T. S. "Rethinking Decentralization and State/Civil Society Distinctions: The State as a Problematic of Governing." *Journal of Education Policy* 11 (1996): 27–51.

Psacharopoulos, G. & W. Loxley. *Diversified Secondary Education and Development: Evidence from Colombia and Tanzania.* Baltimore: Johns Hopkins University Press, 1985.

Ramirez, F. O. & J. Boli-Bennett. "Global Patterns of Educational Institutionalization." In *Comparative Education,* ed. P. Altbach, R. F. Arnove, and G. P. Kelly. New York: Macmillan, 1982, pp. 15–36.

Ranger, T. "The Invention of Tradition in Colonial Africa." In *The Invention of Tradition,* ed. E. Hobsbawm and T. Ranger. Cambridge: Cambridge University Press, 1983, pp. 211-62.

Rogers, S. *The Search for Political Focus on Kilimanjaro: A History of Chagga Politics 1916–1952.* Unpublished Doctoral Dissertation, University of Dar es Salaam, Tanzania, 1972.

Rose, N. *Governing the Soul: The Shaping of the Private Self.* London and New York: Routledge, 1989, p. 1.

Said, E. *Orientalism.* New York: Vintage Books, 1978.

Samoff, J. " 'Modernizing' a Socialist Vision: Education in Tanzania." In *Education and Social Transition in the Third World,* ed. M. Carnoy and J. Samoff. Princeton, N.J.: Princeton University Press, 1990, p. 200–73.

Samoff, J. (with S. Sumra). *Financial Crisis, Structural Adjustment, and Education Policy in Tanzania.* Paper presented at the Annual Meeting of the American Educational Research Association, New Orleans, 4–7 April 1994a.

———. "From Planning to Marketing: Making Education and Training Policy in Tanzania." In *Coping with Crisis: Austerity, Adjustment and Human Resources,* ed. J. Samoff. Paris: UNESCO, 1994b, pp. 134–72.

Shao, I. (ed.) *Structural Adjustment in a Socialist Country: The Case of Tanzania.* Harare: Sapes, 1992.

Spivak, G. C. "Who Claims Alterity?" In *Remaking History,* ed. B. Kruger and P. Mariani. Seattle: Bay Press, 1989, pp. 269–92.

Summers, L. H. *Investing in All the People: Educating Women in Developing Countries.* Washington, D.C.: World Bank, 1994.

Thurnwald, R. C. *Black and White in East Africa: The Fabric of a New Civilization.* London: George Routledge and Sons, 1935.

Todaro, M. P. *Economic Development in the Third World.* New York and London: Longman, 1989.

Wallerstein, I. "The Rise and Future Demise of the World Capitalist System: Concepts for Comparative Analysis." In *Introduction to the Sociology of "Developing Societies,"* ed. H. Alavi and T. Shanin. London: Macmillan, 1982, pp. 29–53.

Welsh, A. R. "The Functionalist Tradition and Comparative Education." *Comparative Education* 21 (1985): 5–19.

World Bank. *Education in Sub-Saharan Africa: Policies for Adjustment, Revitalization, and Expansion.* Washington, D.C.: World Bank, 1988.

Wright, M. *Strategies of Slaves and Women: Life Stories from East/Central Africa.* New York: L. Barber, 1993.

Young, R. *White Mythologies: Writing History and the West.* London and New York: Routledge, 1990.

CHAPTER 11

The Construction of Discursive Space as Patterns of Inclusion/Exclusion

Governmentality and Urbanism in the United States

LISA HENNON

The ministers of knowledge have always assumed that the
whole universe was threatened by the very changes that
affected their ideologies and their positions. They transmute
the misfortune of their theories into theories of misfortune.
When they transform bewilderment into "catastrophes," when
they seek to enclose the people in the "panic" of their discourses, are they once more necessarily right?
—Michel de Certeau, *"Walking in the City"*

One great challenge of the modern nation-state is to develop strategies
for social inclusion at a time when profound changes have occurred in global
economies, patterns of migration, and a rise in long-term unemployment
(Silver, 1994). Social and educational policies seek to devise strategies of
inclusion through reforms of schooling (see, e.g., Istance, 1997). In the United
States, educational reform discourses give the problem of inclusion a geographical sense by targeting urban or inner-city schools for reform. The discourses present the issue as an "urban-suburban" dichotomy and claim to be
offering new ways to devise an inclusionary system of schooling.

However, as inclusion strategies are sought, patterns of exclusion remain
foremost. The urban-suburban dichotomy provides an oppositional framework for inclusionary schemes, but reform campaigns overlook the ways in
which *urbanism* is part of an older trajectory that historically has been a

system to exclude, prompting reform discourses to "panic" about crises in education (to use de Certeau's phrase above). I use the term *urbanism* to refer to discursive patterns that have placed urban in an all-encompassing contrast to something that it is not.

Since the United States was first established, educational reform discourses have attempted to envision the entire space of the nation by invoking geographical divisions that encompass national territory. We can understand the historical trajectory of urbanism as undergoing two shifts. In the eighteenth and nineteenth centuries, urbanism was embedded in discourses of *land* that opposed city to country. By the turn of the twentieth century, urbanism had shifted to discourses about *society* that opposed urban to rural. From about the 1960s, urbanism shifted to discourses of *community* that oppose urban to suburban. While the intent has been to make schooling more inclusive, at each juncture an older form of reasoning—that divides, excludes, and reorders concepts—has created new exclusions.

Urbanism is a historical and conceptual tool of analysis to raise the theoretical question of how to provide a critical framework for comparative approaches to issues of social justice and equality. Discursive deployments of the "city" produce political and moral effects by governing the ways in which we see, think, feel, aspire, act upon, and divide ourselves and others. In other national contexts, American urbanism will not apply, but we should not read the social implications as a provincial issue of education in the United States. A theoretical reading of the analysis through the problematic of governmentality can provide ways to explore the more general question of how oppositional spaces are constructed.

Urbanism and the Metaphor of Land as Nation

From the 1780s to the 1880s in the United States, the discursive space of urbanism tied educational reform movements to land images in emergent discourses of the nation-state. Images of land gave the nation-state a symbolic and physical order, or "landscape," which was mapped onto territory and population. The landscape served to locate problems and to distribute the common school based on patterns of inclusion/exclusion.

The Opposition of City and Country: Cosmopolitan and Pastoral Images

Eighteenth-century discourses of the nation-state constructed a "natural" order to the physical, social, and political world (Becker, 1932; Toulmin, 1990).[1] Drawing upon conceptualizations of Greek city states and Roman republics, a land-based metaphor of geography displaced the religious cosmography of feudalism. The question of a democratic State became how to govern over large distances on a continuous and regular basis. Lands and peoples were envisioned as divided into nation-states that took physical form by dividing surface of territory, or land, into bounded and contiguous entities (see Anderson, 1991).

National space of the new republic was envisioned in multiple ways, for a variety of spatial divisions were available, such as postcolonial regions and constitutionally defined states and territories. In thinking about the educated citizen in relation to land, however, the binary between city and country neatly captured "all" of national space. Country had the double meaning of both the symbolic territory of the nation, and the forests, mountains, pastures, and agricultural settlements within it (see Williams, 1973). Ironically, images of the city made the country, in both senses, intelligible.

We can understand the city and country opposition in two analytic frames, cosmopolitan and pastoral. I use the term *cosmopolitan* to refer to the world order of nation-states and the scaffolding of discourses that went into its construction (Toulmin, 1990). *Pastoralism* is ordinarily understood as a genre of literature or landscape painting, but American pastoralism can be understood as formative of social thought and policy (Marx, 1964). The pastoral image of city and country served as a counterbalance to the cosmopolitan in American thought. Each image contributed key elements to the American landscape.

The cosmopolitan image of city and country established norms of "civilization." The territory outside the original thirteen colonies was considered "unsettled" because it lacked an American stamp on its terrain. The cosmopolitan image of the city helped construct an American landscape by thinking of the city as a microcosm of its geographic territory (Meinig, 1993). Spatial relations of civic, economic, and social elements of the city provided a template for administering and regulating the peopling and settling of territory (see also Foucault, 1980, 1984). Mapping proceeded as though individual states were extensions of the elements found in cities but on a larger scale. All of national space could be understood in its entirety by "seeing" the "country" through the "city."

Cosmopolitan urbanism set up a symbolic relation in which the savagery associated with a harsh wilderness or jungle was the polar opposite to "civilization." The cosmopolitan image associated the city with the achievements of civilization including reason, progress, liberty, and human perfectibility (Williams, 1973). Racial discourses of civilizations placed "races" along an evolutionary road of reason and progress. In the teleology of racial discourses, the destination (and destiny) of reason and progress was the civilization that built cosmopolitan cities (Young, 1995).

The pastoral image of city and country established norms of the nation. Pastoral urbanism adopted Enlightenment beliefs in social harmony and reason but combined them with a Protestant image of the Garden of Eden (Marx, 1964). Pastoralism linked the "progressive" element of cosmopolitan urbanism to human moral perfectibility. The American citizen was constructed to have an exceptional relation to "native soil" as the site of moral conversion. In 1844, the American philosopher Emerson expressed this vision succinctly: "We must regard the land as a commanding and increasing power on the citizen, the sanative [redemptive] and Americanizing influence which promises to disclose new virtues for ages to come" (quoted in Wills, 1994, p. 217).

In the "New World," savagery was associated not only with non-Christians and lesser races of the wilderness; pastoral urbanism associated depravity with populations in European and British cities. A Protestant United States regarded the city as functioning solely for economic ambitions that encouraged political abuses and corruption. The political upheavals abroad and social conflicts in cities threatened the country as a whole. Similar neglect in shepherding populations in the countryside could be fragmenting and destabilizing. In American exceptionalism, pastoral urbanism set up a different symbolic field of positive and negative values that situated the "country" between the wilderness and the city as the norm for nation.

Normalizing Space: Inclusions/Exclusions of a National Landscape

The role of government was to safeguard American democracy by constructing an inclusionary national landscape to encourage ownership of land and by that instill "natural" virtues and collective identity in its citizens. Discourses of cosmopolitan and pastoral urbanism helped normalize the space of the nation-state by stabilizing the meaning of national space as a condition of freedom (see Dumm, 1996). Positive and negative values in images of the city and country created a normative pull on "space." Together they formed ways to imagine a particular locale as linked to the nation. Small farms in the countryside, country estates isolated from yet having access to a city's commerce and civic activities, and villages and towns were organized into a nesting of geopolitical levels of county, state, and territory. In the revisioned landscape, the reasonable American Citizen did not live far from the ameliorative forces of land, either through owning it, or by being schooled to cherish and spiritually thrive within it.

Normative inclusionary categories based on discourses of land established an included/excluded social status in which citizenship embodied and mutually implied both inclusion *and* exclusion, an in-between status that goes unrecognized by invoking the binary of inclusion versus exclusion in political representation (see Popkewitz, introduction, this vol.). When the construction of normative places began to order national space, discursive patterns of social inclusion/exclusion were embedded in the landscape. The "city" and the "local community" are two examples in which schooling played a normative role in ordering national space.

Biological discourses about the city and populational health made it possible for nature to be a part of the city. They compared a healthy pastoral city with a healthy body: streets and roads were the city's arteries and veins, parks and gardens were its lungs (Sennett, 1994). We can read the social movements to build public parks and gardens as ways to naturalize the city. However, reformers believed that city dwellers "outside" the normative vision needed far more than parks and gardens. If they were to be included, they needed technologies of moral hygiene and mechanisms such as the kindergarten and the common school to enable economic and moral citizenship.

The idea of a local community in the countryside seems to capture a universal motif of places where all were on an equal footing. From the perspective of self-government, the local community was thought to give citizens both a sense of autonomy over local affairs and national representation. Conceptualizations of the "local," however, were neither uniform nor unproblematic. In the South, the "county" represented the "local community" where small-plot farmers, traders, and plantation owners met infrequently. In contrast, New England practices of "local community" took the form of the "town" where families from a single Protestant congregation had settled (Meinig, 1986).

The "town" form of "local community" became a normative place in national cartography. The Federal Land Ordinances of 1785 and 1787 surveyed western territories and lay the administrative *groundwork* for regulating land practices (Meinig, 1993). In migrations westward across the northern tier of the United States, people settled into smaller, more densely populated areas. A city system emerged within a transportation network of connection and exchange, giving the North an unforeseen advantage. The more dispersed settlement pattern in the South set up aberrant relations. The southern region was excluded geographically and symbolically in national relations because southern practices of the local developed neither a city system nor civilized pastoral cities.

The more precise telescopic pinpointing of the individual—within the localization of the town as the normative place of local community—brought the body of the population into tighter relations. The vision was of a regulative machinery to penetrate all regions and administer them for the common good (Rose, 1996a). Later, we can read John Dewey's thesis on community in *Democracy and Education* (1916) as an appropriation of northern practices and meanings that he transformed into universal principles of shared values about freedom and obligation.

The common school was an ordering component and normative place that linked the local community to the nation. The land ordinances of the late 1700s required townships to set aside sections to fund construction of schools

and wages for a teacher. We can read the ordinances as remapping the cosmography of schooling into a geography of governing.

Inclusions/Exclusions of National Identity in the "Common" School

The systems of inclusion/exclusion of urbanism mobilized educational
discourses to construct the common school to save a nation careening toward
moral depravity, separatism, and conflict; the purposes of educational discourses were transformative and redemptive (see Popkewitz, 1996). The rhetoric
of inclusion in "common" school campaigns was a nationalist discourse that
attempted to define what was common among those who were *already recognized* as American and to invent strategies for instilling those commonali-
ties within the young. The task seen by common school reformers was to
transform "Carolinians" or far away "Californians," and "settlers," "foreigners," and former "British loyalists," into Americans. The disciplinary role of
schooling was to enable men (with the help of their sisters and mothers) to
raise up the next generation of citizens for participation in self-government.

Specific reforms of common school movements drew upon the mapping
of the reasonable citizen: the American Citizen was Protestant. He spoke an
Americanized English and practiced Anglo or Northern European culture. He
was racially responsive to the "civilizing" benefits of education and was clean
and industrious in thought and demeanor. He demonstrated his allegiance by
being willing to settle within the national landscape.

Within the in-between of included/excluded, pastoral urbanism emerged
as a way to identify deficiencies in city populations. Nomadic, indigent, or
foreign city dwellers, and those who lived a precarious existence on the
periphery, were believed to lack both an economic and moral stake in the
nation. Their "unsettledness" threatened the stability of the landscape, and
their "uncleanliness" and poor health threatened the nation. Schooling for the
children of poor, laboring, and foreign populations in cities would "include"
them by intervening into their lives to make them more "stable" and to give
them skills and dispositions for social inclusion (see also Kaestle, 1983). A
pastoral system of ideas drew together a variety of city schools (e.g. infant,
charity, dame, and monitorial), and appropriated various pedagogies into a
system of moral tutelage (see also Jones, 1990).

Cosmopolitan urbanism located deficiencies of the countryside. Population groups that spoke "incoherent" languages were believed to lack moral
dispositions for national unity. And residents of southern states needed to be
included because they lacked allegiance to the republic. Country schools were
coordinated with city school timetables and curricular technologies: Webster's
dictionaries and grammars regulated language, interdenominational Protes-
tantism organized the subject matter of school texts, and the added curricular
component of national geography disciplined identification with a geopoliti-

cally defined context (Kaestle, 1983). During the painful reconstruction of social collective contexts, those who disagreed argued that parental control of schooling was a fundamental right. Reformers shamed those who objected by labeling them as "provincial" for placing religious or regional values and identities above the nation.

To summarize, from the late 1700s to the decades immediately following the American Civil War in the 1880s, urbanism and discourses of the early common school movement mapped the citizen. The mapping established chains of interaction between the local and the nation by solidifying geopolitical "levels" of state, county, and local supervisory offices. The included/excluded citizen was constructed at the very moment of his inclusion. Wherever the envisioned stability and unity of the national landscape were threatened—by "unstable" populations in cities or by disloyal "provincials"—deficiencies were constructed through a moral and nationalist discourse about identity and its relations to owning land.

Urbanism and the Metaphor of Nation as Society

In contrast to the land metaphor of the early 1800s, from the late 1890s to the 1950s, "society" became the way to imagine the space of the nation-state. The opposition of urban to rural displaced the city-country binary. A new conceptualization of "urban society" was understood as the loss of "rural community." To address the problems of an urban society, education discourses campaigned for mass schooling. Mapping of social differences went into the explicit production of citizens for an urban society.

The Conception of Urban Society as the Loss of Rural Community

We can read the shift to "society" in early discourses of sociology that claimed society as its domain of study. Sociological reasoning at the time conflated "the general notion of 'society' with the empirical phenomenon of territorially bounded social practices" of nation-states (Wagner, 1994, p. 30). From the 1890s to the 1930s, American sociology was concerned with the nature and problems of city life. In 1915, an exhaustive research agenda was proposed in an article entitled "The City: Suggestions for the Investigation of Human Behavior in the City Environment." Sociologists, it was argued, should view the city as a "laboratory or clinic" for the study of "society" (Lindner, 1996, p. 61). A reprint in 1925 changed the title from "City Environment" to "Urban Environment" in an attempt to give "urban society" an empirical *grounding.*

The idea of "grounding" enfolded the metaphor of "land" into a higher empirical form that conflated society with territory. Social and reform-minded investigations were grounded in particular geographic locations: if one wanted to study the distinct ways of living in "society," one's laboratory was the "city." Sociologists and reformers borrowed from the German theorist, Georg Simmel, to assert that the influence of cities spread throughout society. Rural areas were held in opposition to the urban but were ultimately subsumed under the rubric of "urban society." Again, as in the early common school campaigns, the attempt was to "see" national space wholly through a microcosm of the city, but new administrative discourses recast it as "urban society."

An urban-rural dichotomy produced and ordered the opposition of "society" to "community." Community represented the natural or *rural* way to instill dispositions for collective cooperation and social harmony in the individual. In contrast, an urban society represented a complex way of life in which a "heterogeneity" of civic, occupational, ethnic, and professional relations lead to specialization, separation, and conflict (Savage & Warde, 1993; Franklin, 1986).[2] Social problems (i.e., in cities) were understood as the irretrievable loss of a means for social control found previously in rural existence.

The pastoral/cosmopolitan image shifted to an ecological model. Cosmopolitan and pastoral images of the city-country were enfolded into the metaphor of nation as society. Biological conceptions of the city as analogous to the human body became taken as a model for *society* as a whole. A healthy *social body* was compared to a healthy city. For instance, Jane Addams (1912) argued that the "city street" was an unhealthy place for the "spirit of youth" because it provided unregulated intercourse with pleasures found in dance halls, vulgar theaters, alcohol, and cocaine. The pastoral "veins and arteries" of cities became sites of social pathology. Social-biological discourses initiated "ecological" public health reforms in urban design and city planning by locating social deviance and abnormality (Glazer, 1984).

Social science "laws" began to be cast in statistical form and reshaped reasoning about reform. Demographics of ethnicity, occupation, marriage, or age created statistical regularities as populational groups and cleared social space of ambiguities (Wagner, 1994). It became possible to map cities (and society), to correlate groups to other social measures (such as intelligence or birth rates), and to make predictions. A statistics of social difference relocated the citizen in new administrative identities that could be policed within the same system of policing city streets.

Just as bodily pathologies were associated with "alien" organisms and poor hygiene, social pathologies were associated with the immigrant "slum" or "settlement district." New immigrants—from Ireland, Italy, Slovakia, Poland, Turkey, Russia, or China—fared the poorest economically, had to compete for the lowest-paying jobs, and were crowded into housing located next to the foundry, dock, railroad, and factory. They were classified as unskilled or as "peasant stock" similar to the itinerant farm wage-laborer and southern

"Negro" sharecropper. Eugenics and psychometrics discourses calculated the dangers that new immigrants posed to the American "social body" because the groups diluted the "gene pool" and degenerated society's sources of intelligence and morality (Kamin, 1974; Gould, 1981).

The "Burgess Ecological Model" of urban growth emerged as a way to correlate the biological pathologies of the social body to its laboratory, the city (Glazer, 1984). The model conceived of cities as following a general and statistically regular pattern of outward growth. The "wave pattern" of *segregation, invasion, conflict,* and *succession* suggested a narrative of natural processes of assimilation: first, groups sorted themselves into segregated neighborhoods; as one group gained economically, it invaded another area and conflicted with the group already there; after a certain populational "tip point," the new group would replace or succeed the old. Until an immigrant group had been properly assimilated—researchers found it usually took two or three generations—formal means of social control were needed.

The ecological model of the city explained and justified the immigrant "slum" as an inclusionary/exclusionary strategy of internment. Immigrants represented a "viral" threat: the social body needed to be protected from invading and virulent organisms by quarantining its infected areas, treating the disease, and then waiting for the healthy parts of the social body to absorb them.

The ecological model informed educational reforms. The problematic of inclusion situated schooling as a means to treat the "disease" at the local level. The "local" became differentiated according to degrees of pathology, for residents of slums and segregated neighborhoods could not be trusted to exercise their political privileges to elect school officials. Through a revised spatial reasoning, citywide elections of professional superintendents displaced previous forms of city politics based upon neighborhood and ward systems (Tyack, 1974). A second round of common school reforms redefined *common* into *comprehensive,* in which individuals were grouped according to statistical norms. Separate provisions for the "mental defect," stages of "childhood," special needs of "adolescence," and the "truant," "delinquent," or "incorrigible" mapped a new terrain for curriculum (Baker, 1988; Kett, 1977).

The reconstruction of national space into an urban society is significant to an understanding of schooling as a technology of inclusion/exclusion. The shift to discourses of society redefined problems of particular city locations into national terms. The image of an urban society represented a national developmental trend in which the rural became represented as "backward" and "out of step" in thought about *social* problems having *national* proportions (see also Gulliford, 1984). The methods invented to solve problems in cities were extended to the entire territory of society. Social and educational policies that "worked" for the city school were believed to be equally efficacious when applied to the rural school (e.g., intelligence testing and the production of expert knowledges).

The larger point is that historical narratives forget that particular cities, such as Chicago, were the *testing grounds* for generalized applications of social control. An empirically defined and vivisected American society was born out of an amalgamation of discursive practices, statistical operations, and the invention of new administrative contexts that arose in particular pathologized locations.

Inclusions/Exclusions of Societal Identity as Citizenship

We can read the *Cardinal Principles of Secondary Education* (1918) as remapping the citizen. The report's stated purpose was to coordinate the secondary school to newly identified social institutions and administrative identities. The report organized and differentiated the curriculum for the "adolescent" around "adult life performances." A good citizen took on "adult" responsibilities located in the "neighborhood, town, or city, State, and Nation" (p. 14). He did so by acquiring skills in "collective responsibility" as "attitudes and habits important in a democracy" (p. 15). The citizen not only had to recognize his social location but also to follow prescriptions of performance.

The rhetoric of inclusion in the term *collective* worked to exclude by positioning the young as outside and before the space of the reasonable citizen. Although young people participated in strikes, boycotts, and dissemination of dissident literature in various challenges to the social order, the report relocated the young as active performers in the "neighborhood" (see Kett, 1977; Murphy, 1990). Young people's political participation was reclassified as criminal acts or delinquency. Not only were the young regarded as too immature, citizenship itself became a performance. Unlike the natural virtues of citizenship in discourses of land, the shift to society identified citizenship as a role that must be taught. Since society could no longer depend upon rural communities to instill dispositions for self-government, the new configuration of psychology, professionalism, and administration invented pedagogical strategies and psychological identities to regulate citizenship.

To summarize, social and educational reform discourses uprooted and displaced social identities and relocated them in new administrative and psychological mappings of society. Planned and socially organized mechanisms created zoned locations that bound inhabitants into a societal space of regulated freedom (Rose, 1996a). We should not regard the shift in reform discourses as a reaction to social change as much as change itself: other forms of political participation and cultural organization were taken off the map of the citizen. Identification with one's background was subsumed by American identity in which standardized social locations became the collective contexts for inclusion/exclusion.

Governing a Multicultural Society through "Community": Redefining the Problematic of Inclusion

A new urbanism has emerged in current American educational reform discourses of multiculturalism and community. Unlike efforts to assimilate populations in the first half of the twentieth century, multicultural discourses address national and global changes at a time when populational migrations have created a racial and cultural diversity for which the schools are believed to be an instrument of inclusion (see, e.g., Istance, 1997). In the United States, multicultural discourses associate the new diversity with cities, particularly "inner cities." Multicultural discourses racialize "urban" or "inner city" without explicitly designating race. "Urban" acts as a shorthand euphemism for poor "black" and people of color (Lemann, 1991). Rather than regard the shift as a superficial semantic change, the new association of "urban" to "diversity" signals a substantive reordering of the problematic of inclusion.

Social discourses of "society" and "community" remap the "city." The overlay of urbanism and multiculturalism draws in various discourses of society and community which redefine difference and diversity. In an overview of a conference for the American Educational Research Association (AERA), the scaffolding of multiple discourses maps a new landscape. The 1998 theme was "Diversity and Citizenship in Multicultural Societies" (Sleeter and Banks, 1997). I (re)present the overview to highlight the interweaving discourses of urbanism, multiculturalism, society, and community: Educators in *multicultural societies* face a new challenge as the gap between rich and poor widens. *People of color* in *inner city communities* are in *crisis* because jobs have moved to the *suburbs*. Joblessness and poverty impact the citizenship of the *new urban poor* by eroding social and cultural life and robbing young people of *dreams*. The role of education is to develop citizens to be politically *active* in restoring all communities.

To think of an "inner city" as a "community" would have been impossible at the beginning of the century. The idea of the United States as a *multicultural society* has enfolded and reformulated *urban society*. Previously, administrative identities were invented to understand an urban society as a heterogeneous but unitary social body. The problematic for inclusion was internment and assimilation of difference into society. The concept of "multicultural society" redefines the problematic by rejecting assimilation. Multiple communities, it is argued, make up society. The discursive reconstruction has remapped administrative identities of social class and race: *multicultural* poor, and people of color are discursively located in "urban," inner city," or "isolated rural" areas whereas *monocultural*, white, and middle-class populations are discursively located in the "suburb" (see, e.g., Weiner, 1989; Zimpher, 1989). The problematic for inclusion, as stated in the AERA overview, has shifted to how do we reform schooling *in the inner city community* to achieve greater social justice and equality?

The Turn to Community: From Societal Identity to Identity as Lifestyle

A shift to discourses of community engenders a new and salient vocabulary for thinking about the urban school. For instance, school professionals are expected to foster community relations by working closely with the geographic community of the school and also by regarding the school as a "learning community" in which they work to instill a sense of community in their students (see, e.g., Goldberg, 1991).

The turn to discourses of community requires a careful reading. Like the previous motifs of the local and common school, community suggests a separate sphere of autonomy protected from state intervention in which individuals participate equally in determining their lives. Discursively, however, a variety of particular senses of community are used to problematize, analyze, and prescribe collective identity. A "sense of community" can convey Dewey's universal notion of community as shared norms and values to create social harmony, whereas a sense of community activism can connote challenges to the social order, as in the American Civil Rights movements. The idea of community control can also be used to argue against the patronizing and disabling social institutions of the welfare state, which the previous shift to society invented (Cohen, 1985).

In many ways, the ideas of "local" or "community control" shares similarities with the technologies of social control invented at the beginning of the century. If community activism mobilized collective participation to question political and social conventions in the 1960s, today the normative function of society has shifted to community. Citizens in a multicultural society, it is argued, inhabit multiple communities that make claims upon them, of which they need to be made aware. The effort to rescue community and local control from the state emerges, ironically, from the expert discourses that construct community as a means to govern.

We can think of appeals to the citizen's participation in communities as a discursive shift that relocalizes self-government. The site of community, as Nikolas Rose argues, is a discursive space of new moral relations in which individuals have obligations and allegiances to multiple and heterogeneous communities (1996a, 1996b). Community becomes a "micro point of management" of a variety of overlapping networks that are no longer anchored in physical space or the ordered space of society. The community becomes a project of political reflection that aligns the capacities and aspirations of the citizen with the aims of government (Popkewitz, 1996).

The shift to discourses of community has transformed the subject of government by attaching collective identities directly to the life space and life course of the individual. A new citizenship in neoliberal discourses implies a lifestyle related to individual consumption patterns and practices of leisure in which one takes an active role in defining and creating a social identity (Wagner, 1994). A liberal ethos of choice and self-promotion transforms the qualified citizen into one who takes personal responsibility and initiative in managing his or her social destiny and risks. The citizen must be flexible in identifying with multiple communities and, therefore, must be taught the psychological dispositions and capacities for making reasonable choices. At the same time, the newly excluded are subjected to more invasive strategies of community surveillance (see, e.g., Murray, 1995) or are dispersed into a variety of expert pedagogical specialties.

Urbanism and lifestyle intersect in neoliberal discourses of markets. Market discourses assume that all people are situated equally in the community and draw distinctions understood as lifestyle. The self-governing citizen is empowered through an identity as consumer to act within a "local" and private sector. Market discourses emphasize local school decision making and parental involvement in schools (e.g., Powell et al., 1985). However, the suburban lifestyle has become an implicit norm that subordinates the inner city. Chubb and Moe (1990) argue that "heterogeneous" urban schools have "troublesome clientele" who are overburdened by a bureaucracy that doesn't allow them to choose. The authors claim that a more fair and just system of schooling would take as its model the "homogeneous" and "suburban" school in which parents can act as discerning consumers. Political choices are redefined as choices of where to live, to shop, what to eat, where to enroll children in schools, or how to manage a "healthy lifestyle."

Lifestyle as Psychological Biography: Inclusions/Exclusions in Multicultural Pedagogies of Community

Even though discourses of markets and multiculturalism pursue different ideological agendas, they both use the oppositional space of urbanism to distinguish among and hierarchically order communities as markers of life spaces and lifestyles. Multicultural discourses understand the crisis of urban or inner city schools in terms of demographic predictions which identify differences between the communities of the urban child and suburban teacher. For example, a national report on diversity in education finds that up to 70 percent of public school enrollment in the largest school districts are children of color. These children "are more likely to be poor, hungry, in poor health, and to drop out of school than their white counterparts" (Zeichner, 1992, p. 3). In an all-encompassing contrast, teacher education students are portrayed as "overwhelmingly white, female, monolingual, from a rural (small town) or suburban community and . . . come to their teacher education programs with very limited interracial and intercultural experience" (p. 4).

A variety of proposals to remedy the crisis focus upon transforming the prospective teacher. Some argue that we should orient teacher education to urban settings rather than to the "suburban or relatively milder urban school" (Goodlad, 1990, p. 254). Others argue that the focus on the inner city will also apply to suburban and rural areas, but not vice-versa (see, e.g., Weiner, 1989). Still others express doubt that teacher education can transform the "culturally incompetent teacher who might survive in a small town or suburb [but] will not last a day in an urban situation except as a failure or burnout" (Haberman, 1995, p. 92). Implicit in the remapping of individual competencies is a binary of oppositional lifestyle communities.

The binaries that position the "urban" child and teacher are translated into descriptions of their different life courses, life spaces, and lifestyles. A shift occurs from discourses of demographic difference to a psychological register (Popkewitz, 1998a). Issues of racism, gender, and social inequalities are transformed into psychological issues of self-awareness, individual attitudes, and beliefs. The psychological register positions the child and teacher as members of geographic, social, and racial groups, but their group identity is then transformed into psychological biographies.

To understand the "urban" child, multicultural and psychological discourses remap administrative categories of race and social class into biographies of personality, dispositions, and affect. The "urban" child has "street-wise intelligence," "potential," and qualities of "resilience" but lacks confidence, aspirations, and self-esteem (or *dreams*, as in the AERA overview). Psychological discourses construct a separate set of curricular and pedagogical guidelines for racial and cultural differences in rates of development and learning styles (see, e.g., Murrell, 1993). Moreover, in new "constructivist" pedagogies, in which learning is more securely tied to the goal-oriented, active, and choosing individual, the blame for school failure is shifted even further onto the "urban" child (Popkewitz, 1998a).

The discursive space of urbanism has shifted in which the field of symbolic values is reconfigured. What used to be believed as necessary and useful has become the problem. For example, the shedding of one's background identity to be an American is now an inflexible attitude to be corrected by pedagogies of community. Also, to have "street wise intelligence" is a good attribute since the "urban" child cannot be recognized as having a "normal" intelligence. Important changes have occurred that seem to open the school and make it more democratic for urban children, families, and communities, but the binary structure of the discursive field has not changed. The new urbanism has reinscribed a pattern by which new categories of exclusion can be invented.

Closing Comments

The analysis of urbanism through the problematic of governmentality allows us to ask what effects are particular to the United States and more general questions about comparative studies of educational inclusion. In the United States the revised field of symbolic values in a new urbanism seems to draw a more inclusive map of the American Citizen. I have argued that inclusionary reforms structured by the discursive space of urbanism have drawn different maps that historically worked to exclude. We ought to problematize this reasoning, neither because the labels are inaccurate nor because implementation has failed. Urbanism has structured educational reform discourses into binaries that reinscribe categories of exclusion against which the discourses are supposedly arguing.

We can note several important reinscriptions. First, inclusionary rhetoric depends on invoking a collectivity such as "American" or "community" that subsumes other identities. Deficiencies are then identified for which the role of schooling is to invent strategies to include. Second, a new map of inclusion in a multicultural society moves but does not eradicate boundaries of exclusion. Pedagogies of community and psychological biographies have placed the "rural," "inner city," and "urban" outside the space of reason. Finally, the oppositional space of urbanism reinforces the need to police, investigate, and subject to further rigor the space of the urban and bring it under new technologies of discipline. The scaffolding of a new urbanism with discourses of multiculturalism, society, markets, community, and lifestyle produces unrecognized exclusions at the very moment they seek to include.

Urbanism as an oppositional space relates to comparative studies of globalization and regionalization that invoke a dichotomy between global and local or national and "local." An implicit assumption has been that geographic scale helps us to understand issues of social justice and equality. The embedding of geographic scale into populational reasoning invests the state with a sovereign notion of power in which groups of people dominate other groups. The bigger the geographic scale over which privileged groups exert control, it is assumed, the more power is used and abused.

But in the problematic of governmentality, the dichotomy of global-local obscures the productive side of power in which the effects of power are *localizable*. I draw upon an argument by the geographer, Nigel Thrift (1995) to elaborate. To subsume the particular or local under the national or global is a way to exclude. In the case of urbanism, the early metaphor of nation as land helped construct both the "local" and "national" to make government "at a distance" possible. Images of the city and country were used to locate "national" problems by appropriating meanings from particular contexts and invoking them as universal principles to be practiced "locally."

Moreover, the national or global mobilizes large-scale, theoretically totalizing questions and answers that gloss the historically singular and particular effects of power that construct patterns of inclusion/exclusion. Again, in the analysis of urbanism, when discourses shifted to nation as society, the theoretically encompassing rubric of urban society mobilized multiple discourses that subordinated rural and local issues and excluded socially defined groups from American identity. The overlay of urbanism with current discourses of community *relocalizes* the effects of power but neither destroys power nor makes it more equitable.

The discursive localization of the effects of power is important to discussions that use oppositional categories such as the dichotomy of global-local. Global-local distinctions, such as centralization versus decentralization, State versus civil society, or social economies versus markets, are used to frame arguments for social reform but can work to reinscribe new forms of injustice and inequality. That point is that we can understand issues that are of national or global importance while at the same time recognizing that the dichotomy of global-local does not make all issues of democratic freedom intelligible. The dichotomy can work, instead, to obscure the recognition that locally identified governance can be just as effective (and exclusionary) as nationally identified governance.

The reinscription of patterns of inclusion/exclusion relates to a larger issue in comparative studies of education that make assumptions about the relations of the present to its past and future. Historical relations are conjunctural rather than linear. Past formulations form a trajectory that can join at any present moment with newer formulations. Whether the oppositional space of urbanism will produce similar discursive effects in the future cannot be predicted. Therefore, the analysis cannot serve as a guide for educational reform. However, at present, the scaffolding of discourses that come together in the oppositional space of urbanism work to exclude. The analysis can serve a different purpose by excavating unrecognized patterns of inclusion/exclusion in the residue of two centuries of debate about the problems of educating the citizen in the "city."

Notes

A number of people read and commented on earlier drafts. I thank Eva Astrom, Mimi Bloch, Dawnene Hammerberg, Inger Karlefors, Lisbeth Lundahl, and Hannah Tavares for their participation in a series of seminars held in collaboration with Umeå University in Sweden during 1996 and 1997. I also thank Mary Baumann, Katy Heyning, Dori Lightfoot, Jie Qi, and Dar Weyenberg whose work influenced my own as we prepared for our joint presentations at AERA in 1997. Lynn Fendler provided invaluable assistance as I prepared the final manuscript, and members of the Wednesday Group gave it a careful and critical reading. Finally, a special thanks goes to Tom Popkewitz who helped me clarify, tighten, and understand the argument I was groping to make. I am deeply indebted and grateful to him for his help and encouragement.

1. Throughout, the terms *image* or *landscape* can be thought of as a "process by which social and subjective identities are formed" (Mitchell, 1994, p. 1). Representations are discursive practices that enfold and reformulate the collective contexts in which social identities are formed.

2. The notion of *heterogeneity* to describe an "urban society" is different from late twentieth-century usages that signify cultural and racial differences in a "multicultural society." This point is taken up in the next section.

References

Addams, J. *The Spirit of Youth and the City Sreets.* New York: Macmillan, 1912.

Anderson, B. *Imagined Communities: Reflections on the Origin and Spread of Nationalism.* London and New York: Verso, 1991.

Baker, B. "Childhood-as-Rescue in the Emergence and Spread of the U..S. Public School." In T. Popkewitz and M. Brennan (eds.) *Foucault's Challenge: Discourse, Knowledge and Power in Education.* New York: Teachers College Press, 1998.

Becker, C. *The Heavenly City of the Eighteenth-Century Philosophers.* New Haven, Conn.: Yale University Press, 1932.

Cardinal Principles of Secondary Education: A Report of the Commission on the Reorganization of Secondary Education, Appointed by the National Education Association. Department of the Interior, Bureau of Education, Bulletin, 1918, No. 35. United States Printing Office. Washington: 1937.

Chubb, J. & T. Moe. *Politics, Markets and America's Schools.* Washington, D.C.: Brookings Institution, 1990.

Cohen, S. *Visions of Social Control: Crime, Punishment, and Classification.* Cambridge: Polity Press, 1985.

De Certeau, M. "Walking in the City." In *The Practice of Everyday Life.* Berkeley and Los Angeles: University of California Press, 1984, pp. 95–96.

Dewey, J. *Democracy and Education.* New York: Free Press, 1916.

Dumm, T. L. "Freedom and Space." In *Michel Foucault and the Politics of Freedom.* New York: Sage, 1996, pp. 29–68.

Foucault, M. "Space, Knowledge, and Power." In P. Rabinow (ed.) *The Foucault Reader.* New York: Pantheon, 1984, pp. 239–56.

——. *Power/Knowledge: Selected Interviews and Other Writings, 1972–1977.* C. Gordon (ed.). New York: Pantheon, 1980.

Franklin, B. *Building the American Community: The School Curriculum and the Search for Social Control.* London and Philadelphia: Falmer, 1986.

Glazer, N. "Not on Sociological Images of the City." In L. Rodwin and R. Hollister (eds.). *Cities of the Mind: Images and Themes of the City in the Social Sciences.* New York and London: Plenum, 1984, pp. 337–44.

Goldberg, B. "Redesigning Schools: Architecture and School Restructuring." *Radius* 3 (1991): 1–13.

Goodlad, J. I. *Teachers for Our Nation's Schools.* San Francisco: Jossey-Bass, 1990.

Gould, S. J. "The Mismeasure of Man." New York and London: W. W. Norton, 1981.

Gulliford, A. *America's Country Schools.* National Trust for Historic Preservation: Preservation Press, 1984.

Haberman, M. *Star Teachers of Children in Poverty.* West Lafayette, Ind.: Kappa Delta Pi, 1995.

Istance, D. "Education and Social Exclusion." *The OECD Observer* 208 (1997): 27–30.

Jones, D. "The Genealogy of the Urban Schoolteacher." In S. J. Ball (ed.) *Foucault and Education: Disciplines and Knowledge.* London & New York: Routledge, 1990.

Kaestle, C. *Pillars of the Republic: Common Schools and American Society, 1780–1860.* New York: Hill and Wang, 1983.

Kamin, L. *The Science and Politics of IQ.* New York: Halsted Press, 1974.

Kett, J. *Rites of Passage: Adolescence in America, 1790 to the Present.* New York: Basic Books, 1977.

Kliebard, H. *The Struggle for the American Curriculum, 1893–1958.* New York and London: Routledge, [1986] 1992.

Lemann, N. *The Promised Land: The Great Black Migration and How it Changed America.* New York: Alfred A. Knopf, 1991.

Lindner, R. Adrian Morris (trans.). *The Reportage of Urban Culture: Robert Park and the Chicago School.* Cambridge: Cambridge University Press, [1990] 1996.

Marx, L. *Machine in the Garden: Technology and the Pastoral Ideal in America.* New York: Oxford University Press, 1964.

Meinig, D. W. *The Shaping of America: A Geographical Perspective on Five Hundred Years of History. Volume 1, Atlantic America, 1492–1800.* New Haven, Conn. and London: Yale University Press, 1986.

———. *The Shaping of America: A Geographical Perspective on Five Hundred Years of History. Volume 2, Continental America, 1800–1867.* New Haven, Conn. and London: Yale University Press, 1993.

Mitchell, W. J. T. (ed.) *Landscape and Power.* Chicago: University of Chicago Press, 1994.

Murphy, M. *Blackboard Unions: The AFT and the NEA, 1900–1980.* Ithaca, N.Y. and London: Cornell University Press, 1994.

Murray, M. Correction at Cabrini-Green: A Sociospatial Exercise of Power. *Environment and Planning D: Society and Space* 13 (1995): 311–27.

Murrell, P. "Afrocentric Immersion: Academic and Personal Development of African American Males in Public Schools." In T. Perry and J. Fraser (eds.) *Freedom's Plow: Teaching in the Multicultural Classroom.* New York: Routledge, 1993.

Palen, J. J. *The Suburbs.* New York: McGraw-Hill, Inc.

Popkewitz, T. S. "The Culture of Redemption and the Administration of Freedom as Research." *Review of Educational Research* 68, 1 (Spring 1998): 1–34.

———. *Struggling for the Soul: The Politics of Schooling and the Construction of the Teacher.* New York and London: Teachers College Press, 1998a.

————. "Dewey, Vygotsky, and the Social Administration of the Individual: Constructivist Pedagogy as Systems of Ideas in Historical Spaces." *American Educational Research Journal,* 35 (4) (1998b): 535–70.

————. "Pedagogical Ideas in Historical Spaces: 'Constructivism,' and the Governing the 'self.' "

Powell, A. G., E. Farrar & D. Cohen. *The Shopping Mall High School: Winners and Losers in the Educational Marketplace.* Boston: Houghton Mifflin, 1985.

Rose, N. "Governing 'Advanced' Liberal Democracies." In A. Barry, T. Osborne and N. Rose (eds.) *Foucault and Political Reason: Liberalism, Neo-Liberalism and Rationalities of Government.* Chicago: University of Chicago Press, 1996a, pp. 37–64.

————. "Governing Enterprising Individuals." *Inventing Our Selves: Psychology, Power, and Personhood.* New York and Melbourne: Cambridge University Press, 1996b, pp. 150–68.

Savage, M. & A. Warde. *Urban Sociology, Capitalism and Modernity.* New York: Continuum, 1993.

Sennett, R. *Flesh and Stone: The Body and the City in Western Civilization.* New York and London: W. W. Norton, 1994.

Silver, H. "Social Exclusion and Social Solidarity: Three Paradigms." *International Labour Review* 133 (1994/5–6): 531–78.

Sleeter, C. E. & J. A. Banks. "Annual Meeting 1998." *Educational Researcher* 26, 8 (November 1997): 37.

Thrift, N. "A Hyperactive World." In R. J. Johnson (ed.) *Geography and Global Change.* Cambridge: Blackwell, 1995, pp. 18–35.

Toulmin, S. *Cosmopolis: The Hidden Agenda of Modernity.* Chicago: University of Chicago Press, 1990.

Tyack, D. B. *The One Best System: A History of American Urban Education.* Cambridge and London: Harvard University Press, 1974.

Wagner, P. *A Sociology of Modernity.* London and New York: Routledge, 1994.

Weiner, L. "Asking the Right Questions: An Analytic Framework for Reform of Urban Teacher Education." *The Urban Review* 21, 3 (1989): 151–61.

Williams, R. *The City and the Country.* New York: Oxford University Press, 1973.

Wills, G. "The American Adam." *New York Review of Books,* March 6, 1997, pp. 30–34.

Young, R. J. C. D. *Colonial Desire: Hybridity in Theory, Culture and Race.* New York and London: Routledge, 1995.

Zeichner, K. "Educating Teachers for Cultural Diversity." *National Center for Research on Teacher Learning, NCRTL.* Special report, September. Ann Arbor: Michigan State University, 1992.

Zimpher, N. "The RATE Project: A Profile of Teacher Education Students." *Journal of Teacher Education* (November–December 1989): 27–30.

Part IV

Intellectuals, Knowledge, and Educational Change

CHAPTER 12

Critics and Reconstructors

On the Emergence of Progressive Educational Expertise in South Africa

JOHAN MÜLLER

> Are intellectuals prophets and sages; or are they scientists, specialised researchers, or technical innovators? Are they critics of power or expert advisers to politicians, direct or indirect moulders of public opinion? . . . Positions on these questions, and on a host of related ones, are rarely held in full consciousness; they are implicit orientations . . . a permanent substratum of thought, a part of the cultural preconscious, a vital source of the cognitive dispositions at work in the intellectual field.
>
> —Fritz Ringer, 1992, pp. 16, 17

Steve Appel (1993) has argued that educators schooled in theory and reflection are not automatically thereby qualified to offer policy prescriptions. Appel's point is that mastery in the discourse of critique does not necessarily transfer to mastery in the discourse of reconstruction.[1] Appel is here valuably reminding us that each discourse has its own grammar, its own language game.[2] His polemic is against a certain group of educators who seemed to feel entitled to provide policy for the new democratic State in South Africa on the basis of critical credentials and liberation movement membership, rather than demonstrated expertise, in the protocols of the new game.

The question pursued in this chapter is not so much whether theorists (or, in the idiom of this chapter, critics) are or are not suited to reconstructive work; neither is it to establish the epistemological distinctiveness of the two

265

domains of activity (see Appel's [1994] distinction between "theoretical" and "political" social practice); and nor is it to advocate one above the other, as Dale (1993) does when distinguishing between "critical theory" and "problem solving." Obviously the concerns are related. It is rather the sociology of knowledge as one of the conditions under which intellectuals will position themselves in one camp or another, and how this positioning takes place in a concrete instance.

All Is Activism

Civil society as a social-interpretive construction of equality and universality (Balibar, 1990) shares with nationalism, in all its varieties, including national liberation, the virtue and vice of suppressing the potentially divisive interests that lie at the heart of the social division of complex modern societies. To put that another way, it allows for the construction of a wider community and commonality, a shared horizon of striving that goes beyond personal, ethnic, or occupational self-interest, and this allows in turn for a canopy of common sense that highlights common aspirations, while deemphasizing local and particular goals and preoccupations (Tester, 1992). One might note that this way of talking about social-interpretive constructions does not assume that these form a Parsonian "action frame" in any strong sense: in other words, this does not imply that people actually set aside their particular interests for common ones in a civil society imaginary, although this may well happen. It merely asserts that they are predisposed to understand and intervene in the field of social representations in these terms.

In the period up to 1990, intellectuals within the national liberation movement in South Africa, an aspirant civil society and a national-popular imaginary of great power, understood themselves to be waging the struggle in ways that were different only in degree if at all from that of mainstream political activists. Of course many intellectuals were themselves mainstream activists and so their activism and their intellectual work could only have seemed to them all of a piece. But at the height of the struggle in the middle and late 1980s, intellectual work was seen by intellectuals and activists alike as waging the struggle by other means only.

There were a number of entailments to this view. First of all, intellectuals had a sense of belonging to a larger endeavor. This was its greatest advantage and certainly not to be taken lightly in an era of global intellectual fragmentation. But it fudged the distinction between analytical knowledge and strategic knowledge, a feature inadvertently in common with what some postmodernists like Lyotard (1984) advocate. It obscured the occupational boundary between intellectual workers (like academics) and that of other classes: they were all "in the struggle" in the same way at the same time, as it were. It also blurred the boundary between political and social power: "The people" as a bloc, so it was tacitly assumed, would come to rule one day. The possibility that a political elite might come to political power and that a social elite might continue to be privileged could not be voiced in the rhetoric of the national-popular imaginary. It obscured the fact that "national liberation," if not invented by intellectuals (because real popular struggles did construct real histories of reference) was at least shaped and narrativized by intellectuals, for instance by historians both in and out of the South African Communist Party, and especially by sociologists of work who had declared themselves for the working class.

It is self-evident now, but was not so then, that the strong narrative of "people's power" as a political driving force was a construction set out by intellectuals and propagated by leadership elites. They were, after all, the ones with access to the tools of narrativization. To be sure, the best intellectuals were well aware of this.

But in the day-to-day construction of the struggle, the difference between intellectual work and activism proper was blurred, so that to all intents and purposes, all was activism. Insofar as they continued to separate out in practice—since intellectual concerns were not always necessarily strategic—popular wisdom had it that intellectual work should be subordinate to the strategic needs of the struggle, always and absolutely. It is not too much to say that intellectuals were all but invisible as a separate category within the national-democratic movement at this time, except as they obdurately kept surfacing as aspirants to leadership.[3]

In writing about these things in the mid-eighties, Nico Cloete and I (Müller & Cloete, 1987) were inclined to share the ambivalence of George Konrad and Ivan Szelenyi about the social effect of intellectuals who were, as they put it, "on the road to class power," of intellectuals who did not acknowledge their social base and social project within a broader national social movement. At that time, we were somewhat more optimistic than I am now about the prospect for democratizing the process of knowledge production, for minimizing the impact of exclusion through methodological means—through participatory research and other supposedly democratic methodologies (see Müller, 1993, for signs of disillusionment).

It is not the place here to embark on a substantial critique of intellectuals in the struggle in South Africa, but rather to look more specifically at what happens to a loose community of intellectuals in a particular area—education—when the social movement for national liberation that they, in different ways perhaps, felt a part of, changed gear as it did in South Africa in February 1990. This is a story about how such a fledgling community, embedded deep within the bosom of the struggle, is winkled out, and repositioned, by changing social forces and conditions, and how its own strategy in response has, in addition to a host of other things, strengthened the occupational power of educational intellectuals in the postliberation period.

The story will inevitably overhomogenize this group of educational intellectuals. The intention of the present story is merely to establish the contours of the broad trajectory within which subsequent subtrajectories fell. The methodological concern here is to establish how the interpretive interventions of the intellectuals can usefully be analyzed as social constructions in a determinate social field, and how they can be analyzed in their shifts as part of the forces at play in the field and in the wider society.

World-Historical Context

Intellectual fields and subfields of particular countries are increasingly shaped by, and help shape, the world-historical context. Within the globalizing forces at work today, two major and somewhat contradictory dynamics can be discerned which seem to tug the intellectual task in one or other direction: in practice, in both directions, albeit unevenly, at once. The first is an *epistemological* challenge to "strong thought," incorporating:

* antipositivism and a serious vogue for qualitative participatory methods (for example, Lather, 1991);
* a strong assertion of the critical role of intellectuals—for example, Adorno's negative dialectics and Foucault's antiprophetic stance;[4]
* metaphysical critiques of strong thought and of master narratives in postmodernist writings and pragmatic organizational analysis alike (for example, Vattimo, 1988, and Mulgan, 1989).

Yet today, despite the "development" critiques of the seventies, the current internationalizing discourse around "development" is arguably stronger than it ever has been: as can be seen, for example, in the International Monetary Fund, World Bank, and the near-hegemonic status of recent World Development Reports, and so on. "Development" has, in other words, become a polysemic globalizing master narrative in an era resolutely inimical to master narratives.

The second is a *political* challenge to occupational experts, notably an increasing popular suspicion of "expertise" in general and in technical policy in particular, of the "false security of a society from the drawing board" (Beck, 1993, p.119). This suspicion is particularly marked in Eastern Europe, but elsewhere too, especially where IMF conditionalities are causing hardship (see for example Amsterdamski & Rhodes, 1993).

This is undoubtedly fueled by the collapse of planned socialism in Eastern Europe, but also by the unexpected economic successes of the Pacific Rim countries among others. Nevertheless, in all of this, although contested, economism—the priority of capitalist growth—remains dominant. Indeed, despite the critiques, it seems to have grown in influence.

The third is increasing ferment around the *changing role of intellectuals.* This is said to be from "legislators" to "interpreters," in Bauman's (1987) terms, or described as a growing disconnection or "cultural desynchronization" between elites and masses. Intellectuals are widely said to be "specific" or "local" rather than universal.

Nevertheless, the emergence of global problems with effects stretching far beyond national borders, acts against this localizing trend. For example, global warming and other ecological threats, the nuclear threat, and the AIDS epidemic have all contributed to the *rise of the international expert,* the *international development consultant,* and have established the indispensability of the expert and of expertise in thinking through policy dilemmas that are increasingly unthinkable for the ordinary person.

As Ringer (1992) has shown, the way in which intellectuals have situated themselves with respect to these two opposing dynamics, which in this chapter I call, respectively, *"critique" and "reconstruction,"* depends on the structure of the intellectual field and its relation to the field of power in any historical conjunction.

The particular intellectual focused on here, as already mentioned above, is a group of *progressive educational intellectuals* in South Africa—many of them but certainly not all academics—to examine how they responded to the social forces surrounding them, and to look at how they came to change their role as well as their view as those forces came to change.

I will look at the evolution of this community in three phases:

Mid 1980s to 1990
1990 to 1992
1992 to April 1994

In each of these phases I will examine how the tension between "critique" and "reconstruction" was configured and handled. In each case, I will suggest, this was dealt with on the symbolic level by means of a debate between a set of opposites, and it is the shifting terms of this debate that is the main focus of this chapter.

Phase One: Mid 1980s to 1990

There are two general features of the educational environment worth mentioning at the outset. Until quite recently, formal State education, ever since it was taken over by the State in the nineteenth century, has featured in the discourses of the (non-Eastern-bloc) Left, largely by way of a *critique of its social control function.* That is to say, the international New Left has overwhelmingly dealt with education in terms of critique. Secondly, and relatedly, the overriding tenor of progressive educational politics in South Africa has been that of *oppositional politics* since at least Soweto 1976, for entirely understandable reasons. This has only recently begun to change. Together, these two contextual features, against the background of those above, has had a number of distinct effects on the way that progressive educators came to see their job in the early and mid-1980s. In this time, two sets of distinctions that were to emerge later could not be made, such was the homogenizing suction pulling everyone into a central binary vortex, into singular identification with either the "people" or the "State":

These distinctions were:

- the distinction between *political work* and *civic work*
- the distinction between *activism* and *intellectual work*

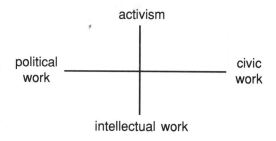

In other words, intellectual work was connected with activism, and civic work connected with political work. As we shall see later in phase two, the terms of the first connection begins to separate out, while the second only begins to separate out in phase three.

Among the many implications of this connection, I will mention only two, by way of example:

1. In the universities where progressive academics taught, those learning to be teachers were given, from the early eighties at least, an astringent diet of marxist reproduction theory. The guiding theorist was of course Althusser, who, with his famous theory of ideology was, in his own context in Paris, trying to theorize the conditions for political action in the wake of the failed revolution of 1968. In South Africa, militant action in the streets was to continue sporadically from 1976 up to 1990, and the students who had become acquainted with Althusser beat the plough-shares of his theories into militant

slogans that fueled their implacable activism and lent it coherence and justification. Althusser might have been flattered but he surely also would have been astonished (see Müller & Tomaselli, 1990). For both intellectuals and activists, at this time, the "road to the state was closed" (Morphet, 1986). The leftwing academics with their borrowed reproduction theory were in effect practicing, on the level of theory, what the activists were doing in the streets—that is, writing the implacability of the State and the need for absolute resistance. The effect was a totalizing standoff between the "people" and the "state," what later was to be called a "violent and unstable equilibrium" (see, for example, Wolpe, 1991).

2. The National Education Crisis Committee (NECC) was formed to break the stalemate. In 1985 a grouping of seasoned political activists, notably Eric Molobi and Vusi Khanyile, organized an umbrella group of parents with teacher and student organizations with the aim of taking the stalemated struggle out of education and getting the youth back to school. This strategy was never really successful, but the founding of the NECC did lead to the establishment of a distinction between *political work* on the one hand, and *civic activities* on the other. At a national NECC workshop at St. Lukes near Johannesburg in August 1989, the distinction was publically made between *political* and *program work*, the latter referring to bursary programs and policy analysis (see below). It was said at the time that the strategic needs of the NECC's political agenda should not hinder the ongoing work of the program work. This prised apart a distinction, albeit hotly contested at the time, of two different forms of struggle. This distinction was later to mature into the political/civil society distinction. Nevertheless, the distinction would take time to filter down into practice.

As the eighties wore on, the NECC leadership had become persuaded of the need for "intellectual assistance" in the struggle, and, in partnership with universities, set up first two, and later a third, Educational Policy Units to do this. Because the issue was never properly clarified, it was completely understandable that the NECC would have one conception and the universities another conception of what the EPUs were supposed to be doing.

The NECC had an activist definition of service to the struggle, one where the EPU's role was to provide intellectual ammunition, that is, to undergird the strategic needs of political struggle. The university, on the other hand, had a conventional definition of scientific work, one where the EPU's role was that of reconstruction and development. The first view was a short-term one; the second a longer-term one. In addition, the NECC was distinguishing only between the first distinction (political and civic work), the university between the second (activism and intellectual work). This unacknowledged difference in orientation led to numerous arguments, and all too often, to a stalemate.

What did the academics and activists working in the EPUs think? They too were confused and torn by conflicting loyalties. And since they could not choose, indeed were not permitted to choose, they shuttled unsatisfactorily back and forth between activism and intellectual work (Müller & Vinjevold, 1991).

The EPUs were effectively paralyzed by this dual and incompatible expectation in this phase. They were never able to provide intellectual ammunition effectively, mostly because by the time they had written their reports the strategic moment had passed; nor were they ever able to do development work efficiently, for a reason I will discuss further below.

So although civic activities were now separated from political work proper, it is fair to conclude that to make any distinction between critical work and reconstructive work was virtually impossible in the political crucible at this time. Those who did try, on a *theoretical* level, distinguishing between Habermas's cognitive and strategic interests, for example, were ignored (see Müller & Cloete, 1987) or on a *practical* level, like those in the Urban Foundation, were suspected of being complicit with the State. The specificity of reconstruction for the struggle was a concept completely unthinkable to the ordinary educational activist, and indeed, for most education intellectuals too, although its time was almost come.

Phase Two: 1990 to 1992

When de Klerk liberalized the political climate on February 2, 1990, he unlocked a series of chain reactions that he could probably never have foreseen. The major one, undoubtedly, was that the bipolar logic of people-State began to unravel and fragment. The people began to split into multiple interest groups, some closer to, some further away from, the State. Another was that groups like the NECC, or at least their national leadership, who had thought of themselves as being in opposition for perpetuity, were suddenly confronted with the possibility of being in government. Indeed, within weeks, they were talking to the state departments, and were being asked to submit plans for emergency budgets. Where would they get these plans? They turned to the EPUs. But remember: the EPUs were stalemated, they had at best done some short-term activist analysis and a little orthodox academic work, so were entirely unpracticed in this new kind of activity, which they soon realized.

So quickly did events move in that intoxicating time that by the middle of the year, the slogan *from critique to reconstruction* was already a cliché. Everywhere, from every side, not only policy think tanks but nongovernmental organizations (NGOs) and academics were being enjoined to leave aside critique and to embrace "reconstruction" (see Chisholm, 1992). We should not underestimate with *what stunned apprehension* this was met by the education intellectuals, both in and out of the EPUs. How were they to do this? It went against their whole training, their conceptual view of knowledge, and their sense of place in society. There was practically no indigenous Left education tradition of reconstruction to draw from, except perhaps in the field of literacy work (Paulo Freire) and Patrick van Rensburg's Education with Production. And they soon became aware that the field of reconstructive policy work had become quite technical with the rapid influx of international consultants in the shape of the Harvard Institute of International Development, the Paris-based International Institute of Education Policy, the World Bank, and other NGO-connected "tourists of reconstruction."

From within the EPUs and in protracted discussion with the NECC national leadership, the idea was born of a fixed-duration national effort at sketching the policy terrain for the progressive movement. By 1991, a fullscale national investigation, the National Education Policy Investigation (NEPI), was set in motion, involving some three hundred educators and activists in and out of universities in twelve research groups. By the end of 1992 the reports were published (see NEPI, 1993).

Because of its heritage, NEPI was not in any position to execute a neat leap from critique to reconstruction, from activist theorizing to technical planning, despite certain strong expectations from some quarters that it would. Indeed, quite the contrary.

The research enterprise, from the guiding committees to the research groups, was set up with the explicit brief to balance intellectual and political inputs, to balance in the policy discourse itself strategic and analytical demands. There were thus activists as well as academics in each work group, at least such was the intention, setting the stage for an explicit confrontation between two purposes of intellectual work that had up to now been latent. And, more important for this story, the intellectuals began to differ among themselves as to which—intellectual or strategic considerations—should play the steering role.

The debate was variously figured: between an ends-based discourse versus a means-based discourse; between a State versus civil society centered discourse; between equity and efficiency (see Parker, 1993). But by far the bitterest contest occurred around the concepts of "equity" (or sometimes "equality") and "development."[5] Equity came to stand for people's needs, aspirations, and struggles, for a composite conception of social justice. And development came to stand for macroeconomic requirements and macroefficiency, for the imperatives of a transforming State system whose needs superseded this or that group which may, as a consequence, be expected to defer their group-specific needs for those of the greater good.

For those groups or intellectuals leaning toward the activist side, equity considerations were incontestably paramount, and the discourse of development was rejected as an excuse for not satisfying the needs of the people. Equity, it was asserted here, was the primary goal of the education struggle. For those leaning toward development, to insist on equity before all else was simply populist ignorance. With the superiority of those who know that the State requires reconstruction more than critique, academics of this persuasion sailed serenely and without any question at all into development and reconstruction, into reconstructive policy work. Where, we may ask with Appel (1993), did they learn it? Largely from the economists who came to sit in quite a few of the research groups and from those isolated individuals, like Peter Buckland, who had found themselves in homeland government before. The rest invented it as they went along.

An editorial group had been given the impossible job of ensuring that each group balanced both "equity" and "development" considerations in their final reports, though quite what *balance* might mean no one clearly knew beforehand.

By and large, and with greater or lesser reluctance, the groups took up the challenge, and a NEPI-wide debate ensued about how the balance should best be effected. This debate can crudely be represented in terms of two opposing positions:

- Proponents of position one—*development< >equity*, construed the two policy goals as irrevocably in tension. They evinced a certain cynicism about the automatic benevolence of development—after all, as long-time theorists, the proponents of this position were steeped in underdevelopment theory and in other critiques of development (see for example Wolpe, 1980), but they nevertheless recognized that some or other view of development was essential in order to locate national priorities (Wolpe, 1992). Proponents realized too that equity of every kind demanded is not realizable (Gerwel, 1992) and that policy poses the question of how to choose.
- Proponents of position two—*development/equity*—assumed, implicitly or explicitly, that it is in principle possible to balance or reconcile developmental criteria with equity demands. Indeed, some argued that it was essential to make this assumption in order to pursue reconstruction while retaining legitimacy in this period (Kraak, 1992). And it is this view too that is reflected in the African National Congress' Reconstruction and Development Programme (ANC, 1993a) and their Policy Framework for Education and Training (1993b) (see also Unterhalter and Young, 1994, p. 8).

Both positions thus implicitly recognized the need to keep development and equity in some or other relation, spurred on as they were by the editorial group at the behest of their executive committee. But position-one proponents wished to retain the tension between the two as a constitutive tension at the heart of the intellectual enterprise of doing policy, while position-two proponents wished in effect to move beyond the uncomfortable tension into some or other relation of accommodation as soon as possible. While this was sometimes done in order to keep as many constituencies within a broad consensus as possible, an in-principle accommodation was also necessary for policy to be amenable to technical solutions. Without it policy debates stall in a standoff over divergent ends, as Weber saw so clearly. It was inevitable then that the debate, while having political and ideological overtones, was in the end not a debate about political ideology so much as a debate about the politics of intellectual work. Discernable in position one is a particular embryonic version of our "critics," in position two, a particular version of our "reconstructors."

The tussle in NEPI was surprisingly heated at times, but in the end, the stake was far larger than NEPI: it had to do not only with how policy should best be done, but also about the political and professional forms that policy work should take. But these material coordinates were only to emerge clearly in phase three. In phase two, the initial jockeying for position in the intellectual field was conducted largely as a debate around equity and development, and this form of jockeying was conditioned largely by the early stage of interest-differentiation characterizing this phase. In other words, because the emergent interest-contests had yet to take on mature institutional and material forms, because the struggle continued to provide a unifying, if diminishingly so, definition of the terrain, the emergent conflict of interests among the intellectuals could best be fought out in symbolic ways only. And yet, the terms of the discursive conflict, albeit locally inflected, are the terms of distinction that divide the terrain of intellectual work in all complex modern societies. For that reason, the equity-development debate in NEPI, if read in this way, provides a particularly revealing case study of the emergence of educational policy expertise, of the emergence of reconstructors in South African educational policy discourse.

There were of course in the NEPI ranks those who propounded an equity-only position. These tended to be either politicians expressing the demands and needs of their constituents, or NGOs who had been founded to deal directly with those expressed needs. On the other hand, there were also those who propounded a development-only position, mainly economists and human resources experts, admittedly in a small minority in NEPI. With hindsight, it is remarkable that the debate was, by and large, joined in terms of some or other *necessary relation* between them. Up until then, the debate between the two positions is the nearest that the national educational debate had got to balancing the intellectual roles of critique and reconstruction. History may well judge that NEPI's greatest success was, for a brief period, to succeed in juggling equity and development, politics and expertise, critique and reconstruction, in the same discursive space, without allowing them to become either conflated or split. If phase one was a phase of fission, phase three was to be a phase of severance. To this extent, NEPI was an exemplary antitechnicist policy endeavor, one perfectly reflecting the time of fledgling but emergent interest-group activity within which it was embedded.

Phase Three: 1992 to April 1994

The third phase places these emergent features of postliberalization civil society—the fragmentation of unified-front constituencies, and the emergence and consolidation of specific institutions, mainly NGOs, taking either "critical" or "reconstruction" positions—into clearer focus.

By 1992, reconstruction had become serious business in South Africa, spearheaded not least by the two major founding activists of the NECC, Eric Molobi (Kagiso Tust) and Vusi Khanyile (Thebe Investments). Especially Molobi was, by 1993, directing European Community (now Union) funding to reconstruction and development projects only, and many education NGOs were either adapting from an equity only position or going to the wall.

What Molobi and Khanyile as the NECC's preeminent activists had learned was the self-defeating effect of collapsing strategic and analytic activities, equality and development considerations. They came thus to pursue development *for* equity of a certain sort, and in so doing, they came to emphasize the technical task of reconstruction. In so doing too, they came to embody the view, if only implicitly, that only by *splitting* the two could reconstruction be promoted.

In the event, neither Molobi nor Khanyile supported NEPI, since both became impatient with the way that the balancing enterprise slowed everything down. They were unimpressed too with the NEPI decision to present policy options rather than a coherent policy model, a decision perhaps more in keeping with the exigencies of the second phase than the needs of the third.

Some academics felt obscurely betrayed when NEPI consciously closed up shop at the end of 1992. It had, after all, been a national rallying and organizing initiative, and had provided a forum for many local and individual voices that might not otherwise have found a national resonance. But any brake on the forward surge of progressive educators by NEPI's demise was more apparent than real. In truth, the field was in more ferment than ever. The discussion below can give only a small flavor of it, and here only in terms of certain broad tendencies. I would certainly not want to claim that all educators now came to define themselves as either critics or reconstructors, but I would suggest that all of them came to define themselves, if only implicitly, with respect to the two tendential roles of academic work, and thereby came to position themselves in a specific relation to both State and civil society.

Numbers of erstwhile NEPI academics returned quite happily to their "critical" colleagues in academia who had been morally marginalized by the first wave of policy work in phase two. From these quarters has emerged a new wave of critique, critical sometimes of prevailing concepts of development (Chisholm, 1992), and sometimes of the idea of policy itself: Appel's (1993) paper is a scholarly version of a more widespread critical received wisdom.[6] A related feature of this critical regrouping is the beginning of professionalization of critical academia. The Southern African Comparative and History Education Society was founded in 1992 and the annual Kenton Conference, long holding out as a "family" rather than an organization, succumbed in 1993 to become Kenton Educational Association (KEA): so too the South African Association of Academic Development and others. It is certainly too early to say how this professionalization will turn out, but it may be surmised that educators taking this route will seek, and find, common cause (because of common material interest) with similar professional associations who, for reasons of political affiliation, they would previously have avoided like the plague: the conservative Pedagogical Society has approached Kenton Educational Association for a possible merger. Both the sociological and psychological communities, split into pro- and antiapartheid organizations, have already remerged. This is what the postideological period (in Offe's, 1990, sense) will mean in practice.

Two other developments also fall within this quadrant. The first is a regrouping among the NGOs that were previously equity driven. These have now begun to form themselves into national proto-professional networks. While many of these may be seen, and may indeed see themselves, as reconstructors, their position is undergirded by a resolute polarization between State provision and civil society provision. Indeed, many NGOs see themselves as the champions of the people ("development is about people") against an uncaring State. The second development is the proliferation of donor-driven program evaluations, written assessments of NGO work in education, commissioned from either academia or from market-based educational consultancies, giving rise to centers of instant educational expertise that sprouted rapidly in this period (Taylor, 1995).

A second group of erstwhile NEPI academics, together with others, perhaps disappointed to have missed out on NEPI, bitten by the bug of policy and keen to pursue it further, looked for and found spaces to pursue these interests in the proliferation of education agencies and think tanks. Others, keen to have a more direct impact on policy, allied themselves to working groups of forums like the National Education and Training Forum and the National Training Board. This work has not emerged as unabashedly technical as that in related sectors like housing, trade policy, and health, although that will undoubtedly still come, especially as quantitative indicators of school quality became the policy fashion of the moment. Nevertheless this work is demonstrably development oriented, engaged in macrosystemic concerns, and is nationally reconstructive in focus. To that extent, it has reached out to power, so to speak, and has cut itself quite adrift from the localist, particularist, needs-oriented, discursive currents that were far more centrally evident in the mainstream of policy work in phase two. To that extent too, this work has forged multiple links with international policy and planning operations, like the Harvard Institute of International Development, International Institute of Educational Policy, the World Bank, and global educational consultants who visit now with increasing frequency.

Willy nilly, this branch of policy work is becoming part of the global mainstream concern with *development* and *reconstruction,* terms popularized, operationalized, and quantified by successive World Bank reports (see World Bank, 1991).

The EPUs survived the transition to the third phase with mixed fortunes, continuing to shuttle rather unsatisfactorily between political and civil society, accepting commissions from both, but continuing to worry about their appropriate role. The cleavage of phase two has not yet compelled them to choose, although it has made their position increasingly uncomfortable.

At the point of political transition in April 1994, the groups of education academics, briefly and disorganizedly cobbled together under the NEPI mantle and forced to accommodate each other, had drifted apart, had differentially organized themselves and their relative reference groups, and had affirmed the split between the two roles or comportments (Hunter, 1993/s4) of intellectual work once again.

Finally, there are those who will claim that, in their persons, they have resolved the tension between critique and reconstruction, and that they are now critical reconstructors. The point being argued in this chapter is not that these individuals are not doing both critique and reconstruction work, but that in their critiques and their reconstruction work respectively, the tension between the two modes is not held in dynamic balance, except perhaps where the policy work is of a very general nature, or in exceptional cases. The more that policy work drives toward planning and implementation, the less can it entertain doubts about its constitutive grounds. Or, in Weberian terms, ends have to be accepted for means to be technically elaborated (Weber, 1949). And yet, just as planning must be practical and strategic, so critique is only coherent when it undertakes a systematic interrogation of those constitutive grounds. This argument is not about conceptual incompatability so much as it is one about the social conditions that enable or constrain specific forms of intellectual work. When the professional associations define "good practice" as a dazzling display, of "high critique," as the annual Kenton Conference does for example (see Christian, 1989, for a critique of such critiques), and when the outside commissioning development bodies and donors will pay only for hard-nosed reconstructive policy, then a balancing act like that accomplished in phase two, however desirable it may or may not be, simply cannot be sustained. Critics and reconstructors can then only comport themselves in separate and separated fields of endeavor (see also Hunter, 1993/4).

Reprise: "Scoundrel Time" Again?

This chapter has tried to capture the flavor of the social movement of a very particular subset of intellectuals, the progressive educational academics in South Africa, over a relatively short period of time, in terms of a set of framing concepts which, it is claimed here, effectively set the terms of operation for the field at the time.

In the first phase, there was a *collapse* of the distinction between analytical activities and strategic activities, between long-term intellectual work and short-term strategic work. The result was that both kinds of activity were hamstrung, and neither was particularly productively pursued in this period, with some individual exceptions of course (Chisholm, Hyslop, Christie, to name only a few).

In the second phase, social justice concerns were separated out from development concerns, with the ensuing debate, cast most often in terms of equity and development, by and large keeping the issues in some kind of dynamic tension or *suspension*.

In the third phase, with the momentous political events beginning to shape the reforming State-civil society relationship, the tension between critique and reconstruction to some extent *snaps*, and agents of the two domains of activity busy themselves consolidating their organizational life and their relative bases of social power. In so doing, South Africa comes back into line with the rest of Western mainstream intellectually at the same time as it does so politically.

The intention has not been to depict a simple movement from social homogeneity to heterogeneity, which would be a fatal but seductive trap. Nor is it to represent, cynically, political liberation as a triumph for unrestrained self-interest jostling in the market place. The concern has been to show that intellectual work and argument is not only historically variable, but that neither the debating terms, nor the values attached to them, are easy to predict as the continuum of intellectual roles is reconfigured within changing historical circumstances, some of which are entirely local, others quite global. Certainly nothing can be read directly off the global trend against certainty in the social sciences, currently called postmodernity. For some, following in the critical-theory footsteps of Adorno, our world is fatally fallen, and to pretend to be able to give a positive reconstructive account of the conditions for equality and social justice is but another round of blind idealism that will trigger mass violence once the masses realize that it is simply another round of "false promises" (Aronowitz, 1993), and they look for a scapegoat upon which to visit their fury.[7] For the unreconstructed critics, therefore, from Adorno and Foucault to Holiday, to pursue positive knowledge of any kind in the world we find ourselves in is to become sucked into the power machine. Here is Breyten Breytenbach (1994, p. 5) articulating this exemplary critical position in his commentary on the April 1994 election and its aftermath: "How can those of us who fought against the power corruption of the previous regime now shirk the responsibility and the sheer joy of opposing without let-up our dear comrades snared in the putrefaction of power under the new rule?" The same sentiment is heard every day in the equity-driven NGO networks. This is war talk, the battle lines drawn, the perennial critical comportment of the intellectual reinvented for a new free South Africa. The honeymoon transition is over, says this view, the State is again the State, and civil society must again gird its loins to oppose it.

But others draw very different conclusions from the loss of certainty. If transcendental truth is gone, then all knowledge, including policy knowledge, becomes wordy and pragmatic, and it falls to intellectuals to find the best possible present set, through research, discussion, and political debate (Taylor, 1992). This is classic Weberianism reinvented for postapartheid South Africa. The reconstructors thus become public or "administrative" intellectuals at the same moment that their critical colleagues retire to the semiprivate spheres of academic conversation. By and large, the split is not mourned by the reconstructors and they are relieved to have the carping critics out of their hair. There is serious work to be done, they seem to be saying, people's well-being depends upon it, and the doubters must keep out of the way. We have had enough of the "schooling of power": it is time to reassert the "power of schooling." The reconstructors in this phase go from analysis, to policy, to power.

No one can win this argument. We are now in what Zizek (1991, p. 188) calls a new "scoundrel time," when the social basis for a mediatory position able to balance the two has disappeared. But to say this is by no means to end by siding with the pessimists. Quite the contrary. Anyway, one intellectual task will always be to look for dialectical play, for redemptive openings precisely at the point of aporia or stalemate (Wexler, 1994). Critics, after all, speaking in the name of an unattained utopia, help to keep "open the 'beyond' of currently unimaginable transformative possibilities precisely in the name of Justice" (Cornell, 1992, p. 182). This may be the exemplary reconstructive role for critics.

Notes

1. "We have no distinctive capacity in this regard—it is bogus to pretend that we do" (Appel, 1993, p. 232).

2. "Our colleagues have given up science for social programmes . . . these academics have . . . changed their tune because they are playing a different game" (Appel, 1993, p. 236).

3. "The priest, the Church, the apparatchik of every country substitutes his own vision of the world (a vision deformed by his own *libido dominandi*) for that of the group of which he is supposedly the expression. The 'people' is used these days just as in other times God was used—to settle accounts between clerics" (Bourdieu, 1992, p. 214).

4. "Knowledge has no light but that shed on the world by redemption: all else is reconstruction, mere technique" (Adorno, 1974, p. 247).

"I absolutely will not play the part of one who prescribes solutions. I hold that the role of the intellectual today is not that of establishing laws or proposing solutions or prophesying, since by doing that one can only contribute to the functioning of a determinate situation of power that to my mind must be criticised" (Foucault, 1991, p. 157).

5. See Gilmour and Soudien (1994) for an argument for the difference between "equality" and "equity." Such an argument could not easily be taken on at this time.

6. Anthony Holiday (1993, p. 178) concludes a thoughtful paper by writing that such (critical) writings "are not calls to action but *curbs on activism*, geared to still enthusiasm and not to stimulate it" (emphasis added).

7. "To try to abstractly portray the conditions of redemption, to give form to the hope of reconciliation as if it existed now, only promotes accommodation to a fallen world" (Cornell, 1992, p. 181).

References

Adorno, T. W. *Minima Moralia: Reflections from a Damaged Life*. London: New Left Books, 1974.

Amsterdamski, S. & A. Rhodes (1993). "Perceptions of Dilemmas of Reform: Remarks and Interpretations Concerning a Study by the Vienna Institute for Human Sciences." *European Journal of Education* 28, 4 (1993): 379–402.

ANC. *The Reconstruction and Development Programme: A Policy Framework*. Johannesburg: Umanyano Publications, 1993a.

———. *A Policy Framework for Education and Training*. Education Department, Johannesburg, 1993b.

Appel, S. "Chalk and Cheese: Reflections on Educational Policy." *Perspectives in Education* 14, 2 (1993): 229–38.

———. "Critical Analysis and Progressive Educational Policy." Mimeo, 1994.

Aronowitz, S. *False Promises*. New York: McGraw Hill, 1973.

Badat, S. "Democratizing Education Policy Research for Social Transformation." In E. Unterhalter, H. Wolpe, and T. Botha (eds.) *Education in a Future South Africa*. Oxford: Heinemann, 1991.

Badat, S., H. Wolpe & Z. Barends. "The Post-Secondary Education System: Towards Policy Formulation for Equality and Development." In B. Kaplan (ed.) *Changing by Degrees? Equity Issues in South African Tertiary Education*. Cape Town: UCT Press, 1994.

Bauman, Z. *Legislators and Interpreters: On Modernity, Post-Modernity, and the Intellectuals.* Cambridge: Polity Press, 1987.

Beck, U. "From Industrial Society to the Risk Society: Questions of Survival, Social Structure and Ecological Enlightenment." *Theory, Culture and Society* 9, 1 (1993): 97–123.

Bourdieu, P. *Homo Academicus.* Cambridge: Polity Press, 1984.

———. *Language and Symbolic Power.* Cambridge: Polity Press, 1992.

Breytenbach, B. "Dogs' bone." *New York Review of Books* 41, 10 (1994): 3–5.

Chisholm, L. "Policy and Critique in South African Education Research." *Transformation* 18/9 (1992).

Christian, B. "The Race for Theory." In L Kauffman (ed.) *Gender and Theory: Dialogues on Feminist Criticism.* Oxford: Basil Blackwell, 1989.

Cornell, D. (1992). *The Philosophy of the Limit.* New York: RKP, 1992.

Dale, R. "Applied Education Politics or Political Sociology of Education? Contrasting Approaches to the Study of Recent Education Reform in England and Wales." Mimeo, 1993.

Foucault, M. Interview. In *The Foucault Effect: Studies in Governmentality.* Eds. G. Burchell, C. Gordon, and P. Miller. Chicago: University of Chicago Press, 1991.

Gerwel, J. "Keynote Address, National Education Conference, Broederstroom, 6–8 March, 1992. (An edited version is published in *Back to Learning: The National Education Conference.* Johannesburg: Sached/Ravan.)

Gilmour, D. and C. Soudien. "Disadvantage in South African Education: The Issue of Transformative Policy and Research." In A. Dawes and D. Donald (eds.) *Childhood and Adversity.* Cape Town: David Philip, 1994.

Holiday, A. "Teaching to Rule: Wittgenstein's Role—Following Considerations and Educational Practice." *Perspectives in Education* 14, 2 (1993): 157–80.

Hunter, I. "Bureaucrat, Critic, Citizen: On Some Styles of Ethical Life." *Arena Journal* 2 (1993/94): 77–102.

Konrad, G & I. Szelenyi. *The Intellectuals on the Road to Class Power.* Brighton: Harvester, 1979.

Kraak, A. "Reinterpreting the Equity-Development Debate and Its Relevance for Higher Education in South Africa." Annual UDUSA conference, Durban, 1992.

Lather, P. *Getting Smart: Feminist Research and Pedagogy with/in the Postmodern.* London : RKP, 1991.

Lyotard, J-F. *The Postmodern Condition: A Report on Knowledge.* Minneapolis: University of Minnesota Press, 1984.

Morphet, A. Response to a paper by B. Parker, *Kenton at Helderfontein,* Johannesburg, 1986.

Mulgan, G. "The Power of the Weak." In S. Hall and M. Jacques (eds.) *New Times: The Changing Face of Politics in the 1990s.* London: Lawrence and Wishart, 1989.

Müller, J. "Beyond Unkept Promises: The Micro-Methodological Challenge in Educational Policy Research." Occasional paper No. 1, Education Policy Unit, University of the Western Cape, Cape Town, 1993.

Müller, J. & N. Cloete. "The White Hands: Academic Social Scientists, Knowledge and Struggle in South Africa." *Social Epistemology* 1, 2 (1987): 141-54.

Müller, J. & K. Tomaselli. "Becoming Appropriately Modern: Towards a Genealogy of Cultural Studies in South Africa." In J. Mouton and D Joubert (eds.) *Knowledge and Method in the Human Sciences*. Pretoria: Human Sciences Research Council, 1990.

Müller, J. & P. Vinjevold. "A Review of the Education Policy Unit, University of Natal." Durban, 1991.

National Education Policy Investigation (NEPI). *The Framework Report*. Cape Town: Oxford University Press, 1993.

Offe, C. "Reflections on the Institutional Self-Transformation of Movement Politics: A Tentative Stage Model." In R. J. Dalton and M. Kuechler (eds.) *Challenging the Political Order*. New York: Oxford University Press, 1990.

Parker, B. "Intellectuals and Education System Change." *Perspectives in Education* 14, 2 (1993): 221–28.

Pieterse, J. N. "Dilemmas of Development Discourse: The crisis of Developmentalism and the Comparative Method." *Development and Change* 22 (1991): 5–29.

Popkewitz, T. S. *A Political Sociology of Educational Reform: Power/Knowledge in Teaching, Teacher Education, and Research*. New York: Teachers College Press, 1991.

Ringer, F. *Fields of Knowledge: French Academic Culture in Comparative Perspective, 1890–1920*. New York: Cambridge University Press, 1992.

Taylor, N. "Party Lines and Penny Pinchers: Implications of a Mixed Economy for Educational Policy Research." Mimeo, 1992.

———. "INSET, NGOs and Evaluation in South Africa: A Review." In P. Vinjevold (ed.) *Report on the NGO Sector for the National Teacher Education Audit*. Johannesburg: JET, 1995.

Tester, K. *Civil Society*. London: RKP, 1992.

Unterhalter, E. and M. Young. "Human Resource Development in Postapartheid South Africa: Some Initial Observations." Mimeo published in the 1995 *World Education Year Book,* ed. L. Bash and A. Green. London: Kogan Page, 1994.

Vattimo, G. *The End of Modernity. Nihilism and Hermeneuntics in Postmodern Culture*. Baltimore: John Hopkins University Press, 1988.

Weber, M. "Science as a Vocation." In H. H. Girth and C. W. Mills (eds.) *From Max Weber*. London: RKP, 1948.

———. " 'Objectivity' in Social Scientific and Social Policy Knowledge." In E. A. Shields and H. A. Finch (eds.) *The Methodology of the Social Sciences*. New York: Free Press, 1949.

Wexler, P. "From New Sociology of Education to New Age." Mimeo, 1994.

Wolpe, H. "Education and Social Transformation." In E. Unterhalter, H Wolpe, and T Botha (eds.) *Education in a Future South Africa*. Oxford: Heinemann, 1991.

———. "Towards a Short-Term Negotiating Policy on Education and Training," NEPI Working Paper, Johannesburg, 1992.

———. (ed.). (1980). *The Articulation of Modes of Production: Essays from Economy and Society*. London: RKP, 1980.

World Bank. *World Development Report 1991: The Challenge of Development*. New York: Oxford University Press, 1991.

Zizek, S. *For They Know Not What They Do: Enjoyment as a Political Factor*. London: Verso, 1991.

CHAPTER 13

The Educational System, Social Reproduction, and Educational Theory in Imperial Germany

PETER DREWEK

On the basis of recent sociohistorical literature, and drawing on exemplary contemporary sources, the author discusses the interactions between the reform of the institutional structures of the German educational system and the emergence of pedagogics as an academic discipline in Imperial Germany. Instead of an empirical-psychological orientation of German university pedagogics *(experimentelle Pädagogik)*, the scientific paradigm of a philosophically grounded culture pedagogy *(Kulturpädagogik)* was adopted, which served, among other things, the political integration of elementary school teachers *(Volksschullehrer)*. The reorientation toward sociological themes and methods that occurred in the course of post-1960 educational expansion, as well as the return to the empirical-psychological issues of the Imperial Era, demonstrate that scientific identity and the semantics of educational science depend to a high degree on the respective historical stage of development of the educational system.

First, in comparing the developmental histories of educational systems in the Western industrialized nations since the late nineteenth century, the most striking common attributes and developments are the external differentiation (in varying measures) of secondary school types; the long-term expansion in (higher) secondary education, the pace of which increased dramatically after World War II, and the resultant increase in the rate of university enrollment.

If, in this context, one chooses to focus on the external structures of secondary education and of the university system, the German school system, with its extensive historical tradition, takes a unique position in the international spectrum. By the beginning of the twentieth century, a process of development encompassing the entire previous century had culminated in the states (or predecessor states) of the German Empire—and in Prussia especially—in a school system whose organization differed in at least three significant aspects from that in comparable countries.

The achieved system encompassed, in a largely coherent structure of State educational institutions, every essential school form: the elementary school *(die Volksschule)*, followed by vocational training schools *(die Fortbildungsschule)*, or advanced secondary schools *(höhere Schulen: das Gymnasium, das Realgymnasium,* and *die Oberrealschule* for boys; *höhere Mädchenschulen, das Lyzeum,* and *die Studienanstalt* for girls), followed by universities or technical institutes. Second, the core of this system, the clearly differentiated secondary school form, was characterized by an unusually early transition to secondary education after only four years of primary education in specialized institutions *(Vorschulen)* separate from the common school. Pupils who did not progress to the intermediate and higher secondary schools were obliged to attend the Volksschule for the duration of the compulsory education period. Third, the disparity between the various secondary school forms, already expressed in differing objectives and corresponding subject profiles or curricula, was further underlined by the widely divergent public and private career prospects made possible by the leaving certificates awarded to pupils of the different schools.

Traditionally, the German educational and employment systems have been closely linked; "authorizations" *(Berechtigungen)* or school-leaving certificates, issued by the one social subsystem are accepted as entrance qualifications to the other. These close ties have meant that, throughout the periods of historical change in social structures and hierarchies, the German educational system acquired a degree of importance unparalleled in other countries (Müller, Ringer & Simon, 1987). The varying curricula and attendance periods within the vertical secondary school structure must be seen as indicative of the disparate opportunities for professional—and therefore social—advancement offered by the school-leaving certificates of the different school types, which have reflected and, from a critical point of view, reproduced the inequalities of the social hierarchy.

Systembildung

An analysis of the relations between education, the State, and society focusing on the development of the German educational system of the late nineteenth and early twentieth centuries reveals a constellation—compared to the post–World War II era—of relatively low complexity. Although in the early nineteenth century one can already observe the early forms of an inherent dynamism in the process of modernization of educational institutions in the context of social differentiation, the educational system at the beginning of the twewntieth century is still to a high degree dependent on particular social contexts.

The term *Systembildung* (systematization), describing a phase model of the legal and social standardization of German educational institutions, is used to define the sociological context of nineteenth- and twentieth-century educational reform in Germany (Müller, 1981). Due to the continued dual structure mentioned above (elementary school/vocational training school vs. advanced secondary school/university), this model is primarily oriented toward advanced secondary education and takes as its point of departure the low degree of institutionalization of the individual schools and school types in the early nineteenth century. As the century progressed, Prussian schools became increasingly interconnected through a developing body of regulations (*Systemfindung*, or " 'rules' of system emergence") relating to access, interschool transfers, and graduation. In the last three decades of the century, the formerly diverse spectrum of advanced secondary schools was aligned (*Systemkonstituierung*, or "system constitution") in a uniform, vertical system of hierarchically differentiated school types. Apart from partial modifications, this organizational form remained largely unchanged throughout the course of the twentieth century. New school types and previously excluded sectors (secondary schools for girls, vocational schools, etc.) were integrated without any profound reform of the existing vertical structure (*Systemkomplementierung*, or "system complementation").

For most of the nineteenth century German advanced secondary schools were characterized by a scientifically oriented curriculum initially based on the classical languages alone. The schools had various names—*Lateinschule, Gelehrtenschule, Gymnasium*—and catered only to male students; the schooling periods were longer than was demanded by official regulations. As well as qualifying pupils for entrance to the higher professional levels in public service and in the private sector, the certificates awarded by these schools served as qualifications for university admission. However, the latter criterion was by no means valid for all institutions of advanced secondary education. Following the (Prussian) *Abitur* edicts of the first three decades of the nineteenth century, which regulated university entrance and standardized grammar school curricula, a group of schools broke away from the other secondary schools and developed their own specific profiles. Despite these differentiations, however, advanced secondary education up to and beyond the middle of the century can be described as a conglomeration *(Konglomerat)* of educational institutions. This conglomeration was first shaped into a secondary education system only later, in the last third of the century.

A rough characterization of nineteenth-century educational history would emphasize that for much of the period the advanced secondary schools can be seen as nonelitist establishments which, with their socially heterogeneous clientele, by no means limited social advancement. Contrarily, it was rather more the case that, for long periods of time and in contrast to subsequent revisionist ideologies, the structures of these schools facilitated social mobility. This was due in part to flexibly organized lessons, which were adapted to pupil ability, and in part to the possibility of leaving school before the university-entrance Abitur level—a procedure which was common until the end of the century—without being stigmatized as school failure and which still qualified pupils for careers in intermediate and higher professions (Müller, 1977).

Until the 1860s and 1870s the Gymnasium had accommodated a socially mixed student body and had provided social mobility for pupils from nonacademic backgrounds. Subsequent rising Gymnasium enrollment rates led to mounting social rivalry between the children of the traditional academic elite and those of the new classes produced by industrialization. Both groups now competed for entrance to the higher professions. Toward the end of the century, this conflict was resolved by the external differentiation of the advanced secondary school system as the core area of secondary education. Two new, modern forms of secondary schools (*Realgymnasium* and *Oberrealschule*), also providing qualifications for university entrance, were established alongside the traditional, humanist Gymnasium. In these schools a significantly diminished value was placed on instruction in Greek and Latin (Müller, 1977).

In the course of the secondary education reforms of the last third of the nineteenth century, the previous structural attributes (socially heterogenous clientele, the flexible organization of lessons, and the promotion of social mobility) were curtailed in the context of the newly constituted system of advanced secondary schools. For much of the century, as institutions with a socially mixed clientele, these schools had facilitated and—due to their open, noninstitutionalized structures—even promoted social mobility. The subsequent phase of system constitution resulted in a socially more homogeneous pupil population in the different types of schools, favoring the differentiated social-reproduction function of academic professional groups by means of the educational system and its more valuable certificates until the 1960s and 1970s.

With regard to the elementary schools, the nineteenth century was characterized by the growing enforcement of the compulsory education regulations that had been decreed in the previous century, the development of the internal structures (multiclass systems, creation and standardization of curricula, partial improvement in teaching methods, etc.), along with a growing awareness of the elementary school teachers of the inadequacy of their professional training. At the same time, the political claims made on the elementary school at different times by the monarchy, churches, political parties, and, not least, the teachers, demonstrate the low degree of social autonomy this school form enjoyed. Throughout the nineteenth century, the elementary schools existed wholly independent of the secondary schools, thus revealing a society of social classes not yet politically integrated. Totally divergent curricula and correspondingly different forms of teacher training institutions— *Seminare,* preceded by *Präparandenanstalten* (preparatory schools) for elementary school teachers; *Studienseminare* preceded by *Universitätsstudium* (purely theoretical university study) for advanced secondary school teachers—are symbolic of the social distance between the Gymnasium and the elementary school. Compared to the increasing interconnection between secondary schools and professional and social structures, the expansion and modernization of elementary schools lagged far behind. Overt political attempts to instrumentalize the elementary school were repeatedly launched in connection with the revolution of 1848 and with the struggle to subdue socialist activities in the late nineteenth century. Elementary school teachers responded to these advances by demanding professional independence through the institutionalization of their training at universities (Kittel, 1957).

Pedagogics and Reform

Although a horizontally organized general (as opposed to vocational) school for all pupils was foreseen in comprehensive social and educational reform plans, in particular by Wilhelm von Humboldt in the early nineteenth-century Prussian reform era, the structural differences between elementary schooling and academic education continued to influence German school development far into the twentieth century, albeit in a modified form.

Due to the dual forms of organization of elementary (lower *Volksschule, Vorschule*) and secondary (upper *Volksschule, Gymnasium*) schools and to the differences in the duration of courses, in curricula, in educational objectives and, finally, in the social value of the respective leaving certificates, the German educational system have proved to be a system functionalized by the academic elites on the threshold of the twentieth century. The institutional identity of the program and the reality of this exclusive higher education seem to reside in just that ideological affinity to the class society and to the imperialist state by which both the education and the schooling of the masses are reduced to social discipline in conformity with the ruling powers and to political integration.

In the historical reviews of German pedagogics since the Weimar era, late nineteenth-century "reform pedagogy"—a highly heterogeneous bundle of innovative approaches to educational reform—is allegedly responsible for breaking up the authoritarian educational conditions of Imperial Germany and initiating a fundamental shift toward educational critique and educational alternatives (Flitner & Kudritzki, 1961). According to this interpretation of the historical developments, the decisive factor in the accelerating process of modernization of German pedagogics between 1870 and 1900 was neither the school nor the state nor the social establishment but the initiatives of educational reformers emerging mostly outside the school and benefiting from critical distance.

If this reconstruction of the educational tradition takes into account only the level of programmatic reformatory discourse and its forms of implementation, then it follows but one line of continuity in German pedagogics, failing to link the historical emergence of pedagogics as an academic discipline, the specific scientific paradigms of "culture pedagogics," and the emergence of "philosophical pedagogics" with the socio- and scientific-historical development of the Empire.

A broader approach shows that educational reform and the institutionalization of pedagogics as an academic discipline emerged directly from the structural development of the educational system itself. Stated simply, three processes which—partly independent of one another—increasingly raised the inner tensions of the educational system throughout the nineteenth century later determined the shape of educational reform in the early twentieth century. First, the new economically and technically successful social elites of the nineteenth century, in the course of the differentiation of the system of higher education, demanded—and were given—access to universities and professions which had until then been reserved for the academic elite *(das Bildungsbürgertum)*. Second, due to the increasingly prominent vocational orientation of the secondary schools and the universities, a growing discrepancy emerged between the traditional philosophical legitimation of higher education on the basis of a neohumanist concept of education *(Bildung)* and the actual social functions of the educational system. Therefore, aside from the structures of the secondary school system, the concept of Bildung itself had to be modernized and redefined in the late nineteenth century to meet the needs of the vocational and employment systems (Drewek, 1995a). Third, this two-fold dynamism of modernization (within the system's structures and within the structures of legitimation) ultimately overlapped with the traditional, politically founded strategies of professionalization of the German elementary school teachers. On the basis of experimental pedagogics and its empirical research methods, the elementary school teachers demanded that teacher education be institutionalized at the universities.

However, both the demand for academic training and the empirical-sychological research paradigm of experimental pedagogics would have uncontrollably accelerated the pace and direction of the modernization of the imperial class-based society and would have negatively affected the newly constituted, socially biased selective functions of the educational system. On the other hand, academic pedagogics of the Weimar era, developed in opposition to these trends, followed a philosophical concept of education that integrates the centrifugal processes of the early twentieth century—feared by the social elites—by drawing on cultural-historical and pedagogical approaches and defusing their socially destabilizing consequences.

Friedrich Nietzsche's Lectures

While the disengagement of the school system from its traditional structures at the beginning of the nineteenth century and its transformation into a modern educational system on the threshold of the twentieth century were both slow processes covering several time periods, the change in the concept of *Bildung* (a philosophical theory of education that has been referred to as the "German tradition of self-cultivation" [Bruford, 1975]) as regards institutional structures was accelerated and became more precipitous only in the last two decades of the nineteenth century. By the time of the founding of the German Reich in 1871, strong discrepancies had arisen between the real modernization trends of the expanding system of higher education and the still tradition-oriented humanistic concept of education. It was now necessary to reformulate the classical German concept of Bildung, which could no longer be reconciled with the structural and functional changes occurring in secondary schools.

One of the most impressive sources for educational thought in nineteenth-century Germany was a series of lectures "On the Future of Our Educational Institutions" delivered in Basel in 1872 by the youthful Friedrich Nietzsche (Nietzsche, 1988 [1872]). In these lectures, hardly noted at the time, Nietzsche declared that the nonutilitarian humanistic conception of education was wholly irreconcilable with the actual social functions of an educational system that primarily served the preparation of careers in the higher professions. "Every education, however, which at its completion holds out the prospect of an office or a livelihood is not an education towards refinement such as we understand it, but merely an instruction as to how to save and protect oneself in the struggle for existence" (p. 715).

In the early 1870s, Nietzsche described the educational claim of the Gymnasium as an ideology which could no longer hide its social function as regards access to higher vocational positions. It can well be considered a proof of this critique that during the 1880s the representatives of the traditional, neohumanist Gymnasium vehemently fought the idea of granting equal status to the *Realanstalten* (schools based on modern languages and the sciences) in order to preserve their own social privileges regarding access to universities.

Nietzsche knows "only of one true opposition, that of institutions of education *[Anstalten der Bildung]* and institutions of the necessities of life *[Anstalten der Lebensnoth]:* to the second kind belong all the existing institutions, the first is the one I am talking about" (p. 717). The late nineteenth-century manifestation of Bildung, having diverged from its tradition, to him represents but a transparent ideology of this system which has nothing at all to do with imparting a true philosophical education. "In order to live, in order to fight the struggle for existence, human beings must learn a great deal; but everything they learn and do to this end as individuals has nothing yet to do with education. The latter begins in an atmospheric layer located high above this world of hardship, of the struggle for existence, of poverty" (p. 713).

Nietzsche transcended contemporary cultural criticism but he was not, however, able to formulate a positive concept of Bildung that could reconcile the traditional ideal with modern institutional developments. Such a reconciliation was first achieved in the 1890s by Friedrich Paulsen. Unlike the elite scholar Nietzsche, Paulsen had started out as a farmer's son and village school pupil and advanced through the Prussian educational system to become a professor of philosophy in Berlin. He was essentially interested in the institutional structures of the German educational system. He attempted to prove that, historically, new social elites had always succeeded in realizing their specific educational ideals within the organization and curricula of advanced secondary education. Therefore, he demanded a school reform that would place the modern or realistically oriented advanced secondary schools on a par with the traditional humanist Gymnasium. Against the background of the educational debates of the 1880s and the period preceding the 1890 School Conference in which he participated, Paulsen brought to the fore—initially in his book *Geschichte des gelehrten Unterrichts (History of Classical Schooling)*—the highly controversial issue of awarding equal status to the realistically oriented schools (Paulsen, 1885; Drewek, 1991).

He linked this question to the cultural-historical process by which, since the close of the Middle Ages, modern society had detached itself from the classical models, a process which included attempts to create—as he later wrote—"a uniform popular education on a modern, national basis" (Paulsen, 1906, p. 73). Paulsen's *Schlußbetrachtung* (summary consideration), which took up only thirty pages of the first (single-volume) edition of the eight-hundred-page *Geschichte,* attracted particularly harsh criticism from classical philologists. Here, in 1885, Paulsen predicted that "what is known today as classical education will one day cease to be the basis of university education for the majority of our scholars" (Paulsen, 1885, p. 762) and that he had "no doubt that the time will come when the German form of instruction will take up its rightful position as the legitimate heir to the Latin" (p. 764). In 1897, Paulsen emphasized that educational developments would be unable to withstand the surrounding social and cultural modernization tendencies in the long run: "The wind blows the way it will. The school cannot dictate the direction of the wind, and so it would be well advised to be guided by it" (Paulsen, 1896/97, p. 649). At the same time, he expanded the neohumanist educational conception of the Gymnasium. According to Paulsen, it was not the substance (the curriculum of the Gymnasium) that shaped secondary education, but the personal effect. He concluded that there is no such thing as a humanistic *Allgemeinbildung* (general education) but only "a particular and personal one" (Paulsen, 1906, p. 57). To Paulsen, this was the "WOHLGESTALT" (*sic*) (the fully developed, integrated form) of education which could not be "imposed upon the individual from outside" (p. 55). "The form, and not the substance, shapes the Bildung" (Paulsen, 1895, p. 419).

If Nietzsche had declared that *Bildung* was no longer possible in the educational institutions, Paulsen went one step further, arguing that *Bildung* should not even be the school's objective: "The school can and should supply the stem with stimulation, opportunity and nutrition for growth; but the school cannot create *Bildung*. [In attempting to create *Bildung*] what it can do is to obstruct the nascent *Bildung* by overwhelming the pupil with subject matter" (Paulsen, 1919/1921 [1896/97], vol. 2, p. 691).

The problem of according equal status to the different forms of secondary educational institutions was resolved in the course of the Prussian school conference of 1900 in favor of a system of different types of secondary schools that accorded more or less the same status to three school types: the *Gymnasium;* the *Oberrealschule* (based on the sciences); and the *Realgymnasium,* a so-called bastard of classical and modern *Bildung* (Willmann, 1988 [1889], p. 387), which at the school conference of 1890 had encountered strong opposition. With this equalization effected by the ("Kiel") Imperial ordinance of 1900, the previously hotly disputed monopoly of the Gymnasium—and thus the dominant role of classical language-based learning in university access—was relativized.

Scientific and Philosophical Paradigms

Viewed historically, the continual process of educational reform in Germany up to the beginning of the twentieth century—remaining intact despite political developments—primarily served to adapt the advanced secondary school structure to the dynamics of a changing social structure. Thus, the existent spectrum of secondary school types became further differentiated in order to integrate new social elites into the advanced secondary educational system. The elementary school system was reformed and incorporated into the composite structure of the educational system only after the secondary school system had acquired a fixed organization and, with this, a specific social reproductive function. The structural transformation of the educational system first changed the advanced secondary education and only afterward the compulsory schools.

A central problem in this chronological sequence was that of confining the integration of new social groups strictly to the advanced secondary educational sector. Integration could only be limited in this way if the system structure allowed in principle the continued existence of a dual lower and higher school structure, even when the conditions for a uniform single system had seemingly been established. In order to function, however, the de facto dual secondary school structure would have had to be reflected by a corresponding dual system of teacher training. This led to a second central problem of educational modernization in Imperial Germany. The duality of elementary and advanced secondary education would have been jeopardized if university training had been extended to teachers from the elementary schools. Thus, the teacher training institutions had to be structured analogously to the dual school organization. This duality had to be legitimized by the formulation of differentiated pedagogic objectives and theories. Despite their objectivity, theories supporting the dual structure of school and teacher training met with a much higher degree of political acceptance and scientific recognition than theories which, no matter how scientifically plausible, could promote and accelerate social integration. On the continuum between these two poles, experimental pedagogics is closer to the latter, whereas philosophical pedagogics corresponds more to legitimation theory.

The strained relation between institutional developments and diverging scientific paradigms here manifest were naively harmonized in philosophical pedagogics. "In educational history the development of theories is inseparable from that of the institutions. Together, the theories and institutions form one large organic unit: mental life creates its own external forms, and these forms are the basis for new directions of life. But the creative element is always reflected in the theory first; for creativity looks beyond the given fact, and drafts the picture of a better future, unconcerned with the minor hindrances and often random distribution of forces in reality" (Spranger, 1960 [1910], p. 1). Eduard Spranger's statement, made in 1910 in looking back on Wilhelm von Humboldt's concept of educational reform, underestimated the interactions between educational theory and the educational system. At the time, it was no longer possible to see the educational "theories" and "institutions" as the twin constituents of Spranger's "organic cultural unit"; in practice, they reflected the diametrically opposed social interests of the elementary school teachers and the academic professionals. Just as the term *system-formation process* can be applied to the differentiation of advanced secondary education in the late nineteenth and early twentieth centuries, the rivalry between empirical pedagogics—as represented by the elementary school teachers—and philosophy-based pedagogics culminated in a similar systematization and hierarchization of educational science at the beginning of the interwar period (Drewek, 1995a).

Ernst Meumann's Experimental Pedagogics

Ernst Meumann, the leading representative of experimental pedagogics, attempted to transfer Wilhelm Wundt's psychological research methods to pedagogics. The field itself was to be redefined as a science based on purely empirical research, and educational studies established as an independent academic discipline.

In 1901, he put it as follows: "In many cases, current educational theory still makes do with a stock of psychological concepts which psychologists themselves have long since rejected as worthless" (Meumann, 1901, p. 65). He further asserted that this theory denied itself the use of "the best research methods currently available, of the systematic observation of other people, of experimentation and statistics. It may even be claimed that all major advances in the liberal arts made through the application of experimental and psychological-statistical methods to the facts of mental life in the course of the last 40 years . . . has had no effect on the mass of pedagogical literature" (p. 65).

Psychology in German universities was undergoing its first phase of expansion when Meumann made this assertion at the beginning of the twentieth century. In the period between the establishment of Wundt's institute of psychology in Leipzig in 1879 and that of the psychological department in the philosophical seminar of the Philipps University in Marburg in 1913, psychological institutes were created in sixteen universities—already almost half of the thirty-five psychological institutes to appear in German universities before 1940. Evaluations of the pedagogic syllabi at German universities between 1910 and 1920 show that the majority of the 1,941 classes offered during this period were experimentally oriented (author's calculations, based on Geuter, 1986; Drewek, 1995b).

Meumann became the leading representative of the experimental movement in German pedagogics before World War I. His collected lectures were published no less than three times in six years (Meumann, 1907, 1911–14, 1914). As the editor of respected pedagogical and psychological journals, he participated actively in the discussion of the continuing school reform after 1910. He was cofounder of the first German institute for psychological research on adolescence, and was awarded an honorary Ph.D. by an American university in 1914, one year before his premature death.

Meumann expected his program for "experimental pedagogics as self-sufficient and uniform research" (Meumann, 1901, p. 66) to result in a "total restructuring of systematic educational theory" (p. 285). However, university philosophers did not grant his treatises the anticipated degree of recognition. Consequently, Meumann established contact with elementary school teachers who had been demanding with increasing force that their professional training should take place at the universities. The teachers saw in experimentalist theory the scientific basis which their cause, inspired at least in part by status considerations, had so far lacked. Meumann also attempted to find a social basis for experimental pedagogics by mainly propagating his "educational theory of the future," not yet established at the universities, among elementary school teachers as "a science more for the learners than the teachers" (p. 285). The elementary school had not been affected by the school reform of 1900. Meumann's proposal that theorists and practicians of school reform should "march separately but fight a unified cause" (Meumann, 1911, p. 1) implicitly supported elementary school teachers who aspired to a higher level of academic training.

If the demands for integration at university level of all elementary school teacher training—supported by Meumann—had been successful, the quantitative balancing of subjects in the departments of philosophy would have required radical revision. Even more significantly, the *praxis-ferne Wissenschaftsmodell* (practice-remote conception) of the faculty and its academic role would have had to be changed.

The effects of experimental pedagogics, however, were not confined to teacher training. It was also shown that a considerable proportion of elementary school pupils were sufficiently qualified to attend the advanced secondary school (Meumann, 1913), thereby confirming that social selection should be replaced by psychological criteria. In the course of his investigations, Meumann had adopted an ever more milieu-theoretical position, in which aptitude was seen as a product of familial socialization, rather than simply a hereditary trait. For this reason, he demanded an increased individualization of teaching, which would above all encourage the abilities of elementary pupils from the lower social classes. Such views, however, were simply not compatible with the structure of the German educational system. The further schooling of 2 percent of highly gifted pupils coming from elementary schools would have resulted in an increase of 25 percent in the number of pupils attending the secondary schools. Above all, it would have meant an enormous increase in social rivalry inside the Gymnasium (Stern, 1914; Drewek, 1989).

Critical analyses by Wundt, Frischeisen-Köhler, and others cast doubts upon Meumann's conception of talent (Wundt, 1910; Frischeisen-Köhler, 1962 [1918/19]). Meumann's critics have argued that experimental aptitude tests could assess elementary physical functions (memory, perception) at most, but that qualitative aspects of intelligence, creativity, and culturally conditioned competencies could not be investigated in the laboratory.

Eduard Spranger's Humanistic Pedagogics

The first protest against these attempts to establish pedagogics as an independent academic discipline came from Eduard Spranger, one of the twentieth century's most prominent German humanist pedagogues. As early as 1910, Spranger described his endeavor to develop a philosophical pedagogy as "an act of self-defense" (Spranger, 1973 [1910]), p. 222) against the psychology-oriented experimental theory.

From 1910 on, the philosophical pedagogy based on the work of Wilhelm Dilthey and propagated by Eduard Spranger in fact emerged as an alternative to the psychology-oriented experimentalist theory. In 1913, Spranger stated his position: "Until now, pedagogics has been conceived narrowly in some quarters, namely as the theory of a teaching technique the significance of which . . . scarcely exceeds the boundaries of the schools and the needs of the teacher. It appears to me, however, that educating is a cultural process rooted in the context of all mental life and that pedagogics is consequently a science which is interwoven with all other cultural areas in its historical, descriptive and normative components" (Spranger, 1913, p. 479). Along with Herman Nohl, Theodor Litt, Wilhelm Flitner, and others, Eduard Spranger belonged to the leading group of humanistic pedagogues who came to prominence during the Weimar period.

In 1917, one year before the end of the World War I, a decision was made that was immensely important for the historical course of pedagogics as an academic discipline. At a conference held by the Prussian ministry of education and culture, experimental pedagogics was clearly rejected (Pädagogische Konferenz, 1917; Schwenk, 1977). One of the reasons stated for this refusal was the irreconcilability of free experimental research and the more important cultural tradition of the German educational system. The chair for pedagogics to be established within the system of the departments of philosophy was to be conceived as "a purely theoretical discipline in the spirit of the entire department, theoretical in the sense of a historical study of the institutions and a general philosophical and cultural-historical foundation of their objectives. Any kind of practical training in the usual sense was to be excluded; psychology was to be discussed only theoretically, in its significance for instruction, without directly applying it" (Troeltsch, 1917a, p. 10). The holder of the chair "should not experiment with all sorts of things as is presently the fashion in American departments of education . . . , as if there existed no established school system and no educational orientation of the nation" (Troeltsch, 1917b, p. 23). "All practical activity remains fragmentary unless it is based on the idea of a culture," the conference proceedings later added "[which] out of the chaos of contradicting trends arrives at a synthesis." The conference centered on "the yet to be grounded culture pedagogy" (Litt, 1917, p. 17), the "science of instruction and education" for the "scientific treatment and systematization of an actually existing institute of the highest social, political, and intellectual importance"—the German educational system (Troeltsch, 1917a, p. 10).

This line of reasoning was reflected in the objectives and final shape of the elementary school teacher training reform in the 1920s. The preparatory institutes and teacher seminars were phased out, while the entrance requirement for the newly established course of study for elementary school teaching was raised (demanding a leaving certificate from an advanced secondary school) through a constitutional ruling. After heated academic and political debate, however, the special model of the college of education *(Pädagogische Akademien)*, as opposed to a university course, was adopted for elementary school teacher training (Kittel, 1965).

During the Weimar era, the two most important documents published on the subject of teacher education, a memorandum by Eduard Spranger in 1920 and another memorandum by the Prussian ministry of education in 1925 (Spranger, 1970 [1920]; Die Neuordnung der Volksschullehrerbildung in Preussen, 1965 [1925]), both reveal an idealization of the teaching profession.

The elementary school teacher above all must be qualified to act as folk instructor and folk educator. In this, pedagogics with its complementary sciences must form the core of his professional training. The elementary school teacher needs to be neither a specialist nor a researcher. But he has to be a *Bildner (Bildung* enabler) who, in direct contact with the people, knows how to awaken and to form intellectual life. Therefore, closeness to life *[Lebensnähe]* must be an essential characteristic of his training. (Die Neuordnung, 1965 [1925], p. 78f.).

This idealization is only comprehensible in light of the above-described academic and political history of experimental pedagogics, which enjoyed increasing success in other countries within and outside of Europe (Depaepe, 1993).

Weimar pedagogics modified the early nineteenth-century neohumanist concept of education. This concept, which had meanwhile been adapted to the changed social conditions and school structures of the early twentieth century, helped to build a new professional ethos for the elementary school teacher, now defined as a Bildner. The external differentiation of the educational system, the function of which experimental theory could not legitimize, was presented in humanistic educational theory as a unit belonging to a higher idealistic level. Bildung, in the nineteenth century a privilege of the upper social classes and now the socialization object of all school types, assumed the quality of a central conception for social integration.

This was especially true for the elementary school teachers themselves. Eduard Spranger quite plainly defined Bildung in the context of educational policy. In 1918, he wrote to the Prussian Minister of Education: "The teacher has learned to work like no one else; but to work for him means to memorize, not to think. Thus, his keen urge to improve his knowledge is led completely astray. He has never been given questions, but only answers; he has not been taught to think and judge independently, but only to 'take in,' he has not been shown a limit to knowledge, but almost everywhere established truths"

(Spranger, (1918) 1971, p. 217). Yet history had shown "that thus Prussian educational policy had merely raised an oppositional teaching force. . . . There is only one way to possibly check the potential threat of the teachers' political radicalism; give them an education, a real education; give them their very own sense of responsibility for what they think; free them from merely intellectual authority; lead them through doubts: let them mentally live through the wealth of possible truths so that they may find their truth" (p. 218).

Conclusion

Studies of the long-term historical development of the German educational system indicate an increasing internal impetus that served to counteract the social reproduction function of the exclusive advanced schools. This development can be presented as a secular process of inclusion which, in the course of the twentieth century, integrated the (initially) socially exclusive Gymnasium and universities (Drewek & Harney, 1982, 1986; Müller & Zymek, 1987; Titze, 1987). This inclusion brought about far-reaching changes in the relationship, originally viewed as static, between educational and social structures. The close links between the educational and employment systems, along with the channeling of advancement-oriented social groups into intermediate schools, led to a steady rise in vocational entrance requirements. Higher qualifications were demanded for entrance to the formerly low and intermediate professional levels in particular, leading in turn to more demand for places at higher-grade institutions. This inclusion of the intermediate and higher secondary schools, which was followed after 1970 by that of the universities, progressively diminished the social reproduction function institutionalized at the turn of the century, and at the same time led to a relative devaluation of the formerly exclusive certificates awarded by the schools.

Parallel to the educational expansion of the 1960s, philosophically oriented pedagogics lost political weight and scientific acceptance. On the one hand, the conditions that undermined the academic predominance of humanistic educational theory in Germany after 1960 evidently emerged from a specific historical context. While the ranks of university theorists included outstanding scholars such as Erich Weniger and Otto Friedrich Bollnow, no major schools of humanistic pedagogy were established—at least partly due to developments in the Third Reich. After 1945, the recruitment of younger pedagogues was extremely difficult. Furthermore, the now older generation of university pedagogues proved unable to participate in the international discourse on education from the 1920s on. On the other hand, the all-important factor was the massive educational expansion that occurred during the period after 1945. This enormous advance in secondary access, a rise from about 10 percent of the age group in 1950 to 40 percent in 1990, required new methods and approaches in the discipline. The new analytical needs could not be met by early twentieth-century pedagogics, which was guided by the object of limiting and channelling access to education. It is revealing that one of the leading postwar theorists of German educational reform, Heinrich Roth, referred to Ernst Meumann rather than Eduard Spranger when he appealed for a "realistic turnabout" in educational science in the early 1960s (Roth, 1963).

References

Bruford, W. H. *The German Tradition of Self-Cultivation: "Bildung" from Humboldt to Thomas Mann.* New York: Cambridge University Press, 1975.

"Die Neuordnung der Volksschullehrerbildung in Preußen. Denkschrift des Preußischen Ministeriums für Wissenschaft, Kunst und Volksbildung (1925)." In H. Kittel (ed.) *Die Pädagogischen Hochschulen: Dokumente ihrer Entwicklung.* Weinheim, 1965, pp. 76–97.

Depaepe, M. *Zum Wohl des Kindes? Pädologie, pädagogische Psychologie und experimentelle Pädagogik in Europa und den USA, 1890–1940.* Weinheim, 1993.

Drewek, P. "Begabungstheorie, Begabungsforschung und Bildungssystem in Deutschland 1890–1918." In K.-E. Jeismann (ed.) *Bildung, Staat, Gesellschaft im 19. Jahrhundert: Mobilisierung und Disziplinierung.* Stuttgart, 1989, pp. 387–412.

———. Bildungsbegriff und Bildungssystem 1870–1920. Zur Reflexion ihres Verhältnisses bei Nietzsche, Willmann, Paulsen, Meumann und Spranger. Köln/ Weimar/Wien 1995a.

——— "Die Herausbildung der 'geisteswissenschaftlichen' " Pädagogik vor 1918 aus sozialgeschichtlicher Perspektive. Zum Strukturwandel der Philosophischen Fakultät und zur Lehrgestalt der Universitätspädagogik im späten Kaiserreich und während des Ersten Weltkriegs." In A. Leschinsky (ed.) *Die Institutionalisierung von Lehren und Lernen: Beiträge zu einer Theorie der Schule.* 1995b.

———. "Friedrich Paulsen." In B. Schmoldt (ed.) *Pädagogen in Berlin: Auswahl von Biographien zwischen Aufklärung und Gegenwart.* Hohengehren, 1991, pp. 171–93.

Drewek, P. & K. Harney. "Beteiligung und Ausschluß." In H.-E. Tenorth (ed.) *Allgemeine Bildung: Analysen zu ihrer Wirklichkeit, Versuche über ihre Zukunft.* Weinheim/München, 1986, pp. 138–53.

———. "Relative Autonomie," Selektivität und Expansion im modernen Schulsystem. Zur Verallgemeinerungsfähigkeit schultheoretischer Annahmen des Qualifikationskrisenprojekts der DFG in Zeitschrift für Pädagogik, 28. Jg., 1982, pp. 591–608.

Flitner, W. & G. Kudritzki (eds.). *Die deutsche Reformpädagogik: Band I: Die Pioniere der pädagogischen Bewegung.* Düsseldorf/München, 1961.

Frischeisen-Köhler, M. "Grenzen der Experimentellen Methode (1918/19)." In *Philosophie und Pädagogik* (intro. H. Nohl). Weinheim 1962, pp. 110–50.

Geuter, U. (ed.). *Daten zur Geschichte der deutschen Psychologie.* Göttingen, 1986.

Kittel, H. *Die Entwicklung der Pädagogischen Hochschulen 1926–1932.* Berlin/ Hannover/Darmstadt, 1957.

———. (ed.). *Die Pädagogischen Hochschulen: Dokumente ihrer Entwicklung (I) 1920–1932.* Weinheim, 1965.

Litt, Th. (without title). In *Pädagogische Konferenz im Ministerium der geistlichen und Unterrichtsangelegenheiten* am 24. und 25. Mai 1917. Thesen und Verhandlungsbericht (1917), p. 17.

Meumann, E. *Abriß der experimentellen Pädagogik.* Leipzig/Berlin, 1914.

———. "Die soziale Bedeutung der Intelligenzprüfungen." In *Zeitschrift für pädagogische Psychologie* 14. Jg., 1913, pp. 433–40.

———. "Entstehung und Ziele der experimentellen Pädagogik." In *Die deutsche Schule* 5. Jg., 1901, pp. 65–92, 139–53, 213–23, 272–88.

———. "Experimentelle Pädagogik und Schulreform." In *Zeitschrift für Pädagogische Psychologie* 12. Jg., 1911, pp. 1–13.

———. *Vorlesungen zur Einführung in die experimentelle Pädagogik und ihre psychologischen Grundlagen.* 1. and 2. vol. Leipzig, 1907; (second edition) vol. 1. Leipzig, 1911, vol. 2 Leipzig, 1913, vol. 3, Leipzig, 1914.

Müller, D. K. "Der Prozeß der Systembildung im Schulwesen Preußens während der zweiten Hälfte des 19. Jahrhunderts." In *Zeitschrift für Pädagogik* 27. Jg., 1981, pp. 245–69.

———. *Sozialstruktur und Schulsystem: Aspekte zum Strukturwandel des Schulwesens im 19. Jahrhundert.* Göttingen, 1977.

Müller, D. K., F. Ringer, & B. Simon (eds.). *The Rise of the Modern Educational System: Structural Change and Social Reproduction 1870–1920.* London/Paris: Cambridge University Press/Editions De La Maison Des Sciences De L'Homme, 1987.

Müller, D. K. & B. Zymek (unter Mitarbeit von U. Herrmann). *Sozialgeschichte und Statistik des Schulsystems in den Staaten des deutschen Reiches, 1800–1945* (= Datenhandbuch zur deutschen Bildungsgeschichte, Band II, Höhere und mittlere Schulen, 1. Teil). Göttingen, 1987.

Nietzsche, F. "Über die Zukunft unserer Bildungsanstalten." In *Die Geburt der Tragödie. Unzeitgemäße Betrachtungen I–IV.* Nachgelassene Schriften, 1870–1873. *Kritische Studienausgabe,* ed. G. Colli and M. Montinari. München, 1988, pp. 641–752.

Pädagogische Konferenz im Ministerium der geistlichen und Unterrichts-Angelegenheiten am 24. und 25. Mai 1917. Thesen und Verhandlungbericht (1917).

Paulsen, F. "Bildung (1893)." In *Encyklopädisches Handbuch der Pädagogik,* ed. W. Rein. 1. vol. Langensalza 1895, pp. 414–24.

———. "Das moderne Bildungswesen." In W. Lexis et al. (eds.), *Die allgemeinen Grundlagen der Kultur der Gegenwart* (= Die Kultur der Gegenwart. Ihre Entwicklung und ihre Ziele, [hg. v. P. Hinneberg] Teil I, Abteilung I). Berlin/ Leipzig, 1906, pp. 54–86.

———. *Geschichte des gelehrten Unterrichts auf den deutschen Schulen und Universitäten vom Ausgang des Mittelalters bis zur Gegenwart.* Leipzig, 1885. (2. edition in 2 vol. 1896/97, 3. expanded edition [ed. and continued with an appendix by R. Lehmann] Leipzig, 1919/1921).

Roth, H. "Die realistische Wendung in der pädagogischen Forschung (1962)." In *Die deutsche Schule*, 55. Jg., 1963, pp. 109–19.

Schwenk, B. "Pädagogik in den philosophischen Fakultäten—Zur Entstehungsgeschichte der "geisteswissenschaftlichen" Pädagogik in Deutschland." In H. D. Haller & D. Lenzen (eds.), *Wissenschaft im Reformprozeß: Aufklärung oder Alibi?* Stuttgart, 1977, pp. 103–31.

Spranger, E. (without title). In *Zeitschrift für Pädagogische Psychologie*, 14. Jg., 1913, p. 479.

―――. "Die philosophischen Grundlagen der Pädagogik (Antrittsvorlesung) (1910)." In *Philosophische Pädagogik*, ed. O. F. Bollnow & G. Bräuer (= Gesammelte Schriften, Band II). Heidelberg, 1973, pp. 222–31.

―――. "Gedanken über Lehrerbildung (1920)." In *Schule und Lehrer*, ed. . L. Englert (= Gesammelte Schriften III). Heidelberg, 1970, pp. 27–73.

―――. "Grundsätzliches zur Umgestaltung der Volksschule (1918)." In F. H. Paffrath. *Eduard Spranger und die Volksschule: Eine historisch-systematische Untersuchung*. Bad Heilbrunn, 1971, pp. 215–25.

―――. *Wilhelm von Humboldt und die Reform des Bildungswesens* (1910). Tübingen, 1960.

Stern, W. "Zum Vergleich von Vorschülern und Volksschülern: Bemerkungen zum vorstehenden Aufsatz." In *Zeitschrift für angewandte Psychologie und psychologische Sammelforschung* 8. Band, 1914, pp. 121–23.

Titze, H. (unter Mitarbeit von H.-G. Herrlitz, V. Müller-Benedict und A. Nath). *Das Hochschulstudium in Preußen und Deutschland 1820–1944* (= Datenhandbuch zur deutschen Bildungsgeschichte. Band I. Hochschulen. 1. Teil). Göttingen, 1987.

Troeltsch, E. "Eröffnungsreferat." In *Pädagogische Konferenz im Ministerium der geistlichen und Unterrichts-Angelegenheiten* am 24. und 25. Mai 1917. Thesen und Verhandlungbericht, 1917a, pp. 9–10.

―――. "Schlußwort." In *Pädagogische Konferenz im Ministerium der geistlichen und Unterrichts-Angelegenheiten* am 24. und 25. Mai 1917. Thesen und Verhandlungsbericht, 1917b, pp. 23–25.

Willmann, O. *Didaktik als Bildungslehre nach ihren Beziehungen zur Sozialforschung und zur Geschichte der Bildung*. Band 2 (1889). Aalen, 1988.

Wundt, W. "Über reine und angewandte Psychologie." In *Psychologische Studien. Neue Folge der philosophischen Studien* V. Band, 1910, pp. 1–57.

Part V
Comparative Strategies Rethought

CHAPTER 14

World System and Interrelationship Networks

The Internationalization of Education
and the Role of Comparative Inquiry

JÜRGEN SCHRIEWER

Internationalization originated as a term of international law.[1] Since the nineteenth century, it has been used to denote limitations of the sovereignty of a State over all or parts of its national territory (such as cities, waterways, or harbors) in favor of other States or the international community as a whole. Only after 1945 did the term take on a more general meaning. At present, *internationalization*—like its more recent twin term *globalization*—is used to describe tendencies toward the intensification of global relations of interaction and exchange, the worldwide interweaving of fields of social communication, and the transnational harmonization of social models and structures (cf., for example, McGrew, 1992). Internationalization and globalization refer to a social reality that increasingly extends into the everyday experiences of individuals as well. However familiar, though, phenomena like international financial interconnections and monetary crises, worldwide ecological interdependencies, the pressures of global migration, or the unforeseen intensification of the worldwide transmission of news may already seem to the late twentieth-century observer, the recent shift of meaning of internationalization indicates that, from the perspective of historical macrosociology, the processes mentioned are, "in evolutionary terms, an absolutely new phenomenon" (Luhmann, 1975a, p. 57).

Nevertheless, as far as education is concerned, phenomena of internationalization and globalization do not seem to be completely new. As early as the beginning 1930s, rather, one can read that "as in economic life, the international interconnection in education has become stronger and stronger as a consequence of contemporary mastery of space; accordingly the international links between educationalists are currently so close, the to and fro so dense, that one can speak of an educational world public." This statement, which is taken from a pivotal treatise published under the title "International Education, Foreign Education, Comparative Education" (Schneider, 1931/32, p. 22), in a sense anticipates developments that were to take on their full shape only in the post–World War II era, if not in the last third of the twentieth century. This anticipation is significant. It throws into relief not only the ambiguous relation, characteristic of educational discourse, between internationalization processes and their interpretation or—to take up a distinction made in the same treatise—between "international interconnection in education" (as an aspect of social reality) and "International Education" (as discourse about that reality); it is linked, moreover, with the distinctive form of international discourse favored by educationists committed to innovation and reform, or concerned with policy and practice (analyzed in greater detail in Schriewer, 1990a). Indeed, if Friedrich Schneider, with this treatise, sought to base the incipient academic institutionalization of Comparative Education in Germany on a sound methodological foundation, by the same token he wanted to prepare the way for the new field to take an intellectual direction, in its subsequent development, that was more to conform to a stance of supranational universalism than to the methodology of cross-national analysis. He clearly favored, thus, a methodological approach through which "cross-national analysis," used as a distinctive method for "discovering general lawlike statements on education" *(komparative Methode)*, was by and large eclipsed by "international consideration" pursued with a view to "exposing major problems, ideas, and currents in world education" *(vergleichende Betrachtung)* (Schneider, 1931/32, pp. 243 and 403f.). Accordingly, the *Internationale Zeitschrift für Erziehungswissenschaft—International Education Review—Revue Internationale de Pédagogie*, launched by Schneider and inaugurated with the article just mentioned, was conceived as a medium of scholarly communication that was meant to foster not so much comparative research across nations and societies, but—as the title implied—the internationalization of educationalists' problem awareness and of educational theory building.

Recent authors have even gone a step further. They explicitly assign to *Comparative Education* or—as some people consciously alluding to Schneider's predilections would prefer—*International Education* the functions of reflecting, supporting, and legitimizing ongoing processes of internationalization of both educational systems and educational theory. In the form of this particular branch of educational studies, they argue, the process of internationalization of education arrives at an awareness of itself. Moreover, according to the historicist rationale underlying such reasoning, the field of Comparative and/or International Education then, as the reflection theory of this process, reacts on it in the sense of further development of internationality (cf. Krüger, 1974; Katz, 1978;

Anweiler, 1977 & 1990; Dräger, 1991, and, from the vantage point of social analysis, Hüfner, Meyer & Naumann, 1987).

In the following, this line of reasoning will be disputed. It is questionable in that it promotes an intellectual attitude that tends to place the emphasis more on confirming and thereby endorsing the increasing intensification of global interconnections implied by the concept of internationalization than on analytically elucidating the complexity of these interconnections. As a consequence— my counterargument runs—the challenges arising for Comparative Education (as for comparative social science in general) from globalization processes and the attendant emergence of a world society are not only disregarded conceptually and methodologically; comparative and/or international educationists, moreover, may be assumed to actively—and, in a sense, politically—contribute to a particular form of "semantic construction of world-society."

The proposed counterargument, however, will not be developed solely on the level of abstract—in this instance: methodological—criticism. Rather, it takes advantage of the possibilities provided by the so-called sociohistorical shift in metascientific discourse (cf. Pollak, 1983) to empirically substantiate, and hence to objectify, methodological arguments. More precisely, the following will be guided by the theses by which Max Weber, in his well-known essay from 1904 about "objectivity" in the social sciences, evoked the fundamental historicity of academic disciplines, and of scientific activity more generally. "Sometime or other" in the course of disciplinary specialization and normalization, Weber suggests,

> the color will change: the significance of uncritically adopted points of view becomes uncertain, the path is fading away into the dusk. The light of the central issues of civilization has moved on. As a consequence, science also prepares to change its position and its conceptual apparatus, and to look at the stream of events from the height of reflection. (Weber, 1973, p. 214)

In this vein, I will start out by confronting—from a perspective drawing on the history of science—the original emergence of the idea of a comparative science of education with the current questioning of that *program*. Against this background, I will then examine at some length contrasting research findings in order to, finally, consider the question of what the possible "position" of the field can be at the end of the twentieth century, and in the face of altered "issues," "points of view," and "conceptual apparatuses."

Stages

At the End of the Eighteenth Century: Outline of a Grand Program

To begin with, I will briefly describe the historical context that saw the emergence of the idea of establishing disciplinary fields of study devoted to comparative research on society, man, and education. This is all the more important as, contrary to inveterate interpretations of the field's development that focus almost exclusively on individual pioneers, the scope of the intellectual project of a comparative science of education will become clear only against the background of the more general transformations in the history of science that took place at the end of the eighteenth century.

The introduction of the comparative method into science was an innovation of the late eighteenth and the early nineteenth century. Comparative research, in that period, represented a *non plus ultra* in modernity. It functioned as an essential element propelling processes of far-reaching restructuring in science, which have been described by the recent history of science as the "emergence of the modern system of academic disciplines" (Stichweh, 1984). The transition from premodern to modern science involved in this restructuring was accompanied by a radical reevaluation of empirical knowledge. In this connection, the comparative approach suggested itself as a means not only for generating, but also for analyzing empirical data.

In this historical context, the project of establishing scholarly fields devoted to the comparative study of language, law, religion, political constitutions, and, eventually, education is one of the earliest and most prominent examples of the transference of a successful methodological approach from the natural sciences—particularly the life sciences—to the human and social sciences. Just as, at first, Georges de Cuvier (1800–1805) did in epoch-making and exemplary fashion for anatomy; Anselm von Feuerbach (1810), a little later, for the study of law; and Franz Bopp for linguistics (Lefmann 1895, pp. 115–18); so, for the field of education, Marc-Antoine Jullien de Paris (1817) drew up—about 180 years ago—the program for transforming, by way of empirical investigation and comparative analysis, heterogeneous and unconfirmed quantities of knowledge into a distinct and increasingly autonomous discipline. The "normative ideas"—to use Max Weber's term—that underlay this launch of Comparative Education aimed, thus, at nothing less than the positivist reformulation of hitherto merely speculative educational doctrines, and the development of educational theory on the basis of methodically conducted research. The very originality of this 1817 text, the earliest in the French language to use the term *science de l'éducation*, stems precisely from the fact that it constituted not only a manifesto in favor of establishing Comparative Education but also a program for developing a Science of Education as such.

It was in the same historical context, ultimately, that the subsequent theoretical and methodological problems associated with the transference of a successful research approach from the life sciences to the social sciences and humanities had been given consideration. In fact, considerations of this kind did not appear in the writings of Jullien, a representative figure of the late French Enlightenment who, after receiving an up-to-date training in comparative zoology, was mainly committed to political and social reform;

they were, however, given attention in the reflections of a scholar of comparative linguistics who had been trained in philosophy, and who, apart from holding high office in public administration and diplomacy, devoted his life entirely to the study of the humanities. I refer to Wilhelm von Humboldt, and to the *Plan einer vergleichenden Anthropologie (Outline of Comparative Anthropology)* he wrote in 1795. In this treatise, Humboldt discussed the methodological issue of how to systematically mediate between "historical objects"—which are anthropology's preexistent "empirical material"—and these objects' "theoretical treatment," the latter being geared to grasping explanatory relationships and ascertaining causal knowledge. Humboldt considered, moreover, the additional theory problem—the "peculiarity" as he called it—encountered by the comparative social sciences exactly because of the fact that they reach far beyond the material world of anatomy. This problem arises from the difference, fundamental to the object domain of all social science, between purported "laws" of human nature and man's "indispensable liberty"; between the regularities rooted in human genus and social systems as such and—as Humboldt put it—man's "spontaneous energy" (Humboldt, 1964, pp. 36 and 42ff.). In a sense, Humboldt anticipated contemporary theory debates related to the contrasts between general cause-effect relationships and man's fundamental historicity open to unknown futures, or, couched in terms yet more modern, between causality and self-reference.

By highlighting these two strands of problems, Humboldt, at the same time, pointed out the lines of reference for the continuous methodological debates that have accompanied the development of Comparative Education as an academic field up to the present day. This is not the place to review these debates in detail; suffice it to note that even under the conditions of academic institutionalization the comparative subdiscipline—or "aspect" discipline (Diemer, 1970)—of education remained entangled in a net of conflicting expectations, contrasting functional assignments, and hard-to-reconcile methodological options (Schriewer, 1982; Epstein, 1983). Resultant controversies spring, for instance, from the difference between widely held ideas of International Education and the classical program for Comparative Education. They arise from the conflicting expectations of reform-oriented policy research and theory-oriented scientificization. They repeatedly flare up with regard to the discrepancy between the widespread practice of synthesizing international development trends with a view to orientation and the requirements of comparative methodology defined in accordance with the logic of scientific discovery. Ultimately, such controversies result from contrasting modes of perceiving the Other: from the contrast, which in turn is constitutive in shaping the distinctive subject-matter of study, between minimizing sociocultural differences with a view to facilitating pragmatic understanding and thoroughly exploiting these same differences for purposes of social science analysis (cf. Schriewer, 1990a).

At the End of the Twentieth Century: The World as the Unit of Analysis

What is radically new about the present situation—the situation at the end of the twentieth century—is that demands are no longer just being raised for improved versions of the methodological form of Comparative Education. Rather, some of the field's fundamental theoretical and methodological assumptions as such are being called into question.

Recent research and theory developments do indeed amount to the unravelling of the largely unquestioned subject matter of Comparative Education: the world conceived of as a multitude of separate regional or national societies which, as autonomous entities, as historically distinct configurations, constitute one another's mutual environments. The immediate consequence of such an epistemic elimination of the field's subject matter is that its defining methodological procedure as well—comparison applied to a multiplicity of independent units of analysis—is deprived of its meaning. Comparison, then, is replaced by historical reconstructions of wide-reaching processes of cultural diffusion or by global analyses of transnational interdependence (McMichael, 1990; Wallerstein, 1987). Finally, two different strands of theoretical reasoning, namely retrospectively construed theory critiques and prospectively fashioned "world system" models, interlink in such conclusions.

The kind of theory critiques referred to have been presented by, among others, Friedrich H. Tenbruck (1981). The title of his study, "The Birth of Society out of the Spirit of Sociology," contains his theses in a nutshell. According to Tenbruck, if the formation of a specifically sociological communication network can be conceived of as an intellectual response to the radically novel social reality that emerged, at the end of the eighteenth and the beginning of the nineteenth century, from the dissolution of the corporative, estate-based, social structures of early modern Europe, then the conception of a society subsequently favored by that sociological discourse—that is, the abstract concept of a multiplicity of mutually independent, quasi-autarkic, and to that extent comparable societies—is context bound in several respects and, therefore, of questionable theoretical validity. Not only had this concept of society, Tenbruck further relates, the imprint of the theoretical requirements of a discipline patterned on natural-science models; it also took as immutable a certain, merely transient, "contemporary state of affairs, namely the self-image of ninteenth-century nations concerned about their cultural individuality and political autonomy for which . . . the identity of the people, culture, nation and state was an obvious lesson of history" (Tenbruck, 1981, p. 348). But, Tenbruck continues, a concept of society with that pretension should have been, in fact, empirically disproven long ago by internationalization phenomena and large-scale processes of transcultural diffusion.

What makes these theses particularly pointed, in their antagonism toward the comparative approach, is—beyond their reanalysis of social and intellectual history—the fact that Tenbruck developed them by way of an intense discussion of the works of Emile Durkheim. In repudiating Durkheim he, at the same time, repudiates the one theoretician of comparative social science who more than anyone else was responsible for translating, at the end of the nineteenth century, the grand program of the late eighteenth century into a rigorous scientific methodology. In so doing, Durkheim also showed the comparative method to be the substitute—peculiarly suited to the social sciences—for macrosocial experiments, thus laying the foundations for a tradition of comparative social science research that has continued to be of crucial importance up to the present day. Suffice it to recall here the well-known passage from Durkheim's *Rules of the Sociological Method* (first published in 1895) where, taking up an idea first conceived during the period of the far-reaching restructuring of science a century earlier, he reiterates the connection between comparative research and the formation of scientific disciplines: "Comparative sociology is not merely a particular branch of sociology; it is, rather, identical with sociology itself to the extent that it ceases to be purely descriptive and aims to account for the facts" (Durkheim, 1986, p. 137).

While critical reconstructions of social theory have thus historically relativized, not merely the basic assumptions regarding its specific subject matter, but, in so doing, the comparative social sciences project proper, this project is currently being overtaken—in terms of evolutionary theory— within the framework of world-system analyses. And just as classical sociology saw itself as a response to the altered social reality of the ninteenth century, world-system models for their part claim that social macrostructures in the late twentieth century can be adequately grasped only by taking into consideration the global context of worldwide relations of interdependence which have intensified in novel ways (cf. So, 1990, pp. 169ff.). This claim also extends to the analysis of particular fields such as national education systems. Their structures, development potentials, and social functions, it is argued, can be fully explained only if their respective positions in a worldwide structure are systematically taken into account:

> Analyses of education within the context of closed, national systems fail to capture the position of a country within the international system. It is this situation which conditions the effects of intranational economic, political, and socio-cultural factors on educational development or underdevelopment . . . This global perspective enhances our understanding of the origins, evolution, and implications of educational practices, combining the micro and macro levels of analysis, and linking provincial occurences to national and international events. (Arnove, 1980, pp. 50 and 54)

The state of theory building regarding the parameters that are decisive for the construction of world-system models is at present incomplete (cf. Bornschier and Lengyel, 1990, pp. 3–15):

- The dominant work in this area has taken shape as a result of Wallerstein's resumption of Braudelian investigations into economic history (i.e., broadly conceived, long-term process analyses of large-scale networks of transcontinental exchange relations) interpreted in the light of the political economy of capitalism and dependency theory (Braudel, 1979; Wallerstein, 1976, 1991).

- Models using arguments that are not so much economistic as based on modernization theory and cultural sociology, developed by a research group headed by John W. Meyer and Francisco Ramirez at Stanford, focus on the universalization of sociocultural organization patterns, and especially of the nation-state (Meyer & Hannan, 1979; Boli, Ramirez & Meyer, 1986).

- Conceptualizations based on the theory of social differentiation, finally, seek to explain the emergence of a "world society" in terms of the dynamics intrinsic to functionally specific subsystems of society—particularly the economy and scientific research—which tend toward intensifying their special communication links irrespective of the boundaries of territorially organized political systems (Luhmann, 1975a, 1982a).

In the following, the basic idea of the world system as a paradigm will be characterized with reference to a theoretical version that can be traced back to the Wallersteinian tradition and its grounding in economic history. The selected text, authored by Albert Bergesen, particularly exemplifies the history-of-science dimension of the replacement of the perspectives predominant in international social and educational research by the world-system paradigm (Bergesen, 1980).

In this text, Bergesen recapitulates the fundamental paradigm shifts that, since the eighteenth century, have successively gained acceptance in the history of social theory. In so doing, he demonstrates that each of these theory shifts has corresponded to an inversion in the basic model of social order. Thus, he draws parallels between, on the one hand, the transition from (i) the individual-based interactionist models characteristic of late eighteenth-century utilitarianism to (ii) the holistic conceptions of order characteristic of the sociological systems developed in the late nineteenth century and, on the other hand, a theoretical revolution that is due to occur at the end of the twentieth century. Bergesen indeed claims that (iii) the early forms of the world-system paradigm, which had been developing since the 1950s within the framework of dependency theory, still conceived of the disproportionate world division of labor as a result that had gradually emerged from the interactions—the exchange relations and economic processes—between the core states and peripheral areas; that is, between a small number of highly developed industrial nations and a large number of more or less developing, dependent countries. However it is time, according to Bergesen, to proceed to yet another radical change in the conceptualization of global order, and to conceive of the world system as (iv) an emerging reality sui generis, as a "collective reality exogenous to nations":

> The final paradigm revolution will come when we invert the parts-to-whole framework of the world-system outlook and move to a distinctly whole-to-parts paradigm which posits *a priori* world social relations of production which in turn determine the core-periphery relations of trade and exchange.

The world system, consequently, "has its own laws of motion that, in turn, determine the social, political, and economic realities of the national societies it encompasses" (Bergesen, 1980, pp. xiii, 10). *Sociology*, the science of society, is therefore to be replaced by *Globology*, the science of "the collective reality of world order" (Bergesen, 1980, p. 8).

Does this mean, then, that "the light of the central issues of civilization" has—again recalling Max Weber—irrevocably shifted? Has, in other words, the right to represent scientific modernity to which the comparative social and human sciences quite rightfully laid claim at the beginning of the nineteenth century passed, at the end of the twentieth century, to analyses of the single world system as a global network of interrelations and interdependencies that have intensified in hitherto unknown ways?

Findings

The Emergence of a World Educational System

To empirically substantiate metascientific arguments means—in complement to their historicization—resolving such issues not ad hoc or according to speculative conjectures, but by sifting through the body of research and carefully considering the findings and problems that are revealed in the process—and these findings are unexpectedly rich in contrasts.

First, I shall briefly enumerate major research results that have been produced within the framework of the world-system paradigm and that have in turn contributed to further elaborating world-system models in the field of international educational research. These results indicate astonishing processes of global alignment that have taken place at different levels, and in different dimensions, of education:

1. To begin with, the last four decades have seen a *uniform worldwide educational* expansion that has embraced all levels—primary, secondary, and tertiary—of the educational system (cf. Komenan, 1987; Kurian, 1988, pp. 15–36). This expansion has been so massive and so uniform that it can no longer be plausibly explained in terms of the varying contextual conditions, social demands, or economic trends prevailing in quite different national settings: "Comprehensive statistical analyses of educational expansion, the incorporation of women, constitutional specification of educational rights and duties, and so on," Ramirez and Boli-Bennett sum up, "reveal that varying national characteristics had little or no effect on these dependent variables during the postwar period. Hence there is little support for any of the numerous, much-debated theories attempting to account for these developments. In their stead we offer the view that education has become an important element of the transnational social system" (Ramirez & Boli-Bennett, 1982, pp. 32–33; Meyer et al., 1977). Compared to educational growth in general the trend toward expansion is even more marked in the case of universities. Irrespective of the divergent political systems, economic development levels, or public policy priorities of the individual countries, the worldwide increase in university enrollment has turned out to be the most important individual international development trend of the postwar era (Altbach, 1991c, p. 193; cf. Ramirez & Riddle, 1991).

2. This expansion goes hand in hand with the global acceptance of a largely standardized *model of institutionalized schooling* as a blueprint for orienting and assessing educational policies worldwide. The standardized model is a combination of the distinctive structural features of the modern educational system, the nineteenth-century European development of which has been described in detail as a "system formation process" or "systematization" in recent comparative-historical research (Müller, Ringer & Simon, 1987). The worldwide dissemination of these structural features is considered by many to be a salient indicator of cultural globalization processes (Boli & Ramirez, 1992; Ramirez & Boli, 1987). These features include:

   • a general administrative framework usually founded, controlled, and funded by the State;
   • a school system internally differentiated according to successive levels, diverse courses of study, and corresponding end-of-schooling examinations;
   • the organization of teaching and learning processes in the classroom according to distinct age groups and uniform time units;
   • the governmental or public regulation of such teaching and learning processes through more or less detailed requirements in the form of syllabi, directives, and examination plans;

- the shaping of distinctive roles for teachers and pupils, and to a certain extent the professionalization of teachers and teaching methods; and finally,
- the use of certificates, diplomas, and credentials to link school careers with occupational careers, connecting selection in schools with social stratification.

3. Furthermore, a *"world-level developmental cultural account and educational ideology"* (Fiala & Lanford, 1987) has emerged which parallels, supports, and reinforces the above-mentioned expansion and globalization processes. Within this framework, institutionalized schooling is considered to be an integral component and an indispensable lever of societal modernization processes. The underlying programmatic ideas are rooted in some guiding principles that have determined the self-interpretation of European modernity since the nineteenth century, namely (i) individual personality development, citizenship, and participatory competence; (ii) the equalization of social and political opportunities; (iii) economic development; and (iv) political order guaranteed by the nation-state. These ideas, in turn, are reflected—in a global standardization and with increasing intensity over time—in the educational goals and the general mandates concerning childhood, family, and education that can be found in the constitutions of a rapidly growing number of countries on all continents.

4. Finally, the dissemination of this semantics of modernization—as well as of the corresponding model of "the modern school" (Adick, 1992)—would not have been possible without the social and institutional infrastructure provided by an *international communication and publication system in the realm of the social sciences and education* (cf. Altbach, 1987, 1991a, 1991b, 1994). This includes, on the one hand, the broad array of international organizations committed to policy development and implementation in the areas of education and culture such as the World Bank, UNESCO, the International Bureau of Education, the International Institute for Educational Planning, or OECD. Large-scale international organizations such as these not only provide institutionally secured role definitions for an immense international educational establishment—which in part sees itself as decidedly supranational (cf., e.g., the autobiographical account by Hoggart 1978)—but also well-funded publication facilities and thus extraordinary opportunities for international distribution and influence. The scientific communication system, on the other hand, has become strongly hierarchized between the core—today nearly synonymous with Anglo-American academia and peripheral areas. A handful of wealthy industrialized nations in North America, Europe, and Japan and a number of large multinational publishing companies such as Macmillan, Pergamon, Harper and Row, Prentice Hall, Elsevier,

Hachette, or Bertelsmann make up—to use Philip Altbach's graphic phrase—"a kind of OPEC of knowledge" (1991b, p. 122). With their research potential and academic personnel, and through specialized journals and textbooks, the rich nations and the multinational publishing companies, respectively, control the production, legitimation, and distribution of what is regarded as relevant scientific knowledge throughout the world. In fact, studies on certain subfields of educational research have produced sufficient evidence to show how even the problem conceptualizations and theoretical frameworks, the classificatory schemes and statistical categories, the quality assessments and normative evaluation standards that are current in international organizations and in Anglo-American academic circles put pressure on researchers worldwide to adapt their work to these criteria—and this pressure is all the more successful as it is not even perceived as such (Hüfner, Meyer & Naumann, 1987).

Suffice it to mention just one illustrative example of this three-way alliance between the hierarchized system of science, the international publication infrastructure, and the global dissemination of a particular developmental and educational ideology. The authors of the ten-volume *International Encyclopedia of Education* (Husen & Postlethwaite, 1985) are overwhelmingly members of the Anglo-American educational research establishment. Of the 1,175 authors, nearly half (N = 564) come from the United States and roughly three-quarters (N = 855) come from the group of English-speaking industrial countries taken as a whole. If one adds to these figures the authors from countries such as India, South Africa, or Sweden who increasingly use the English languge as the accepted idiom of scholarly communication, the proportion of English-speaking authors increases to nearly 80 percent. One of the editors-in-chief, in a later retrospective, attempted to justify this Anglo-American dominance by the sheer weight of American research capacities. According to his assertions, nearly half of the world's research literature in education was produced in the United States during the planning period of the encyclopedia; additionally, more researchers in education worked in the United States during this period than in all European countries combined (Husen, 1990, p. 68). Despite its self-definition as "international," this encyclopedia is in fact a soapbox for the dissemination of Anglo-American or Anglo-American-influenced educational research. Therefore, internationalization, in education as in other fields, may be tantamount only to the "universalization of a particular world view" (Casanova, 1993).

Nevertheless, the worldwide distribution of this large-scale educational encyclopedia is guaranteed by the financial and advertising capabilities of Pergamon, which has branches on almost every continent and is among the largest of the above-mentioned publishing firms. First published by Pergamon in 1985, the *International Encyclopedia* has since been marketed in the form of two reprint editions (Husen & Postlethwaite, 1988, 1991), a compact disc, and a number of more specialized partial encyclopedias on selected subfields.[2] As a further indication of its prevalence, a largely updated and expanded twelve-volume edition was published in 1994. The very publishing success of the encyclopedia is thus instrumental in explaining the nearly boundless dissemination of supposedly transnational ideology. Indeed, the original and reprint editions from 1985 to 1991 contain no less than 180 entries pertaining to "educational planning," "development and modernization," and the "economics of education," to fields, in other words, that largely correspond to the "world-level developmental cultural account and educational ideology." An entry that would systematically delineate the structure of education in its own right, transcend a mere instrumentalist view of education and, in so doing, link up the encyclopedia with traditions in educational theory prevailing in parts of the world other than the English-speaking countries—namely, the entry "education"—was, however, not included.

Against the background of such mutually corroborating pieces of evidence regarding the global expansion of education, the worldwide dissemination of models of institutionalized schooling, the acceptance of a particular developmental and educational ideology, and the workings of international scientific communication and publication structures, diagnoses originating in other contexts and based on different evidence become intelligible. A survey of different fields of comparative policy research shows indeed that in no other area of public policy, neither in economic, nor in social or environmental policy, does there exist such a high degree of global standardization of organizational structures, policy-relevant models, and reform discourse as in educational policy and policy-oriented educational research (Weiler, 1987). One must conclude, therefore, that educational systems and educational research are, unlike other areas of social interaction, not simply a fixed component of more general processes of the internationalization and globalization of cultural patterns. Rather, they seem to be especially susceptible to the dynamics of increasing internationalization. According to a thesis formulated in Parsonian terms, therefore, schools—in the sense of the structural model referred to—are an "evolutionary universal" of the social and cultural development of modernity (Adick, 1988, p. 353 after Parsons, 1964; cf. also Adick, 1992).

Education as a Component of Varying Interrelationship Networks

With such findings and conceptualizations concerning the emerging world system in mind, one has now to review the results of cross-cultural comparative research proper. More precisely: What results has a comparative social inquiry that makes use of comparison as a distinctive method of analysis—

and does not merely turn out descriptive surveys or synthetic interpretations of international developments—produced?

In the following section, major results of recent comparative research regarding social problem areas that in different countries have been, or continue to be, characterized by largely similar challenges to both educational and social policy will be summarized. These are, at the same time, areas that have been or continue to be interpreted in pronouncedly universalist terms within the framework of relevant social theories; areas which because of the predominant prognostic models have led to expectations of converging problem-solving patterns; problem areas, then, which have been assumed to be determined by almost law-like macro-social causal or functional relationships. In point of fact, however, comparative research has unearthed an impressive range of international variation regarding the problem-solving patterns and strategies that have been realized in diverse historical and cultural settings.

a. Such findings apply, first of all, to the intricate whole of *employment and labor-market policy* that is increasingly interwoven with *social and educational policy*. Comparative outcomes analyses of the strategies followed in order to guarantee full employment have not only shown that such strategies—further education and training for the employed, migrant worker policies, avoidance of moral hazard in the social security system, wage flexibility, etc.—are employed to a considerably varying degree even among the advanced industrial nations committed to free enterprise, but also that they result in extraordinarily diverse outcomes (Schmid, Füglistaler & Hohl, 1992). Additionally, such studies reveal a variance in the economic-performance measures, structural-adaption policies, and economic-management priorities of individual countries for which there is, contrary to the assumptions of macroeconomic theories, "no single straightforward economic explanation." Whereas all countries taken into consideration "were exposed to the same external economic shocks, their responses could hardly have been more different. . . . There seems to be no obvious correlation between rates of economic growth and rates of inflation, between inflation and unemployment, or even between economic growth and employment growth. Instead, it seems that in a generally worsening world-wide economic environment individual countries have chosen specific national profiles of economic performance, favoring or neglecting specific measures of performance" (Scharpf, 1984, p. 259).

Just as the predictive power of 1960s-era convergence theories—arguing the evolutionary convergence of the development patterns of modern industrial societies as a consequence of the functional imperatives imposed by the purportedly universal exigencies of technological and economic rationality—was refuted by comparative evidence pointing to the persistence, in those same societies, of distinctive national profiles of social and economic organization (Goldthorpe, 1984; Kumon & Rosovsky, 1992), more recent comparative studies show how the sweeping pressure to increase productivity is met, in all these countries, by varying strategies of innovation which in turn are rooted in clearly divergent labor-market and industrial policies (Sabel et al., 1987; Naschold, 1992). An illustrative example of this is the Japanese model of new work organization, known since the 1980s as "Toyotism." Instead of merely following this supposedly culture-free and superior model, the industrial countries of Europe and North America, by taking into account nationally different patterns of industrial relations institutions, labor market conditions, and educational and training systems, show preference for "different roads" with "different outcomes":

> Now, with the collapse of the communist regimes of Eastern Europe, economic integration in Western Europe, and the contemporary dominance of free-market ideology, new convergence theory becomes tempting. But entrenched national institutions and particular market circumstances make national and local diversity as important now as ever. (Turner & Auer, 1992, p. 28)

b. Similar conclusions have been drawn on the basis of an extensive body of comparative research dealing with the interconnections between *vocational education and training systems, qualification structures of the labor force,* and *work organization in large-scale manufacturing units.* One learns, thereby, to thoroughly distrust the thesis—posited by industrial sociology and the economics of education—stating that qualification requirements and educational and training structures are largely determined by technological change, economic development, and the exigencies of a universal rationality intrinsic to industrialism (Maurice, 1980; Heidenreich & Schmidt, 1991). These studies have shown, rather, that vocational education and training as well as the utilization of human labor are, even within the ranks of technologically advanced industrialized societies, to a large extent defined by societal and cultural factors. (cf. Dore, 1973; Iribarne, 1989)

Comparative indepth analyses of closely matched industrial companies in France, Great Britain, and Germany are salient exemplars of this strand of research. They show convincingly that these companies, while being very similar in terms of branch of industry, size, products, production technology, and competitiveness in the same markets, nevertheless structure their workforces according to distinct national patterns of company organization and division of work. Such differences are particularly conspicuous between French and German companies. While French companies in general systematically utilize a marked division of work, both horizontally and vertically, the pattern of work organization predominant in German companies is characterized by a significantly smaller number of hierarchic levels of supervisory and managerial positions; smaller wage differentials; a less rigid division of work; a higher degree of professional and technical expertise among the lower levels of Meisters, foremen, and workers; and, consequently, wider opportunities for craft judgement-based decision making and continual upgrading of professional qualifications even among workers engaged in subordinate activities (Lutz, 1976). British manufacturing plants are organized on a pattern that is no less nation-specific and, in a sense, intermediate between the French and German models (Maurice, Sorge & Warner, 1980; Sorge & Warner, 1987). Soviet-Russian *kombinats*, on the other hand, once operated on patterns of organization that, because of their high degree of functional differentiation and vertical hierarchization, were rather closer to the French model, although the Russian patterns had developed out of very specific social and historical circumstances (Pietsch, 1980). The impact, finally, of "nationally divergent manufacturing cultures" (Maurice, Sorge & Warner, 1980, p. 65) is conspicuous even when comparing the local branches of multinational companies established in various countries and on different continents (Hofstede, 1986; Hirata, 1991).

The deeper insight encouraged by these studies furnishes conclusive proof that there is a close, and not arbitrarily modifiable, interdependence between nation-specific patterns of industrial work organization, qualification structures of the labor force, systems of education and training, nation-specific patterns of mobility and career progression, and developed institutions of industrial relations. Above all, it is the respective institutions of education and training that play, in this context, an especially important role. They operate as a largely autonomous subsystem that, by shaping their social environment, induces other subsystems (such as large industrial firms) to adapt. Accordingly, the highly inclusive model of apprenticeship-based vocational education and training traditionally predominant in Germany has favored, until the recent past, the broad transmission of technical-practical expertise and thus the lateralization of interprofessional communication within the firm (e.g., between workers, foremen, and technicians) encouraged by this common background. It is characteristic of vocational education patterns based on full-time schooling, in contrast, to promote the hierarchization of courses of study and corresponding degrees which is later reproduced in the ordering of career patterns and employment positions. Cases in point are France, where vocational education structures are subject to the pull of gravity and the criteria of selectivity of a school-system committed to the virtues of general education and abstract knowledge, and Britain, where the emphasis is on basic notions of experimental science and technology rather than practical, professional expertise.

In each of the cases mentioned, interrelationship networks develop which, while remaining consistent *intranationally*, vary significantly when examined *internationally*. These networks—between training relations, organizational relations, industrial relations, and collective-order relations—have evolved, reciprocally adapted to one another, and structurally solidified in long-enduring processes. Such socially and culturally determined networks of interrelationship are in turn likely to determine the differentiated forms and strategies of the subsequent utilization of novel technologies, thereby maintaining the rich diversity of historical-cultural patterns (Lutz, 1976; Maurice, Sellier & Silvestre, 1979; Deppe & Hoss, 1984).

c. International comparative research into the *connections between education, modernization, and development* reveals largely similar findings. An examination of the voluminous body of research demonstrates that these connections are considerably more complex than the assumptions of modernization theories—based on the economics of education, political science, or social psychology—would lead one to expect (Fägerlind & Saha, 1985; Grellet, 1992). This applies all the more to models suggesting linear causal links between *modernizing institutions* (i.e., schools or firms), *modern values, modern behavior, modern society*, and *economic development* which have been constructed with a view to suggesting strategies for developmental policy (Inkeles & Smith, 1974). In each dimension relevant to developmental policy—education and economic growth, education and sociopsychological modernization, education and political mobilization—these connections are neither direct nor linear, nor do they produce the same effects in different societies. Instead, they are as a rule not very pronounced, only partially effective, basically dysfunctional, or purely and simply counter-productive. In any case, they are "highly problematic" and can only be understood in terms of interrelationships.

"Education"—in the sense of Western-type schooling—"is both determined and a determinant of the society in which it is located; . . . both an agent of change and in turn is changed by society; . . . it acts both as a producer of social mobility and as an agent for the reproduction of the social order" (Fägerlind & Saha, 1985, pp. 88, 195).

These interrelationships are for their part embedded in, and reshaped by, more encompassing social relation networks. Thus, the impact of schooling that is observable in different countries, as well as the structures of "modernity" attained in each of them, are the consequences of the varying contextual conditions dominant in different societies and in turn impinge upon these contextual conditions in varying ways.

What the three strands of comparative research have in common, then, is that their results demonstrate an observable multiplicity of varying interrelationship networks and developmental paths. Although at a general level these networks and developmental paths may be conceptualized within the framework of system models and systemic typologies, their essential complexity must be further elucidated through long-term, comparative analysis. The general conclusions which may thus be drawn from these strands of comparative study recall the work of Samuel Eisenstadt in historical-comparative modernization research (Eisenstadt, 1973, p. 362, and 1992); they are further supported by research accumulated in fields such as comparative politics and comparative sociology of organizations. Surveys of this body of research do indeed diagnose the dissolution, in the face of comparative evidence, of concepts based on a supposedly universal rationality of industrialism (Heidenreich & Schmidt, 1991) and of conceptions that assume a unidimensional logic of development (Menzel, 1991). Not only does the so-called Third World, once construed as such in the framework of development theory and policy, break down into the hardly conceivable multiplicity of *newly industrializing countries*, *least developed countries*, *most seriously affected countries*, *threshhold countries*, *low-income countries*, oil-exporting versus oil-importing countries, land-locked versus coastal countries, and large versus mini or island states; not only does the culture-bound diversity of political institutions and organizations further increase, contrary to the anticipated convergence toward a universal—say a Western—model; what is more, the all-encompassing theories that claim universal validity—be they rooted in modernization or dependency theory, structural functionalism or Marxism—can no longer account for the breadth of variation of what Humboldt once called social science's "historical objects." In other words, the "crisis of universalism" (Badie & Hermet, 1990, pp. 19–44) corresponds to the "failure of the grand theories" (Menzel, 1991; Boudon, 1992).

"There are"—French comparativists sum up—"no universal determinants; individual historical processes are too numerous, too complex, and, in effect, too independent of one another" (Badie & Hermet, 1990, p. 10).

Perspectives

Reconciling History and Comparison

The preceding examination of various fields of comparative and international social and educational research has thrown into relief the conspicuous contrast between the global spread of transnationally standardized educational models and the persistence of varying sociocultural interrelationship networks. Beyond nation-specific information, it is this contrast which is the most significant result of comparative research and, relevant to theory, the most pertinent. In the following, this will be systematically extended in three different respects.

1. This transition to a more systematic point of view is facilitated by the very results of comparative research, especially those concerning the development of higher education, the sciences (particularly the social sciences), and the international states system. Thus, on the one hand, these results show, indeed, a considerable increase in the international alignment of expansion processes and a marked homogenization of organizational features. Furthermore, it becomes clear that the European university is the one institution, aside from the school, whose worldwide dissemination (including the establishment of branches of American, as well as French and Japanese universities in other countries) has been more self-evident and has taken place with a greater "lack of alternatives" than is the case for most other institutions characteristic of societal modernity (Stichweh, 1998; cf. also Altbach, 1991c).

In contrast, however, to global alignment processes at the organizational level, recent research has demonstrated that it is precisely the global expansion of universities into large-scale systems that results, not in growing convergence, but in further national differentiation. To the extent that higher education systems lose their elite character, the evidence suggests, their concrete integration into the varying nation-specific patterns of social stratification, labor force qualification structure, administrative regulation, and public policy is strengthened (Goldschmidt, 1991a, 1991b; Kerr, 1991; Teichler, 1988).

Contrary developments appear, likewise, in the social sciences. Comparative sociology-of-knowledge analyses have shown the persistence of historical semantics based on national language and of academic cultures imprinted by tradition in spite of scientific rationality's claim of universal validity (cf. Ringer, 1992; Harwood, 1992). They demonstrate, additionally, how particular disciplines—despite the intensification of international communication between scientists—continue to draw, and even renew, their major paradigmatic orientations out of the spirit of their respective theory traditions (cf. Schriewer & Keiner, 1992 and 1993, in the field of educational studies, and Schulze, 1989, in the field of history).

Furthermore, in reaction to the global Anglo-American dominance (documented above) in the area of scientific research and dissemination (cf. Chekki, 1987), controversial debate has recently appeared concerning the conflicting tendencies of *internationalization* versus *indigenization* in the social sciences (Genov, 1989, pp. 1–17), and the development of culture-specific *indigenous sociologies* in contrast to a *Universal Social Science* (Albrow & King, 1990).

Analyses from comparative politics, finally, turn up findings which point to an almost "dialectical" interlocking of supranational integration and intranational fragmentation (McGrew, 1992, p. 23; Smith, 1992). They demonstrate how attempts at supranational integration, primarily European, parallel not only the maintenance but also the strengthening of the nation-state and the extension and intensification of its penetrating capability (Sharpe, 1989; Milward et al., 1992). By the same token, they support the idea that increased efforts at transnational integration go hand in hand with the dynamization of processes of regional—linguistically, ethnically, or culturally imprinted—diversification (Grant, 1981; Charpentier & Engel, 1992; Scardigli, 1993).

As comparative research in higher education, social sciences, and the international states system makes clear, therefore, the contrary phenomena of internationalization and nation-specific structural elaboration do not simply occur side by side, unrelated. Rather, they are connected to one another as challenges and reactions, as processes and unintended consequences. They refer equally to relationships constituted in time and to the potential for diversification inherent in such relationships; to overarching developmental processes and to the complexity generated by such processes. They emphasize, in other words, the macroperspective regarding large-scale, area-encompassing historical processes that is characteristic of the world-system approach; in so doing, however, they disabuse us of any notion of a unilinear, let alone evolutionistic, goal-determined rationality that might be attributed to such processes.

> It would . . . be inaccurate to conceive of globalization as some kind of teleological process. The idea that globalization incorporates some predetermined historical logic which is leading inexorably either to the creation of a world society or to some form of world government is simply not tenable. The historical evidence is ranged against it. For globalization stimulates forces of opposition which may just as readily lead to an increasingly fragmented world, since greater mutual awareness and interconnections between different societies may simply sow the seeds of conflict and tension. (McGrew, 1992, p. 23; cf. Smelser, 1991, p. 89)

2. Also fruitful, when considered systematically, are insights arising out of analyses of the transnational processes of migration (of scholars and experts) and diffusion and reception (of ideas and models) which pervade with increasing intensity the European—and later the worldwide—history of education from the nineteenth century on. Beyond illuminating the conflict-laden character of internationalization and globalization processes, the particular advantage of such analyses is that they show the mediating steps taken by the individual actors and/or social groups of which these processes are composed. The significance attributed to these analyses, contrary to the marginal role assigned them within the context of traditional comparative education, lies in the fact that they serve as an empirical critique of theoretical

approaches and interpretive models committed to a supposed world-historical developmental logic. In contrast to the assumptions on which such a logic is based, rather, they underscore both the nonlinear, contingent nature of globalization processes and the impact recurringly provoked in such processes by deviation-generating potentials. Characteristically, the transcultural diffusion of knowledge, organization models, problem-solving patterns, or policies is met by the receiving cultural or national groups with specific reinterpretation and adaptation procedures. As a consequence, models offered transculturally are, in the new environment, selected according to prevailing interests, adapted to specific situations and needs, reinterpreted along cultural lines, and—to historically varying degrees—transmuted into structural reformations.

The aforementioned worldwide dissemination of the European-style university, the history of the social sciences, and the spread of Western principles of political order and State organization provide a multitude of examples of these adaptive procedures. Comparisons, for example, of Japan and Brazil show that the reception and institutional implementation of the European university model in non-European countries has followed quite different patterns despite similar modernization challenges. In Japan, the selection of eclectic elements taken from various (primarily French, American, and German) university models, and their subordination to modernization and qualification requirements defined under authoritarian rule, led to an adaptive transformation—an *indigenization*—of the Western models while simultaneously immunizing the Japanese *Imperial Universities* against the unwelcome symptoms and effects perceived in the foreign examples. In Brazil, on the other hand, the relative weakness of modernizing and industrializing elites favored the lingering cultural and ideological dominance of French influence in general, and of the French tradition of maintaining independent faculties and institutions for advanced technological learning in particular (Cowen, 1988). Findings from the history of science support similar conclusions. Even a superficial overview of this research—from the spread of nineteenth-century German philosophy and philology throughout Western Europe (Espagne & Werner, 1988, 1990); to the adoption of Weberian sociology in France, the United States, and Southeast Asia (Pollak, 1986; Kantowsky, 1982); to the genesis of modern pedagogy in Japan (introduced by a Herbartian theorist since forgotten in Germany) (Terasaki, 1989)—shows the reception of scientific theories and innovations to form an endless series of interpretations and reinterpretations, filtered by prevailing interests and channelled into preexisting discourse constellations. The same holds true for the dissemination of Western democratic principles and political institutions throughout non-Western countries (Badie, 1992a). Again, as in the Japanese example, the institutions adopted merely formally are interwoven with previous layers of political behavior, social meanings, and culture-specific patterns of the exercise of authority. In this process of restructuring into a "system without a core" these institutions change their significance and the way they function (Wolferen, 1989).

The multitude of "adaptation logics" hinted at by such examples and the underlying deviation-generating cultural frameworks, differing notions of time and truth, and collective experiences sedimenting in the course of history

> unmask the highly ideological visions proclaiming the end of history [due to a supposedly irresistable convergence toward the Western model of liberal capitalist society] as purely illusory. Such a claim can at best refer to surface-level phenomena and to the impression of Westernization looming in certain processes of transmission. Behind this front, in reality, is dissimulated a complex play of importations and appropriations, and also of resurging popular modes of political action and ancient cultures which the comparativist is obliged to take into consideration: the Chinese, Indian, and Japanese trajectories are made just as much of pure overlay as of measured appropriations and the re-actualization of millenial cultural traditions. (Badie, 1992b, pp. 366–67)

Comparative research insights into the complexity of diffusion and reception processes, then, can be immediately fused with the equally complex findings previously detailed concerning the global spread of transnationally standardized educational models on the one hand, and the persistence of varying sociocultural interrelationship networks on the other. There is, to conclude in general terms, an abstract universalism of transnationally disseminated models which fans out into multiform structural patterns wherever such models interact, in the course of institutional implementation, with different State-defined frameworks, legal and administrative regulations, forms of the division of labor in society, national academic cultures, context-bound social meanings, and religious worldviews. In other words, the school as an "evolutionary universal" turns out to be not so much universal as socioculturally particular as soon as one systematically analyzes the multiple interrelationships between educational credentials and the privileges they bestow; between educational accomplishment and career success; between education and employment; between selection in schools and stratification in society; between the structures of schooling and public law; between university study and the collective ethos; between learning processes and social change; and between scientific rationality and the self-evolutive momentum of historical semantics.

Such references to state, law, culture, and collective experiences, to worldviews mediated through religion, national language, and historical semantics, indicate deviation-generating and -amplifying potentials which give rise, historically, to ever new sociocultural configurations. Systematically, such references also reactualize the insights that are lasting contributions of comparative social research from Lorenz von Stein (1868) to Stein Rokkan (1970);

from Max Weber (1920–21) to Pierre Birnbaum (1988); and from Norbert Elias (1978) to Ernest Gellner (1988).

3. Against this background, finally, the divergent methodologies discussed in earlier comparative educational debate—contrasting nomothetic with idiographic orientations; variable-oriented with case-oriented approaches; or, in other words, contrasting a *positivist* paradigm using comparison as a quasi-experimental procedure of theory testing with a *historicist* paradigm stressing the comprehensive explanation of culturally defined phenomena or configurations—present themselves as considerably less irreconcilable than portrayed by their respective proponents. These distinct contrasts indeed become levelled out to just the extent that Comparative Education research accepts the challenge raised by the macrohistorical perspective that has taken shape in response to globalization processes and world-system approaches. To meet this challenge means, beyond identifying specific relationships between variables, and complementary to holistically reconstructing sociocultural configurations, incorporating both methodological procedures into more encompassing analyses of large-scale societal modernization and transcultural diffusion and reception processes.

Such a broadening of analytical perspective is suggested by our sifting through the results of the various fields of comparative research; indeed, it is forced upon us in the very interweaving of contrary currents:

- of *internationalization* and *indigenization*;
- of *supranational integration* and *intranational diversification*;
- of *"evolutionary universals"* and *sociocultural configurations*;
- of *global diffusion processes* and *culture-specific reception processes*;
- of an *abstract universalism of transnationally disseminated models* and of *deviation-generating structural elaboration*; and
- of the *global spread of standardized educational models (regardless of differing societal settings)* and the *surprising diversity of sociocultural interrelationship networks (in spite of the universalist assumptions of grand theories)*.

It is this interweaving, then, that marks the common ground where issues of schooling, education, and training intersect—practically and politically—with what Max Weber referred to as the "central issues of civilization" in a changing world; moreover, this interweaving of contrary currents designates a hard core of unavoidable problems of empirical analysis and theoretical explanation which Comparative Education is called upon to resolve. These explanatory problems form the context which Comparative Education, toward the end of the twentieth century, will be obliged to take into consideration when it prepares—as Weber would say—to (i) clarify its guiding "points of view," (ii) explicate its methodological approaches, and (iii) identify its "conceptual apparatus." This presupposes, however, that Comparative Education as a field refuses to answer to the short-lived cycles of educational policy making or to be replaced without protest by the pretensions of an emerging world science *(Globology)*; that, on the contrary, it defines itself—just as the late eighteenth-century ideal implied, and as more recent epistemological considerations claim—as the comparative (as opposed to systematic or historical) "aspect"discipline (Diemer, 1970) of a Science of Education as such. The consequences of such conclusions at the level of scientific practice are threefold. Comparative Education that intends to throw fully into relief the complexity of its domain has no choice but (i) in *perspective* to conceptualize its subject matter equally in terms of societal modernization trajectories, sociocultural configurations, and transcultural diffusion and reception processes (cf. McMichael, 1990).[3] As a consequence of this dovetailing of perspectives, comparative inquiry becomes associable with the theses of world-system theoreticians; by the same token, comparative inquiry contributes to the empirical elucidation (by way of detailed historical reconstructions) of the encompassing global character of internationalization processes, and checks (by way of methodical comparisons) evolutionary universalism's claim to validity. In this dovetailing of perspectives, Comparative Education is compelled (ii) in *method* to "reconcile history and comparison," parallelling the growing consensus that has emerged from the debate in historical sociology (Badie, 1992b, p. 364). This reconciliation is not merely the merging of cross-cultural comparison and historical process analyses into comparative-historical research (Schriewer, 1984), but also implies the temporalization of the very explanatory concepts (problem definitions, background variables, causal configurations, etc.) and analytical models (cf. Castles, 1989). Finally, such consequences stress the need for Comparative Education (iii) in *concept* to rely on theoretical orientations and conceptual systems that are capable of incorporating the considerable array of methodological points of view and analytical perspectives and of informing corresponding research; which is to say, are capable of integrating the insights generated in the various fields of comparative research into interrelationship networks and system dynamics, deviation-amplifying mechanisms and complex causality, and into structural elaboration and the dependency of recursive structural change on previous structures.

Theories that both incorporate and elaborate such insights have been developed on the basis of research in the natural sciences, life sciences, and social sciences throughout the past two decades. Under headings such as "self-organization" or "morphogenesis," they delineate an interdisciplinary research program of growing importance (cf. Krohn, Küppers & Paslack, 1987). They have not only informed research in such disparate fields as meteorology, management theory, and urban development; they have also inspired theoretical reorientations in comparative technology research, industrial and organizational sociology, and the historical-comparative sociology of education. The major authors representing such theory developments include Margaret S. Archer, writing in English (cf. Archer, 1982, 1985); Edgar Morin, in French (cf. Morin, 1981–85); and, in German, Niklas Luhmann (Luhmann 1970–90, 1982b, 1984, 1990). I wish to take up, here, just a few aspects of these theory developments, not least because—returning to a history-of-science approach—one can show that they present certain parallels to previous *problematiques* while, at the same time, offering new answers.

Not unlike the late eighteenth-century grand program of comparative science, self-organization models appearing in the sphere of the social sciences represent yet another theoretical innovation taken from the life sciences. Yet the particular significance of Luhmann's theory of self-referential social systems emerges from his appropriation of the fundamental ideas of general systems theory, cybernetics, neurophysiology, and communication theory and, at the same time, his reformulation of these concepts with reference to the "peculiarity"—in Wilhelm von Humboldt's phrasing—of the social sphere. In so doing, Luhmann precisely elaborates the differences between "living systems" and "meaning-generating systems" and, among the latter, between "psychic systems" (constituted on the basis of consciousness) and "social systems" (constituted on the basis of communication) (cf. Lipp, 1987). Thus, Humboldt's *problematique*, emerging from the antagonism—inherent in the particularity of the social object domain—between purported "laws" of human nature and man's "spontaneous energy," is given an answer compatible with present-day social science.

A further advantage of Luhmann's work arises from the interweaving of systems theory with evolutionary theory, or, more specifically, a theory of social communication with a theory of social differentiation (cf. Luhmann, 1975b). This framework provides the conceptual tools for grasping both the specificity of sociocultural fields of action (such as education) and their relations to the societal environment (cf. Schriewer, 1987, 1990b); moreover, it offers the conceptual options for making understandable these fields of action (or subsystems) in their evolution within the context of more encompassing sociohistorical differentiation processes—including the contemporary world-societal intensification of specialized communication.

Such a theoretical framework makes possible, then, a conceptualization of historical-comparative research which is complex enough to allow the analyzation of the assumed "evolutionary universals"—not in the abstract, but as historically concrete—that is, embedded in processes of societal differentiation, social interaction, and global diffusion. Furthermore, it makes possible a taking up again of opposing lines of interpretation which pervaded the developing comparative disciplines from their late eighteenth-century inception. Indeed, the opposition between genealogical-*cum*-evolutionary and ecological-*cum*-culturalist approaches—personified in the historic *Académie* dispute of 1830 between evolutionist Etienne Geoffroy Saint-Hilaire (publicly supported by Goethe) and catastrophe theorist Georges Cuvier—was only later neutralized in the eclipsing of the former by decidedly scientistic methodologies giving priority to the latter.

Semantic Constructions of World Society

The guiding concepts of self-reference, reflexivity, and reflection—constitutive of Luhmann's theory—are fundamental to the development of one final argument. They conceptualize meaning-based sociocultural processes as a social reality that observes and describes itself, and which uses this self-description to organize itself. In essence, these concepts—from the outset—imply a sociology-of-knowledge perspective. This perspective emerges in response to the disjunction between structural developments and semantic developments, as well as to the (not haphazardly varying) interrelations between them in particular areas of social action, such as education. The interrelations so assumed, between "structures of society" and "semantics" (Gesellschaftsstruktur und Semantik) (Luhmann, 1980–1995, especially vol. 1, pp. 9–71), between patterns of social order and corresponding meanings recorded in written form, and between organizations and ideas, provide an explanatory framework for those findings of comparative research which give emphasis to the importance of interpretive schemes, "social meanings" (Ringer, 1979), and "the order-maintaining and order-transforming capacities of the symbolic dimensions of human activity" (Eisenstadt, 1995, pp. 306ff.) in the varying processes of system formation and modernization. They serve, then, as a conceptual link suitable for the recombination—according to Ringer (1992)—of "social history" and "intellectual history."

More importantly, these interrelations invite renewed attention to a distinction, made by Friedrich Schneider, which can be made fruitful for further analysis of internationalization processes. The distinction between "International Education" (as a form of educational discourse) and "international interconnection in education" (as an aspect of social reality), mentioned previously, is indeed applicable to a differentiation between levels that has been implied throughout the course of this chapter—for example, the difference between an "abstract universalism of transnationally disseminated models" and "multiform structural patterns"—and which now will be brought into focus. Largely independent of the factual internationalization of typical patterns of educational organization and expansion, there has been—and continues to be—ongoing discussion of internationality in educational reform debate. Couched in constructs such as "world models" (e.g. Chalker & Haynes, 1994), "international standards" (illustrated by Hanf, 1987), or "global development trends'" (systematized by Roselló, 1978), moreover, the discussion tends to precede the fact of internationalization. In other words, the realm of sociohistorical processes (characterized by tension-filled complexity and designated by the terms *internationalization* and *modernization*) must be distinguished from the realm of educational discourse (which not only reflects, but, in turn, takes a life of its own and impinges upon, these processes). This differentiation requires a corresponding differentiation between two analytical approaches. The first has been developed, in the preceding section, by redefining the perspectives of a Science of Comparative Education commensurate to the problem dimensions of its object domain. What now remains to be specified, beyond this redefinition—and complementary to it—is the conceptual focus of the sociology-of-knowledge analysis of pedagogical contributions to the semantic construction of world society.

The theory of self-reference (or, more precisely, the sequence of concepts "reflection," "interruptions in relation of interdependence," and "externalization") proffers the conceptual tools for this analysis. Informed by these concepts, indeed, a sociohistorical reexamination of the very products of institutionalized Comparative Education itself supplements the empirical analysis of world-societal phenomena.[4] Underlying this approach is the presupposition that educational theory primarily develops, not as a *scientific theory* (produced according to the commitment of pure science to criteria of truth), but as a *reflection theory* (formulated within each of society's specialized subsystems with a view to fostering the self-understanding and self-steering capacities of these systems). Educational theory, then, is the reflection theory *of* the educational system developed *within* the educational system. In discussing its object domain, educational theory discusses itself as a component of its object domain—and, in so doing, discusses its own self-discussion. Like *all* forms of self-referential closure, therefore, reflection theories developed in the contexts of particular subsystems are in need of interruptions of their circular relations of interdependence. Such interruptions typically take the form of systems opening themselves to their respective external environments—however selectively this may be done. It is through the incorporation of "supplementary meaning" as extractable from external points of reference that circular self-reference becomes amenable to specification.

For education—conceived of as the reflection theory of the educational system—Luhmann and Schorr (1979, p. 338ff.), without claiming to be exhaustive, have identified three major patterns of externalization: the appeal (i) to general principles of scientific rationality; the appeal (ii) to values; and the appeal (iii) to organization. The authors, moreover, clarify the functions these forms of externalization fulfill with regard to the stabilization of education as a corpus of theoretical knowledge that is both committed to the problem agendas of the educational system and concerned with academic status and reputation. Thus, reference (i) to general principles as formulated by philosophies of science dispenses education from the need for a priori or dogmatic assumptions to validate its purported scientific nature. Reference (ii) to values, or value-based ideologies, externalizes the justification for action—especially in educational reform and policy decision making. Reference (iii) to organization, finally, by shifting the blame for failures onto politics or administration, marks out "a focus to which to ascribe the more disagreeable aspects of social reality" (Luhmann & Schorr, 1979, p. 341f.); it constitutes a feature of educational thinking that externalizes disappointments while, at the same time, stimulating claims for alternatives in educational organization.

These structural features correlative to the self-referential nature of reflection theory set the stage for the sociological examination and reinterpretation of a large body of educational literature which, although weak in terms of comparative methodology and questionable in terms of relevance to theory building, is by convention assigned to Comparative Education. Indeed, this literature, when so considered, is given a new (and unexpected) significance. It meets the structural need for externalization intrinsic to reflection theory, particularly in the case of reformative reflection on education. From a point of view internal to a given national system of education and committed to that system's practical concerns, references to "examples abroad," to "world experiences," or to "world situations," are indeed understood to be something more than objectively documented contemporary histories of education as it is practiced in other countries. Rather, such references are expected to serve as lessons, to provide stimulative ideas and new impetus to policy definition, or to outline a frame of reference for the specification of options for reform. The act of "looking beyond one's frontiers at comparable countries" is thus conceived, in terms particularly indicative of the intended absorption of supplementary meaning through externalization, as a "system opening itself outwards . . . to external stimuli" (Schorb, 1970, pp. 16, 20).

This type of reference to examples abroad and to a supposed "realm of internationality"—however unexplicitly in terms of theory and methodology—can be viewed, then, as a form of appeal to the external environment that is complementary to Luhmann and Schorr's three patterns of externalization. Such externalizations to world situations relevant to education involve, accordingly, not the comparative analysis of sociocultural differences pursued with a view to promoting social-science knowledge; they involve, rather, the minimization of such differences by suggesting an orientation (first, at the level of reformative ideas and models, and then at the level of practical policy) toward international "reference societies" (Bendix, 1978)—be these "países que están al frente de la civilización del mundo" as a mid-nineteenth-century Spanish author characteristically stated (Pedro, 1987, p. 163f.) or, in late twenieth-century terms, "the ten world class countries" (Chalker & Haynes, 1994). In so doing, they rely—in terms of Friedrich Schneider's distinction—not on the "method of cross-national analysis" *(komparative Methode)* used as a distinctive approach to theory building and/or explanation; rather, they endeavor to achieve an "international consideration" *(vergleichende Betrachtung)* pursued with the intention of "exposing major problems, ideas, and currents in world education" (Schneider, 1931/32, pp. 243, 403f.) In other words, the suitability of the externalization to world situations for yielding supplementary meaning is related, not to the utilization of social science methods of comparison (whose inherently critical potential is bound to the complex techniques of establishing relations between relationships or even patterns of relationships), but to its resorting to the very surrogate of comparison, to its methodological *pis-aller*, namely to the international perspective (organized according to an observer's discretion on the basis of the simple operations of identifying similarities or discerning more/less or sooner/later relations between observable facts).

Historical accounts of the development of comparative and/or international studies in education substantiate this argument. Whether it was concerned with extending the Progressive Education ideals into a World Education Movement or identifying a common Western European Idea in Education; whether educational structures were perceived as dependent upon the increasing convergence of industrialized societies or an ongoing scientific and technological revolution; whether the debate hinged on democratization or comprehensivization, on the revival of values education or on world perspectives in adult education: all of these varying forms of internationalizing reform discourse and educational policy that were developed within particular national settings "have served both to support the commitment of like-minded individuals who shared the positions in question and to provide justification against opposition. Demonstrating the internationality of one's own demands for reform has meant defending them against the reproach that they are biased and partial and, indeed, qualifying them as universal and indispensable" (Zymek, 1975, p. 348f).

In so doing, the externalization to world situations in a sense objectifies value-based rationales for reform policy. This justificatory performance is accomplished in the form of historical descriptions and/or statistical surveys that are recognized as scientific. Moreover, as a good many of the International Reformative Reflection literature is focused on defining and further developing institutional structures and models of educational organization, this pattern of making reference to externality by indicating possible alternatives is well designed to overcome the disappointments educationists encounter, again and again, in a social world determined by organization. The externalization (iv) to *world situations*, in other words, neutralizes the obligation of direct recourse (ii) to *values* or *value-based ideologies*; it redoubles reference (i) to *principles of science*; and it reinforces the externalization (iii) to *organization*. By thus combining justificatory, foundational, and ascriptive aspects, externalizations to world situations provide a remarkable degree of self-regulated dynamism to reformative reflection on education. Consequently—as is apparent equally in the initial ambiguities implied by Friedrich

Schneider's methodological program and in the later development of the field—it is the type of theorizing specific to educational system reflection itself that, perpetually renewed, has transmuted the grand program of Comparative Education into its surrogate form, International Education. Externalizations to world situations are not constructed in a vacuum. Rather, they are embedded in a global reality—the "interstate system" according to the institutionalist strand of world-systems research (Ramirez & Boli-Bennett, 1987)—which is characterized equally by its differentiation into a multitude of territorially organized political systems and by multiple clusters of interrelations (of competition, rivalry, conflict, dominance, cooperation, or alliance) between these systems. The competitive impulses arising from the workings of this interstate system imply, then, the multiplication of externalizations to world situations along the distinctive system/environment perspectives corresponding to the numerous nation-state-defined educational systems (and system-related contexts of reformative reflection on education). One (politically-*cum*-linguistically defined) context of systemic self-reflection externalizes, in other words, to other education systems and their self-reflections; these contexts, in turn, refer to still others, with the consequence that they make up models, and provide stimulative ideas, reciprocally for one another.

Out of the accumulation of relations of cross-system observation and externalization of this kind emerges a web of reciprocal references which takes a life of its own, moving, reinforcing, and dynamizing the worldwide universalization of educational ideas, models, standards, and options for reform. This web becomes incorporated—as an essential component—into self-sustained world-level educational reform discourse. Viewed from a sociology-of-knowledge perspective, finally, this transnational discourse acts as much as the semantic counterpart of ongoing evolutionary processes propelled by the dynamic restlessness intrinsic to functionally differentiated modern society as it reacts, as the semantic construction of world society, upon social structures in the sense of further harmonization, standardization, and homogenization.

Notes

1. Major parts of this chapter were presented as the Claude Eggertsen Memorial Lecture, which I was invited to deliver in the frame of the Thirty-Ninth Annual Conference of the Comparative and International Education Society, held in Boston, Massachusetts, March 29 to April 2, 1995. I am grateful to Jack Michael Halverson, Humboldt University, Berlin, whose perceptive remarks and linguistic skills were extremely helpful in finalizing a readable English version of the chapter.

2. Cf. among others, *Economics of Education. Research and Studies*, ed. George Psacharopoulos (1987); *The Encyclopedia of Comparative Education and National Systems of Education*, ed. T. Neville Postlethwaite (1988); *Educational Research,*

Methodology, and Measurement: An International Handbook, ed. John P. Keeves (1988); *The Encyclopedia of Human Development and Education*, ed. R. Murray Thomas (1990); *The International Encyclopedia of Educational Evaluation*, ed. Herbert J. Walberg and Geneva D. Haertel (1990); *The International Encyclopedia of Curriculum*, ed. Arieh Lewy (1991).

3. The concept of sociohistorical modernization is not used here in the sense of a Westernization inherent in a purportedly inevitable logic of world history; rather, it serves as an "umbrella label," as a "functional expression of those interlinked processes of secular social, political, economic and cultural change (such as industrialization, democratization, bureaucratization and urbanization) whose effects are experienced worldwide, albeit in a highly uneven way. . . . Accordingly, modernization does not imply the emergence of some kind of world society in which cultural homogeneity or cosmopolitanism prevail. Rather, because its effects are unevenly experienced throughout the globe and because it promotes resistance wherever it permeates, it is more accurate to conclude that modernization reinforces the tendencies towards both integration and disintegration in the contemporary global system" (McGrew, 1992, 25–26).

4. The following paragraphs are drawn from a line of reasoning developed in greater detail in Schriewer (1990a, pp. 62ff.) and based upon extensive bibliographical references; here, this corresponding literature is referred to in a summarized form.

References

Adick, C. "Schule im modernen Weltsystem." *Zeitschrift für Kulturaustausch* 38, 3 (1988): 343–55.

———. *Die Universalisierung der modernen Schule*. Paderborn: Schöningh, 1992.

Albrow, M. & E. King (eds.). *Globalization, Knowledge and Society*. London: Sage, 1990.

Altbach, P. G. *The Knowledge Context: Comparative Perspectives on the Distribution of Knowledge*. Albany: State University of New York Press, 1987.

———. "Textbooks: The International Dimension." In *The Politics of the Textbook*, ed. M. W. Apple and L. Christian-Smith. New York: Routledge, 1991a, pp. 242–58.

———. "Third-World Publishers and the International Knowledge System." *Logos* 2/3 (1991b): 122–26.

———. "Patterns in Higher Education Development." *Prospects* 21, 2 (1991c): 189–203.

———. "International Knowledge Networks." In *The International Encyclopedia of Education*, ed. T. Husen and T. N. Postlethwaite, 2d ed., vol. 5. Oxford: Pergamon-Elsevier, 1994, pp. 2993–98.

Anweiler, O. "Comparative Education and the Internationalization of Education." *Comparative Education* 13, 2 (1977): 109–14.

———. "Die internationale Dimension der Pädagogik." In Anweiler, O. *Wissenschaftliches Interesse und politische Verantwortung: Dimensionen vergleichender Bildungsforschung*. Opladen: Leske and Budrich, 1990, pp. 225–35.

Archer, M. S. "Theorizing about the Expansion of Educational Systems." In *The Sociology of Educational Expansion. Take-off, Growth and Inflation in Educational Systems*, ed. M. S. Archer. Beverly Hills and London: Sage, 1982, pp. 3–64.

———. "Structuration versus Morphogenesis." In *Macro-Sociological Theory. Vol. 1: Perspectives on Sociological Theory*, ed. S. N. Eisenstadt and H. J. Helle. Beverly Hills and London: Sage, 1985, pp. 58–88.

Arnove, R. "Comparative Education and World-Systems Analysis." *Comparative Education Review* 24, 1 (1980): 48–62.

Badie, B. *L'Etat importé. Essai sur l'occidentalisation de l'ordre politique*. Paris: Fayard, 1992a.

———. "Analyse comparative et sociologie historique." *Revue Internationale des Sciences sociales* 133 (August 1992b): 363–72.

Badie, B. & G. Hermet. *Politique Comparée*. Paris: PUF, 1990.

Bendix, R. *Kings or People: Power and Mandate to Rule*. London and Berkeley: University of California Press, 1978.

Bergesen, A. "Preface" and "From Utilitarianism to Globology: The Shift from the Individual to the World as a Whole as the Primordial Unit of Analysis." In *Studies of the Modern World System*, ed. A. Bergesen. New York: Academic Press, 1980, pp. xiii–xiv and 1–12.

Birnbaum, P. *States and Collective Action: The European Experience*. Cambridge: Cambridge University Press, 1988.

Boli, J. & F. O. Ramirez. "Compulsory Schooling in the Western Cultural Context." In *Emergent Issues in Education: Comparative Perspectives*, ed. R. F. Arnove, P. G. Altbach, and G. P. Kelly. Albany: State University of New York Press, 1992, pp. 25–38.

Boli, J., F. O. Ramirez & J. W. Meyer. "Explaining the Origins and Expansion of Mass Education." In *New Approaches to Comparative Education*, ed. P. G. Altbach and G. P. Kelly. Chicago and London: University of Chicago Press, 1986, pp. 105–30.

Bornschier, V. & P. Lengyel (eds.). *World Society Studies*, vol. 1. Frankfurt a.M. and New York: Campus, 1990.

Boudon, R. "Grandeur et décadence des sciences du développement: Une étude de sociologie de la connaissance." *L'Année sociologique*, IIIe série, tome 42 (1992): 253–74.

Braudel, F. *Civilisation matérielle, économie et capitalisme*, XVe-XVIIIe siècle, 3 vols. Paris: A. Colin, 1979.

Casanova, P. "La *World Fiction*: Une fiction critique." *Liber—Revue européenne des livres*, 16 December 1993, pp. 111–15.

Castles, F. G. (ed.). *The Comparative History of Public Policy*. Cambridge: Polity Press, 1989, especially the Introduction, pp. 1–15.

Chalker, D. M. & R. M. Haynes. *World Class Schools: New Standards for Education*. Lancaster, Pa.: Technomic Publishing, 1994.

Charpentier, J. & C. Engel (eds.). *Les régions de l'espace communautaire*. Nancy: Presses Universitaires de Nancy, 1992.

Chekki, D. A. *American Sociological Hegemony: Transnational Explorations*. Lanham and London: University Press of America, 1987.

Cowen, R. "The Importation of Higher Education into Brazil and Japan." In *International Currents in Educational Ideas and Practices*. Proceedings of the 1987 Annual Conference of the History of Education Society held jointly with BCIES, ed. P. Cunningham and C. Brook. Evington: History of Education Society, 1988, pp. 41–49.

Cuvier, G. de. *Leçons d'anatomie comparée*, 5 vols. Paris: Crochard, An XIV-1805.

Deppe, R. & D. Hoss (eds.). *Work Organization, Incentive Systems and Effort Bargaining in Different Social and National Contexts*. Frankfurt: Institut für Sozialforschung, 1984.

Diemer, A. "Zur Grundlegung eines allgemeinen Wissenschaftsbegriffs." *Zeitschrift für Allgemeine Wissenschaftstheorie* 1, 2 (1970): 209–27.

Dierkes, M., H. N. Weiler & A. Berthoin Antal (eds.). *Comparative Policy Research: Learning from Experience*. Aldershot: Gower, 1987.

Dore, R. *British Factory—Japanese Factory: The Origins of National Diversity in Industrial Relations*. Berkeley: University of California Press, 1973.

Dräger, H. "Der interessierte Blick in die Fremde." In *Erwachsenenbildung im Kontext: Beiträge zur grenzüberschreitenden Konstituierung einer Disziplin*, ed. M. Friedenthal-Haase. Bad Heilbrunn: Klinkhardt, 1991, pp. 208–25.

Durkheim, E. *Les règles de la méthode sociologique*, 22e édition. Paris: PUF, 1986.

Eisenstadt, S. N. *Tradition, Change, and Modernity*. New York: Wiley-Interscience, 1973.

———. "A Reappraisal of Theories of Social Change and Modernization." In *Social Change and Modernity*, ed. H. Haferkamp and N. J. Smelser. Berkeley: University of California Press, 1992, pp. 412–29.

———. *Power, Trust, and Meaning: Essays in Sociological Theory and Analysis*. Chicago and London: University of Chicago Press, 1995.

Elias, N. "Zur Soziogenese der Begriffe 'Zivilisation' und 'Kultur.' " In N. Elias, *Über den Prozeß der Zivilisation*. Frankfurt a.M.: Suhrkamp, 1978, pp. 1–64.

Epstein, E. H. "Currents Left and Right: Ideology in Comparative Education." *Comparative Education Review* 27 (1983): 3–39.

Espagne, M. & M. Werner. "Présentation." *Revue de synthèse* IVe série, no 2, April–June 1988, pp. 187–94.

———. (eds.) *Philologiques I. Contribution à l'histoire des disciplines littéraires en France et en Allemagne au XIXe siècle*. Paris: Editions de la Maison des Sciences de l'Homme, 1990.

Fägerlind, I. & L. J. Saha. *Education and National Development: A Comparative Perspective*. Oxford: Pergamon, 1985.

Feuerbach, A. von. "Blick auf die teutsche Rechtswissenschaft" (1810), reproduced in Feuerbach, A. von. *Kleine Schriften vermischten Inhalts*. Nürnberg: Otto, 1833, pp. 152–77.

Fiala, R. & A. G. Lanford. "Educational Ideology and the World Educational Revolution, 1950–1970." *Comparative Education Review* 31, 3 (1987): 315–32.

Gellner, E. *Plough, Sword and Book*. London: Collins Harvill, 1988.

Genov, N. (ed.). *National Traditions in Sociology*. London: Sage, 1989.

Goldschmidt, D. "Idealtypische Charakterisierung sieben westlicher Hochschulsysteme." *Zeitschrift für Sozialisationsforschung und Erziehungssoziologie* 11, 1 (1991a): 3–17.

————. *Die gesellschaftliche Herausforderung der Universität. Historische Analysen, internationale Vergleiche, globale Perspektiven.* Weinheim: Deutscher Studienverlag, 1991b.

Goldthorpe, J. H. "The End of Convergence: Corporatist and Dualist Tendencies in Modern Western Societies." In *Order and Conflict in Contemporary Capitalism*, ed. J. H. Goldthorpe. Oxford: Clarendon, 1984, pp. 315–43.

Grant, N. "European Unity and National Systems." In *Education in the Eighties: The Central Issues*, ed. B. Simon and W. Taylor. London: Batsford Academic and International, 1981, pp. 92–110.

Grellet, G. "Pourquoi les pays en voie de développement ont-ils des rythmes de croissance aussi différents?" *Revue Tiers Monde* 33, 129 (1992): 31–66.

Hanf, T. "Die Schule der Staatsoligarchie." *Bildung und Erziehung* 33, 5 (1980): 407–32.

Harwood, J. *Styles of Scientific Thought: A Study of the German Genetics Community, 1900–1933.* Chicago and London: University of Chicago Press, 1992.

Heidenreich, M. & G. Schmidt (eds.). *International vergleichende Organisationsforschung. Fragestellungen, Methoden und Ergebnisse ausgewählter Untersuchungen.* Opladen: Westdeutscher Verlag, 1991.

Hirata, H. S. "Brasilien, Frankreich, Japan: Unterschiede und die Suche nach Bedeutung." In Heidenreich and Schmidt 1991, pp. 180–89.

Hofstede, G. *Culture's Consequences: International Differences in Work-Related Values*, 2d ed. London: Sage, 1986.

Hoggart, R. *An Idea and Its Servants: Unesco from Within.* London: Chatto and Windus, 1978.

Hüfner, K., J. W. Meyer & J. Naumann. "Comparative Education Policy Research: A World Society Perspective." In Dierkes, Weiler, and Berthoin Antal, 1987, pp. 188–243.

Humboldt, W. von. "Plan einer vergleichenden Anthropologie" (1795). In Humboldt, W.von. *Schriften zur Anthropologie und Bildungslehre*, ed. Andreas Flitne. 2d ed. Düsseldorf and Munich: Küpper, 1964, pp. 32–59.

Husen, T. *Education and the Global Concern.* Oxford: Pergamon, 1990.

Husen, T. & T. N. Postlethwaite (eds.). *The International Encyclopedia of Education: Research and Studies*, vols. 1–10. Oxford: Pergamon, 1985; reprint editions 1988 and 1991; 2d ed. in 12 volumes 1994.

Inkeles, A. & D. H. Smith. *Becoming Modern.* London: Heinemann, 1974.

Inkeles, A. & L. Sirowy. "Convergent and Divergent Trends in National Educational Systems." *Social Forces* 62, 2 (1983): 303–33.

Iribarne, P. d'. *La logique de l'honneur: Gestion des entreprises et traditions nationales.* Paris: Seuil, 1989.

Jullien de Paris, M.-A. *Esquisse et vues préliminaires d'un ouvrage sur l'éducation comparée.* Paris: Colas, Delaunay et al., 1817.

Kantowsky, D. "Die Rezeption der Hinduismus/ Buddhismus-Studie Max Webers in Südasien. Ein Missverständnis." *Archives Européennes de Sociologie* 23, 2 (1982): 317–55.

Katz, J. "Chronologie de l'Année Internationale de l'Education et du Conseil Mondial des Sociétés d'Education Comparée." *Conseil Mondial des Sociétés d'Education Comparée: Bulletin* 6, 1 (1978): 6–11.

Kerr, C. "International Learning and National Purposes in Higher Education." *American Behavioral Scientist* 35, 1 (1991): 17–42.

Komenan, A. G. *World Education Indicators*, Education and Training Series Report No. EDT 88. Washington: Worldbank, 1987.

Krohn, W., G. Küppers & R. Paslack. "Selbstorganisation: Zur Genese und Entwicklung einer wissenschaftlichen Revolution." In *Der Diskurs des Radikalen Konstruktivismus*, ed. S. J. Schmidt. Frankfurt a.M.: Suhrkamp, 1987, pp. 441–65.

Krüger, B. *Bildungswesen und Pädagogik im Prozess ihrer Internationalisierung.* Münster: EdD Dissertation, Pädagogische Hochschule Westfalen Lippe, 1974.

Kumon, S. & H. Rosovsky (eds.). *The Political Economy of Japan*, vol. 3: *Cultural and Social Dynamics.* Stanford: Stanford University Press, 1992.

Kurian, G. T. (ed.). *World Education Encyclopedia*, vol. 1–3. New York and Oxford: Facts on File Publications, 1988.

Lefmann, S. *Franz Bopp, sein Leben und seine Wissenschaft*, pt. 2. Berlin: Georg Reimer, 1895.

Lipp, W. "Autopoiesis biologisch, Autopoiesis soziologisch." *Kölner Zeitschrift für Soziologie und Sozialpsychologie* 39 (1987): 452–70.

Luhmann, N. *Soziologische Aufklärung*, vols. 1–5. Opladen: Westdeutscher Verlag, 1970–1990.

———. *Gesellschaftsstruktur und Semantik: Studien zur Wissenssoziologie der modernen Gesellschaft*, vols. 1–4. Frankfurt a.M.: Suhrkamp, 1980–1995.

———. "Die Weltgesellschaft." In N. Luhmann, *Soziologische Aufklärung* 2. Opladen: Westdeutscher Verlag, 1975a, pp. 51–71.

———. "Systemtheorie, Evolutionstheorie und Kommunikationstheorie." In N. Luhmann, *Soziologische Aufklärung* 2. Opladen: Westdeutscher Verlag, 1975b, pp. 193–203.

———. "The World Society as a Social System." *International Journal of General Systems* 8, 3 (1982a): 131–38.

———. *The Differentiation of Society.* New York: Columbia University Press, 1982b.

———. *Soziale Systeme. Grundriss einer allgemeinen Theorie.* Frankfurt a.M.: Suhrkamp, 1984.

———. *Essays on Self-Reference.* New York: Columbia University Press, 1990.

Luhmann, N. & K.-E. Schorr. *Reflexionsprobleme im Erziehungssystem.* Stuttgart: Klett-Cotta, 1979.

Lutz, B. "Bildungssystem und Beschäftigungsstruktur in Deutschland und Frankreich. Zum Einfluss des Bildungssystems auf die Gestaltung betrieblicher Arbeitskräftestrukturen." In *Betrieb—Arbeitsmarkt—Qualifikation I*, ed. H.-G. Mendius et al. Frankfurt a.M.: Aspekte, 1976, pp. 83–151.

Maurice, M. "Le déterminisme technologique dans la sociologie du travail (1955–1980). Un changement de paradigme?" *Sociologie du travail* 22, 1 (1980): 22–37.

Maurice, M., F. Sellier & J. J. Silvestre. "La production de la hiérarchie dans l'entreprise: Comparaisons France-Allemagne." *Revue française de sociologie* 20, 2 (1979): 331–65.

Maurice, M., A. Sorge & M. Warner. "Societal Differences in Organizing Manufacturing Units: A Comparison of France, West Germany, and Great Britain." *Organization Studies* 1, 1 (1980): 59–86.

McGrew, A. G. "Conceptualizing Global Politics." In McGrew, Lewis et al. 1992, pp. 1–28.

McGrew, A. G., P. G. Lewis et al. *Global Politics. Globalization and the Nation-State.* Cambridge and Oxford: Polity Press and Blackwell, 1992.

McMichael, P. "Incorporating Comparison within a World-Historical Perspective: An Alternative Comparative Method." *American Sociological Review* 55 (1990): 385–97.

Menzel, U. "Das Ende der 'Dritten Welt' und das Scheitern der großen Theorien." *Politische Vierteljahresschrift* 32, 1 (1991): 4–33.

Meyer, J. W., F. O. Ramirez, R. Rubinson & J. Boli-Bennett. "The World Educational Revolution, 1950–1970." *Sociology of Education* 50 (1977): 242–58.

Meyer, J. W. & M. T. Hannan (eds.). *National Development and the World System: Educational, Economic, and Political Change, 1950–1970.* Chicago and London: University of Chicago Press, 1979.

Milward, A. S. et al. *The European Rescue of the Nation-State.* London: Routledge, 1992.

Morin, E. *La Méthode, tome 1: La Nature de la Nature; tome 2: La Vie de la Vie.* New edition. Paris: Seuil, 1981–85.

Müller, D. K., F. Ringer & B. Simon (eds.). *The Rise of the Modern Educational System.* Cambridge: Cambridge University Press; Paris: Editions de la Maison des Sciences de l'Homme, 1987.

Naschold, F. *Den Wandel organisieren. Erfahrungen des schwedischen Entwicklungsprogramms "Leitung, Organisation, Mitbestimmung" (LOM) im internationalen Wettbewerb.* Berlin: Sigma, 1992.

Parsons, T. "Evolutionary Universals in Society." *American Sociological Review* 29 (1964): 339–57.

Pedró, F. *Los precursores españoles de la Educación Comparada. Antología de textos.* Madrid: Universidad Nacional de Educación a Distancia, 1987.

Pietsch, A.-J. *Die Interdependenz von Qualifikationsbedarf und Arbeitsorganisation, untersucht am Beispiel der Sowjetunion im Vergleich mit Frankreich, der Bundesrepublik Deutschland und der DDR.* Munich: Osteuropa-Institut, 1980.

Pollak, M. "From Methodological Prescription to Socio-Historical Description." *Fundamenta Scientiae* 4 (1983): 1–27.

———. "Die Rezeption Max Webers in Frankreich: Fallstudie eines Theorietransfers in den Sozialwissenschaften." *Kölner Zeitschrift für Soziologie und Sozialpsychologie* 38, 4 (1986), 4: 670–84.

Ramirez, F. O. & J. Boli-Bennett. "Global Patterns of Educational Institutionalization." In *Comparative Education*, ed. P. G. Altbach, R. F. Arnove and G. P. Kelly. New York and London: Macmillan, 1982, pp. 15–36.

———. "The Political Construction of Mass Schooling: European Origins and Worldwide Institutionalization." *Sociology of Education* 60 (1987): 2–17.

Ramirez, F. O. & P. Riddle. "The Expansion of Higher Education." In *International Higher Education: An Encyclopedia*, ed. P. G. Altbach. New York and London: Garland, 1991, vol. 1, pp. 91–105.

Ringer, F. K. *Education and Society in Modern Europe.* Bloomington and London: Indiana University Press, 1979.

————. *Fields of Knowledge: French Academic Culture in Comparative Perspective, 1890–1920.* Cambridge: Cambridge University Press; Paris: Editions de la Maison des Sciences de l'Homme, 1992.

Rokkan, S. et al. *Citizens, Elections, Parties: Approaches to the Comparative Study of the Processes of Development.* Oslo: Universitetsforlaget, 1970.

Roselló, P. *La teoría de las corrientes educativas: Cursillo de Educación Comparada Dinámica,* 2d ed. Barcelona: Ediciones de Promoción Cultural, 1978.

Sabel, C. F. et al. *Regional Prosperities Compared: Massachusetts and Baden-Württemberg in the 1980s.* Berlin: Wissenschaftszentrum Berlin für Sozialforschung, 1987.

Scardigli, V. (ed.). *L'Europe de la diversité: La dynamique des identités régionales.* Paris: Editions du CNRS, 1993.

Scharpf, F. W. "Economic and Institutional Constraints of Full-Employment Strategies: Sweden, Austria, and Western Germany." In *Order and Conflict in Contemporary Capitalism,* ed. J. H. Goldthorpe. Oxford: Clarendon, 1984, pp. 257–90.

Schmid, H., P. Füglistaler & M. Hohl. *Vollbeschäftigungspolitik: Der Wille zum Erfolg. Ein Ländervergleich der Schweiz, Deutschlands, Österreichs, Schwedens und Japans.* Bern: Haupt, 1992.

Schneider, F. "Internationale Pädagogik, Auslandspädagogik, Vergleichende Erziehungswissenschaft." *Internationale Zeitschrift für Erziehungswissenschaft* 1 (1931/32): 15–39, 243–57, 392–407; and 2 (1932/33): 79–89.

Schorb, A. O. "Der internationale Vergleich als Instrument der Bildungspolitik." In *Pädagogische Forschung und pädagogischer Fortschritt,* ed. W. Hilligen and R. Raasch. Bielefeld: Bertelsmann, 1970.

Schriewer, J. "'Erziehung'und 'Kultur': Zur Theorie und Methodik Vergleichender Erziehungswissenschaft." In *Die Pädagogik und ihre Bereiche,* ed. W. Brinkmann and K. Renner. Paderborn etc.: Schöningh, 1982, pp. 185–236.

————. "Vergleichend-historische Bildungsforschung: Gesamttableau oder Forschungsansatz?" *Zeitschrift für Pädagogik* 30, 3 (1984): 323–42.

————. "Funktionssymbiosen von Überschneidungsbereichen: Systemtheoretische Konstrukte in vergleichender Erziehungsforschung." In *Pädagogik, Erziehungswissenschaft und Systemtheorie,* ed. J. Oelkers and H.-E. Tenorth. Weinheim and Basel: Beltz, 1987, pp. 76–101.

————. "The Method of Comparison and the Need for Externalization: Methodological Criteria and Sociological Concepts." In *Theories and Methods in Comparative Education,* ed. J. Schriewer and B. Holmes, 2d ed. Frankfurt: Lang, 1990a, pp. 25–83.

————. "Comparación y explicación en el análisis de los sistemas educativos." In *Los Usos de la Comparación en Ciencias Sociales y en Educación,* ed. M. A. Pereyra. Madrid: Centro de Publicaciones del Ministerio de Educación y Ciencia, 1990b, pp. 77–127.

Schriewer, J. & E. Keiner. "Communication Patterns and Intellectual Traditions in Educational Sciences: France and Germany." *Comparative Education Review* 36, 1 (1992): 25–51.

Schriewer, J. & E. Keiner. "Kommunikationsnetze und Theoriegestalt: Zur Binnenkonstitution der Erziehungswissenschaft in Frankreich und Deutschland." In Schriewer, Keiner, and Charle 1993, pp. 277–341.

Schriewer, J., E. Keiner & C. Charle (eds.). *Sozialer Raum und akademische Kulturen: A la recherche de l'espace universitaire européen.* Frankfurt, Bern, New York: Lang, 1993.

Schulze, W. *Deutsche Geschichtswissenschaft nach 1945.* Munich: Oldenbourg, 1989.

Sharpe, L. J. "Fragmentation and Territoriality in the European State System." *International Political Science Review* 10, 3 (1989): 223–38.

Smelser, N. J. "Internationalization of Social Science Knowledge." *American Behavioral Scientist* 35, 1 (1991): 65–91.

Smith, M. "Modernization, Globalization and the Nation-State." McGrew, Lewis et al. 1992, pp. 253–68.

So, A. Y. *Social Change and Development: Modernization, Dependency, and World-System Theories.* Newbury Park and London: Sage, 1990.

Sorge, A. & M. Warner. *Comparative Factory Organization—An Anglo-German Comparison of Management and Manpower in Manufacturing.* Aldershot: Gower, 1987.

Stein, L. von. *Das Elementar- und das Berufsbildungswesen in Deutschland, England, Frankreich und anderen Ländern.* Die Verwaltungslehre. Fünfter Theil: Die Innere Verwaltung. Zweites Hauptgebiet: Das Bildungswesen. Stuttgart: Cotta, 1868.

Stichweh, R. *Zur Entstehung des modernen Systems wissenschaftlicher Disziplinen. Physik in Deutschland 1740–1890.* Frankfurt a.M.: Suhrkamp, 1984.

———. "From the Peregrinatio Academica to Contemporary International Student Flows: National Culture and Functional Differentiation as Emergent Causes." In *Transnational Intellectual Networks and the Cultural Logics of Nations,* ed. C. Charle, J. Schriewer, and P. Wagner. Providence, R. I. and Oxford: Berghahn, 1998.

Teichler, U. *Convergence or Growing Variety: The Changing Organization of Studies.* Strasbourg: Council of Europe, 1988.

Tenbruck, F. H. "Emile Durkheim oder die Geburt der Gesellschaft aus dem Geist der Soziologie." *Zeitschrift für Soziologie* 10 (1981): 333–50.

Terasaki, M. et al. *Oyatoi Kyoshi Emil Hausknecht no Keukyu.* Tokyo: University of Tokyo Press, 1989.

Turner, L. and P. Auer: *The Political Economy of New Work Organization: Different Roads, Different Outcomes.* Berlin: Wissenschaftszentrum Berlin für Sozialforschung, 1992.

Wallerstein, I. *The Modern World System: Capitalist Agriculture and the Origins of the European World Economy in the Sixteenth Century.* New York: Academic Press, 1976.

———. *Unthinking Social Science: The Limits of Nineteenth-Century Paradigms.* Cambridge: Polity Press, 1991.

Weber, M. *Gesammelte Aufsätze zur Religionssoziologie,* vols. 1–3. Tübingen: Mohr/Siebeck, 1920–21; 6th and 7th ed. 1978–1983.

———. "Die 'Objektivität' sozialwissenschaftlicher und sozialpolitischer Erkenntnis" (1904). In Weber, M. *Gesammelte Aufsätze zur Wissenschaftslehre,* 4th ed. Tübingen: Mohr, 1973, pp. 146–214:

Weiler, H. N. "Introductory note to chapters 8–9." In Dierkes, Weiler, and Berthoin-Antal 1987, pp. 186–187.

Wolferen, K. van. *The Enigma of Japanese Power: People and Politics in a Stateless Nation.* New York: Alfred A. Knopf, 1989.

Zymek, B. *Das Ausland als Argument in der pädagogischen Reformdiskussion.* Ratingen: Henn, 1975.

Index

SUNY Series: Frontiers in Education
Philip G. Altbach, Editor

List of Titles

Class, Race, and Gender in American Education—Lois Weis (ed.)

Excellence and Equality: A Qualitatively Different Perspective on Gifted and Talented Education—David M. Fetterman

Change and Effectiveness in Schools: A Cultural Perspective—Gretchen B. Rossman, H. Dickson Corbett, and William A. Firestone

The Curriculum: Problems, Politics, and Possibilities—Landon E. Beyer and Michael W. Apple (eds.)

The Character of American Higher Education and Intercollegiate Sports—Donald Chu

Crisis in Teaching: Perspectives on Current Reforms—Lois Weis, Philip G. Altbach, Gail P. Kelly, Hugh G. Petrie, and Sheila Slaughter (eds.)

The High Status Track: Studies of Elite Schools and Stratification—Paul William Kingston and Lionel S. Lewis (eds.)

The Economics of American Universities: Management, Operations, and Fiscal Environment—Stephen A. Hoenack and Eileen L. Collins (eds.)

The Higher Learning and High Technology: Dynamics of Higher Education and Policy Formation—Sheila Slaughter

Dropouts from Schools: Issues, Dilemmas and Solutions—Lois Weis, Eleanor Farrar, and Hugh G. Petrie (eds.)

Religious Fundamentalism and American Education: The Battle for the Public Schools—Eugene F. Provenzo, Jr.

Going to School: The African-American Experience—Kofi Lomotey (ed.)

Curriculum Differentiation: Interpretive Studies in U.S. Secondary Schools—Reba Page and Linda Valli (eds.)

The Racial Crisis in American Higher Education—Philip G. Altbach and Kofi Lomotey (eds.)

The Great Transformation in Higher Education, 1960–1980—Clark Kerr

College in Black and White: African-American Students in Predominantly White and in Historically Black Public Universities—Walter R. Allen, Edgar G. Epps, and Nesha Z. Haniff (eds.)

Textbooks in American Society: Politics, Policy, and Pedagogy—Philip G. Altbach, Gail P. Kelly, Hugh G. Petrie, and Lois Weis (eds.)

Critical Perspectives on Early Childhood Education—Lois Weis, Philip G. Altbach, Gail P. Kelly, and Hugh G. Petrie (eds.)

Black Resistance in High School: Forging a Separatist Culture—R. Patrick Solomon

Emergent Issues in Education: Comparative Perspectives—Robert F. Arnove, Philip G. Altbach, and Gail P. Kelly (eds.)

Creating Community on College Campuses—Irving J. Spitzberg and Virginia V. Thorndike

Teaching Education Policy: Narratives, Stories, and Cases—Hendrick D. Gideonse (ed.)

Beyond Silenced Voices: Class, Race, and Gender in the United States Schools—Lois Weis and Michelle Fine (eds.)

Troubled Times for American Higher Education: The 1990s and Beyond—Clark Kerr (ed.)

Higher Education Cannot Escape History: Issues for the Twenty-first Century—Clark Kerr (ed.)

The Cold War and Academic Governance: The Lattimore Case at Johns Hopkins—Lionel S. Lewis (ed.)

Multiculturalism and Education: Diversity and Its Impact on Schools and Society—Thomas J. LaBelle and Christopher R. Ward (eds.)

The Contradictory College: The Conflicting Origins, Impacts, and Futures of the Community College—Kevin J. Dougherty (ed.)

Race and Educational Reform in the American Metropolis: A Study of School Decentralization—Dan A. Lewis (ed.)

Professionalization, Partnership, and Power: Building Professional Development Schools—Hugh Petrie (ed.)

Ethnic Studies and Multiculturalism—Thomas J. LaBelle and Christopher R. Ward

Promotion and Tenure: Community and Socialization in Academe—William G. Tierney and Estela Mara Bensimon (eds.)

Sailing Against the Wind: African Americans and Women in U.S. Education—Kofi Lomotey (ed.)

The Challenge of Eastern Asian Education: Implications for America—William K. Cummings and Philip G. Altbach (eds.)

Conversations with Educational Leaders: Contemporary Viewpoints on Education in America—Anne Tumbau-Lockwood

Managed Professionals: Unionized Faculty and Restructuring Academic Labor—Gary Rhoades

The Curriculum, Second Edition—Landon E. Beyer and Michael W. Apple (eds.)

Education/Technology/Power: Educational Computing as a Social Practice—Hank Bromley and Michael W. Apple

Capitalizing Knowledge—Henry Etzkowitz, Andrew Webster, and Pat Healey (eds.)

The Academic Kitchen—Maresi Nerad

Grass Roots and Glass Ceilings—William B. Harvey (ed.)

Community Colleges and Cultural Texts—Kathleen M. Show (ed.)